BY JAMES LORD

Six Exceptional Women

Picasso and Dora

Giacometti: A Biography

A Giacometti Portrait

Six Exceptional Women

FURTHER MEMOIRS

SIX
EXCEPTIONAL
WOMEN

FURTHER MEMOIRS

JAMES LORD

FARRAR STRAUS GIROUX

NEW YORK

Library of Congress Cataloging-in-Publication Data
Lord, James.
Six exceptional women / James Lord.—1st ed.
p.   cm.
Includes index.
1. Women—Biography.   I. Title.
CT3203.L67   1994   920.72—dc20   93-42384 CIP

IN MEMORY OF

LOUISE BENNETT LORD

CONTENTS

Where the Pictures Were

[GERTRUDE STEIN &

ALICE B. TOKLAS]

1

Picasso had many visitors at his studio in the rue des Grands-Augustins when I arrived there that March morning in 1945. But he got around to me eventually. I said good morning. He said, "Do you know Gertrude Stein?"

"No," I answered with surprise, though even then I should have learned in Picasso's case to be wary of surprise.

"Well, you should meet her," he said. "After all, you're both American, and it will be interesting. I'll telephone her right now and arrange it. She lives very near here."

Why Picasso determined on this particular day that Miss Stein should serve his need to clear the studio of an excess admirer, I have no idea. He was not usually so urbane. In any case, as I was able to appreciate later, he probably felt little care for the possible pleasure and satisfaction of either an old friend or a new one.

"Gertrude!" he said into the telephone, and that un-Latin name had a comical resonance in the lilting Spanish accent of Picasso's French. They talked for a minute, then he said, "There's a young American soldier here who wants to meet you. I'm going to send him over." Pause. A toss of Picasso's head, an impatient gesture of his arm. "Well, it doesn't matter if it's time for your bath or not. I'm going to send him over anyway."

Having done with the telephone, he turned back to me, and as I went with him through the pale, dusty sunlight toward the door, he said, "You'll see, Gertrude is a very interesting woman. Then there's her friend, Alice Toklas, too. Everybody should know them. It will be very interesting."

Down the semicircular stairway and outside in the rue des Grands-Augustins, I wasn't so sure. To me an introduction from Picasso may have seemed a categorical imperative, but Miss Stein was apparently of another mind. And yet I knew that on the far side of timidity and intimidation Picasso himself had not proved too formidable for a semblance of friendship. Besides, in that diamond spring no twenty-two-year-old's fantasy seemed unreasonable in Paris.

As one walks away from the Seine, the rue Christine is to the right of the rue des Grands-Augustins, between it and the rue Dauphine, a short street lined on either side by tall, antique houses, in none of which despite persistent legend lived that mannish queen, Christine of Sweden. Number 5 is in the middle of the block on the south side. Its courtyard used to be disfigured by a cheap shed. The staircase still has a tracery balustrade of wrought iron and a high, atmospheric serenity. When I went there, the steps were always glossy with wax, of which the thin, unforgettable odor still embodies my diffident pride and excitement as I went up that first day. My finger on the bell made a tinkling in the distance, and I waited, mirrored as an awkward presence in the highly varnished door. It opened.

A beaked nose, dark bangs above dark, direct eyes, and a dark wisp of mustache, short, rather stooped, dressed all in gray—this was Alice B. Toklas. She said, "You're the young man from Picasso, aren't you? Then come in."

The entrance hall had height and sunshine, and a quantity of unframed paintings—obviously by Picasso—hung against the white paneling. There were also some large, dark pieces of antique furniture, and I tried to appreciate the profusion without appearing as overawed as I felt. Miss Toklas took me through to the salon, asked me to sit down, and said that Miss Stein, who was having a bath, would presently join us. But she was already there. Whether present physically or not, whether alive, indeed, or dead, Gertrude Stein always inhabited that room as long as it contained all the possessions that so vividly, historically and imperatively substantiated her presence. These, above all, were the pictures. Where the pictures were, Gertrude was.

The pictures were by Picasso. A few by Juan Gris, and one or two, hung in obscure corners, by Sir Francis Rose and Marie Laurencin, simply emphasized that all the others were by Picasso. The celebrated portrait of Miss Stein hung above the fireplace against the inset mirror of the chimneypiece. Opposite the two high windows hung the famous Blue period painting of a nude girl holding a basket of red flowers. Above a heavy commode between the windows hung a Cubist picture. Facing Miss Stein's portrait from across the room, a muted rose nude gazed passively outward, her hands joined. Among these four most important paintings hung a quantity of other, smaller ones, a dozen or more, all of exhilarating quality, still lifes, figures and landscapes of the early Negro and Cubist periods.

I sat on an overstuffed sofa upholstered with shiny brown horsehair. It was very comfortable, but I was not. Miss Toklas sat silently facing me in a small armchair also upholstered with horsehair. We waited. She made a few observations about the military life, then added, "Miss Stein and I are very fond of General Grant."

"Oh. What outfit is he with?" I asked.

"General Ulysses S. Grant," she replied severely.

"Oh yes," I said, but since at that time it seemed preposterous to me, an enlisted man, that anyone, especially a writer, might admire an officer, living or dead, especially a general, I let it go at that.

"General Grant is one of the greatest men of American history," said Miss Toklas. "We quite prefer him to Lincoln."

I said, "Oh."

Soon a large, shaggy, white but not very clean French poodle plodded into the room—Basket. Then Miss Stein came in. She had a heavy, decisive step and her presence commanded attention. At once and always her figure in those shapeless tweed suits made me think of a burlap bag filled with cement and left to harden. She was not much taller than Miss Toklas but so sturdy and solid within herself that she seemed very large. Her bold head, hard, short gray hair and deeply creased features were serenely imperious. As I rose, I felt afraid that Miss Toklas might tell her friend how I had failed the General Grant appreciation test.

She merely said, "Lovey, this is the young man from Picasso."

When we had shaken hands and said hello, Miss Stein announced, "I have to go and do some errands and walk my dog for half an hour and that's all the time I can spare today. If you want to come with me, you may."

This was obviously not an invitation but an ultimatum, and I accepted immediately. Miss Stein took a leash, attached it to Basket's collar and went toward the door. I followed.

In the stairway Miss Stein matter-of-factly said, "Now tell me everything about yourself." Her voice was resonant and expressive, the voice of authority.

"Well, there really isn't much to tell," I diffidently replied.

Miss Stein stopped, her hand on the faceted glass newel knob at the foot of the stairs. "Now listen to me," she said. "If that's the kind of answer you're going to give when I ask you a question, then it's quite obvious that you and I will never have anything to say to one another and you might as well run along right now."

Appalled and yet determined, if possible, not to be found wanting in this crisis of identity, I said, "All right, I'll tell you about myself."

Miss Stein shrugged but nodded and went along through the courtyard with her dog. I went along beside her, and I said, "I'm twenty-two years old. I was born in Englewood, New Jersey, and I went to school there until I was about eight."

"How interesting," said Miss Stein. "That's a very curious coincidence, because I happen to know already a young man from Englewood, New Jersey; he takes very beautiful photographs, and his father was a clergyman in Englewood." As we turned left in the rue Christine, she continued for a time to talk about the young man, whose name was George Platt Lynes, then shifted to another topic, which led to another and then another.

I was never again required, or invited, to talk about myself, or to talk, in fact, very much about anything whatever. Miss Stein, as always, did all the talking. That first day, while we walked up to the rue de Buci and across the Boulevard St.-Germain, stopping occasionally to make purchases for the shopping bag I carried, Miss Stein talked endlessly and rather aimlessly about anything that occurred to her. I don't remember now, and didn't write down then, everything she said, but I do remember the vitality, curiosity and exuberance of her talk. She told me about Paris and France and the war and, above all, about herself, her impressions, feelings and thoughts. She talked well. Certainly she knew that she was Gertrude Stein and that that made a difference, but at the same time she was so keenly and obviously interested in everything she said that it seemed impossible not to share her interest. One of the sources of her charm, I think, was her naïve, almost childlike absorption and pleasure in her own being. She plainly assumed that the whole world was exactly as she believed it to be, which was a comforting conviction, and she communicated that sense of comfort to others. She had about her something of the schoolteacher, a homespun, sibyl-like and autocratic schoolteacher. And as is true of many schoolteachers, the subject that interested her most and which she consequently taught best was herself. For responsive students she was therefore able to feel true affection, though only so long as they took care not to confuse familiarity with equality and remained attentive to the sole legitimate source of understanding.

The quality of my attention that first day with Miss Stein must have seemed acceptable, for when we had made our way back to the rue Christine I was invited to return as often as my military duties might allow.

Gratified with whatever intimations of personal adequacy or even significance I may naïvely have drawn from this experience, I reported to Picasso that my meeting with Miss Stein had been a success and a pleasure. He did not seem in the least interested. I thought this odd, but it would never then have occurred to me to question Picasso.

Many, many American soldiers visited Miss Stein and Miss Toklas in the rue Christine during the spring and summer of that year, I among them. The two women had been escorted in an army plane around Germany, where Gertrude made several speeches to the troops, and she had spoken as well in Paris at a number of meetings organized for soldiers by the Red Cross. The GIs enjoyed her no-nonsense, didactic but maternal talk. We were encouraged to accept Miss Stein as a famous but folksy mother of us all. Fresh from experiences which cried out for both expression and understanding, hundreds of aspiring GI writers and intellectuals were on the lookout for someone of consecrated achievement and authority around whom to crystallize their personal longings and who would offer them in return a vicarious intimation of attainment. Gertrude Stein was ready, willing and able. She had already given proof of her aptitude to a previous generation, and with celebrated results. Moreover, Miss Stein was the one and only person available for the role, a situation perfectly in keeping with her notion of appropriate natural selection. It suited the GIs well enough, as a matter of fact, for those favored by her attention were able to enjoy the sentiment of benefiting by it solely as a result of her omniscient discrimination and not at all as the incidental by-product of a world war. The presence of all those soldiers—like all those Picassos—in Miss Stein's salon seemed to everyone concerned a delightful and self-evident demonstration of cultural inevitability.

Miss Stein, as I recall, hardly ever talked about the pictures. They were there. They formed a prestigious backdrop for her monologues. They attested with admirable seriousness to her clairvoyance in the past. And they consequently served notice that the utterances of the present were not to be taken lightly. There was no need to talk about them. Besides, Gertrude had not painted them.

Superlative collections of art almost always dominate the personalities of their possessors. Even when the acquisitive motive has been so pure and noble as to purge all taint of ostentation, vanity or greed, few collectors are by their own intellectual and spiritual sovereignty able to live as equals with the overpowering presences on their walls. Miss Stein was one of these. To her mind the ownership of those Picassos was no accident. The providential inner chime which announced the proximity of genius had sounded just as clearly for Gertrude, after all, as it had for Pablo, and if she had no doubts about who had actually painted the pictures, she was equally certain of her own vital part in the ultimate acknowledgment of the greatness and worldwide fame of the one who had.

To achieve this halcyon modus vivendi with masterpieces, Miss Stein may also have had at her command, strange as it may seem, a certain basic indifference to the visual arts. Though she had written word portraits and word genre pictures, though she had bizarrely presumed to transmute into literature the "sensation" of Cézanne, she had not, in fact, ever painted a painting. And in the arbitrary world of her aesthetic judgments, it was her private, subjective experience alone that determined the character of her objective convictions. Despite the unerring discrimination of her taste as a young woman, she may always have been more interested in painters than she was in painting, particularly if the painters were prepared to accept her artistic dominion. As she grew older, this disposition led her to praise the works of men who had only their personal admiration for her to offer as proof of creative distinction, and the pity is that she evidently found the proof persuasive.

Miss Stein's personality dominated her collection. And likewise, her portrait dominated all the pictures surrounding it. That one painting seemed to unite forever in a single work of art not only the artist and his model in their joint quest for immortality but also in an intimately independent way two beings of genius and both of their separate, incommunicable personalities. Its presence in that room was insistent and unforgettable, because in its own way it seemed to be Gertrude, while she in her own way seemed to be it. One could never ignore her portrait, because one could never ignore her. It was there, as she was, with overpowering and indomitable immediacy. Hanging as it did above the fireplace, it hung higher than any of the other pictures, as if to remind them that they were, as they were, lesser works of art. And it appeared to remind us, too, that we were mere humans, living things that would die, while it, being a great work of art, would endure and survive us all, supreme in the mastery and self-possession of its abiding presence. It is no accident that throughout the years of absence from Paris during the Occupation, Miss Stein's portrait was the only Picasso that kept her company in her rural hiding place to remind her of the many that had been left behind. Where it was, she was. "For me," she wrote, "it is I, and it is the only reproduction of me which is always I, for me." She often stood in front of it while talking, as if to demonstrate by the juxtaposition that in the end the real and the ideal might be made one, after all. Her portrait by Picasso was a vivid, tangible demonstration and embodiment of her own genius and her own immortality.

Gertrude talked, the soldiers listened and everybody was happy. I wondered about Miss Toklas. She sat quietly by, seldom participating in any occasion other than to pass the delicious cookies she had made or, when pressed for an opinion, to agree automatically with some pronouncement of Miss Stein's. Occasionally, however, she did make a waspish, irrelevant remark, and this obviously irritated Gertrude Stein and sometimes her guests. But for the most part Miss Toklas seemed rather out of it, neglected and ignored. To be sure, the GIs had no wives for her to talk to, as she had in bygone years talked to the wives of the great men who were conversing with Gertrude. But none of the GIs were great men either. Still, the striking imbalance in the social status of the two women was disconcerting. Whatever their private relations may have been, in public Alice was the inferior, and

9

everyone who came to the rue Christine seemed constrained to acknowledge it. That sense of constraint at times made me uncomfortable, for I felt that it must at times have made Alice uncomfortable, too. But Gertrude's naturally expansive and peremptory manner left no option. Indeed, as I returned regularly to the rue Christine, I had become more and more aware of Miss Stein's monolithic egotism, which seemed to take substance from the whole universe and to express itself with indefatigable self-sufficiency.

What she talked about I did not record, but the topics were probably not of great moment, and, in any case, would change nothing of our opinion or understanding of Gertrude. Whatever she may have said, she was talking about herself, and it is she who remains unforgettable. In her beautiful and interminable voice she talked and talked and talked, and her talk was very like her writing. It ran on regardless of conventional usage and syntax, yet most of the talk—unlike much of the writing—made perfectly good sense. Miss Stein was nobody's fool, and she took care to let one know that. Like all remarkable performers, she was mindful of her audience. She lectured and admonished us but she amused us. Although she always held the center of the stage, her spectators were made to feel that their role, passive as it might be, was no less vital than her own. For this she was willing to take great pains, though these could never be extended to the acknowledgment or acceptance of her youthful guests as individuals. Still, she rarely turned away any who wished to be admitted. And for some of those who showed cause why they should be invited to return, she even offered to read and criticize manuscripts, which she did with painstaking conscientiousness. It was made clear, however, that no one else was expected, or would be allowed, to share the spotlight. The wings, perhaps, at best. I remember very well how summarily she dealt with any who were so foolhardy as to interrupt or, worse, so insolent as to contradict her. Glaring at the offender, she would simply repeat what she had already said but in a louder voice. If the transgressor presumed to insist, she would repeat herself again and in a still louder voice, then if necessary yet again and louder still. No one was disposed to enter into a shouting match with an elderly lady. As very young men, we were expected to say yes, and little more.

Miss Stein was interested in the GIs because they were interested in her. That was her natural state of being. But it was also natural to her to assume that because she saw them at all, she saw them as they really were. In this she was mistaken. She couldn't understand them because she had no interest in them for their own sake. And yet she wrote a book about them: *Brewsie and Willie*. It was her last book and one of her worst, because it presumes to speak for once of people other than herself. She completely failed to express the concerns or to portray the spirit of even the rather specialized GIs whom she met.

Some of us may have fancied at the time that we were another Lost Generation. Miss Stein was not of that opinion. I once asked her what she had meant by her famous remark, and when she had explained requested her to write out for me the explanation. She did.

"I only repeated what a Frenchman said, that between the ages of seventeen and twenty then human beings become civilized, and if they have no civil life they miss the moment of becoming civilized and are a lost generation. Not this time, though, for other reasons."

She didn't trouble to specify what those other reasons might be, and I was not so bold as to inquire. But it doesn't matter, because even if she had had an answer, it would have been an abstraction of her own devising, not a reasoned judgment based upon study or understanding of the generation in question.

And yet upon occasion she could be feeling and generous. She asked whether I would like her to read something I had written. It was a play based on a wartime incident described some months before in the French newspapers. The next time I went to the rue Christine, Miss Stein took me aside to tell me her reaction. She had read the play with evident diligence and care. Though she could hardly have found it entertaining, for it was plodding and conventional, yet she made it her business to commend as well as to criticize, and she did both with a thoughtful seriousness not in the least condescending. At the last she said, "Your writing reads well, and maybe someday writing will be a reality for you, and I have one piece of advice to give you that every writer who is going to be a real writer must be given sometime by somebody, and it is to consider your emotions more carefully. A real writer must be very sure of his emotions before putting a pen on paper, so that is what I advise you to do, to consider your emotions more carefully."

It was excellent advice, which I have tried to heed. Miss Stein was gracious and kindly. I thanked her. Perhaps she did believe I might eventually become a real writer, but I am sure she never fancied for an instant that I might one day have the temerity to wonder in print whether she was capable of practicing what she preached.

The last time I saw her has with the years been made especially memorable by regret. Not alone for what happened but even more for the fact that it was, indeed, the very last time I ever saw Gertrude Stein and consequently had no opportunity afterward to try to redeem the memory of that afternoon from my own rudeness and ignorance.

Picasso had introduced me not only to Miss Stein and Miss Toklas but to a number of other people as well, among them a young Russian-French painter of exceptional promise named Chapoval. He later killed himself, aged only thirty-two, but that is another story. Chapoval did not know Gertrude. But he knew about her collection, of course, and wanted to see it. Never stopping to wonder why Picasso himself might not have arranged this, I blithely assured Chapoval that nothing could be easier and that I would simply take him along with me one day to the rue Christine. That I did so may be construed as evidence not only of my callow nonchalance but of the extraordinarily free and easy etiquette which Miss Stein allowed to prevail. To be sure, it had been rather the same in the old days at 27, rue de Fleurus, where even those who presented themselves on Saturday evenings without pretending to be a friend of a friend were usually admitted.

Therefore, with Chapoval alongside me, I confidently went one afternoon to ring the familiar bell. It was a rainbow day of late summer, when any youth in Paris can feel that he holds the world in his hand simply because he has accomplished the miracle of being alive.

Miss Stein in person, which was not at all her custom, opened the door. She nevertheless greeted me amiably enough. I introduced Chapoval to her, then said I hoped our visit was not inopportune and explained that we did not mean to disturb her but only wanted to have a look at the pictures.

The grossness of my blunder became clear immediately. Frowning, she said, "This is no museum. You can't just come round here to gawk anytime you feel like it. Besides, it's not convenient."

"But Chapoval is a friend of Picasso," I absurdly protested.

"Then let him go and ask Picasso to see some Picassos," retorted Gertrude at once. "Picasso has a lot more Picassos than I have. Go and ask him to show them to you, and then maybe you'll see what sort of a man Picasso is, too, if you don't know it already, and then you'll see something about Picasso. But you can't come bursting in here."

Embarrassed, humiliated, I stood back on the landing in clumsy, flushed silence.

"Well," said Gertrude after a pause, "I'm going out to do an errand in a minute, and you can both walk with me if you like. You just wait here, then we'll go down and you can walk with me while I do my errand."

She closed the door. We awkwardly stood and fidgeted but waited. Miss Stein returned presently with Basket on a leash and we went down the staircase. In the street we turned right and then right again along the narrow sidewalk of the rue des Grands-Augustins. The dog walked in front, then his mistress, then I, beside her but a little behind her, while Chapoval came a few paces in back of us. I can't remember what we were talking about. My notebook doesn't say. Gertrude was talking, no doubt. When we reached the rue St.-André-des-Arts and turned left there in the lemon sunshine, she said something about the number of GIs who were already being shipped home for discharge, the war being at last over. Their visits had begun to weary her, but she nonetheless felt sorry to see them go. And it was sad for them, too, she added, it was sad that they had to go home and take off their uniforms and be done with war and the army, because never again in their lives would they be so happy.

At that moment, of course, there was hardly an American in uniform who didn't long to shed it as quickly as possible. We were all sick of the war, sick of the army. We only longed to sit in hometown living rooms and eat apple pie. I disagreed with Miss Stein, and said so.

She stopped abruptly and faced me on the sidewalk in the sun. She irritably repeated what she had already said and added that it didn't matter what I thought at the moment, or what all the GIs thought, indeed, since their wartime experiences were ones they would look back on all their lives with pleasure and nostalgia, because then they had been carefree among other men and because men loved fighting.

But not dying, I thought, not suffering. I had done no actual fighting myself, but I had seen some of it. I had seen dead men and dying men. I had seen prisoner-of-war camps, the abjection, misery and despair breeding in the filth and mud. I had seen too much and all of it was too recent and too overwhelming for me to be able to understand or to acknowledge in what way Miss Stein was, of course, right. I said again that I disagreed with her.

She frowned sternly at me, solid as cement in her tweed suit, and she said, "Well, it doesn't matter whether you think so or not. What matters is that I'm right, and you'll think so in due time, and that's all that matters, but you're too young, you're too young and inexperienced now to understand."

I stood there. And then I said, "But you're not right. You're wrong. And you're a stupid old woman and you don't understand anything."

I turned away. Without waiting for her to answer me, I turned away abruptly and left her standing there in the street with her white dog on the leash. I walked quickly toward the rue des Grands-Augustins without once looking back. I went round the corner, and I never saw Gertrude Stein again.

I was trembling. With anger, with amazement at my own temerity, and even then, I trust, with some sense of regret. Chapoval had come along behind me, but after talking for a minute about what had happened, we parted in the street.

My feeling at the moment was principally one of indignation at the idea of an elderly woman presuming to understand better than I the true nature of my recent experiences, and to talk down to me about them. As I walked back along the rue des Grands-Augustins, approaching No. 7, I made up my mind to go and see Picasso to tell him what had happened. Since it was the afternoon, and not the time when he usually received visitors, I had to ring at some length in the half-darkness at the top of the staircase. Finally Picasso himself muttered through the heavy oak door, asking who was there.

"It's Lord," I said.

He opened a crack but didn't let me in. It was obvious that my unannounced arrival was not to his liking, and he irritably asked what I wanted.

"I've just left Gertrude Stein," I explained. "We had a dispute. I wanted to tell you about it."

Immediately the door opened wide. He said, "Come in, then." We went through the narrow passageway and to the left past the kitchen into the high, rectangular room where visitors habitually had to wait in the mornings to see him. He sat on the edge of a table and eagerly said, "Tell."

While I explained in detail what had happened Picasso grew angry and excited, muttering repeatedly, "The slut!" and "The pig!"

When I had finished, he jumped from the table and said, "So you see what she's like. I must say it took you long enough to realize it. That very first day, when I sent you over there to see her, I expected you to come right back in half an hour and tell me what a slut she is. That pig! A real fascist, what's more. She always had a weakness for Franco. Imagine! For Pétain, too. You know, she wrote speeches for Pétain. Can you imagine it? An American. A Jewess, what's more. And she's fat as a pig. You know, she once sent me a photo of herself standing in front of an auto, and you couldn't even see the auto. Gertrude took up the whole photo, that pig."

I was dumbfounded by this outburst, and couldn't understand why, if Picasso felt as he said he did about Gertrude, he had ever sent me to see her in the first place. But I didn't know him very well then.

Picasso was still talking. "And all she says about me and my painting. To listen to her anybody would think she's manufactured me piece by piece. But if you want to see how much she really understands about painting, all you have to do is look at the crap she likes now. She says the same things about Hemingway, too. Those two were made for each other, though. I never cared for him, never. He never had the true understanding of bullfights the way a Spaniard truly understands them. He was a phony, Hemingway. I always knew that, but Gertrude didn't know it. He came to see me at the Liberation, and he gave me a patch from the tunic of an SS man with 'SS' embroidered on it, and he told me he'd killed the man himself. That was a lie. Maybe he killed lots of wild animals, but he never killed a man. If he had, he wouldn't have had to pass out souvenirs. He was a phony, and that's why Gertrude liked him. All the rest of us always liked Fitzgerald. He was the one we all thought had the real talent. As for the Toklas, that little witch, do you know why she wears her hair in bangs?" Picasso laughed loudly. "She had a horn," he said. "In the middle of her forehead. A growth like a rhinoceros. So they made the perfect couple, Gertrude and Alice, the hippopotamus and the rhinoceros. But then Alice had the horn cut off, and her bangs are supposed to cover up the hole." He kept on laughing for a time, and then he said, "So now you know what Gertrude is like, that slut."

Suddenly he turned away. He seemed to have lost all interest in the subject of Gertrude and Alice. It was apparent that he wanted me to go, and I had the peculiar impression that for him it was as though everything I had just told him, and everything he had just said to me, as well as I myself, were all at once nonexistent. He explained that he was busy and that I would have to leave.

I walked back toward my billet across the courtyard of the Louvre and up the Avenue de l'Opéra, surprised, perplexed and rather awed, to write down what had happened in my schoolboy's notebook with its green oilcloth cover.

Gertrude Stein, it is true, was quite reactionary in her political thinking, inasmuch as she thought politically at all, which was very little, since she essentially recognized no authority other than her own genius and felt that the workaday world could hardly do better than to follow her example. In this, of course, she was like most artists, particularly great ones, and Picasso in his own way was a far more flagrant example of such temperament than Gertrude ever was. In any case, I was amazed by the idea that she might have written speeches for Marshal Pétain. That such a stolid, vainglorious martinet might in times of national calamity have chosen to address his countrymen in the convoluted and prolix style characteristic of Miss Stein seemed to me utterly preposterous. I found out later that, in fact, for reasons I do not know but which were obviously good enough for her, Gertrude had simply translated some of Pétain's speeches into English.

The sequel to Picasso's abusive outburst of that afternoon occurred almost ten years later, and it was typical of him. One spring evening in Provence he and I found ourselves together as guests for dinner in the same house. His behavior on that occasion was a model of the perversity and malice to which all those who knew him had to become accustomed. During dinner he was rude and insulting to me. Afterward in the salon I sat on a chair to the right of the fireplace. Picasso settled at the near end of a couch beside me. Offended and angry, I did not look at him, pretending to be unaware of his presence, not an easy affectation to bring off. The conversation meanwhile came round to Gertrude and Alice. Our host expressed a low, contemptuous opinion of both Gertrude's work and her personality. I objected, naming qualities of the individual and her writings which I thought admirable.

Picasso patted me familiarly, even affectionately, on the arm. "You're quite right, my little Lord," he said. "Gertrude was an extraordinary being. If she came into a room, suddenly it was full even when it was empty. And she understood painting. She bought my pictures when no one else in the world wanted any. She was a friend. And she was a writer of the first importance. Think what she did. Well before Joyce. You're quite right," he repeated, patting me again. "You're intelligent, Lord. Gertrude had rare qualities. And Alice, too. Alice and Gertrude were the same person in a way, only different parts. Poor Alice. It must not be very amusing for her now day by day. I guess she's having money troubles. A pity. She had to sell a bunch of my old drawings. Some weren't signed, so they were brought to me to be signed, and I signed them. I was glad to do that to help Alice."

And then two years were still to pass before I learned the story of the radiators. It was a matter long done with by that time, yet in retrospect seems to cast some legitimate light backward. It was told to me by Catherine Dudley, an American from Chicago who had lived in Paris since the twenties. She had at one time been the mistress of Pascin and knew almost everyone in the Parisian art world, including Gertrude, Alice and Picasso. In fact, it was she who with another friend had been instrumental in finding the apartment in the rue Christine. And at the end of the Occupation, having been released from the internment camp where, unlike Gertrude and Alice, she spent the war years, it was Catherine who supervised the preparation of their home for her friends' return. The paintings were all safe, but a quantity of indispensable household appointments were missing. Most of these had been stolen. Some had merely been borrowed.

Throughout the entire Occupation, heating was an urgent problem in Paris. Fuel for stoves became virtually unobtainable, and gas was in too short supply to be used for anything but cooking. However, electricity, though rationed, did remain available. An electric radiator became consequently a possession without price, and even Picasso found it impossible to obtain enough of them to heat his enormous studio. In his surrealist play *Desire Trapped by the Tail*, written in January of 1941, he had feelingly evoked the prevalence of chilblains and the dearth of central heating. Genius seems to exacerbate rather than to alleviate the discomforts and displeasures of daily life. Picasso happily recalled that Gertrude's nearby apartment, standing empty, contained not only more than two dozen of his paintings but also several perfectly good electric radiators. He communicated with his old friend in her country hideout and asked whether she might arrange for him to borrow them. She agreed.

It was mid-December of 1944 when Gertrude and Alice determined to return to Paris. After a cold and difficult journey they finally arrived, bearing with them, in addition to priceless butter and eggs, Gertrude's portrait by Picasso. They were relieved to be home at last and to find all their treasures safe. Picasso came to see them the day after. The reunion was happy and sentimental. But the winter of 1944–45 proved to be exceptionally cold and long. The two elderly ladies in their high-ceilinged apartment were quickly reminded by the weather of their absent radiators. They asked Picasso to return them. He promised to do so. They waited. The radiators were not forthcoming. They asked again. Picasso apologized and promised again to return the radiators. Still they did not appear. Yet again, and with asperity no doubt, Gertrude requested the prompt return of her property. Picasso promised yet again to oblige. But he was exasperated by the insistence of his old friend. "She wants me to freeze to death," he complained to his newly acquired young mistress, Françoise Gilot. However, he did not use the radiators very often, for electricity in post-Liberation Paris was extremely expensive, and despite his fabulous wealth Picasso liked to spare expense. When the radiators finally came back to the rue Christine, it was spring.

2

In 1946, when Gertrude Stein died, I was in the United States. I remember the brilliant marine blue of that July day on Cape Cod when a chance acquaintance told me of her death. I did not feel bereaved, certainly, nor even very sad, but I was sorry again that I would never have an opportunity to try to make amends for having called a true artist a stupid old woman.

I had not been particularly friendly with Alice Toklas, and indeed on more than one occasion had written in my notebook that I found her presence irritating. I had from the first, as a matter of fact, felt Miss Toklas not to be a friendly person. This seeming lack of warmth may have been merely a by-product of Gertrude's all-consuming egotism. With intimate friends Alice may have been affable and demon-

strative. I had no idea. In any case, some weeks after Miss Stein's death
I wrote a letter to Miss Toklas, expressing what could only have been
the most conventional of condolences.

She replied. Her letter, written on September 10, was short and
formal, penned in that painstaking, arachnid script which seemed so
strangely inappropriate to her quiet and self-effacing person. She
thanked me for having remembered her and written. Then there was
one brief sentence which stood out immediately with arresting intensity
on that half page of cheap paper: "I am staying on here alone." That
sentence seemed to bear beyond distance and time the feeling and
significance of a living lifetime. "I am staying on here alone." It was
moving and unforgettable, but I had no idea then, nor could she herself
have guessed, of the cruel exactitude with which her purpose would
be fulfilled. Miss Toklas concluded her letter by asking that I come to
see her when next in France, and I promised myself to do that.

It was in the early spring of 1947 before I again spent any time
in Paris. Then I telephoned to the rue Christine. DANton 65-06. I
remember the number even now. Miss Toklas answered. She asked
me to come and see her in the afternoon a few days later.

It was the same. The high, eighteenth-century calm of the staircase, the smell of wax, the brightly polished brasses of the door were
all the same. A maid opened for me and led me through the hall hung
with Picassos. It was the same. Miss Toklas came to the salon door to
greet me, smiling but formal, a little more stooped than before, perhaps,
and yet the same. We went together into the salon, and it was the
same.

Except that Picasso's portrait of Gertrude was gone. Which is to
say that the room was utterly, irreparably and desolately different. The
entire apartment was different. And nothing, nothing even in illusion
for an instant, could ever possibly be the same again. Gertrude was
gone. And not only Gertrude herself but also the ideal, immutable
image and symbol of her was gone; the one reproduction of her that
had always been Gertrude for Gertrude, and consequently for Alice as
well, was gone. They were separated in the mind as well as in the flesh.
Gertrude had gone to join the immortals, and in substance she had
taken with her the all-embracing evidence of her immortality. It was
lost forever to the home and the life which for thirty-eight years she
had shared with Alice, and in which it had dominated every other

material thing. Gertrude had taken good care before dying to make sure that her portrait should afterward without delay be housed in a place where the august presence of other masterpieces would corroborate the very concept of immortality and shed added glory forever upon that embodiment of her genius. It hangs today in the Metropolitan Museum of Art in New York, a city where Miss Stein herself was never at home, but there in the greatest museum of her homeland it is appropriately kept company by the effigies of pharaohs, deities of every variety and sundry other immortals, and every year millions of people pass before it who have never heard of Alice B. Toklas.

"I am staying on alone," she had written. Alone, indeed. In that apartment where they had long lived together, Alice was now alone. It abounded in reminders and memories of Gertrude, certainly, but the one presence which had always been Gertrude more than any other save Gertrude herself was absent. And it was none other than Gertrude who had determined that this should be so. When Alice stood in the salon and looked at the place above the mantel where the painting had hung, she no longer saw the portrait of her lifelong friend and companion; she saw another painting by Picasso which she had hung there in the hope of compensating for the presence now irretrievably lost, with the result, she said, that the room seemed emptier than ever. "They took the Picasso portrait for the Metropolitan ten days ago," she wrote to a friend. "It was another parting and completely undid me."

Miss Stein had made her will four days before her death. There is no reason to believe that she knew she was so soon to die. Yet that eventuality can hardly have been absent from her mind as she lay ill in the American Hospital, aged seventy-two, and prepared to make final disposition of her possessions, of which the importance had been so vital and evident to her. At last she was in a position to consider conclusively the importance to her life of the people who were also to remain behind, to weigh as best she could their feelings and to determine accordingly their appropriate relationship with the possessions. She could no longer think of herself, her own existence and her own significance as constituents of unlimited experience and undiminished awareness. For the first time in her life, perhaps, and for what little of it was to remain, life itself could only be visualized in terms of the beings and things that would survive her. But things, unlike beings, have an arbitrary and intractable existence of their own, unaffected by the desires and oblivious to the feelings of their possessors, whose feelings and desires they nevertheless frequently embody and consequently control.

Alice, as always, was at hand. Gertrude may have discussed with her the terms of the will. But Alice would certainly not have offered any objection to them. Not then. Not when her friend, as she knew even if Gertrude didn't, lay mortally ill. Not after a lifetime of accommodation and acquiescence. The property, like the will, was Gertrude's. And the word "will" abruptly in this context assumes a far-reaching and inflexible connotation.

Gertrude bequeathed her portrait by Picasso to the Metropolitan Museum of Art. To Yale University went all her private papers and manuscripts, with instructions to her executors to provide for publication of all writings—and these were plenteous—not yet published. To Alice was left everything else. The legacy, however, bore a decisive restriction. The money, the securities, the personal property and above all the pictures were not unreservedly Alice's to do with as she saw fit. She was to be the trustee only, merely the custodian, enjoying Miss Stein's belongings until her own death, when the entire estate would pass to Gertrude's nephew, Allan, or to his heirs, upon whom no restriction was placed.

The practical purpose underlying this condition was presumably to avoid double payment of inheritance taxes. And yet Gertrude Stein more than most people must have appreciated that death provides for no afterthoughts and that life is fraught with unforeseeable contingencies. She must have known that money very often brings out the worst in people. She must have realized that no human relationship is secure from the eventuality of estrangement. But perhaps she was unable to imagine that the future after her death might be other than it had been during her lifetime.

Being Gertrude Stein, she may never have fancied that Alice might take it upon herself to survive for twenty years. After the decades of deference and service, she may simply have assumed that her friend would naturally not leave her alone for long and would be content throughout eternity to sit in a corner talking to Xanthippe while she discoursed with Socrates.

However it may have been, there was a vital failure of imagination.

In her life Gertrude had wished to prolong beyond the grave the works of her living imagination, but she proved incapable of imagining or foreseeing the needs of those who would remain on the near side of that grave. Throughout her entire career as a writer she deliberately put theory before feeling. Perhaps in her life that same disposition prevailed. She worried and wrote interminably about the elusive nature of her own identity. The quality and fate of Alice's may not have caused her equivalent concern. Of her own emotions she may not have been a very severe or serious judge.

Having quested after immortality in her art, Gertrude contrived in her personal life strangely to do the same. Whether consciously or unconsciously, she did succeed in prolonging after death the subservience in which Alice had lived for so long, which had had a point and a purpose while Gertrude lived but which with her loss became purposeless and pointless and ultimately added grievance to Alice's grief. Perhaps Gertrude cared very much for her nephew. Some atavistic sense of the responsibility of kinship may have moved her. It is beside the point. No tie of consanguinity, no familial responsibility can compare to the bond created between two beings by thirty-eight years of uninterrupted devotion and intimacy. If Gertrude and Alice had been man and wife, of course, the problem and its poignant aftermath would in all likelihood never have arisen. But man and wife were precisely what they were not, and no determination of affection apparently could undo the ambiguity of nature.

To be sure, it was specifically stated in Gertrude's will that the executors were authorized to make payments to Alice, and for that purpose if necessary to sell paintings, "insofar as it may become necessary for her proper maintenance and support." But the executors, in addition to a Baltimore attorney, were Alice herself and Allan Stein, the very two individuals whose immediate and ultimate interests in the disposition of the estate it would have been reasonable to assume might one day come into conflict.

And so it was, after the cooking of all those meals and the typing of all those manuscripts, after the providing of comforts and the devising of pleasures, after the aiding and the abetting, after the days and the nights, that Alice B. Toklas found herself not the proprietor but merely the keeper of all the possessions which by their secure and familiar presence might in her bereavement and loneliness have as-

sured her of her own continuity and diminished the anguish of sep-
aration. The things were not really hers, not even as much hers now
as they had been before Gertrude died. To accept this, to adapt to it
an entire notion of life and the future would have been difficult for
anyone. For Alice it proved impossible. She remained as she had been,
as she had become by living with, and for, Gertrude, and her relationship with Gertrude's former possessions remained as it had been
during Gertrude's lifetime. But Gertrude was no longer there to decide
and sanction, and she had not bequeathed that entire authority to Alice.
It was the one legacy that might have made the end of Alice's life less
sad, less desolate and less deprived than it was. For she could not
change. Her folly, as certain of their oldest friends called it, was simply
that she remained true to the self and to the life that had been dear
to Gertrude Stein.

These considerations may seem unimportant and irrelevant today.
But they are not, because Gertrude is not. She has achieved her ambition. Of all the steps on the endless path toward immortality the most
treacherous and arduous is the first. Gertrude has taken it with ease.
For two generations after her death she has remained vividly present,
and so by the same token has Alice. Whatever concerns them is of
legitimate concern, for seldom has the work of any writer been more
profoundly and decisively inseparable from the character and temperament of its author. Her subject matter was her subject matter itself,
its raison d'être was its selfsame raison d'être, and her own being was
the entire raison d'être and subject matter of her being. Alice made
the vital contribution of her lifetime to this chain of necessity. She
provided for Gertrude the artful, living link between life and art which
alone can reconcile the artist to his life. It is essential, and its raison
d'être, too, is simply that it has to be. Alice added to literature, for she
added to Gertrude.

It has been suggested by some, by Hemingway and others, that
beneath Alice's outward deference lay a ruthless will of her own and
the shrewd faculty to use it. Perhaps. I find this difficult to believe. It
accords not at all with Alice's lifelong public behavior and is contradicted both by Gertrude's work and by her will. Neither before Miss
Stein's death nor in the years afterward, when I saw Miss Toklas
frequently, did I ever observe anything to suggest, even by implication,
that she might in private have attempted to dominate the ménage. Can

it have been merely the accident of alphabetical precedence which caused the name of Miss Stein to stand above that of Miss Toklas on their joint calling card? Alice herself later said to one of Gertrude's biographers, "I am a person acted upon, not one who acts." She may at times have been contrary or demanding, to be sure. Most people are. But the life which the two women lived out together must have been essentially as it appeared. Such remains the wonder, the virtue and the pathos of it.

So it was, as I've said, not quite a year after Gertrude's death that I first came back to the rue Christine. I sat on the horsehair sofa as I had on my first visit two years before, which then seemed so long, long past, and Miss Toklas likewise sat opposite me in the small armchair. To her right was a side table holding an ashtray and a teacup, to her left a high window that shed late light, accenting her forthright Semitic features. I tried to see beneath her bangs the hole Picasso had mentioned, but neither then nor afterward did I ever discern any trace of it.

We had tea, and I didn't know what to say. This was the first time since our first meeting that I had ever been alone with Miss Toklas. I remembered having failed to understand which General Grant she and Gertrude admired, and I wondered whether she, too, remembered. Not knowing what to say, I looked around, and it seemed easy to talk about the pictures.

Over Miss Toklas's right shoulder, hanging to the right of the fireplace, was a small Picasso watercolor of a single apple. I spoke of it admiringly, and Alice told me that Picasso had painted it especially to console Gertrude for the loss of a small Cézanne still life of apples which Leo Stein had insisted upon having when he and his sister divided their joint collection before World War I. I asked how the collection had actually been divided. It had been very simple, Alice explained. "Gertrude was in one room, and Leo in another. They weren't speaking at the time. I went from one to the other with the paintings until the selection had been made." And it had been equable enough, she added, for the Cézanne apples had turned out to be the only picture that both refused to part with. But Gertrude finally let it go, Alice said, because Leo was absolutely adamant, and when Gertrude didn't know what to do, he sent word that she should think of it as an act of God.

Talking about the paintings, looking from one to another, it seemed natural to me to speak of the portrait. How it might have seemed to Alice I didn't stop to think at the moment, and afterward it was too late. I said, "The room doesn't seem the same without the portrait."

"No." She twisted round and glanced above the fireplace, as if to take stock yet again of that irremediable absence. Then she said, "I wanted to keep it here as long as I could. I asked them to leave it as long as possible. But they had to have it at last, and they have it now. In fact, I received a letter only a few days ago to say that the portrait had been placed on exhibition in the entrance hall of the museum. Gertrude would be pleased. That's what she wanted. But it's not the same. You're right. Without the portrait it's not the same here at all. But nothing at all is the same, anyway."

I was embarrassed. Miss Toklas, however, seemed composed. We talked about other things, about some of the other GIs who had come to the rue Christine in 1945 and what they were doing, about what I was doing, about one thing and another. We sat in that high, serene room with its masterpieces and memories, we drank tea, smoked cigarettes, and presently I realized with surprise and pleasure that we were having a conversation. It was something that had never happened to me before in that place. It was delightful.

Miss Toklas liked to talk. She did it well, without restraint and at length. But she enjoyed being talked to as well, and her own pleasure in expressing herself seemed to depend on the readiness and ability of her listener to do likewise. In short, she was a conversationalist. She delighted in telling stories, too, recounting in great detail picturesque anecdotes and vivid reminiscences of people and places. Her voice was throaty, a little hoarse, lower than Gertrude's, sometimes melodious, sometimes rasping, but always expressive, even when at the end of her life its vibrancy and volume had gone. She accompanied her talk with little gestures of her cigarette and nods of her head. She laughed easily, often at her own remarks, of which she unaffectedly enjoyed the pointed and frequently irreverent wit. To talk with Miss Toklas was a pleasure, and she herself seemed to accept with candid satisfaction that this should be so, as if from the beginning it had never been otherwise.

Many people came to see Alice in the rue Christine during those first years after Gertrude's death. Some were old friends. Some were acquaintances. Some were those who despite the absence of the star wished to see the stage upon which she had performed, to meet the great woman's handmaid and alter ego and, perhaps, by identifying themselves with the locale and the survivor of an illustrious past, to achieve some enhanced identity of their own. Miss Toklas cordially welcomed them all, and her identity, too, as the years passed, may have seemed to be enhanced. Without Gertrude the days and the months were fundamentally empty, to be sure. That was the basic fact upon which every other fact rested, and Alice said so. Still, there were letters to be written, books to be read and meals to be cooked. There were people to be seen. There were many people, and all of them were coming to see her, to be with her, to talk to her. She knew perfectly well that some of them saw in her only the Alice B. Toklas who had lived with Gertrude Stein, but that, of course, was what she had been all her life, and to find herself assigned to the auxiliary role even after Gertrude's death can hardly have been a surprise whenever it occurred. She enjoyed her guests. With them in conversation she could relive the celebrated past and appreciate the unforeseen present, in which she surprisingly found herself called upon to do most of the talking. Little by little it seemed that Alice without Gertrude was not less Alice but more.

Through these years, living mostly in Paris as I did, I saw Miss Toklas regularly. In the late afternoon or, more often as time passed, in the evening, I would go to the rue Christine to eat, drink and converse with her. Alice usually sat in the same little armchair between the fireplace and the window, a package of Pall Mall cigarettes tucked beside her, from which with evident relish she frequently selected and lit one. I no longer sat on the sofa but on a chair closer to her, for as the years passed she grew harder and harder of hearing. In the fine room at night the lighting was not bright. The pictures, objects and furniture merged into a noble but featureless background. Beside Alice's chair there was a lamp, focusing upon her and what she said the entire significance of the moment.

Of my many conversations with Alice Toklas I unfortunately recorded few, writing down next to nothing at the time. But Alice herself is easy to remember. She made herself memorable by contriving with candor and exactitude to be herself. And it is this above all which through the years I gradually came to understand, and which I remember still with emotion and respect.

The lives of most people are shaped by mindless and uncontrollable chance. I never felt this to be true of Alice Toklas. As she talked and talked of the past and of her life with Gertrude Stein, I became convinced that it had been as it had been because she had had the wit and self-possession to sense from the beginning what might be, and had purposefully and deliberately chosen to live the life which she and Gertrude lived together for nearly forty years. Only that sort of lucid and forceful resolve, coupled, of course, with an emotional crystallization that gives it daily relevance, can provide the vital momentum that keeps a lifetime secure from chance and sustains its intrinsic fulfillment. From the first Alice must have decided that her part was to serve Gertrude, to serve above all Gertrude's sovereign compulsion to write, and to serve accordingly the being who led a life separate from theirs and who eventually became the world-famous author Gertrude Stein. In doing so and by becoming consequently indispensable, Alice served her own purpose as well. Nothing is indispensable to an artist save what *is* indispensable. To be and to provide this service for Gertrude was Alice's particular genius. Only someone who knew her can appreciate how utterly vital to *The Autobiography of Alice B. Toklas* Alice B. Toklas actually was. And it was Alice's capital concern to try to sustain this vital link with her friend's creative life after Gertrude's death by providing for the publication of all those unpublished writings which had been left behind. That is principally what she needed money for, and that is mainly why her material circumstances became first precarious and finally tragic.

Alice liked to go out as well as to entertain at home. In particular she enjoyed fine restaurants, where her justly famous gourmet tastes could receive their due. Her comings and goings in public during the late forties and early fifties did not pass unnoticed, for her attire seemed devised to accentuate, if not to flaunt, the singularity of her appearance. I remember one morning in the rue Jacob seeing ahead of me on the sidewalk an outsize, flat-brimmed black hat festooned with a luxuriance of black ostrich feathers. It was set squarely on top of a diminutive person wearing a black coat that fell almost to the ground, and by the extravagant disproportion of its size the hat appeared to be propelling its wearer along the street rather than vice versa. Curious, I hurried ahead to see who it was, and of course it was Alice. On another occasion I recall meeting her at a concert. She was wearing openwork leather sandals over her stockings, a long black skirt, a long black lace shawl over her white shirtwaist and a hat in the form of a wreath made of gold lamé leaves interspersed with red celluloid berries. She carried a very large white handbag and a black cane. People stared. If they did not realize who it was, they inquired, and when they had been told, they said, "Oh yes." Everywhere that Alice went everyone had heard of Alice B. Toklas. For a time during those years she was a celebrated personage in her own right, a condition which she obviously enjoyed and which gave pleasure to those to whom her friendship gave pleasure.

But then the years passed. The visitors grew fewer. Alice grew older and her financial resources grew less, while the publication of the unpublished writings continued to call for cash. It was to earn money that she had written her famous cookbook, in which the recipe for pithy reminiscence and irreverent witticism is presented as capably as the recipe for boeuf bourguignon or hashish fudge. Though reluctant to deplete her friend's collection, need of money nonetheless compelled her to sell a picture, dutifully obtaining beforehand the appropriate legal permission. It was not a major work. Allan Stein had died only five years after his aunt, having achieved in all his lifetime, as Alice acidly observed, no greater distinction than to have been painted by Picasso and Matisse. His three children were now the expectant heirs to the artistic, and monetary, riches hanging on the walls of the rue Christine. The material preservation and financial appreciation of this prospective bonanza became the abiding care of these three and especially of their mother, the widow of Allan Stein. It so absorbed them that they felt no sympathy for the person and, as it turned out, no concern for the "proper maintenance and support" of the aged lady who had been lifelong companion to the original collector of the treasures. Nor were they ever moved to contribute so much as a tittle to the posthumous glory of their future benefactress by financing publication of her unpublished writings.

Alice repaid in kind the indifference of her friend's eventual heirs. She knew perfectly well, having been on hand, that Gertrude had all her life sold pictures when in need of extra cash, and certainly without troubling to ask anyone's permission. Alice serenely proceeded to do likewise. Finding herself short of money once more and determined to continue publication of the posthumous works, she blithely sold a score or so of Picasso's drawings without bothering about legal niceties. That the terms of Gertrude's will might have induced her to be more circumspect gave her no pause. After all, the money was to be spent on Gertrude.

Allegations have been made to the effect that Alice was extravagant not only in her passion for expensive foods and fine restaurants but also in the carelessness with which she sold works of art, accepting for them far less than she should have. Gertrude had never bought paintings as a financial speculation. Indeed, she once said that no one guided by such motives could ever form a first-class collection. When time vindicated her aesthetic acumen, she no doubt thought it perfectly natural, but the stupendous increases in the value of her collection must have surprised—and definitely delighted—her. It enabled her to live as she pleased in great comfort and to publish her own works if she felt like it. When she sold a painting, she bore in mind the difference, usually enormous, between what she had paid and what she was being paid. She did not try to drive the hardest bargain, nor could she have succeeded in doing so, as she usually did business with Kahnweiler, famed for being a pincher of pennies. Alice did the same. As a businesswoman she was doubtless naïve, even nonchalant. After a lifetime of familiarity she probably took the pictures rather for granted, which does not mean for a minute she didn't love them. In any case, it was absurd to expect that she might have been a shrewd and resourceful bargainer. And art dealers are not celebrated for the ethical fastidiousness of their professional practices. The ones to whom Alice sold the drawings made a killing, and by so doing they added a further dimension of sorrow to the eventual demise of the vendor.

In 1954 the apartments in the building at 5, rue Christine were offered by the landlord for sale, with the occupants of each apartment given first opportunity to purchase it. Alice certainly had no desire to move, but she just as certainly had no ready money to buy her apartment. There were the pictures, of course, but the Stein heirs had made it plain that they were not disposed to authorize sales. Alice was seventy-six years old. She doubtless counted on her advanced years to avoid ever being obliged to move out of the apartment even though she did not own it. French housing law at that time was such that an owner or landlord could compel his tenant to leave an apartment only after protracted, arduous and unpredictable legal proceedings, and aged tenants were accorded special prerogatives. In any case, Alice did not buy the apartment in the rue Christine, and someone else did.

And so she was older and the visitors were fewer and she went out less and less. When I called to make an appointment to see her, Alice now sometimes urged me to come that very evening. It became obvious that she lacked occupation and companionship. However, in her increasing solitude some solace did prevail. She had become converted to Catholicism and, though she never spoke to me of religion, I suppose it must have been agreeable to her to accept the notion of life after death and thus to entertain the prospect of being reunited with Gertrude. Alice's conversion had been encouraged and her convictions were feelingly confirmed by Dora Maar, who had found God's presence her ultimate consolation in Picasso's absence. The two women saw each other often. They were compatible. Both had been beloved by geniuses, and in time nature and fate had taken both geniuses from them. Picasso had painted Gertrude's portrait. Dora painted Alice's. It is delicate and feminine, as it should be, but penetrating and expressive also, as both women would have willed it to be. For them both the experiences of the past must have been almost unbearably present as the one posed and the other painted. And it is easy to imagine Dora assuring her model and friend that faith would ultimately make right the wrongs of fate and nature.

Meanwhile, Alice's health had begun to fail. I can't remember now the precise chronology or sequence of all her maladies and accidents. But at one time she suffered a severe attack of pernicious jaundice, then her eyesight and hearing grew progressively poorer and poorer and she gradually became crippled with arthritis. Though she had begun to walk with a cane even in the apartment, she fell several times, breaking her hip once, then on another occasion, I believe, her pelvis, and then her wrist. Little by little came the decline. And yet Alice remained resiliently alive. Her wit and mental vitality never left her.

Alice has been accused of being spiteful and malicious. At times she was. Those characteristics were ones she shared with Gertrude, who for her own self-protection and partisan purposes had made good use of Alice's ability to be brusque and caustic. Upon occasion she expressed sarcastic, harsh judgments of others, but generally these were accurate, and she did not make fun of people's weaknesses. Moreover, when she came to write her memoirs she did not say in print any of the severe things she sometimes said in conversation. Especially, for example, she was generous toward Hemingway, of whom her private opinion was contemptuous. But he, of course, was too petty and vindictive to return the favor when he came to prepare the tasteless feast of his own memoirs. To young people, including myself, who sent her their books and manuscripts, Alice was indefatigably gracious and kind, offering encouragement and praise which were often proof more of her tolerant generosity than of her critical discrimination.

In 1960, recuperating from one of her injuries or illnesses, Alice went for an extended sojourn to Rome, where she lived in a pension run by Canadian nuns. She appreciated the mild weather, enjoyed herself and remained away longer than she may have originally intended. During this lengthy absence the person who had bought Alice's apartment saw an opportunity to try to evict her, claiming that the apartment was unused by its tenant and should therefore be freed for occupancy by the proprietor. Eviction, however, was an eventuality that would have to linger long in the courts, outcome unsure, hence not a pressing cause for concern.

Immediate danger came from another quarter. The Stein heirs had also seen an opportunity, though they wished to deprive Alice not of the apartment but of its contents. They cared where the pictures were, not where Alice was. Having learned of the unauthorized sale of the drawings for less than maximum value, outraged at the thought of money lost and fearful lest additional portions of treasure slip through aged and careless fingers, they thought about what could be done. The paintings were not only unguarded in Alice's absence but uninsured, and as their value multiplied the heirs' worry did likewise. Alice was in no position to pay costly insurance premiums. Besides, Gertrude had never done so. Considering the cost prohibitive, she had said that in order to keep the paintings insured she would have had to part with them one after another to pay the premiums. She preferred to enjoy them and trust in fate. But her heirs were interested in cash, not paintings. They meant to enjoy the collection by selling it, and were disposed to trust neither in fate nor in Alice. Her prolonged absence gave them the opportunity for which they'd been waiting. On the grounds of precious property left vulnerable in a vacant apartment they obtained a court order. Entering the apartment where Gertrude and Alice had made their last home, they removed every picture of value from the walls, and Alice never laid eyes on them again.

Far away in Italy she could do nothing. But even if she had been in Paris, she might simply have accepted the inevitable as inevitable. Throughout her life with Gertrude she had done so, and this event was also, however indirectly, of Gertrude's making. Alice was her own self with particular singleness and entirety. Neither Picassos nor dollars would have caused her to be otherwise. And, after all, she wanted nothing more than to be left in peace to live as she pleased and continue with the publication of Gertrude's unpublished works. Perhaps that was folly. To satisfy it, however, a single medium-sized Picasso would have been more than enough. It would have paid for plentiful publications, plus all the creature comforts, fine foods and medical expenses that any woman of eighty-three could conceivably need for the rest of her life. But Gertrude's heirs were not inclined to be as indulgent— or obedient—as their relative and benefactress had desired and willed them to be.

No doubt Gertrude had never foreseen that things might come to this. It is easy to imagine her reaction had she been present. But she was not, and she couldn't come back from the grave or descend from the walls of the Metropolitan Museum to undo what she had done. Nobody can blame Gertrude for the sordid behavior of her relatives. But that they happened to be her heirs was her responsibility alone.

And so, when Alice returned from Italy in 1961, the pictures were gone. After half a century of familiarity, after all the intimate association which added to the meaning of masterpieces the meaning of a lifetime, they were gone. First Alice had lost Gertrude herself, then Gertrude's portrait, and now Gertrude's pictures, the things of all the things still remaining that had most vividly made it seem that Gertrude remained. But acceptance had always been Alice's part, and she accepted, though whenever she looked at the bare walls, she saw their barrenness more plainly than even she could possibly have expected. The apartment had not been repainted for more than fifteen years, with the result that where each picture had hung a discolored area of its exact size now remained. Like drab and disconsolate ghosts, these shapes were far more insistent and inexorable presences than the paintings themselves had been, because they never for a moment allowed one to forget that what had been was now no more. But Alice accepted. She couldn't afford to have the rooms repainted, and she made no effort even to rehang the few pictures that were her property so as to conceal or camouflage the evidence of her privation. The walls remained as they were. Alice lived face to face with absence and emptiness.

The collection of Gertrude Stein meanwhile was sequestered in the vault of the Chase Manhattan Bank in Paris, where, safe alike from the eccentricities of old women and the admiration of connoisseurs, it could serenely increase in value till Alice died. So long as she lived, the Stein heirs could not dispose freely of their treasure. And she lived long. They grew impatient with her durability. As it turned out, though, she did them a favor—inadvertently, one may be sure— for the value of the collection multiplied by more than ten times from the date of Gertrude's death until at last Alice went to join her in the Cemetery of Père Lachaise. And when the pictures were finally resurrected from their venal tomb, the astute and devious negotiations by which they were eventually sold to the highest bidders for six and a half million dollars bore no resemblance to the impulsive and artless salesmanship of the two deceased ladies. The decades avenged them both, however. Had the avaricious Steins sold their two dozen paintings by Picasso and seven by Juan Gris one by one instead of as a lot, saving the finest till last, they would have found themselves far, far richer than in the greediest of their dreams. But greed is always in a hurry.

For the time being Alice remained obdurately alive, and the heirs had to make the best of it. The best of it for them, however, was far from the best for Alice. Deprived of the pictures, she had no means, aside from her own sadly inadequate royalties, of assuring her "proper maintenance and support." The heirs had agreed to grant a minimal monthly allowance, and their Parisian lawyer was designated to have charge of relations with Alice. He was later to become famous for dealing with the estates, and widows, of artists, and he attempted to arrange some sort of deal to settle things despite the inconvenience of an aged woman's will to live. But Alice would have none of it. His attitude toward her was one of overbearing punctiliousness tempered by uncompromising concern for the sole welfare of his clients.

Visits to Alice in those years became poignant and sad. Almost an invalid, she walked very slowly, leaning with shaky care on her cane and on a friendly arm, if there was one. She could no longer hear well enough to speak on the telephone. She could barely guide a pen. Her voice was losing resonance and her eyes strength. The cheerless impression of Alice's own infirmity, when one went to see her, was aggravated by the neglect, disrepair and cumulative deterioration of the apartment. The walls bore those bleak silhouettes of the confiscated pictures. The horsehair furniture, bought in London before World War I, sadly showed its age. The carpeting in many places was worn to the cord, and I wondered whether it might not have caused Alice's broken bones.

But she sat in her armchair and talked with her friends as long as she could. Stooped, her head forward between her shoulders, her eyeglasses set on the beak of her nose, her cigarette dropping ash all round her, she talked on in her fading voice, and laughed, and told stories, and she was herself with resolute and sharp-witted tenacity.

"It's sad," I said to her one evening, though I could hardly have doubted that she felt otherwise, "it's sad to see all those blank spots where the pictures were."

"Oh, not to me, dear," said Alice. "I can't see them. But I can see the pictures in my memory. I remember each one and where it was. I don't need to see them now."

And yet she could see me. And yet she could see flowers, furniture and clouds in the sky. But memory, it is true, did serve her. Memory served her, for example, to recall that she had loved the pictures, and that when Gertrude had sold Picasso's *Girl with a Fan*, she wept. Memory must have served Alice for very much in those years, being toward the end just about all she had. It served, in any event, for the gratifying awareness that Alice B. Toklas alone had served the memory, and honored the last will and testament, of Gertrude Stein as the writer had most wished: by seeing to the posthumous publication of eight volumes of her work. In death, as in life, Alice had served Gertrude by dint of unsparing self-denial. If in her poverty and bereavement she felt entitled to damn her friend's heirs, she never breathed a word of reproach against Gertrude herself.

More than once I asked Miss Toklas why she did not write her memoirs, for the stories she told of the people and the times she had known were always interesting, amusing, alive. She would reply, "Gertrude Stein said everything I have to say." At last, however, again in need of money, she did write *What Is Remembered*. One has only to compare that book with the witty and vivid reminiscences which intersperse the recipes of *The Alice B. Toklas Cookbook* to know that she had waited too long, which is a pity. Then, perhaps, but only then, one may feel that it is too bad she didn't need more money sooner, and for herself.

The Stein heirs, and their lawyer, proved less businesslike about remitting to Alice the promised stipend than they had been about taking from her their property-to-be. The expectation of millions made it easy to forget about the needs of a sick and lonely old woman. The pictures all were safe, yes, but at the time of their removal a couple of trinkets had been overlooked. One of these was a small black-and-white metal sculpture by Picasso that had stood on the mantel beneath Gertrude's portrait. The other, also by Picasso, was a folded and painted paper construction in a shadow box which had stood under the Cubist picture on the commode between the windows. Alice sold the black-and-white sculpture through a friendly dealer, who—in this case, at least—obtained for her a reasonable and sorely needed sum. The heirs' lawyer learned of this and immediately delivered himself of protests, demands, warnings. He insisted that the sale be rescinded and the sculpture sent to join its erstwhile companions in the bank vault. But the purchaser happened to be named Rothschild, and for once the heirs didn't get what they wanted.

Remittances of the stipend were slow, irregular and above all inadequate. Finding it unthinkable that Alice should simply be abandoned to her invalid and lonely fate, a group of her old friends agreed among themselves to assure the "proper maintenance and support" which Gertrude's relatives could not be bothered to provide. They principally contributed money, knowing that it would never be repaid. Some of those who lived in Paris also ran errands, supervised servants and, when necessary, sent for doctors. They did everything they could to make life pleasant as well as tolerable for Alice, but they occasionally complained about her. She could be difficult and demanding. She expected things to be as she wished them to be simply because that was her wish, and when, of course, they turned out to be otherwise, she was displeased. Displeasure was a state of being Alice knew how to express with eloquence.

There were long periods now when she lay bedridden. Very few people saw her. No doubt she was sometimes impatient and irritable. Inaction and tedium must have been very trying for her, as her mind remained clear and her spirit was unaffected by ill health. She was intensely and emotionally grateful for any attention that came to her from beyond the limited confines of her daily existence. Such attentions grew gradually fewer and fewer. Alice could neither telephone nor write letters. These were written for her when possible by a kindly friend named Joseph Barry. A Spanish maid haphazardly took telephone messages. But more and more Alice lived cut off from all life outside the place and conditions of her own survival. And the world that still remembered Gertrude Stein forgot about Alice B. Toklas. She had known for some years after Gertrude's death a time of plenitude and appreciation in her own right. It was past. Aged and decrepit in the shabby, denuded apartment, Alice stayed on alone in an aloneness that was each day more profound and abiding.

Then in 1964 came the final calamity and ultimate deprivation. She was obliged to leave the rue Christine. Having at last won legal jurisdiction, the owners of the apartment did not hesitate to evict the eighty-five-year-old invalid who had known no other home for more than a quarter of a century.

Alice had nowhere to go. Apartments were difficult to find, expensive, and she was incapable of searching for one. Her friends with considerable difficulty finally found a small apartment in an ugly modern building on the rue de la Convention. The neighborhood is drab and far off on the other side of Paris from the handsome, picturesque Sixth Arrondissement where Alice had always lived with Gertrude. By a curious coincidence this new apartment was in the same street and in a building very like the one where Picasso's lifelong companion and secretary, Jaime Sabartés, had an apartment as small and impersonal as Alice's, and where he, too, eventually died alone.

Though she submitted as best she could to her eviction, Alice hated the rue de la Convention. Not because the neighborhood was ugly, for she never went about in it, or because the apartment was small and uncongenial, for she never made any attempt really to live in it, but simply because Gertrude was not there. The rue Christine may have become threadbare and dingy, but Gertrude had lived there in her lifetime, and in Alice's memory she lived there still. The walls there may have been bare, disfigured by cupidity and loss, but they still held Gertrude. In the rue de la Convention, Gertrude was absent with overwhelming absence, she was dead with absolute and unmerciful deadness. No attempt was ever made to arrange that apartment as a place in which someone might someday enjoy an expectant or pleasurable life. The furniture stood around awkwardly under the too low ceilings, unused and incongruous, as if the movers had indifferently placed it where it now stood when they first carried it in. The pale plaster walls were unadorned. No rugs lay on the floors or curtains hung at the windows. Alice lived in that apartment with regret and desolation. Most of her life there was spent in bed. If she did not always thank fate, or her friends, for having installed her in the rue de la Convention, it is —unhappily—little wonder.

Before Alice's last move, I, too, had moved, returning temporarily to live in the United States. But on a visit to Paris in 1965 I was able to arrange, after several telephone conversations with a maid, to visit the rue de la Convention.

I arrived late in the afternoon. The maid received me with the practiced officiousness of a servant who is accustomed to give the orders in a household rather than to obey them. I was told to wait a few minutes while Miss Toklas was being prepared to receive her visitor.

Then the maid led me into Alice's bedroom. Half of it was occupied by an old-fashioned brass bedstead. Alice lay in it, very small and wasted, her thin, thin hands stretched before her on the white counterpane, holding a black rosary. The maid said, "Here is your visitor." She spoke with hearty condescension, as if addressing a person of lesser prerogative and questionable understanding. To me she added, "You mustn't stay too long. That would tire Miss Toklas."

I said hello to Alice. She greeted me and thanked me for coming. I sat on a chair by her bedside. The maid remained in the room, standing at the end of the bed, watching us, and I wondered whether for some reason it would be necessary for her to stay during my entire visit. But after a moment she went out, closing the door loudly.

No sooner had she gone than Alice raised herself slightly in bed, staring hard at the closed door, her eyes glinting, and exclaimed, "I hate her!"

"Well, how are you?" I asked.

"I'd be fine if it weren't for that dreadful woman," said Alice. "If it weren't for her, I'd be cured. I'd be sturdy and cheerful, as I like to be. She knows how I hate to have her slam the door, so she does it every time. She makes life miserable for me in every way she can, and I'm at her mercy."

"Well," I said. But the cares of the sick make strangers and foreigners of the healthy. I felt inadequate and ill at ease. I told Alice about a recent trip I had made to Russia. She asked whether I had seen there a large Picasso of the Blue period in which a young girl is balancing on a ball. I had. That painting, she said, had long ago belonged to Gertrude Stein, who had sold it just before World War I, after which the Bolsheviks confiscated the collection of the rich Russian merchant who had bought it. She said, "I can remember it so well. I can remember all the pictures. I used to dust them all. The maids were never allowed to touch them. When I think of the rue de Fleurus and the rue Christine, I always remember where the pictures were."

We talked of other things. Alice asked me questions about myself, about my life in America. She said that she thought I had been wise to go back there to live. She felt that she herself had been fortunate to live away from America before it became the most powerful country in the world, because she thought it would be difficult for anyone to live abroad and find fulfillment there if he were leaving behind the most powerful country in the world. I am naturally not so sure as she was about that. I asked whether Miss Stein had felt likewise, and Alice said, "Gertrude never left home in the same way I did. She was always at home through the language, but I was at home only through her."

I said something, but there was in fact nothing I could say. And then before long the maid returned. I hadn't been in the room more than twenty minutes. The maid said, "Miss Toklas must rest now." She spoke with the authority of those who exercise dictatorial control over things which happen incidentally to be people.

I rose, pressed the hands that held the rosary and said goodbye. Alice made a smile and a nod. I went out of the room, followed by the maid, who closed the door loudly. In the entryway she said, "It's necessary to take precautions with her. Because of her weakness. One never knows." I said I understood, though I didn't, and then I went out into the drab November of the rue de la Convention.

That was the last time I saw Alice B. Toklas.

But she lingered on in that dispiriting apartment for more than a year. Finally she died in the month of March 1967, only a few weeks before her ninetieth birthday. She left few possessions, none of which excited contention or even much interest among those who survived her. She also left a will. One of its provisions is interesting. Having specified that she wished to be buried in the same tomb as Gertrude Stein in the Cemetery of Père Lachaise, she added that her own name, date of birth and date of death were to be inscribed on the back of the stone monument already standing there. On the front Gertrude's name would consequently forever appear alone. In death, as in life, there was to be no mistake about the order of eminence.

So at long last Alice was borne to the grave where her beloved friend had lain waiting for more than twenty years. And there they lie together now, united forever in fact and in memory, each having served in her own indomitable and creative way the human hunger for art and the artist's craving for immortality.

Mademoiselle Atmosphère

[A R L E T T Y]

April in Paris. 1947. My first sojourn in the city since the end of the war, thus my first as a free man. Pale green in the Tuileries. Chestnut trees in bloom along the boulevards. Of the beauty of the future there was not a doubt. I stayed at the Hôtel de France et Choiseul and found in a junk shop an early proof of Rembrandt's *Hundred-Guilder Print*. At the Brasserie Lipp, I had lunch with Picasso and Françoise Gilot. Alice B. Toklas gave me tea and talked mournfully about Gertrude Stein. I had a couple of pals from the army who had elected to be discharged in France. We sat in the Café de Flore and evoked all the good times we had relished at the expense of the U.S. Army. One of these pals introduced me to a French ballet dancer then enjoying some celebrity named Roland Petit. He said that I reminded him of a prize-fighter, though I have never in my life used my fists. He called me *"mon petit boxeur."* Our intimacy was brief, but one day the following September, he invited me to lunch, stressing that I would, or should, always be grateful to him for introducing me to the remarkable actress who was to be his other guest. I am. She lived at that time in one of Paris's grandest hotels, the Plaza-Athénée, just across the Avenue Montaigne from the far less splendid establishment where Roland resided. We went over under the green trees, and there she was, waiting for us in the foyer, attired all in white, Arletty.

Of course I knew who she was and had seen her on the screen, perhaps at that time only in *The Children of Paradise,** her finest film

* So called because the topmost of theater balconies was in the nineteenth century called the "paradise."

and arguably the finest ever made in France, which by 1947 I had certainly seen at least twice. Though not yet fifty, she was already then a legendary figure. No other actress in France, either then or later, possessed a comparable aura of inscrutable allure, fortified by proletarian self-assurance and a humorous sense of irony. Some people called her "the French Garbo," but she possessed a far more vibrant and versatile personality than the reclusive Swede, though in fairness it must be recognized that she was less hauntingly beautiful. Wonderfully beautiful nonetheless, and, as an individual who lived her legend to the bitter end, certainly haunting.

She laughed when we shook hands and said to Roland that his *petit boxeur* didn't look quite ready for combat. Her laughter was a silvery titter, very high-pitched, girlish, like the hilarity of a child, delightful in contrast to her speaking voice, which had the velvety resonance of the viola played by a virtuoso. And yet her manner of being herself was so spontaneously natural, whether on the screen or in the street, that one never thought of her as a make-believe creation. She was the unaffected personification of herself, and to those who knew her it was nearly impossible to distinguish between the actress who played a role and the woman who lived a life. Her secret, I thought, when we became more closely acquainted, was that all her talent was simply the self-evidence of her character.

That first day it was warm. We strolled down the avenue in the pale blue sunshine and had lunch on the terrace of a brasserie facing the Place de l'Alma, then still disfigured by Bourdelle's hideous bronze monument to the Polish patriot and poet Adam Mickiewicz. Roland and Arletty did most of the talking, as they had dozens of acquaintances in common, all of whom apparently gave plentiful grist for titillating gossip. I wasn't entirely ignored, however. Arletty appreciated the novelty of strangers, enjoyed asking questions that could be considered indiscreet and was perfectly prepared to respond with candor to similar queries. It was flattering to have caught the interest of the famous actress, if only for a moment. At that time I knew next to nothing of her troubles, having heard only rumors to which I had paid scant attention. Still, I did remember talk of guilt and punishment having to do with the war. And these were matters which had obsessed me already for several years, and still do.

After lunch we sauntered back up the avenue. Roland, having a rehearsal to attend, left us. Arletty stood by the glistening entrance to her palatial hotel and said that if I had nothing better to do . . . Coffee, I must understand, was almost unobtainable, not to mention cigarettes. I didn't drink coffee then, and was familiar with few vices save those I had learned in the army. But one could always take pleasure in a little chat, she added, in the privacy of her room. The employees of the hotel were all her very special friends. This was hardly the variety of invitation to which I was accustomed. Not from a woman, anyway, and she was plainly amused by my timidity. She laughed—the girlish, trilling titter—and took my arm. The ease of her physical familiarity, which ventured nothing but camaraderie, was irresistibly engaging.

We went up to her room on the fourth floor, large but plain and dim, with one window opening onto an enclosed courtyard. A silken suggestion of luxury came when the lights were turned on. She had been in this room for just one year and would remain there four years longer. There hung on the wall an interesting but not outstanding Dufy of the Fauve period, also a sepia of the inevitable barouche by Constantin Guys and a sketch by Dunoyer de Segonzac of Colette outstretched in the grass. I stayed all afternoon.

What is charm? The power to please by force of personality and intellect, an instinct for the persuasiveness of sympathy, the indefinable effect of an enchantment? Arletty possessed all this. And with such physical simplicity. I don't know what we talked about. I seldom noted down our conversations. What I knew when I left the Plaza that afternoon was that I had found a friend. She told me to call her and come back to see her, but she needn't have. I was foolish. It never occurred to me that a woman so famous, beautiful, delightful could be lonely, nor might I have guessed the reason. I did go back to see her. We went for walks downriver, crossing over the Pont Mirabeau to come back along the Left Bank. Who could have dreamed that forty-five years later she would end her life in pitiable circumstances very nearby? She had heard of Kafka, then nearly unknown in France, and thought he sounded interesting, so I brought her a copy of *The Trial*, a fact she recorded in her autobiography. *The Trial*, to be sure, if only I had known it—but I didn't—was of all the works by Kafka the single one that would have had the most profound and personal resonance for her. I was to learn that she was a character made of sterner stuff than the bewildered and doomed Joseph K.

Mademoiselle Atmosphère

The stay in Paris that September lasted only ten days. My French domicile was then three hundred and fifty miles west of the capital, in Quimper, an unspoiled, charming, boring town at the tip of the Breton peninsula, where I was the guest of the chief doctor at the local insane asylum. So I said goodbye to Arletty, Roland and my other Parisian playmates and took the train from the Montparnasse station. The doctor and his family were impressed to hear that I had made friends with the famous actress, an acquaintance they considered far more prestigious than Picasso or Alice B. Toklas, though the doctor was himself a gifted producer of mediocre paintings. Despite the remoteness of Quimper from the center of French cultural and political life, those of its inhabitants who presumed to constitute an intellectual elite—and my friend the doctor was very confidently of their company—took pains to keep abreast of what went on in Paris. In the Breton backwater, where nothing sensational ever occurred, a breath of scandal inspired far livelier interest than reports of long-winded debates in the National Assembly. Consequently it was normal that superficial accounts of Arletty's troubles were to be heard among the residents of Quimper, all of whom knew only too well that their names would never appear in the press except in very small print in announcements of births and deaths, if then. Their version of the actress's history, therefore, I took to be inevitably tipped by the venom which provincial envy so often aims at newsworthy hearsay from the capital.

Arletty had been a girl of the streets, so they said, and found her way onto the stage via the zigzag and opportunistic paths pursued by persons of her ilk. About her talent there could be no dispute, though it was unfit for the consecration of France's greatest thespian challenges: Racine, Musset, Hugo, etc. In short, a gifted showgirl who had had the good luck to get memorable roles in a handful of movies directed by masters of the medium and co-starring actors of established skill. Oh, she was good, unique, even captivating, no question of that, and the fame and fortune and admiration that came her way were as rightfully hers as the next girl's. But then intervened the folly and transgression that sometimes confound those who get above themselves, mistaking their high attainment for license to defy the discipline required of exceptional prominence.

The war came. France fell. National ignominy was imposed upon the prostrate land by its conquerors. The head of state shook Hitler's

hand. Jews were arrested by the French police, their future entrusted
to the Germans. Persons residing near premises requisitioned by the
Gestapo complained that their sleep was troubled by screaming in the
dead of night. Hostages were taken and, if unlucky, shot. It was before
the backdrop, so to speak, of such atrocious conditions that the famous
actress, by this time a popular embodiment of spirited Gallic pluck,
found nothing better to do than become the mistress of a German
officer. Now, many French women found lovers in the enemy army,
and for having done so many were cruelly tormented by lawless mobs
at the end of the war, but they were for the most part obscure non-
entities. Arletty was too well known for the mere humiliation of having
her head shaved, her naked skull tarred with a swastika and in this
abject state paraded through the streets to confront the jeers and spittle
of the mob. Prison would be none too good for her, people said, looking
forward to severe retribution for the moral treason of which they found
her guilty. And that indeed had been her lot.

Such was the skeletal account of Arletty's troubles that could be
heard in Quimper. The war had ended only two years before. I remembered all too well the vengeful frenzy that had run rampant
throughout France as soon as it was sure that retaliation from the Nazis
no longer need be feared. Summary executions, pitiless beatings and
brazen robberies had been carried out by self-appointed posses that
had joined the Resistance movement when next to no enemies remained to resist. As a member of the Military Intelligence Service, I
had been in a position to know far more about these lawless atrocities
than I would have liked. So I thought it sensible to pay but half-
hearted attention to the stories concerning my actress friend.

The doctor was not one of those who judged her severely. Within
the walls of the asylum he had had nothing to do with the war or the
Germans, no fighting having taken place in Quimper. One of his medical friends, however, Dr. Destouches, a celebrated novelist as well as
a physician, known by the nom de plume of Céline, had been as famed
during the war for his sympathy with the Nazis and hatred of the Jews
as for his literary achievements. Fleeing France with the retreating
Germans, he had made his way to Denmark, where he was in prison.
Letters from him came occasionally to the asylum, brilliant in style
but vile in their rabid anti-Semitism and paranoiac hatred of liberal
democracy. My host, much entertained and rather flattered to receive

these missives, seemed not a bit indignant at their contents, though by this time all the world knew of the monstrous enormities perpetrated by men in sympathy with Céline.

In mid-November I returned to Paris, this time en route to the United States, accompanied by my doctor friend and—as he was fond of calling her—his concubine. His legal wife had some years before leapt from a third-floor window, exclaiming that she was on her way to heaven, but had gone instead to Sweden, her homeland, taking with her their son, a virtuoso, as I recall, on the oboe. We had a good time in Paris. I didn't think it suitable to introduce them to Picasso but felt they would be amused to make the acquaintance of Arletty. The four of us had lunch, which was decidedly a success, much laughing occurred, and it came out in the course of casual conversation that Arletty, too, was a friend of Louis-Ferdinand Céline. Due to the turmoil of their mutual troubles, however, she had lost track of him and didn't know how to reestablish contact. The doctor said that nothing could be simpler than to provide her with the fugitive's address. He promised to send it as soon as he returned home, which he did.

I went to America, got rid of my appendix and set about writing a very long, unpublishable novel, much of which was set in a Nazi concentration camp. I heard occasionally from Arletty, who wrote, "I have good news from Ferdinand." The best news she could have had from him was that he continued to avoid extradition to France. Passions had begun to cool, and it is unlikely that Céline's life would then have been in danger, but he certainly had far less to fear in Copenhagen than in Paris. I also heard from my friends in Quimper, who urged me to return there as soon as I could. But I lingered in America for eighteen months. It was mainly on account of my novel, for which I had expectations in keeping with my age. When it was clear that these would be unfulfilled, I went aboard the *Queen Mary* in mid-March 1949 and arrived in Paris five days later.

The very first person I went to see was Arletty, still resident at the Plaza, and I found her delightfully unchanged, her laugh girlish as ever, conversation rippling, the inimitable accent a magic alloy of the prosaic and the ineffable. During my absence she had acquired a tiny automobile, so small that it was almost a toy and could accommodate only two passengers. We went for drives in the nearby countryside and had lunch in cheap restaurants where Arletty was sometimes recognized and made much of. It was during these moments alone together that I began to learn the outline of the story of her life.

The childhood of the future movie star seems to have been happy enough, though humble almost to the point of poverty. Léonie Bathiat was her name, born May 15, 1898. Eighteen years later, after little schooling and a variety of uninteresting jobs, one winter evening she saw her father brought home on a stretcher, having been run down by a streetcar. He held his daughter's hand, said, "I'm done for, little fellow," and died before dawn. It hardened her heart. Not long afterward a rich industrialist whom she had met in the casual manner which often leads to a casual relation invited her to be his guest in a suburban mansion. Her mother said, "If you leave, it's forever." And so it was. But her residence in the suburban mansion was not of long duration. She went to live in little hotels in the vicinity of the Madeleine, a neighborhood known still today for the facility offered by its sidewalks to ladies and gentlemen in search of transitory companionship. She did a bit of modeling, adopting as her professional name Arlette, heroine of a story by Maupassant which had impressed her. One day on the boulevard she was accosted by a man who described himself as a connoisseur of art and suggested that she might become a model. The proposition did not please. Then what about the theater? The stage was not appealing either. Nonetheless the would-be benefactor took out a couple of his calling cards and scribbled on them the names of two theatrical producers who might be interested in such an attractive young woman. His name: Paul Guillaune. Not merely a connoisseur, he was one of the most perspicacious, successful and wealthy art dealers of his era, and in addition a discriminating fancier of beautiful women. An introduction from him was a valuable asset. Arlette did not know this and had no expectation of becoming an actress. But one afternoon, as she was passing fortuitously one of the theaters recommended by Guillaune, whose cards still lay in the depths of her handbag, a whim prompted her to go inside and ask for the director. He looked her over, was amused, and suggested that she sing something. As the war had ended only nine months before, she chose "It's a Long Way to Tipperary." Hired on the spot, she was just twenty-one. The theater director didn't care for the name Arlette, so he replaced the final *e* with a *y*, proving again his acumen, for Arletty is a name much easier to make famous than Arlette. But it was by the original name, selected for herself, that she was always known to her friends. None of us ever called her Arletty, and she always signed her letters Arlette.

Stardom did not come overnight, and sometimes Arlette and her comrades in need of pocket money reverted to the localities and expedients of the life before Paul Guillaune. But she discovered that she loved the theater and that she had only to be herself in order to make theatergoers love her. Most actors and actresses are schooled to adapt themselves to a variety of roles and teach themselves trademark tricks, but Arlette needed no schooling and her downright lack of histrionics was the innate trick of her stagecraft. Despite the considerable variety of roles that she played, especially in films, the public always recognized, and admired, Arletty as herself before being captivated by her semi-impersonations. At thirty she was famous, a celebrity sought after by both aristocrats and plutocrats. The Aga Khan gave her diamonds but demanded no deference in return. She had a happy love affair. Her working-class youth had been left behind but was not forgotten. Vanity, pride, arrogance were not in her nature, and it would have been a defeatist indeed who might have predicted then that precisely at the midpoint of her life good fortune would conclusively forsake her.

I had bought a motorcycle and took it with me to Quimper. It gave me a freedom which I had never had before to roam the nearby countryside, then still completely unspoiled, some impoverished peasant villages unchanged for centuries. I visited the coastal towns of Concarneau and Douarnenez, Pont-Aven and Le Pouldu, where Gauguin and his followers had worked for several years and where some of their sketches still hung in a tavern they had frequented. I was particularly pleased one day in mid-April, when the camellia bushes in the gardens were red and white and the sky had momentarily turned milky blue, to receive a telephone call from Arlette. She was at Belle-Ile-en-Mer, an island off the southern coast of Brittany, facing the Quiberon Peninsula, about seventy miles from Quimper. I knew that she owned a small house there, given her by an admirer not long before, the same admirer, in fact, who often helped her with bills at the Plaza, a wealthy manufacturer of paper products named Michel Bolloré. As the house was not yet habitable, she was staying in a pension, and asked me to come there to keep her company for a few days. I was delighted to get away for a while from the asylum, especially as I planned to leave within a fortnight for six weeks in Italy.

The seventy-mile ride on my low-powered motorcycle was lengthy and bumpy. From Quiberon a ship took only forty-five minutes to cross the rough strait to Le Palais, the principal locality of the island. Arlette was on the pier to meet me, smiling, waving, her white raincoat flapping backward in the breeze like the wings of an excited swan.

My motorcycle she thought preposterous, maintaining that I ought to travel in a convertible auto made in the U.S.A. It greatly gratified her when I acquired one a few years later, particularly as it was white. But her own little car was black, like a large and cumbersome beetle. It didn't go even as fast as my deplorable bike, and the solitary three-hundred-mile journey from Paris must have been very tedious for her. The pension where she was staying was in a little fishing port called Sauzon at some distance along the coast. Belle-Ile is, or was, wild and picturesque, with high cliffs of variegated rock along several stretches of its coast, views frequently painted by Claude Monet and a number of his Impressionist colleagues. The interior of the island is a broad, undulating plateau dotted here and there with a few clusters of little white houses and the occasional tower of a disused mill, all bathed in the gentle marine radiance of an endless sky. As I came to know the island I felt that it possessed an antique, Arthurian enchantment. And it is a fact that that part of the world shared much of the same mythology as nearby England and that famous Breton minstrels had spread the legend of Arthur and his knights across Europe in the Middle Ages. This awareness added much to the magic and exhilaration of Belle-Ile in the midst of its silvery sea.

Sauzon is a small, white village built along one street that rises steeply from a port which in those days sheltered half a dozen rather run-down fishing boats. Its simplicity and tranquillity were the sole attractions it had to offer to an occasional visitor. In 1949 there were no foreigners, and even the few French families with children and mothers-in-law appeared only in July and August. The Pension Le Mouroux was the single establishment offering bed and board, though in emergency the excess visitor could usually find accommodation with an obliging local family.

Arlette, needless to say, had the finest room in the pension, with a wide, far-reaching view from her window. My room was just across the landing, spacious though modest and without a view. She was anxious to show me her house. It was on the other side of the island in a little village, barely more than a hamlet, called Donant, and the last house in the place before the road began its descent to the scrap of sandy beach caught between the cliffs far below. Small, plain and in a state of very mediocre repair, the interior particularly needing extensive restoration and remodeling, the house did not make much of an appeal to my imagination. Even later, when it had been entirely refurbished and provided with a number of good pieces of antique furniture, I never cared much for it. It was a lonely, solitary dwelling in its windswept isolation, the residence of a hermit. And of course that is in a very real sense what by force of circumstances Arlette became. But I tried to show as much enthusiasm for the little house as I could, agreeing that the dim and musty rooms could be made cheerful and attractive, because Arlette was so conspicuously happy to have it. I was slow to realize that her happiness must be due to the fact that this small house and her even smaller car, plus the few possessions in her room at the Plaza, were all that she could call her own. She had some money, though I never knew just how much, but it was not enough to spare her the necessity of financial assistance from rich people like Bolloré and René de Chambrun, husband of Josée Laval, thus son-in-law of the wartime prime minister.

Arlette was an excellent guide to the beauties and curiosities of the island, wanting her friends to care as feelingly for the locale of her retreat as she did. So we drove through the pearly afternoons all around the island, stopping often to admire a view painted by Monet or a secret beach hidden between monolithic boulders. She was not the only actress who had been drawn to the well-named isle. Sarah Bernhardt had built a grand house overhanging the sea. Nothing remained of it then, but there was a seat carved out of the cliff where the tempestuous tragedienne had loved to come and contemplate the huge crashing of waves. Arlette also liked that spot and went there often. One day as we were returning to the little car, she said, "I used to have a Packard, but naturally they took it, along with so much else." I made no reply, because I realized that for the first time in my presence she was alluding to her troubles. Though curious, I didn't want to appear to pry and thought, besides, that the less inquisitive I seemed the more likely I

would be to learn her own version of what had happened to her. I was
right. Little by little, through evocations of an incident here, an anecdote there, occasional memories, I believe I came to know as much
as is interesting to know of Arlette's wartime liaison and the dramatic
consequences caused by it. The knowledge did not come chronologically, of course, but for the sake of a coherent narrative it makes sense,
I think, to recount it, along with my own observations, as if the whole
story had originally been told to me just as I shall endeavor to tell it
now, half a century after the facts.

December 1940. France had fallen six months before. Hitler's
troops occupied the northern half of the country. German soldiers
paraded in Paris, sat in cafés and restaurants, attended the Opéra and
Folies-Bergère. It was the era of "politeness," when the French wanted
to believe that their enemies, after all, were very well behaved, courteous to ladies, kindly to children, and that military catastrophe might
not ravage the integrity of national life. This unrealistic and, indeed,
reprehensible delusion led many people to condone circumstances
which it would have cost them nothing to condemn and to turn a blind
eye to evidence which confirmed evil times to come. In this somber
context there were few actresses in France more prominent, both
professionally and socially, than Mademoiselle Arletty. She was feted
and admired not only by her colleagues but also by duchesses, fi-
nanciers and important political figures. Of these the most notable was
Pierre Laval. Being an intimate friend of Laval's son-in-law and
daughter, Arlette consequently had close and frequent contacts with
the father. Even before the war Laval, a brilliant orator and commanding personality, had advocated Franco-German cooperation.
After the defeat he championed collaboration, eventually assumed dictatorial powers, authorized a fascist militia and instituted a rule of
terror over his prostrate homeland. Laval was definitely not the sort of
man that a principled patriot would have wanted as a friend under
such circumstances. But Arlette put friendship before patriotism, and
in a certain sense felt entitled to do so because she accepted herself
so positively as a personification of what the French call "La France
Profonde." Her family, like Laval's, had its origins in Auvergne, a
harsh, mountainous territory, the inhabitants of which are reputed to
be stubbornly self-reliant and more attached to their province than to
the nation of which it forms one of the poorest regions. During the

Occupation, Arlette also became friendly with Céline, whom she considered the greatest author of modern times. Their affectionate sympathy for one another was immediate, lasting until the writer's death, and they, too, shared an identification with "La France Profonde," as their backgrounds were both associated with the same working-class suburb of Paris, Courbevoie. So it would not be inaccurate to say that during a time of deep trouble for what was most profoundly French Arlette counted among her friends a number of persons who were famous for their sympathy with the makers of that trouble. This was unseemly—and, worse, reckless—for an individual so conspicuously in the public eye. But Arlette was blind to all propriety, even to all expedience, which did not proceed from the rule of her own personality. She did not yet know this. And then came a crucial moment which transcended friendship.

One evening she went to a concert with Josée de Chambrun, who introduced her to a German officer seated beside them. Hans Soering was the son of a diplomat, born in Constantinople, fluent in French, having studied in Grenoble. He and Arlette ran into each other here and there. He was able to do her a few favors. Younger than she, good-looking without being sensationally handsome, he was a suave man of the world. Arlette had met many like him, but he cannot have met many like her. Yet they fell in love. As everyone knows, there is little choice and much chance at work when it comes to falling in love. For the officer the affair must have seemed like luck incarnate. For the actress it was the role that introduced her to misfortune. She played the part with the sincerity and élan which had made her famous, and it was her fame that brought about the unhappy denouement. Had she performed the great classical dramas, she might have had some premonition, but her repertory had till then been lighthearted and ephemeral. The challenge of an enduring and somber performance was biding its time.

To find a woman who seemed to the French at that time more quintessentially French than Arletty would have been difficult. In 1938 she had appeared in a film called *Hôtel du Nord*. Her role was not the principal one, but she became the enduring star of the production by virtue of a single word: *atmosphère*. In a crucial scene she and her partner, Louis Jouvet, are together crossing a bridge above the Canal St.-Martin in northern Paris, he on his way to go fishing, when he tells her that he would prefer to go on alone, as he feels that she does not contribute satisfactorily to the "atmosphère" which suits his mood. Whereupon Arletty furiously replies in the inimitable accent of the Parisian suburbs, "*Atmosphère! Atmosphère! Est-ce que j'ai une gueule d'atmosphère?*" ("Have I got a mug made of atmosphere?") Overnight that one word—*atmosphère*—became indelibly associated with Arletty, remaining so to this day, and by semantic magic it added a dimension of symbolism to her legend. In cafés and châteaux all over France men and women would exclaim to each other, "*Atmosphère! Atmosphère!*" and burst out laughing, some of them, perhaps, unaware of the metaphorical significance of their hilarity. That Arlette created a unique environment, not only in *Hôtel du Nord* but also in her own presence and existence, was a fact acknowledged almost universally in her native country, the word that consecrated her celebrity ideally suited to the origin and constitution of it. Of this, too, she was at the time probably not yet aware. Had she been shrewd, clairvoyant, introspective it would have saved her much torment. But then she would not have been the Arlette known, cherished and admired by her friends.

To be the mistress of a German officer while France was occupied by the German army put a woman in a position that was, to say the least, ambiguous. Had Arlette been a private person, and the affair kept as private as such liaisons can be kept, which is never very private, then the consequences might have been no more annoying than the discomfort caused to the individual consciences of those involved. Arlette, however, was anything but a private person, nor did she or her lover endeavor to conceal the liaison. They went about together in public as if no opprobrium could conceivably stigmatize the conspicuous display of their attachment. To exacerbate matters, moreover, Soering was an officer of high rank, a colonel in the Luftwaffe, entrusted with crucial responsibilities and familiar with the highest officials of the Reich; he was an associate of Hermann Goering, chief of the Luftwaffe and a Nazi from the founding days, creator of the Gestapo and for some years its chief, a porcine, ruthless creature guilty of crimes against humanity beyond the reckoning of any tribunal. But neither the officer nor the actress appears to have felt an instant's misgiving, not to mention qualm, about the possible implications of their conduct. Arlette gladly attended a reception at which Goering and his cronies preened. Her lover contemplated marriage and felt constrained to elicit the approval of the Reichsmarschall, who in turn put the question to the Führer. "Be careful," Hitler is reported to have replied, "she is too friendly with Laval." In short, Arlette was responsible for nothing that concerned either the prosecution of the war or the persecution of the Jews, but she was very conspicuously friendly with the enemy, thus by implication a permissive witness to the sufferings of her countrymen, and for a personage in her position hurtful to their morale. So it might have been alleged that she was a traitor to "La France Profonde," and such was the view held by many.

The chance of a lifetime came to Arletty in the midst of the war, as if chance were capable of awareness and realized that this would be its last opportunity. She was chosen for the role of Garance, heroine of *The Children of Paradise*. Garance is a girl of easy virtue, if not quite of the streets, whose complex amorous affairs form the principal subject matter of the film, which recounts her failure to establish an enduring relation with the actor who loves her—for the highly theatrical action of the film dramatizes the life of the theater—and whom she loves in return. To avoid a threat of trouble with the police she accepts a liaison with a rich aristocrat. In the end, after the murder of her haughty benefactor and a brief reunion with her true beloved, since married, she is seen alone in a carriage being driven toward a destiny which it seems safe to assume will not be happy. Upon this haunting image, which shows Arlette's beauty to have been, indeed, heartbreaking, the cinematic, theatrical and representational curtain falls.

By the time the filming of *The Children of Paradise* was finished, the curtain had also begun to fall on a spectacle infinitely more dramatic as it became increasingly clear that the war begun by the Nazis would end in their defeat. Those who had been their friends in conquered lands started to worry, because the imminent victors promised punishment to fit every transgression, and it was assumed that vengeance would take precedence over due process of law. Arlette learned that she had been condemned to death in absentia by a tribunal in Algeria. But she was not of the breed to be intimidated. Whatever test of character might be assigned by circumstances, she could be certain of her ability to do justice to the challenge of the scenario. And to do so alone. Her German officer was no longer present to provide moral or material support, having been transferred to Italy, and his presence might only have made the situation of his mistress more precarious.

The pace of the approaching debacle quickened. On the Norman coast the Allies' invasion was bloody but successful. Laval, Pétain and the remnants of their mongrel government fled to southern Germany. Céline went with them, accompanied by a host of others, some of whom disappeared en route. Arlette was then living in an apartment on the Quai de Conti, close by the Institute and facing the Louvre on the far bank of the Seine. One night, when the Liberation of Paris was but a few days distant, a troop of armed men gathered in front of her building, shouted obscene insults and shot several bursts of machine-gun fire into the windows. Arlette happened to be at home. She and her maid lay on the floor while bullets tore through the draperies, shattering mirrors and chandeliers.

Though anything but timorous or defeatist, Arlette was not one to leap heedlessly into the thick of strife either. Leaving the Quai de Conti, she went to stay with friends in several out-of-the-way places, thus managing to avoid unpleasantness during the Liberation of Paris and for some time thereafter. Eventually, however, she knew that she was sure to be arrested and compelled to appear before an *épurateur*. This word means either purifier or purger and the second definition was more suited to the function of the unofficial officials who determined what punishment would best fit the ostensible misconduct of those whose guilt was taken for granted. Arletty was arrested sometime in the late autumn of 1944, incarcerated with both men and women from every variety of background in several places of detention, all of them insalubrious, reeking of inadequate sanitation, the straw mats on which the inmates slept infested with bedbugs and cockroaches. This interval of confinement, lasting for approximately two months, was the most unpleasant period of her purgation. When the time came for her "hearing," the *épurateur* decreed that she should be placed under house arrest in some locality at least fifty kilometers from Paris for an unspecified length of time. And forbidden to work, which meant that she had no means of earning a living.

In adversity there are sometimes golden instances of good luck that redeem the indignity of misfortune. During the war Arlette had made casual acquaintance with a couple named Jacques and Lelette Bellanger. Rich, retired, they resided in a château called La Houssaye on the outskirts of a village just fifty kilometers east of Paris. Learning of the arbitrary sentence of the *épurateur*, they came forward and proposed that their residence might serve as the house of arrest for the condemned actress. She had thought of installing herself in a small, remote hotel and hesitated to accept the charity of virtual strangers. The *épurateur* decided the matter by asking a foolish question. Had Monsieur Bellanger, he inquired, been a member of the Resistance? Arlette sensed the challenge and said yes. "Then that's where you'll go," said the *épurateur*, "and it will serve you right!"

The Château de La Houssaye, not one of France's grandest, is nonetheless a lovely and imposing structure of tan masonry and rose-colored brick in the pure Louis XIII style, surrounded by a moat and set amid an extensive park. It was to this amiable place, than which none could have seemed less like a prison, that Arletty brought her few remaining possessions in December 1944 to serve out the period of detention. The moment of her arrival was peculiarly ambiguous, for at the same time the Germans were waging their ferocious counter-attack in the Ardennes, which appeared at first to have a chance of breaking through the overextended Allied line, and a shiver of anxiety coursed through France. But the sally was repulsed in a month, though at the cost of 75,000 casualties. Then it was clear that the final defeat and humiliation of Germany could only be a matter of time. What emotions this prospect may have roused among the inhabitants of La Houssaye is a matter for conjecture. The "prisoner" had never been, and never was, an individual to whom the contingencies, complexities and consequences of politics were of much meaning or moment. She concentrated thought and feeling on personal relations, the eventu-alities of her profession and the very private perpetuation of her own dignity. One may allege that it was grossly frivolous of her to have lived in such close proximity to political causality and remained indifferent to or, worse, unaware of its effect on human lives. For this frivolity she was being punished, and for once with some justice it can be acknowl-edged that the punishment fit the offense. This was to be the decisive test of her famous "atmosphère."

Arlette's hosts, Lel and Bel, as she came to call them, were de-cidedly of conservative opinion, but in their remote château had had nothing to do either with the Germans one way or another or with the war itself save for enduring the attendant hardships in obtaining food, fuel, clothing and even such necessities as toilet paper. One may won-der why they voluntarily offered their splendid residence as a house of

arrest for someone they knew but slightly and who brought with her
the odor of disrepute and shame. What motivated their hospitality, I
think, was the glamour, however tarnished, of a famous and novel
personality and a rather romantic inclination to come to the aid of a
beautiful damsel in distress. Lel may have had more personal, private
motives. It was no secret that Arlette had had lesbian attachments. Bel,
a dreamer, had spent the war years lying on his back on a high scaffold,
fastidiously restoring the painted seventeenth-century ceilings of his
château. They were superb.

The winter of 1944–45 was particularly severe. The large, high,
many-windowed rooms of La Houssaye were emphatically cold. The
moat froze over. From the nearby village and neighboring farms came
only the barest necessities of food. Discomfort added to the displeasure
of confinement. Lel and Bel could go to Paris. Not Arlette. Every week
she was required, no matter what the weather, to walk four miles to
the local police station to report her continuing presence under house
arrest. The people in the village, most of whom had never set foot in
Paris, and who knew nothing of the cinema, had no idea who she was.
The real name recorded on the obligatory identity card was Léonie
Bathiat. She was proud of that name, because she was proud of her
working-class origin, which strengthened the self-reliance needed to
bolster against all odds the conviction of an indomitable integrity.

Springtime, however, eventually came. Greenery sparkled across
the park, while beside secluded walls violets bloomed. Migratory flights
of birdlife winged through the blue. And then one day the war in
Europe was over. With peace, one might have thought, would come
the time of clemency, compassion and reprieve. But no. Victory, it
seems, is more triumphant when for a time, at least, the defeated are
made to pay the indemnity of humiliation. Arlette was condemned to
serve a further full year of house arrest, though at first it had been
implied that her detention would be a mere matter of two weeks. And
after that year another hearing would be required to determine when,
and if, she might be allowed to resume her professional activity.

"It was the best time of my life," she told me. "It gave me the
opportunity and the initiative to become myself."

At one corner of the area enclosed by the moat stood a lone tower,
vestige of a fortress dating from medieval times. It was here that Arlette
spent in solitude much of the time of her confinement. The library at

La Houssaye was well supplied with books. She did much reading, especially of Proust and Pascal, not such unlikely literary companions when one considers their basic attitudes toward the condition of humankind. It was Pascal in particular whose *Pensées* she read and reread, meditated on and weighed. That she should have found interest as well as solace in the writings of the great scientist and philosopher is logical, for she had every reason to believe that reason is inadequate to solve man's difficulties or to satisfy his hopes, and that a profoundly mystical disposition is essential to any understanding of the world and man's place in it. Which is not to say that she became a fatalist but, on the contrary, that she became able to accept a principle of existential commitment which took for granted the responsibility of every human being in his elemental solitude to act in mitigation of the solitude of others. In short, she saw that she had been blind to her own frivolity and failure of imagination. It was a revelation. Her "atmosphère" had become the environment essential to a spiritual evolution. To say that this was simply good luck would be to discount the potential of determinism in all of our lives. In any event, after eighteen months of house arrest and the companionship of Pascal, Arlette was a transformed individual. As a woman, an actress and an embodiment of the imagination. She did not yet know to what extreme extent this transformation would lead her in order to see that it was genuine.

The second "hearing" took place six months after her release from house arrest, its outcome merely a reprimand, and then technically Arlette was free to pursue her profession. But the climate had changed as much as she had. The triumphant success of *The Children of Paradise* did not bring the proposals that would inevitably have followed had there been no trouble. There were a few timid suggestions, but these produced no positive results. So she waited patiently in her room at the Plaza-Athénée, and it was at this time that we became acquainted.

2

A letter from Arlette came to Quimper in mid-July, saying that she planned to leave soon for Brittany and would be in touch with me. It was not more than a week later that I received a telephone call from Belle-Ile. Arlette asked whether I could come there the very next day in time for lunch. As I was just then trying to finish a short story, the only acceptable piece of fiction I've ever written, entitled "The Boy Who Wrote NO," I hesitated to say yes. But she insisted. "I need your help," she said, "and it's urgent." She didn't say why she needed help, or of what sort, but the appeal was impossible to refuse. I couldn't guess what help I might conceivably give that would be of any good in a situation that Arlette deemed urgent. I told her that she could count on me, and that is how I happened to be witness to an incident that might have occurred in one of her prewar films, an incident, moreover, that may have been one of the last in which the Arletty of a former day played a part well suited to a previous persona.

I arrived in Quiberon on my motorcycle just in time to catch the noon boat. Arlette was on the pier. She said, "We'll have to hurry to get back to Sauzon in time for lunch. I'll tell you everything then, but in the dining room watch out for the fat lady. If she stares at us, ignore her." With that she got into her midget car and I followed along behind.

The Pension Le Mouroux was run by three sisters, two of whom were women of a certain age, conservatively attired and of inconspicuous appearance. Nothing less descriptive could have been said about the third, the youngest, short, stocky, with close-cropped hair, mannish and always clothed in the same blue jacket and trousers worn by the local sailors, whose work she frequently shared. Her name was Marie and because of her unconventional attire she was known in Belle-Ile as Marie-Trousers. She and Arlette had grown particularly friendly, in part because much of the renovation of the little house in Donant had been capably supervised by Marie-Trousers, who did a good deal of the work herself.

Foreign tourists were still endearingly rare in the summer of 1949, but the French had by then sufficiently recovered from the hardships of wartime to go on vacation. The Pension Le Mouroux was consequently packed with tourists from the mainland, mostly families with children, whose toy boats and pails and shovels and celluloid swans littered the hallways and stairs. They crowded the dining room, creating a considerable din. Arlette and I had a table in a corner next to the window looking onto the garden. I had no difficulty spotting the fat lady. She sat at a table by herself in the far corner from ours and was decidedly adipose, though not yet obese, a woman of dark complexion and black hair drawn back sleekly into a bun, her dark eyes heavily made up, lips and fingernails crimson, attired in black, a figure conspicuously incongruous in a vacation dining room populated by half-naked children, parents in sportswear and mothers-in-law in bright frocks with patterns of seagulls and sailboats.

"Don't look," said Arlette. "That's just what she wants."

"Who is she?" I asked. "And what in the world is she doing here?"

"She's a princess," said Arlette. "Ottoman, I think. Or is it Armenian? I get them confused. Or maybe it's the same thing. I'll tell you what happened."

This princess, she explained, whose actual name I never learned, also resided at the Plaza and had manifested much, and almost too much, sympathy for the lonely, out-of-work actress. Perhaps, Arlette acknowledged, she had been impulsively and imprudently responsive to the friendliness of the Muslim noblewoman. They had dined together a number of times and taken a few excursions into the nearby countryside in the princess's hired limousine. Then Arlette had been pressed to accept a number of gifts, pieces of relatively inexpensive jewelry, the most important item of which was a small clock in gold, lapis lazuli and rose quartz, which, as a matter of fact, was even then on Arlette's bedside table upstairs. However, she had taken care never to allow the semblance of friendship to develop into anything like an intimacy, had avoided introducing the princess to her friends and never invited her to visit La Houssaye. But when the prospective trip to Belle-Ile came up, the princess pleaded to be taken along for a few days of innocent repose by the seaside, and Arlette, thinking she had no acquaintance on the island except Marie-Trousers to witness this exotic relationship, acquiesced. So the two ladies had set out in the little black car, barely capacious enough to accommodate their persons and their baggage. In the warmth of the brilliant July morning the physical proximity imposed by the cramped interior of the automobile had almost inevitably brought forth from the princess gestures, and declarations, which, though they can hardly have come as a surprise, Arlette found unwelcome. If the princess had counted on the long trip to provide for unbridled expressions of sentiment, however unwelcome, she had seriously misconstrued the temperament of her chauffeur. When they arrived in Chartres, just fifty miles west of Paris, Arlette drove straight to the railway station and ordered her passenger to get out of the car and take her baggage with her. The princess was plaintive and penitent, promised to behave irreproachably in future and begged to be allowed to continue the journey. But Arlette was adamant, remarking as she drove away that the train service was frequent and with luck the princess could be back at the Plaza in time for a late lunch.

Relieved to be rid of her too demonstrative passenger, Arlette drove on contentedly between poplar trees and wheat fields toward Le Mans. But she had not reckoned with the implacable tenacity of the Orient. Not very far from Chartres a large taxi drew up alongside her, the princess inside making imploring gestures through the window. Annoyed but by nature tolerant, Arlette came to a halt, whereupon the princess scrambled out of the taxi and got down on her knees on the pavement in front of Arlette's car, not an easy feat for the overweight noblewoman, pleading to be permitted to resume the journey, promising to behave with impeccable propriety and vowing to remain on the highway on her knees until her plea was granted. It must have been a ludicrous spectacle, viewed with astonishment not only by the taxi driver but also by passing motorists compelled to slow down as they went by. No more pleased than the next person to appear ridiculous, Arlette relented, took in the repentant princess and her baggage and once more set off toward Quiberon. As to conduct, the princess was as good as her word, and the two ladies arrived without incident just in time to catch the last boat for Belle-Ile. At the Pension Le Mouroux their arrival caused some excitement, no princess, not even an Oriental one, having heretofore honored those homely premises. The best rooms had of course been reserved for them, the two at the top of the house, almost adjoining, separated from one another only by the narrow landing. Arlette immediately recognized the tactical blunder, but it was then too late to do anything about it, the pension being already overcrowded.

During dinner princess and actress chatted amicably, in no way behaving in such a manner as to excite the interest or even arouse the curiosity of the other diners. But it was after dinner, when it came time to retire to the bedrooms, that, as Arlette foresaw, the crucial moment might come. And indeed on the landing at the top of the stairs there was a brief scuffle. Arlette, however, more lithe and agile than her adipose friend, managed to slip into her room and lock the door. This maneuver was predictably followed by plaintive protests and a persistent rattling of the doorknob. When after a time this minor disturbance brought no positive result, the princess went into her room. Now, it happened that the two bedrooms at the top of the house had been recently constructed in the former attic, and though they were spacious the materials used had been subject to severe economy, with the result that the partition between the rooms was thin. By cupping her hands against it to create a megaphone, the princess was able to make herself clearly heard in the adjoining room. She pleaded and complained, insisting that she meant no harm, yearned only to voice her veneration and vowed to bring no unpleasantness to the person she revered. To all of this Arlette would have liked to turn two deaf ears, and she damned herself for having been too clement with the fat lady on her knees in the highway. Silence being the only policy, she waited for the princess to tire, but the supplications and imprecations continued on the other side of the wall for close to an hour, growing louder and louder, approaching almost the decibel of scandal in the peaceful pension, till finally with an ostentatious sob they ceased.

Assuming the princess to be a late riser, Arlette was up early the next morning to make preparations for what she expected to be something of a siege. Marie-Trousers was naturally enlisted as principal ally and strategist. It would unfortunately not be possible to move the princess to another bedroom, as the pension was full, but she could be placed at a distant table in the dining room. And at night Marie-Trousers would sleep on a mattress in front of Arlette's door. During the day they could slip away to Donant or Port-Goulphar, hoping that in their absence the princess might have the good idea to depart. It was then that Arlette thought to introduce me into the imbroglio as an additional element of defense and, of course, deception.

I was twenty-seven that summer and probably not the worst-looking young fellow ever to come along on a motorcycle. Arlette was fifty-one, but that made no difference in the sensual equation, because we knew what it was and, most particularly, because the princess didn't. I understood at once that I was to serve as a pseudo buffer in this emotive entrenchment, a prospect that quite amused me. As the pension was full, a pleasant room had been prepared for me in the house just next door, belonging to a congenial elderly couple. Arlette and I spent that first afternoon visiting her house at Donant, which I found no more attractive or cheerful than before, and driving about the island, returning to Sauzon just in time for dinner. We chatted and laughed while eating. Few people could be more entertaining than Arlette. The remarkable effervescence of her vitality, punctuated beautifully by the cadenza of laughter, was in itself witty and diverting. In her far corner of the dining room the princess glowered but made no disturbance. That, Arlette assumed, would probably come later, when she and I were alone together in her bedroom, where it had been settled that we would spend the remainder of the evening, with Marie-Trousers on guard outside. It didn't occur to me then that perhaps I was a too willing accomplice to a provocation which made a mockery of honest emotion and true distress.

In Arlette's bedroom we had a bottle of sauterne, sweet and cold, and she told me how profoundly she had been influenced by the *Pensées* of Pascal during her detention. She had learned quite a number of them by heart, which was not too difficult a thing for an actress, and recited one of the most famous: "What a chimera then is man! What a novelty! What a monster, what a chaos, what a contradiction, what a prodigy! Judge of all things, feeble worm of the earth, depository of truth, a sink of uncertainty and error, the glory and shame of the universe." I was impressed, and thought that, after all, she might have been Phèdre. As we sipped the sauterne our conversation somehow came round to Kafka. *The Trial* had remained with stark clarity in her mind and she feelingly observed that it was only too true to life, as she herself had been convicted and punished without due process of any kind. I asked whether she had read any other works by the melancholy author. Oddly enough, she hadn't, and so I set out to tell her the terrible tale of "The Metamorphosis," a work I believe to be Kafka's masterpiece, the story of a man who wakens one morning to find himself transformed into a monstrous cockroach. For some reason, incomprehensible to me but to her compelling, Arlette found this tragic fable irresistibly funny. She laughed and laughed, especially at the detail of the rotting apple embedded in the chitinous integument of the wretched Gregor Samsa.

It was this hilarity which aroused the ire of the princess. She couldn't have heard what I was saying, as I spoke in a normal conversational tone, and she would doubtless have been astonished to learn what it was that so amused her inaccessible friend. At all events, she can only have assumed that we were having a good time, from which she was excluded, and that was enough to make her furious. She began to pound on the wall and shout through the partition. "I know what you're doing," she shrieked. "It's disgusting, vile, degenerate. I hate you. I was a fool ever to believe in your friendship. You're a false friend, a viper, a traitor. They were right to put you in prison, and it's only too bad they didn't keep you there. I curse the day I ever met you. I curse you, too, and your American gigolo. You're both disgusting and vile and I despise you." And all the while she kept pounding on the wall, creating a commotion which was certainly audible throughout the tranquil pension and probably beyond. Marie-Trousers, on guard on the landing, was not intimidated by the princess. Knocking forcefully on her door, she announced that if the disturbance did not cease immediately, the person responsible would have to leave the pension at once and find other accommodations for the night. That warning had an immediate effect. On the other side of the partition there was some muffled muttering and perhaps some tearful snuffling, then silence.

"That woman could be dangerous," said Arlette.

I had finished the recital of Kafka's somber parable and the bottle of sauterne was nearly empty. Bidding Arlette good night, I went out quietly past Marie-Trousers on her mattress and with relief repaired to my bedroom in the house next door.

One of the older sisters Le Mouroux told me when I arrived for breakfast the next morning that Arlette and Marie-Trousers had already left for Donant to supervise some work in the house but would be back in time for lunch. While I was drinking tea and eating a croissant the princess appeared. Coming straight to my table, she said, "What's your price?"

Startled, I replied, "For what?"

"To leave this island immediately," she said, her tone peremptory, "and stay away from my friend Arletty for good."

"Mademoiselle Arletty is also a friend of mine," I retorted, "a very good friend. Your suggestion is offensive, and I have nothing further to say to you."

"I'm rich," the princess announced, "very rich. I notice that you travel about on a motorcycle. Surely you would prefer to have an automobile."

"Not from you," I loftily replied. "And I don't think Mademoiselle

Arletty would be very pleased to know that you have had the nerve to speak to me this way."

"Arletty is a wicked woman," cried the princess. "When I said she ought to be in prison, I wasn't joking. And maybe you ought to be there with her. It's obvious you're a cheap bit of trash."

"Oh, shut your trap, you fat old bag," I exclaimed, losing patience and manners.

At that the princess to my relief did withdraw.

Arlette and Marie-Trousers returned just in time for lunch. Angry and humiliated, having had all morning to brood upon the princess's rude presumption, I was imprudent. I should have kept the confrontation to myself. But I didn't. While we ate I told Arlette what had happened and been said. She was furious. "I'll not let it pass," she said. "There will be redress. Here and now. In front of everyone." Thereupon she leapt to her feet, overturning her chair, and strode across the room toward the princess's table.

The princess, however, must have been watching and anticipated that Arlette's approach would be hostile, for with an agility surprising in one so cumbersome she left her table and retreated toward the front of the dining room. In the center of this room stood a large circular table occupied by a youngish father and mother, three small children and one grandmother. It was around this table that the two women, one vengeful, the other fearful, circled, while every eye was fixed upon them, not a mouthful of food was eaten and breathless silence gripped the room. It was definitely a bizarre spectacle, ludicrous but disquieting, the two women circling that table, first in one direction, then the other, Arlette the pursuer, the princess her quarry, and of all the spectators I was the only one to know what caused the obvious anger of one and the fear of the other. It didn't take more than a minute or two for Arlette to catch the princess, and it was very possible, I think, that the captive desired nothing more than to be captured, though she may not have bargained for the harsh humiliation that followed. Gripping the prisoner hard by her fleshy forearms, Arlette propelled her forcibly across to our table, where I remained seated, and then commanded, "On your knees!" When the princess was slow and obviously reluctant to obey, her captor forced her down by digging her fingernails into her arms and yanking her forward, loudly repeating the command "On your knees!" so that the hapless noblewoman came down with something of a crash and a gasp of pain onto the wooden floor. The onlookers, who had doubtless never witnessed—or even imagined—such a scene in real life, also gasped.

"Now ask for pardon," ordered Arlette. "Ask for pardon or I'll rip off your wig."

"I ask your pardon," the princess plaintively murmured, her head bowed in submission, not looking at me.

Then Arlette took her place at the table and said, "Now disappear from my sight!" Whereupon the unhappy princess scrambled to her feet and fled the room.

"That was a rather severe retribution," I observed.

"Oh," said Arlette with a Gioconda smile, "it might have been far more so if I hadn't been so angry."

The other occupants of the pension resumed their interrupted meal, now and again eyeing us with overt curiosity.

We saw no more of the princess that day. She had not left the island, however, for in the evening we heard noises from her room, as if she were moving the furniture about. But she created no disturbance. Arlette was very satisfied with her victory and anticipated no further annoyance. Unfortunately she seriously underestimated her adversary.

The next morning when I went to the pension for breakfast I immediately became aware that a considerable commotion was in progress upstairs, and soon one of the elder sisters hurried in and said, "There's trouble. The police are here. The princess has accused Mademoiselle of stealing her jewelry. You'd better go up, because she says that you're Mademoiselle's accomplice. It's ridiculous, of course. But so disagreeable, so disagreeable."

There was a crowd in the stairway. Two policemen in uniform, an inspector in plain clothes, Marie-Trousers, the other sister Le Mouroux, Arlette, the princess. Arlette was explaining to the inspector that the jewelry supposedly stolen had been received as gifts from her accuser, a perjurer of the basest species. The princess haughtily retorted that the items could easily be found by searching the room of the actress or, perhaps, of her gigolo and accomplice, she added, pointing at me. The inspector came down a few steps and asked to see my papers. I had none with me, as Americans are not accustomed to keep identity papers always on their persons, and I have never carried my passport unless preparing to cross a national border. Arlette said that I was an American writer, a friend of hers, a person of impeccable repute, residing for the summer in Quimper, and that she would vouch for me. "Isn't that just what the guilty party would claim?" cried the princess. The inspector didn't like the absence of papers. It was equally clear that he didn't like anything about this business, and I suspected he must have found it fishy from the first. Undoubtedly he had already heard the story of the grotesque scene in the dining room. For some reason he decided that it would help the situation to eliminate me from it. So he advised me always to carry identity papers in future, said that I was free to go and would do well to leave Belle-Ile immediately.

"But you can't just let him go free," shouted the princess. "He might be guilty. I'm sure he's guilty."

"Madame," said the inspector, "if you wish this investigation to proceed, you will do well to remember that I am in charge and require no advice from anyone. And allow me to remind you that you have made a formal complaint against Mademoiselle Arletty. If it should come out that there is no basis for this complaint, your own situation, especially as a foreigner in France, could be seriously compromised. Do I make myself clear?"

The princess nodded, scowling. I said goodbye hurriedly to Arlette, kissed her on both cheeks, made my farewells also to the sisters Le Mouroux and took my leave, content to be on my motorcycle in the warm morning air and well out of a ridiculous predicament. That I had been used by Arlette to some ambiguous end in her relations with the princess was perfectly clear, but rather than taking it amiss I considered it an affirmation of friendship and trust, and the fact is that thereafter we were closer than before. Without my participation in that strange imbroglio I don't think I would ever have come to know Arlette as well as I did. Leaving Belle-Ile that day, I wasn't in the least worried about what might be happening in Sauzon, assuming that all would be settled—probably to the satisfaction of everyone concerned—before I reached the mainland.

I heard nothing, in any case, from Arlette.

Three weeks later I was alone in the asylum save for all the inmates and the concubine's mother, as the doctor and the rest of his family had gone to spend the month of August in a concrete bungalow at a nearby seaside resort. Not relishing too much solitude, I invited to

Quimper a young Englishman named Andrew Gordon, whom I had met in Paris in June. Even in the doctor's absence, but especially in the busybody presence of the concubine's mother, I wouldn't have lodged a lover in the apartment. And since there was little to do in Quimper I thought what a good idea it would be to go to Belle-Ile. Andrew was all for it. I telephoned the sisters Le Mouroux. The pension was full, but as I was a friend of Mademoiselle Arletty, who had long since departed, a pleasant room would easily be found for me somewhere in Sauzon. We set out, the two of us on the motorcycle, on August 15, the Feast of the Assumption, one of the great religious holidays of Catholic Europe. Our room was in a house on the far side of the little port, so we had to be rowed back and forth. The water was phosphorescent and at night it dripped from the oars like long strings of diamonds.

I asked one of the elder Le Mouroux sisters about Arlette and the princess. What had happened in the case of the so-called stolen jewelry after my departure? "Oh, they made up, of course," said Mademoiselle Le Mouroux. "The inspector stayed for lunch with Mademoiselle Arletty. And later she went with the princess to Auray to visit the antique shops, and the princess bought half the furniture for the house in Donant."

I remarked that this seemed perfectly incredible after what had happened.

"Oh, monsieur," sighed the spinster sister, "one must understand that the people of the theater are not like you and me."

Early in September I gave myself a definitive discharge from the asylum and went to live permanently in Paris. Arlette and I laughed about the scene with the policemen at Sauzon, and she said that she had not had the heart to continue being unkind to the poor princess but neglected to mention the antique dealers in Auray or furniture for the little house. She invited me to go with her to La Houssaye for weekends, showed me the tower where she had spent so many months reading Pascal and the police station where she had had to go every week to report. We went inside together. The officers were still the same. She said, "It's a pleasure to come and say hello when I no longer am obliged to." They all laughed and called her by her real name, Bathiat. That was the first inkling I had that she aspired to win back the esteem, even the affection, of "La France Profonde" by the simple affirmation of her "atmosphère" and that against odds more adverse than we could have imagined she would live to succeed.

The Bellangers appeared to be kindhearted, hospitable people who enjoyed the lively company of Arlette and her friends. There was never, I noticed, any talk of politics at La Houssaye. In the splendid château surrounded by its moat, one might almost have thought oneself to be living in a tale by Perrault.

It was during that autumn and winter that Arlette finally reappeared before the public. In a role, however, that would not have been thought appropriate for the beautiful, self-possessed heroine of *The Children of Paradise*. And yet she chose it for herself: the role of Blanche DuBois, pathetic, weak, defeated by circumstances and finally deranged, in Tennessee Williams's melodrama *A Streetcar Named Desire*. Something better suited to her previous persona would surely have presented itself sooner or later, but Arlette wanted to play Blanche. What was it, I wondered, that she found compelling in a character so unlike her own? Perhaps she felt that the play, a sensational success in New York, would provide her dormant career with the revived impetus it badly needed. Perhaps she obscurely felt that by performing in Paris the part of a woman ultimately led to her doom by weaknesses of the flesh she would be undertaking an act of contrition. I don't know. In any case, the part of Blanche did not display her talent to good effect, but the notices were favorable and the play was a success. I saw it often, as I used to go the theater, wait for the final curtain and then accompany Arlette to some bistro for supper, which frequently lasted till the night was more than half over.

One Tuesday that winter, the only day when *Streetcar* was not performed, Arlette asked me to go with her to a showing of *Hôtel du Nord* at a cinema club in the suburb of Malakoff. I had then never seen the film or the famous "atmosphère" scene and was glad to have the chance. Arlette explained that Malakoff was a fanatically Communist district. "A good place to take my temperature," she said. The theater was drab, located in an out-of-the-way street. We were seated in a box at the rear of the auditorium. The film is not one of Carné's best, as the saccharine love story which forms its central structure is banal, implausible and insipidly performed. All the force, and vitality, of the production emanates from the secondary plot, in which Arletty is cast as a spirited girl of the streets and Louis Jouvet as her capricious pimp. The "atmosphère" scene is, indeed, of unforgettable brio and humor, one of the superlative moments of cinematic art, and it received loud, appreciative laughter. When the film was over, the lights in the theater came on and the president of the cinema club stood up in our box, called for attention and announced that Mademoiselle Arletty had honored that evening's showing with her presence. There was considerable applause, but there were also some loud whistles, an expression of contemptuous disapproval in France. Arlette smiled and waved. Then the applause overcame the whistles. The president, a slight, bald man of middle age—certainly old enough to remember the war, even to have had some part in it—apologized for the unpleasantness. Arlette said, "I expected it to be much worse. I'm grateful to you for this opportunity to test the health of my 'atmosphère.' " We all laughed and went into the lobby. Several people asked for her autograph, which she gave with a gracious flourish, asking each person's name.

In the car on the way back to Paris she said, "If Madame Raymonde* had been there tonight, she would have whistled a lot louder than those Commies. I count the evening a smash hit. Now maybe I can make it back to the big team. Carné, Prévert, Gabin, Jouvet."

But she never did make it back to the big team. Neither, for that matter, did Prévert or Carné, and Jouvet died not long after. Only Jean Gabin went imperturbably on from one success to another. Arlette was given smaller and smaller roles in less and less important or challenging films, and the inevitable assumption was that she accepted them mainly because she needed the money.

One day in the spring of 1950 Arlette invited me to go with her to lunch at La Houssaye. It was a special occasion, she said, for there would be someone there likely to interest me. She didn't say who this person was, and I enjoy surprises, so I didn't ask. There were ten people present that day, six women and four men. The afternoon was lovely, spangled with bumblebees and songbirds, and we ate outside on the bridge spanning the moat. Of the four women and two men who were strangers to me I couldn't guess which one was likely to be of particular interest. So I asked Arlette after lunch, while we were having our coffee. "It's the dark glasses," she said. I had noticed but paid slight attention

* Her name in *Hôtel du Nord*.

to a man of middle age and medium height, with thinning brown hair, who, indeed, had kept on a pair of dark glasses throughout the entire meal.

"And so?" I asked.

"My German officer," she said, and explained that he had come to France especially to see her although he was not legally entitled to be in the country. "Marriage on his mind," she added. "But not on mine. He's going to be made an ambassador. Can you imagine 'Mademoiselle Atmosphère' becoming 'Madame l'Ambassadrice'? Not I."

I agreed that such a transformation would seem incongruous.

"Are you impressed by him?" Arlette asked.

"We haven't said anything except hello," I replied. "So it's impossible for me to judge."

"He did me a great service," she said, "by making it possible for me to make so much trouble for myself. Some people say that it ruined my life. It certainly ruined my career and made a mess of my reputation, but thanks to him I discovered the self in myself. And yet when I see him today I can't see what it was that led me to that discovery. The discovery was a marvel, while the man was only an affair. I thought it would interest you to see him."

"Oh, yes," I said. "But the interest isn't in him."

Arlette shrugged and we moved away from the parapet where we had been chatting alone. The following summer—on July 31, 1951, to be precise—Lel Bellanger died. It was a drastic loss for Arlette, for Jacques even more shattering. And it was the end of an era for Arlette. In December she finally left the Hôtel Plaza-Athénée and installed herself at 31, rue Raynouard in an apartment offering a fine view across the city. The building was solidly bourgeois, comfortable but impersonal, her apartment there spacious but rather bare, uninviting and austere, I felt. She thought so herself, for in her memoirs she wrote, "I was to live there for seventeen years, solitary and without happiness."

And indeed this was the beginning of the long period of solitude and unhappiness that would prove to be the ultimate demonstration of Arlette's "atmosphère," the test of the self she had found within herself and the cruel apotheosis of her will to triumph over troubles. To prove, to test, to endure so much takes time. In the event it took forty-two years.

3

There were friends, of course. She was not forgotten. A personality such as hers, a character as intransigent, candid and outspoken, commands the dynamo of remembrance. Friends did what they could to help. But it wasn't much. The small parts in second-rate films and supporting roles in occasional plays only emphasized that a five-year fracture in the career even of a major talent can disable it forever. Arletty remained a name to be conjured with, certainly. She was a celebrity, her appearance at balls and receptions sought after, she was invited to the Carnival in Rio and the April-in-Paris ball in New York, where she met Queen Juliana and Greta Garbo. She visited Berlin and the Pacific islands painted by Gauguin. The film festival in Cannes invited her to sit on the jury. It became increasingly clear, however, that the actress who had moved, amused and fascinated all of France was destined never to do so again. That knowledge, of which no mention ever was made by her, must have contributed like the gradual cessation of a vital function to the solitude of the barren apartment in the rue Raynouard.

She had not been living there long when a hint of adversity fell to her lot. It touched that part of an individual's physical constitution most immediately and profoundly expressive of personality and spirit: the eye. For some time Arlette had been troubled by a weakening of vision in the left eye. Having characteristically ignored it longer than she should have, she finally consulted a specialist, whose examination showed that a prompt operation now offered the best hope of saving partial sight, at least, in that eye. I never knew exactly what the trouble was, not liking to risk indiscretion by inquisitiveness. The operation was not a success, leaving the left eye very nearly blind. The other one remained as strong as ever, but from that time onward Arlette would be permanently obliged to care for both eyes by putting drops in them morning and night, not the same drops in each eye, however—one kind in the left eye in hopes of preserving what sight remained, another kind in the right eye to protect it from deterioration. A slight saving grace in this misfortune was that, though she was nearly blind in one eye, her expression remained unchanged, her gaze as captivating as ever, and she was able to continue performing small roles on the stage and in films. Whenever outside, especially in sunlight, she took care to wear dark glasses. And in Belle-Ile during the summer months she wore a hat with a wide brim that further shaded her eyes. The little house facing the ocean at Donant had gradually become her true home, where she was content with her books, her radio and occasional visitors. And it was there, as if fate had not yet had its due in putting her to the tests of destiny, that disaster once again forced the issue.

One night in July 1962 she came home tired from a formal dinner and made a fatal mistake. Into her left eye she put the drops meant for the right eye, into the right those meant for the left. The drastic consequences soon made themselves felt. But Arlette did not resist the determination of circumstances. She did nothing, waiting stoically for the consequences of her self-imposed harm. It was only by chance that a doctor friend, coming to call two days later, discovered what had happened, and he immediately had her transported by plane to a clinic in Nantes. It was too late by then to undo the damage done by the wrong drops. Still, it was possible to avert total blindness. She could see but poorly, could read but only for a short time and occasionally. Two months after the accident, guided and attended by a compassionate cast, she was able to act in a mediocre film called *Le Voyage à Biarritz*. It was her last.

In 1962 I returned to live temporarily in America. But every year I came back to France, usually in the summer, for a lengthy visit, and if I did not see Arlette, I had news of her. She had attempted to perform in a play, *The Hostage* by Brendan Behan, but had had to give it up. Another operation, by a celebrated specialist in Lyon, gave promising results. With the aid of contact lenses her sight was sufficiently restored for her to contemplate a return to the stage. The play, *Les Monstres Sacrés* by Cocteau, was a success but the strain on the actress too great. On November 11, 1966, Armistice Day, she awoke in total darkness, blind. An emergency operation was performed the next day. It failed. The prognosis was grim. Nothing further could be done. She would be more or less totally blind, and rather more than less, for the rest of her days. "In a situation like this," she said, "there are only two solutions: combat or cyanide." Given her temperament, it was not even a matter of choice. She fought. She had been an actress, after all, a sovereign of the arts of make-believe, and she would make them serve her now.

In those years there was a cabaret near the Opéra called Le Grand

Eugène. Arlette had heard that the show there was unusually original and entertaining. "I'd like to see it," she said. "You'll take me, won't you, my Lord." So we went with a friend. If guided with care and warned in advance of what was coming, she moved with extraordinary grace, holding her head high, never betraying that she couldn't see where the next step would take her. During the performance, of which she was able to hear the music and singing, of course, she continually asked in a whisper to be told what was taking place on the stage. When I told her, she would occasionally exclaim aloud in her inimitable accent, "Oh, that's very good! They've got real style, haven't they!" As if she could see just as well as the rest of us, and it was almost possible to believe that she could. She laughed when we did and applauded with no less enthusiasm than anyone else. Her performance, indeed, was far more gifted and inspiring than the one on the stage. When we stood up to leave, a few people in the audience who knew her or recognized her came up to say hello. To each one she held out her hand and said, "How good it is to see you again." If she realized who the person was, she asked for news of the theater, friends in common, etc. When we got back to the rue Raynouard, she told us to leave her at the door. "From here," she said, "I can see my way without my eyes. I've become a real expert at transforming darkness into daylight."

She was not expert enough, however, to transform her material circumstances from night into day. Though not precisely poor, she was anything but rich, and the bare but spacious apartment in the rue Raynouard now cost more than she wanted to afford. Anyway, she could no longer see the view across the Seine toward the domes of the Invalides and the Panthéon. In the winter of 1969 friends arranged for her to move into a small two-room apartment at 14, rue Rémusat in a large, ugly building reserved for persons of limited resources. It was a far, far cry from the effulgent luxury of the Hôtel Plaza-Athénée, or, indeed, from the imposing nobility of the Château de La Houssaye. But that was all the same to Arlette. Her universe had shrunk to what she could hear and touch. Flavors and odors were also clues to the continuity of the veiled world, but food and perfume were low on her list of priorities. The small rooms of her apartment were poorly furnished. In the living room were a couch, where she usually sat, with her telephone and radio close at hand, a few chairs, a table and a clutter of books, boxes, vases of flowers and bottles. She had developed a taste for champagne. A bottle of Veuve Clicquot or Dom Pérignon was always a welcome gift, but I never once sensed that Arlette had had a drop too much.

There were many visitors, especially at first, sometimes too many to be seated in the small room. "I've never seen so many people since I went blind," Arlette remarked. She was always gracious, cheerful, alert. She politely received the many journalists anxious to take advantage of her excellent memory, for now as she neared eighty she had become one of the last witnesses of a vanished era. Of the numerous other visitors some were old friends, some bare acquaintances, and some complete strangers who had solicited the favor of a meeting by telephone. She always left her number in the book, responding with equal sympathy and good humor to the calls of friends and strangers, many of these also blind, to whom in their distress she was glad to offer a little encouragement and laughter. Of her visitors she said, "Their eyes are my windows on the world." Not all of them, alas, were as courteous and discreet as she. Many of her possessions, some of them precious, disappeared: books, bits of jewelry, bibelots, every single letter of the many from Céline. "You have to admit these thieves have good taste," she remarked, adding, "But I did prize my father's watch, the only family souvenir."

After the move to the rue Rémusat there were always people who came during the day to perform housekeeping chores and help Arlette with any personal grooming which in her darkness she was unable to do for herself. I never knew who they were, how they came to be there or who, if anyone, paid them. But there they were, always attentive and helpful but discreet and retiring. Arlette held the center of her poorly diminished stage until the end. And despite the journalists, despite the visitors, despite the thieves, despite the helpers, it was a very, very lonely stage, becoming lonelier and lonelier as the years ground by. But never was there a murmur of complaint. She said, "The affliction of the eyes is a noble one, the affliction of Oedipus. I have had a tragic destiny. It's not the destiny of Garance, to be sure, but it *is* a destiny." The affliction of Oedipus, of course, was deliberately self-imposed as penance for his transgressions, whereas Arlette's affliction was hardly to be regarded as penance. Transgressions had been imputed to her, and she had accepted the consequences without objection, but she felt no guilt. She was without hubris.

Though the rue Rémusat was far away from my Left Bank ivory tower, I went to see Arlette regularly, usually for lunch, which we always had at a nearby restaurant called the Hameau d'Auteuil. Well known there, she was pampered by the staff. Her food was served already cut into small pieces, and I marveled at the delicacy and fastidiousness with which she ate. Anyone not knowing that she was blind would have to have observed her with searching scrutiny to become aware of it. Once she even ventured as far as my apartment, where I had invited a few other actresses and actors to have lunch with her. One of them wept with emotion. Arlette had become a legend, though she ridiculed both the fact and the idea.

The municipal council of the Parisian suburb of Courbevoie, where she had been born, decided to name a street in her honor. She gave her consent, she said, because it would have pleased her parents. There was a ceremony. She cut a red, white and blue ribbon, then went back to the rue Rémusat. The little house in Belle-Ile had had to be abandoned long before.

She did not live in fear of her eventual fate. "When the poems of Baudelaire or Verlaine are constantly in your thoughts," she said, "you aren't afraid of tomorrow."

Nor was she fearful of her solitude, which as she grew older and older became more and more absolute. "It's an indispensable companion," she said. "I love it. More than a need, it's become my source of energy, of meditation."

She sang. All alone in the darkness of day or night she sang the old songs she'd learned thirty, forty, fifty years before. "It's my therapy," she said. She remembered them all, words and music, and they helped her to sustain the self she had created. Perhaps she worked harder now at being Arletty than she ever had before, and no doubt it was now more important than ever that she should succeed in maintaining her unique and famous "atmosphère." And she did. She dictated a volume of memoirs, amusing and incisive. The verve of her conversation, the music of her laughter, the brilliance of her personality remained changeless. Or almost so. Sometimes the effort required for her to be herself, the self she had always been, became visible, but it was only the more moving and noble for being perceptible.

She listened a great deal to the radio. "It's practical," she said. "You only have to turn the knob when it gets bad." And the radio, as if aware that she relied upon it, made free to repay her reliance by inviting her to record a series of interviews in which she recounted her career, her life, her memories. They were a notable success. She was outspoken, witty, sometimes inflexibly frank, but never cynical. She bore no grudges, felt no self-pity. "I'm incomplete," she said, "I don't know hatred."

And then as time wore on and on Arlette was ninety years old. Much attention was paid to her anniversary by the press, and her famous films, now classics of the cinematic art, were shown on television. No mention was made of the long-ago troubles. "La France Profonde" had forgiven and forgotten, welcoming her back with emotion to the glory of its Gallic heart. She was moved, but she had no illusions. She said, "The bird who puffs herself up thinking, 'I'm admired by everybody, I'm immortal,' is an idiot. Anyone who thinks that in three centuries people will pay to hear her laugh is a dreamer." Arlette was no dreamer. She knew what was coming. It did not intimidate her, and she only hoped that it would not entail an excess of suffering. "When people ask me what I'd like to have said about me after I die," she declared, "it's 'That broad, she was the real thing.' "

The apartment in the rue Rémusat had grown shabby and dusty. Arlette herself was no longer so immaculately groomed and attired as she had always been in the past. However, she could not see the change, and perhaps that was the only blessing of her blindness. And there were occasionally days when she simply could no longer succeed in being Arletty. But for those who remembered, who could see her still as Garance, Madame Raymonde, and hear the famous cry of *"Atmosphère"*—for us the memory was more than enough to compensate for any ravage. Now, more often than not, a half-empty bottle of champagne stood on the floor beside the little couch where she always reclined. She urged her visitors to share a sip with her. It would be brought by one of the young men or women ever present to wait on her, and all too often the glass would look as if it hadn't been washed for a week or two. But no matter. The champagne was Arlette herself, almost until the end. Then there were moments of vagueness. She would repeat what she'd said but a few minutes before. She tired easily. Still, she valiantly endeavored to adhere to her motto: Keep smiling!

Mademoiselle Atmosphère

The last time I saw Arlette was on a Sunday afternoon in March 1991, having telephoned in advance to be sure that my visit would not inconvenience her. The woman who answered said that Arlette was always glad to see me but that I would find her in bed, as she had fallen and broken her wrist three weeks before. On the way to the rue Rémusat I stopped at a florist's and bought a bunch of red roses, thinking that if she couldn't see them she might at least smell them. While the florist was wrapping up his bouquet he had a radio playing in the shop, and by one of those miracles that one can hardly believe to be coincidental Arletty's voice issued from the loudspeaker. It was a replay of one of her interviews. I mentioned this extraordinary co-incidence to the florist, telling him that his roses were for the woman whose voice he now heard, and he said, "She's really somebody." I also had with me a bottle of Dom Pérignon. There were two young men and one woman to admit me to the apartment when I arrived. I'd seen one of the young men and the woman before but still had no idea who they were or by what manner of arrangement their presence was assured.

I found Arlette in her small bedroom in a narrow hospital bed, the sort with large rubber wheels and the chrome fences that can be raised at night to prevent a patient from falling out. Her left wrist was tightly wrapped in a gray net bandage. I kissed her right hand, very brown with liver spots. Her hair was completely white, in some disarray, her teeth stained, face puffy and wrinkled, yet she didn't look like a woman of great age. She had on a white nightgown with a pink wool sweater over it, none too clean. Indeed, nothing in the whole apartment was clean or neat. The paint was worn and dirty, curtains also. One had a sense that since she could see nothing everything was let go. Over her bed hung the ink drawing of Colette reclining in the grass. There was also a small etching inscribed to her by Braque and the Fauve Dufy of a boat deck. All of these I remembered from previous residences. Her voice was a bit faint and the wonderfully trilling laugh now sounded decidedly forced. Yet it was a sign of her indomitable determination to be herself. I told her of the remarkable coincidence of hearing her voice on the florist's radio and his remark. She said, "Everybody is somebody. The trouble is it's so hard to find out who."

We didn't have a real conversation. There were silences, when I wondered whether she was still aware of someone else's presence. We talked about Belle-Ile, Roland Petit, Lel Bellanger, other people we'd known in the past. I mentioned Colette because of the sketch above Arlette's bed, and she said, "A real force of nature, that woman. What's she doing now?" I didn't answer, not wanting to pretend that Colette was still living nearly forty years after her death. We talked about the weather. I told Arlette that I was leaving for New York on Wednesday. Only a minute or two later she asked when I was going to London. The radiance of her gaze had now completely vanished. Her left eye stayed in the far left corner of the socket, the right one in the center, but both veiled. She had some difficulty moving her head and limbs. I asked whether she had to remain in bed all the time and she quickly said no, anxious, I thought, to make it clear that she was not altogether bedridden. I stayed for barely half an hour. Standing up to leave, I kissed her on the cheek and said goodbye.

"Au revoir, James, au revoir," she cried, her voice rising and yet once more musical for a moment. "You'll come back soon, won't you? You'll come back very soon."

"Yes," I said, knowing that in all likelihood I never would. And I never did. For that last instant, though, I had heard the incomparable voice of "Mademoiselle Atmosphère."

She lived on in her darkness with her radio, her telephone and the unforgotten songs sung at three o'clock in the morning for sixteen lengthy months, dying at last—peacefully, I was told—on July 23, 1992, aged ninety-four. Her departure caused a stir. "La France Profonde" realized that it had lost a precious and irreplaceable personification of its vital spirit. Both sentiment and intellect were prodigally expended in the press to say so. Had the authorities been left to decide, Arlette would no doubt have been interred in the Cemetery of Père Lachaise, where many of the most eminent dead of France repose. But she had expressly made it known that she wished her remains to return to Courbevoie, the working-class suburb where her family lay buried, and her wish was respected. The hearse conveying her there made a detour en route to pass by the Hôtel du Nord, the locale of her most celebrated scene, if not of her finest performance. And there was a large crowd of emotional mourners in front of the obscure hotel to pay homage as she passed. Their presence, and hers, constituted something of an irony, for all of the scenes supposed to have taken place in the hotel had actually been filmed in sets constructed at the faraway studio in Billancourt. Thus the reality of the film is, as it should be, a thing of artifice. But the broad who played in it, made it famous and sacrificed her fame for her destiny: she definitely was, and still is, the real thing.

La Mère Ubu

[M A R I E - L A U R E   D E   N O A I L L E S]

1

"I don't want to die," she shrieked. "I don't want to die. I don't want to die."

But already a funereal hush had fallen upon the palatial house where she had been born, and her raucous, furious reluctance to be parted from it forever sounded a final tribute to its fabulous contents and a creative echo of the supreme themes of art and song. In the salon beyond the deathbed room hung her portrait by Picasso, canvases by Degas, by Géricault, by Braque, in the adjoining gallery by Watteau, Chirico, Delacroix, by Klee, by Van Dyck and Goya in the grand staircase, in the vast rooms above by Rubens, by Rembrandt, by Simone Martini alongside numerous other portraits of her by illustrious artists of the twentieth century, not to mention many, many paintings from her own hand. The statuary, in addition, including a gilded bronze by Bernini, was resplendent, also the rare tapestries and magnificent furniture, the thousands of volumes in precious bindings and the priceless manuscripts by celebrated poets, novelists and notorious men and women of letters, one of whom, not the least, was her notorious ancestor, the Marquis de Sade, and another was his scandalous descendant, herself. Is it any wonder, then, that she violently fought shy of her impending encounter with death? What she had to lose, however, must surely have seemed to count for more than all the accumulated treasure of her possessions and for more even than the fame of her name, which was Marie-Laure de Noailles, née Bischoffsheim, viscountess by virtue of marital misadventure. Nonetheless, at eleven o'clock on that chilly Parisian morning, January 29, 1970, having been stricken but the previous evening, aged only sixty-seven, Marie-Laure expired, while her eldest daughter, two doctors, her personal maid and her very last lover were left, as they always had been, in some bewilderment as to the rationale of her obstreperous behavior.

Immortality is a condition fairly difficult to come by, though the longing for it is in one way or another almost universal and considered by some, therefore, to be beneath one's dignity. Men and women, however, who have made deathless reputations for themselves have not by and large been very bothered about their dignity. But many of them have longed to be loved. Even about Shakespeare, of whom we know so little, we know that. Marie-Laure's grandmother, a very grande dame, whose aspirations ascended to the acme of social *bienséance* but little higher, came by this superhuman condition without even trying to and probably without much understanding of what it was made of or how it functioned. She received lots of mail and kept a wastebasket prudently at hand while perusing it. Her granddaughter never forgot how feelingly the old lady would sometimes sigh as she threw away a half-read missive and murmured, "Another letter from that bore Marcel." This reliable provider of ennui was Proust. The novelist knew, of course, that most people do not have enough strength of character to become creatures of the imagination and so his letters to the Countess de Chevigné would have benefited little from the entertaining legerdemain which made her a model for the Duchesse de Guermantes in his masterpiece. And certainly he realized, if ever anybody did, how the recapture of time gone by can create an infinite future. Jean Cocteau used to claim that Proust had besought him to intercede with the countess, whose good friend the chic poet presumed to be, and persuade her to read his books. "But why bother?" Cocteau claimed to have said. "After all, Fabre didn't expect the insects to read his." The famous entomologist was writing for humans, however, not for insects, and like Proust, let alone Cocteau, counted on the finesse of his style to guarantee the survival of his discernments.

Madame de Chevigné may have thought the assiduous author tiresome. Perhaps she also surmised that his scrutiny could transform the private tedium of ennui into the public bother of embarrassment. Though of inestimable lineage, the countess, née Laure de Sade, was poor, and this was prejudicial in a milieu where money made most of the difference between prestige and prominence. To go out and work for a living did not present itself to anyone of the Chevigné mentality as a viable option. Then, as now, however, breeding could name its price in the marriage market. Maurice Bischoffsheim was the offspring of an immensely rich Jewish banking family, who, like the Rothschilds, had been assimilated into the structure of European aristocracy while still sustaining unassailable ties to the fate of persecuted forebears. The selling of Marie-Thérèse de Chevigné, daughter of the countess, to the young Bischoffsheim must have involved negotiations made almost intolerably painstaking by the pretense that marital felicity might be part of the bargain, but a capacity to tolerate considerable pain in the pursuit of pretense is intrinsic to the enjoyment of high society. Anyway, the mortification of a mercenary marriage was not unduly prolonged, for the rich husband was tubercular. Madame Bischoffsheim hardly had time to take stock of her sumptuous household and attend a few receptions for visiting royalty when she became pregnant and gave birth to a girl named Marie-Laure, whereupon the infant's father fell ill and, the costliest care notwithstanding, expired, aged only twenty-eight. Everything he had, which was so much that nobody could ever quite calculate the muchness, multiplication being its principle, went to the child, the mother left a mere trustee till her daughter's coming of age.

The eighteen-month-old heiress was delicate. Fear that she might have inherited not only a fortune but a fatal frailty hovered over her formative years. Nurses and governesses strictly sheltered the little girl from those frightening French drafts and saw to it that she never did anything risky. The climate in Paris was deemed a bit insalubrious, therefore much of her youth was whiled away in the South of France at Grasse, a town set well back from the risqué resorts of the coast and where nothing more exciting than the manufacture of perfume went on. Her upbringing was exceedingly proper even by the starchy standards of that polite and hypocritical age. When she was eight, her mother remarried, this time to a husband of her own choice, a popular playwright named Francis de Croisset, charming and worldly, much beloved by his stepdaughter. Her health improved as she grew older, and by the time of her adolescence a certain whimsical willfulness of character began to appear. One of her most passionate desires as a girl was to see Nijinsky dance, but Madame de Croisset forbade it as improper. She was encouraged to be bookish, remaining exceptionally so all her life, while a discerning interest in the visual arts was early developed by intimacy with masterpieces of painting and sculpture in her own home. This intimacy led to a desire to collect works of art of her own choice. An immense fortune, an original personality, lively intelligence, a respect for cultural values, absolute insulation from the cares of the workaday world and a decided disregard for convention all were hers. Only physical beauty was lacking, a deficiency bound to be deeply disturbing for one to whom aesthetic criteria would always be essential. Not that she was ugly, merely plain. To disguise this inopportune fact, there was much that could be done by hairdressers, dressmakers, jewelers and ingenious artisans of material splendor, but the fact remained evidential and contributed its teasing significance to the evolution of things.

To get Marie-Laure married, prestigiously married and, if possible, happily married, was of course a priority for Madame de Croisset. Having herself been sold to Maurice Bischoffsheim, she doubtless looked out for a match not too indebted to the pecuniary. The situation was slightly complicated by the young woman's sentimental fondness for Jean Cocteau, but his poetical fancy fed on boys. This was rather a pity, for telling similarities of temperament might have made a match between them more satisfactory than the one ultimately concluded, a suggestion which at the time would no doubt have seemed scandalous to all. But both Marie-Laure and Jean Cocteau came to thrive on scandal. A suitor of patrician lineage, personable appearance, impeccable politesse and acceptable affluence presently came upon the scene. His name, one that rang loud with historical and courtly resonance, was Viscount Charles de Noailles. He seemed made to order to satisfy the needs, desires and aspirations of everyone concerned, and any semblance as ideal as this naturally breeds a plentiful potential for adversity.

The honeymoon was a voyage to Cuba, where Marie-Laure gave a little hint of things to come by declining to disembark at Havana in order to continue her study of Freud's *General Introduction to Psychoanalysis*. The viscount made his cultural contribution to their young married life by arranging to have Picasso execute a portrait drawing of his wife, a likeness which, though large, was not particularly emblematic of the artist's genius. In order to avoid hustling her mother and stepfather too ungraciously out of the magnificent mansion which was now hers, Marie-Laure first set up housekeeping in smaller quarters in the rue de la Baume. During all their married life, no matter which of their residences they happened to be occupying, the couple never shared the same bedroom. Such contiguity might have seemed a trifle common to the aristocratic sensibility. To a young wife, however, the situation was disconcerting, for the viscountess soon found that her husband's visits to her bedroom for moments of conjugal felicity were far less frequent than she had hoped and expected. Nor was there anything she could do about this, decorum decreeing that intimate initiative be the prerogative entirely of the male. But it does not seem unreasonable to conjecture that those lonely and disappointing nights may have fostered in the young woman, perhaps unconsciously, a nascent resolve, no more than an intimation of an intimation at first, to obtain someday for herself privileges and liberties and satisfactions all her own and dependent upon no one else.

Nonetheless two children, both girls, Laure and Nathalie, were presently born, and the Charleses, as they were known by all in those luxurious, optimistic years, set themselves up in the grand mansion on the Place des Etats-Unis. There they received in lavish splendor the very proper nobility and the merely rich who by virtue of his lineage and her fortune constituted their appropriate milieu. Then they thought that their status called for a secondary residence. So they bought a hilltop crowned by the ruins of an ancient Saracen fortress in the South of France at a place then fashionable called Hyères. Their neighbor round the flank of the hill was the American novelist Edith Wharton, than whom hardly anyone could have been more fashionable or respectable. Within the fortress's ruined walls an immense folly of reinforced concrete in the Cubist style was built by an architect modish at the time named Mallet-Stevens. The place was called St.-Bernard. It contained about forty bedrooms, plus salons, dining rooms, library, swimming pool, squash court, gymnasium, hairdressing salon, vast kitchens; it was filled with works of art by contemporary artists and stood in its rambling immensity amid terraced gardens decorated with sculptures by Giacometti, Laurens, Lipchitz, Zadkine, et cetera. In short, a showplace, from the topmost tower of which fluttered a banner bearing the Noailles armorial colors.

Having created this extravaganza, the Charleses seem to have felt that the staid Parisian social life of the Faubourg St.-Germain, that tame menagerie made microcosm by Proust, was a bit too tame for them. Exciting things were going on in Paris, and the young couple possessed everything needed to participate in the excitement save the slightest concern or concept as to its effect. This was the heyday of Surrealism, make-believe anarchy and fun-house revolution. The Surrealists took themselves very seriously; they thought to transform the circumstances of life on earth by liberating the human unconscious and its expression through hallucinations and dreams. Scorning logic, religion, morality and above all the bourgeois order of society, they aspired to create a universal utopia and thought that a heady dose of scandal, nihilism and, if necessary, violence would hasten its coming. This was all quite diverting and perfect nonsense, as never for an instant did it threaten the established regime, because the Surrealists had no political program. So a self-important and innocent good time could be had at a minimum of risk. This was just the thing for the Charleses, who made it their business to become friendly with the Surrealist legion. That they represented the very epitome of everything that Surrealism most acrimoniously decried made not a scrap of difference. Youthful anarchists were impecunious, whereas the Charleses, who could eat off gold dinner plates with gold knives and forks whenever they felt like it, were affably prepared to subsidize the denunciation of their way of life. They paid the expenses of Surrealist publications, bought paintings and sculptures by members of the group and welcomed them to their resplendent residences.

In the twenties and thirties photography, though nothing new, was all the rage, the cinema likewise. If it was to become a form of art, however, daring benefactors had to be found. Already in 1928 Salvador Dali and Luis Buñuel had produced a film called *Un chien andalou*, a rather shocking work which had delighted the Surrealists but made little impression on the public. They were anxious to try again, determined the next time to perpetrate an authentic outrage. But they needed a million francs, no niggardly sum at the outset of the Great Depression. Charles de Noailles produced the money as if it had been plucked from a tree, his manners, as always, so exquisite as to suggest that the courtesy came to him rather than from him. He assuredly did not foresee that he was underwriting the seismic upheaval of his entire existence.

Buñuel and Dali got busy and pretty soon had produced an authentic shocker entitled *L'Age d'or*. The mansion on the Place des

Etats-Unis contained an opulent ballroom, all gilt and mirrors transported piece by piece from a palace in Palermo, with a ceiling painted by Solimena, and the Charleses at great expense had arranged that without altering the room's usual appearance films could be shown there. Thus it was in a setting of rococo splendor that *L'Age d'or* had its first showing before a group of aristocratic guests. The film, especially in view of the conventions of that era, was blasphemous, indecent and scandalous, conceived to give offense and successful in doing so. There was no coherent sequence of events, one bizarre image following another, and as a climax Marie-Laure's outrageous ancestor, the Marquis de Sade, so beloved by the Surrealists, was invoked. The principal figures of his most shocking work, *The Hundred and Twenty Days of Sodom*, were presented, not as themselves, but as Jesus Christ and his disciples. Perhaps the Charleses regarded all this as a lark, while their friends were too polite to tell them that it was bound to make trouble. Consequently a public showing of the film took place in December 1930. Scandal had been sought, and it was forthcoming. The first showing brought about a minor riot, fascist toughs threw stink bombs, ripped up the seats, splashed purple ink onto the screen, slashed Surrealist paintings hanging in the theater and injured a number of the spectators. So *L'Age d'or* immediately became an issue between liberal and conservative newspapers, with the latter promptly victorious, the film banned a week after its first showing, all available copies confiscated by the police. In short, the makers of the film had gotten what they wanted: the goat of the bourgeoisie. The producers, however, can hardly have bargained for the commotion which their philanthropy brought upon them. It was tactfully suggested to Charles that he might henceforth avoid appearing at the Jockey Club, that sanctum of exclusive *bienséance*, an affront from his peers not to be taken lightly by a nobleman of his standing. There was even talk of excommunication, no laughing matter in society said to be polite, but this was not a serious threat. The upshot of so much brouhaha was that the Charleses were no longer as welcome as they had been in the staid *hôtels particuliers* of the Faubourg St.-Germain. They had been infected by scandal, which was rightly considered contagious, and henceforth, if not exactly outcasts in the highest circles of society, they were treated and regarded with a circumspection not lacking in condescension. This may have been their great good fortune, because it allowed them—it virtually condemned them—to create their lives from resources within themselves rather than from those which chance had so prodigally provided. This, of course, represented a very considerable challenge, fraught with risk. Marie-Laure was intimidated by neither, but her husband was far less audacious. The interesting story is therefore hers, though in fairness it may be intimated that he had cause to be cautious.

Meanwhile, the luxurious life went on, and there is nothing like luxury to help one forget the mishaps brought about by the best of intentions. And it is likely that both enjoyment and forgetfulness came more easily on the hilltop at Hyères, far from reminders of embarrassment and humiliation. The guests were no longer the same who had played bridge and charades. Now they were artists, writers, musicians and bohemians whose only talent was to be entertaining. The games they played were decidedly more fun. Even so reserved an individual as André Gide was amused, recording in his journal some details of a visit to St.-Bernard with his young friend Marc Allegret:

Gymnastics, swimming in a vast pool, new games whose names I don't know, played with a shuttlecock, balls, balloons of every description— one in particular played by four of us (the very congenial professor of gymnastics, Noailles, Marc and myself) with a medium-sized ball which each team tried to keep from hitting the ground on its side of the high-strung net. We were playing more or less in the nude, then, all sweaty, we'd plunge into the tepid water of the pool. This game amused me more than I thought it possible, amused me like a child or like a god, and all the more so that I didn't feel myself awkward.

It does, indeed, sound like good fun and perhaps one may be forgiven for perceiving in the childlike or godlike pleasure of the sixty-year-old novelist, himself a scandalous figure consequent to his courageous defense of homosexuality, a reminiscence of pleasures described in antiquity by Petronius. So much pleasure, especially in a setting of sumptuous privacy, is likely to lead to delectable relaxation of restraints and forgetfulness of inhibitions. Such was the case at St.-Bernard, both then and later.

One afternoon Marie-Laure walked into her husband's bedroom and found him in bed with "the very congenial professor of gymnastics." Little imagination was needed to know what was happening.

Needless to say, there was no scene. Marie-Laure left the room. She and her husband never once spoke together of what she had witnessed. Employment was found elsewhere for the professor of gymnastics. So far as appearances were concerned, the incident might never have occurred. But it had. And if Marie-Laure did not speak of it to the viscount, she spoke to others. When she described it to me thirty years later, the aftershock remained intense, for as a consequence of what she had seen that day it had come to her as a revelation that her life henceforth must be her own creation, that she must have the strength, the courage, the imagination to make of herself the leading character in the drama of a memorable existence. Homosexuality as such did not scandalize her, being virtually banal in her milieu, but it was traumatic to have to recognize why so many of her nights had been so lonely. And the force of this trauma can only have added vitality to her desire to become a personality, as the French say, à part entière, ready to run the risks of her own whims and weaknesses.

Thus the Charleses ceased to exist as a social entity, becoming the Viscount and Viscountess de Noailles, Charles and Marie-Laure, separate individuals who from that time onward led mostly separate lives, often under the same roof, and who remained nonetheless closely bound to one another. What the viscount may have thought or felt in the wake of his wife's untimely appearance in his bedroom I have no idea, and I wager it was not a topic he broached very freely, if at all. Urbane, supremely polite, a charming conversationalist, he seemed to all of us to personify the ideal of the eighteenth-century nobleman, exquisite but aloof, and it was unthinkable that he might have made small talk of his feelings. Perhaps he was relieved to have Marie-Laure find out something that his temperament would have prevented him from telling her. And it may have helped him to accept, even, perhaps, to enjoy, some of the more extravagant escapades of her career. As for himself, he was content to remain more and more in the background. His interest in the avant-garde vanished. He returned to the milieu which had previously been his, became passionately addicted to gardening, an authority on horticulture, and created an extraordinary garden on his estate in the South of France at a comfortable remove from Hyères. He was waited on and kept company by a series of exceptionally handsome chauffeurs, valets and secretaries. It was he who mainly took on the responsibility for the upbringing and education of his daughters, since their mother was busy becoming an autonomous and prominent personality. Having wished for sons, he had the two girls taught by select tutors as boys would have been, and their father may have surmised that a portion of masculine self-sufficiency and resourcefulness would stand them in good stead. He was right, but it didn't do much good. He must also have hoped that both would make brilliant marriages. They didn't. Toward the end of his life the viscount became friendly with Queen Elizabeth, the Queen Mother of England, and went for little trips with her to visit unusual gardens, and it does not seem frivolous to assume that these royal interludes may have been the most pleasurable of his life.

Marie-Laure meanwhile felt that the first order of business was to make up for serious arrears in the sexual department. Her intelligence, her inventiveness, her erudition, her humor, generosity and hospitality all were prominent components of the exceptional Marie-Laure persona, but the sexual craving was also an essential motivating force of the theatrical production in which she played the leading, true-to-life role. It *was* a purposeful and vigilant creation, which is its interest and vindication, saving it from the negation of the average and endowing the outcome with something like Aristotelian catharsis, for Marie-Laure did possess the strength of character to become a creature of the imagination. Her folly, her absurdity, her triviality, greed and malice—in addition to so many happy and positive traits—were all intrinsic to the largeness of her life, which is why we loved and admired her.

Can it be entirely coincidence that the first and last of her lovers were homosexual, also a considerable number, though by no means all, of those in between, not to mention a great number of her friends? It is a notable fact that wealthy ladies past middle age very often find their firmest friends among homosexuals. Heterosexual men have little time to spare—or should one say waste?—on older women, no matter how rich, unless there is a convincing likelihood of appropriating their money, whereas homosexuals enjoy the refinements of costly sociability and elegance for their own sake. The very first lover, then, of the viscountess is said to have been an Englishman named Edward James, the son of very rich parents, an eccentric art collector, especially keen on the works of Dali (who had not yet become a venal charlatan). Their affair was doubtless brief and probably unsatisfactory. Edward was

pretentious and unpredictable, prone to self-dramatization and ostentatious gestures. In later years he secluded himself in the wilds of
Mexico, built a palace there and eventually died.

That Marie-Laure was seriously and sincerely devoted to her husband, and to many other men besides, is indubitable, but it may be
that she was truly and passionately in love only once. And here too
she was unlucky. All along the lengthy line of her love affairs, as a
matter of fact, luck eluded her. It eluded her, indeed, so consistently
that one wonders why. Perhaps the explanation may suggest itself in
the evocation of her life. This might even suggest something provocative and valid about the principle of love as a wherewithal of life for
us all. Marie-Laure would have liked that.

Igor Markevitch entered her existence with the nonchalance of a
born genius. And that is simply what he presumed to be, encouraged
in this presumption by no less an authority than Sergei Diaghilev. The
sophisticated impresario had an unerring appreciation of comely
youths as well as of creative talent, and though Markevitch had from
childhood possessed extraordinary musical ability, it was as a lover that
the sixteen-year-old adolescent traveled around Europe with his ailing
countryman, who had but one more year to live. This glamorous, if
scandalous, liaison gave the young fellow entrée not only to the select
musical circles of Nadia Boulanger and Alfred Cortot, where he willingly acquiesced in the assumption that great things were to be expected
of him, but also to the salons of wealthy and elegant patrons of the
arts, where his charm and self-assurance encouraged others to concur
in his high opinion of himself. Naturally he came to be acquainted
with Charles and Marie-Laure de Noailles. Shrewd beyond his years,
too shrewd, perhaps, for his own good, he perceived that the viscount
was an unusually permissive and not very possessive husband, while
the viscountess wanted nothing more than to be possessed. Just how
the affair began between the would-be prodigy and the lonely noblewoman is unclear and irrelevant. It began. The date seems to have
been sometime early in 1933, Markevitch then twenty-one, Marie-
Laure ten years older. The young composer's mother had a modest
home in Switzerland. Marie-Laure rented a house nearby for the son
and herself, bringing along two automobiles, two chauffeurs, a cham-
bermaid, and a score of trunks and suitcases. As it had been for Diaghilev, money was always a problem for Igor, though he had no need

to be as lavish, but again like the prodigal impresario he always seemed to find generous patrons when urgently required. Much leisure was necessary for the conceiving and composing of the ambitious works by which he proposed to prove his genius. It was rumored that before his affair with Marie-Laure he had utterly ruined a prominent Parisian architect. At all events, the viscountess had more money than anyone could count and was happily prepared to part with it in this fashion. She and Igor appear to have enjoyed an idyllic existence together. While Markevitch composed, she wrote letters to her husband and daughters, read countless books and conscientiously kept a journal. (The fate of which her descendants decorously refuse to disclose.) It seems to have been during this period that she conceived the desire to do creative work of her own, the first efforts being literary. Perhaps the young musician persuaded her that she, too, possessed the talent and temperament of an artist.

Atavistic instinct may also have impelled the young woman to believe that hers was a true creative temperament. Her grandmother had been born Laure de Sade, and her own forename perpetuated the nominal relation to a nearly mythic personage of the fourteenth century, none other than the famous Laura who had inspired the most sublime love poems of Petrarch. The poet never revealed her surname, and little is known with certainty about her life save that she was approximately the same age as Petrarch and of a noble family. That is all. But Provençal tradition has for centuries maintained that she became the wife of Hugues de Sade, a woman of rare cultivation who wrote verse herself, bore seven children and died of the plague in 1348. Present-day research tends to dismiss as unfounded any connection between Petrarch's Laura and Marie-Laure's distant forebears, but it is idle to speculate now about the accuracy of a legend which has been the ancestral cult of a famed and illustrious family for six hundred years, continuing to the present day. Was not the Charleses' first child named Laure? For generation after generation, then, the prestigious presence of Petrarch's Laura in their past seemed to preside like the spirit of genius and the symbol of intellectual distinction over the future of the Sade dynasty. Marie-Laure always drew a laurel leaf beneath her signature when signing a letter or painting, and sometimes allowed that sign alone to identify her. That she could look back in her ancestry to the example of a woman so supremely inspiring can hardly have failed to influence her concept of the role that she herself might play on the immortal stage of art.

Markevitch in his memoirs maintains that his affair with Marie-Laure did not constitute a scandal. This is nonsense. It was scandalous to the nth degree for a member of Paris's most select society, bearer of one of France's grandest names, the mother of two young daughters who would one day be expected to make respectable, indeed illustrious, marriages, to have run off with a young and impecunious musician who had yet to demonstrate his genius, and live openly with him, spending uncounted amounts of money. And all this after the *Age d'or* furor had hardly been forgotten. It marked Marie-Laure once and for all as an individual who could not be counted upon to respect the rules and formalities, however hypocritical and fraudulent, which then determined the code of aristocratic conduct, now a forgotten aberration. It gave her, in short, her freedom. Henceforth the entire responsibility for her development as a personality was to be hers alone. If this frightened her, it must have elated her as well, because few women have been more resolved than she was to create herself as the leading character in the performance of her life.

The affair with Markevitch lasted ecstatically enough for a couple of years. Then there was trouble. Marie-Laure became pregnant. If she kept the child, it would have to be legally and socially considered the progeny of Charles, an unacceptable eventuality. An abortion was agreed upon with melancholy. Then there was talk of a check given Igor by the viscountess to which the resourceful composer added a zero or two. In any case, it was felt in Marie-Laure's family that far too much money had been spent already, and partly as a consequence legal steps were taken to prevent her henceforth from ever enjoying free access to her capital. As for Igor, creative fulfillment did not come to him as inevitably as expected, and he sought to salvage his distinction by becoming a conductor. The intimacy with Marie-Laure had wilted. And then he married the daughter of Diaghilev's most miraculous protégé, Nijinsky, returning in spirit, as it were, under the fabulous wing of his original mentor. Markevitch thereafter, having counted for a great deal at first, ceased to count for much at all in the life of Marie-Laure. He didn't count for much in the world of music either, despite numerous recordings and guest appearances as the conductor of minor orchestras. He had known a moment of putative greatness at age sixteen, afterward great expectations indefinitely deferred.

Then there were other lovers, none so important to her as Igor had been. There were also balls, cocktail parties, luncheons, dinners, excursions in the country. This was the era of café society, a phenomenon repugnant to the aging denizens of Proust's microcosm. And so Paris received the likes of Elsa Maxwell, Cole and Linda Porter, the Murphys, Fitzgeralds and Miss Hoity Wiborg, not to mention South American millionaires such as Arturo Lopez, the Anchorenas and Patiños, all of them determined to have a good time and none too concerned about decorum. Marie-Laure was sought after, feted and admired in this milieu, where her scandals scarcely counted as trifling peccadilloes. She became the café society queen. To the newcomers she was able to introduce Dali, Max Ernst, Giacometti, Picasso, Francis Poulenc, Eluard, Aragon, et al. She published a volume of stories entitled *Ten Years on Earth*, and it may have seemed to her that her true terrestrial existence had begun barely a decade before. If so, it would have been perfectly natural to anticipate willful whims and a stubborn determination to do precisely as one pleased, the normal impulses, to be sure, of childhood.

Meanwhile, symptoms of impending calamity became more and more frequent on three of France's frontiers, most especially to the north. In retrospect it seems that one would have had to be desperately dense not to realize well before Munich what Hitler was up to, and particularly would clairvoyance have seemed imperative for Jews. A madman, of course, could never have foreseen the entire horror, but prudence was obviously indicated. Charles de Noailles was supremely prudent. His wife was the daughter of a Jew, but this man had himself been but half Jewish, his mother a Brahmin from Boston named Paine. Marie-Laure was therefore but a quarter Jewish and married to an Aryan, which would technically exempt her from any persecution under the infamous Nuremberg Laws. The viscount nonetheless took the precaution of having a very detailed and official genealogy drawn up in case of any emergency. His prudence was repaid under circumstances so ironic as to be for him, a Frenchman whose ancestors had fought for Louis XIV and with Lafayette in the American Revolution, bitterly humiliating.

Then came the war, so quiet at first on the Western Front as to be deemed "*drôle*." But what took place in Poland was deadly serious, a rehearsal for Belgium and France, and it must have been a very intransigent Germanophile or vicious member of the Anti-Jewish League who could without grief watch Nazi soldiers parading on the Champs-Elysées while swastika banners floated over Paris. But the Occupation was a fait accompli, about which nobody in France could do much, the Resistance as an effective movement materializing only when the eventual outcome of hostilities began to look like a sure thing. Meanwhile, life went on as best it could, and for those who could afford the best it went on without intolerable inconvenience. Still, there were restrictions, curfews, shortages, nuisances, and the effect of these was to exacerbate the inclination of everyone to have a good time insofar as possible. It seemed, indeed, a means of putting a defiant face on the national catastrophe. Women's dresses, and especially their hats, turned into extravagant creations. Sly means of circumventing restrictions immediately became widespread, theater and cinema flourished, the shrewder Jews slipped out of sight and people gave parties, in Paris at least, as never before. Parties provided forgetfulness, and if sometimes the forgetfulness went too far, one must be mindful of how desperate was the need to forget. The aristocratic world, like the artistic one, knows no frontiers, and shrugs off the prohibitions of the rank and file. So it was not uncommon, once the initial shock of defeat had passed, to encounter German officers at the most elegant receptions. Besides, many of these men bore names quite as patrician as any to be found in France; some, indeed, were relatives and many were artists and writers. Even so famous an antifascist and "degenerate" artist as Pablo Picasso did not turn away German admirers from his studio door or disdain to be seen in the houses where they were to be met. Marie-Laure's mansion was one of these, the Anchorenas' vast apartment on the Avenue Foch was another, and as a practical consideration it was worth remembering that these grand establishments provided food that could not be had elsewhere. The Anchorenas kept a cow on the roof of their building so as to have plenty of butter and cream, and they used to say that the three men they most admired in the world were Hitler, the Duke of Windsor and Picasso, order of preference optional.

And yet . . . it is vital never to forget that while these Nazi officers went about their business, which in certain cases they honorably endeavored to make as innocuous as possible, while they attended the fashionable parties, had dinner at Maxim's and flocked to the Folies-Bergère, their colleagues were supervising the installation of unthinkable facilities in distant and occult locations, the names of which history will forever hold in horror: Dachau, Buchenwald, Belsen, Ravensbruck, Treblinka and, ultimately, Auschwitz, not to mention many more. Of all this the defeated citizenry remained unaware. However, the officers knew as little or as much as their duties required, but they knew, and it is not surprising that they refrained from revealing this knowledge in conversation. As for the man in the street, even he could not for long remain unaware of the persecution of Jews, the execution of hostages and the infamous activities of the Gestapo.

It was ineluctably—like it or not—against the background of all this that relations between the French people and their enemies would ultimately have to be judged. And if the judgment was sometimes more severe than many thought fair, or sometimes less so, this was simply further fortuity in the unequal chances of war. Marie-Laure might have seemed one of the last persons likely to be guilty of a transgression which for a French woman with Jewish antecedents might be judged reprehensible. Yet she was guilty, and the transgression unfortunately was precisely of the sort most easy, tempting and treacherous: the carnal. Many of the wearers of the enemy uniform were magnificent young men, and it is a truism that soldiers are particularly prone to lust. So Marie-Laure took a German lover. It was said, and insinuated by herself to be a mitigating circumstance, that he was in fact Austrian, but everybody knew that many Austrians outdid Germans in their enthusiasm for the Third Reich. The identity of the young officer seems to have been forgotten by everyone, probably with relief, but there is no uncertainty either about his existence or about his affair with the impetuous viscountess. Evidently it never occurred to her that the outcome of *this* scandal—for that was how it was certainly judged even by people foreign to the Faubourg—could lead her into serious trouble. One can only conclude that her conduct was ruled by the conviction that no criterion could apply to her save her determination to do as she pleased. No effort seems to have been made to conceal this affair. It would have been in vain anyway, for the couple were involved, along with the composer Georges Auric, in an automobile accident serious enough to become public knowledge. No grave injury was sustained, but Marie-Laure's nose was damaged, causing her ever afterward to breathe through her mouth, with the result that her laughter became a highly humorous snuffle and she snored very loudly when asleep.

Numerous French women—and men—gladly met with pleasure, affection, even love in the company of the enemy forces occupying their country. The populace in general harshly condemned these affairs. To be sure, they did involve not only emotional and social issues but ethical considerations as well. And even in time of war, when every ethical principle would seem blasted by the whirlwind of conflict, yet there are standards of rectitude which survive. They may be little observed, if at all, but they endure, and sooner or later, and more or less, everything being relative, they prevail. It was not in Marie-Laure's nature to be discreet. On the contrary. But she was neither courageous nor rash, possessed a normal amount of common sense, and therefore probably refrained from making a public display of an affair with a Nazi officer. Or perhaps it was the viscount who succeeded in persuading her to be prudent. In any case, she suffered no unpleasant official retribution. A moral judgment, however, was passed by those who had the sentiment or principle to find her guilty, at best, of frivolous indifference to circumstances of the utmost gravity. That Marie-Laure pondered these ethical issues seems unlikely, as she was not given to musing upon matters unpleasant to her or unfavorable to her reputation. But the issues existed, and anyone who would take account of Marie-Laure's life must be mindful of the moral impeachment which they proclaim. Of course no one mentioned to her face anything of the sort. Her station, her fortune, her nonchalance itself made her immune to disagreeable aspersions, and the German affair does not seem to have lasted much more than a year, perhaps eighteen months.

How ironic that sometime during this period, late one night—insidiously, as always, choosing the most vulnerable hour—representatives of the Gestapo came pounding at the door of 11, Place des Etats-Unis to arrest the Jewess Bischoffsheim. It so happened that the viscount was absent, but the servants had received orders in case of emergency and knew what to do. They called the elder daughter, Laure, then aged about eighteen, and it was she who produced detailed genealogical documents for inspection. Frustrated no doubt, though perhaps awed by the grandeur of the surroundings, the Gestapo men had no choice but to depart, while Marie-Laure slept on, undisturbed.

Not long after, she took another lover, a haughty and temperamental cellist, a musician of second-rate competence named Maurice Gendron. Then one day the war was over and the Noailles found that it had not caused them much inconvenience save for the fact that while its horrors and devastation made havoc in half the world they had become middle-aged amid their tapestries and bronzes and gold snuffboxes.

2

In the month of June 1950, I was posing for a drawing in a cheap hotel room on the Ile de la Cité. Though born in Berlin, the artist was an Englishman of exactly my own age named Lucian Freud, grandson of the world-famous psychoanalyst. We had met in London the previous autumn. Posing for Lucian was quite a painstaking chore, because he insisted on absolute immobility and worked very slowly. I was happy, however, to undergo some discomfort, because I admired Lucian's work—both then and now—and greatly enjoyed his entertaining, cultivated company. The drawing he made is exceptionally fine, even for him, a good likeness besides, and though to his eye unfinished and of moderate size it required several sessions of posing. Toward the conclusion of one of them he told me that he was going to have dinner that evening with a friend of his named Marie-Laure de Noailles and suggested that I join them if I had nothing else to do. Even had I had another engagement, which I hadn't, I think I would have abandoned it in favor of Lucian's suggestion. In 1950 still a relative newcomer to Paris, I had nonetheless heard of Marie-Laure. I had already heard of her, as a matter of fact, in 1945, when as a soldier I spent six months in the French capital. So I knew that she was immensely rich, equally eccentric, a patroness of art and literature, possessor of masterpieces of painting and sculpture. And I told Lucian that I would be delighted to go along and have dinner with him and his friend.

Marie-Laure and Lucian had recently traveled together to Vienna in order to be present at the dedication of a plaque on the building at 19 Berggasse to commemorate the momentous explorations of the human psyche which Sigmund Freud had for decades conducted there.

While in Vienna they went one evening to a café, where an incident occurred that was typical of Marie-Laure's witty and inventive response to the unexpected. They fell into conversation with a fellow client, a man who proved to be congenial, and eventually it came out that his name was Sacher-Masoch, whereupon Marie-Laure at once asked whether he might be a descendant of the famous Leopold von Sacher-Masoch, whose name had come into general usage to characterize certain sexual abnormalities. Upon being told that he was, she immediately exclaimed, "*Ich bin Sade, du bist Masoch, er ist Freud!*" It was indeed an evocative coincidence that three direct descendants of men associated in theory to one another by the vagaries of sexuality should have found themselves face to face, a coincidence made to order to have symbolic implications for Marie-Laure, and for Lucian, both of whom regarded vagaries of sexuality as perfectly prosaic.

We took a taxi. I wasn't very well dressed, but neither was Lucian. The light beneath the chestnut trees in the spacious Place des Etats-Unis was fading emerald, the great gray houses like stone mastodons petrified on either side. Number 11 was a huge pile in the late-nineteenth-century style, unadorned but grandiose. Lucian rang and the portal popped open. We came in beneath a vaulted porte cochere. To the right a pair of glass doors opened onto a vast, high-ceilinged entrance hall. A butler in black greeted us impassively. I was aware of a marble staircase, Corinthian columns and crystal chandeliers above, sculpture, paintings, tapestries, but it was impossible to take in very much of this as we passed through into a gallery hung all around with paintings up to the high ceiling. I was overawed. It is fair to say that no one, even those well acquainted with palaces, ever entered that house for the first time without some sense of marvel and thrill. At the far end of the gallery, where glass doors gave onto a garden, the butler opened a door to his right, standing aside, and we passed into an octagonal salon. Marie-Laure awaited us here, came forward in a flowered silk frock, smiling, shook hands, very amiable and informal, as if to put one promptly at ease. And her desire to do so seemed quite sincere. No sincerity on her part, however, could put one very quickly at ease with the sumptuous surroundings which constituted the setting intrinsic to *her* ease, and while it would be sardonic to suggest that so much treasure had been accumulated to provide social advantage to its possessor and to intimidate visitors less affluent, it was impossible to avoid the assumption that such a room had been knowingly arranged as a setting in which its proprietor's existence and personality could most dramatically be displayed. In a word, her stage. Its effects were splendid beyond description but some modest descriptive effort is nonetheless necessary to the narrative. Of the paintings, three were by Goya, two of these among his most marvelous, life-size portraits of his son and daughter-in-law. There was one by Rubens, one by Braque, and scattered among them numerous drawings by Picasso, Prud'hon, Balthus, including the large Picasso of Marie-Laure. On side tables of marble and gilt bronze lay a score of gold, gem-encrusted snuffboxes, etuis and eighteenth-century *cartes de bal*. Tanagra figurines, Renaissance bronzes and Byzantine ivories stood on the chimneypiece and bookshelves. The furniture was superb, the chandelier of rock crystal. Presently the butler returned, without having been summoned, bearing a silver tray with an opened bottle of champagne and three cut-crystal goblets which he set down in front of the fireplace on a low table of which the top was a large slab of jade. In silver vases were luxuriant bouquets of white lilies, and one of my most evocative memories of that first evening is of the heavy scent of those flowers in the pale green light that filtered through from square and garden.

Hardly had we sat down and taken a few sips of champagne when the telephone buzzed. The viscountess picked it up, listened for a minute or two, spoke a few words and put it down. "That was Roro," she said. "He's with Cecil and wants to join us for dinner, so I said it was all right."

Lucian would be happy to see Cecil, he said, as they had some sort of arrangement about a portrait that was hanging fire and needed clarification. I had no idea who either of these persons might be.

Roro must have been just around the corner when he phoned, and very sure of Marie-Laure's goodwill, because it wasn't more than fifteen minutes before he was ushered into the salon. The viscountess in the meantime had gone into an adjoining room and soon returned wearing long white gloves and carrying a red pocketbook. Roro—whose name was Robert Veyron-Lacroix—was dark-haired, Latin in appearance. He kissed Marie-Laure on both cheeks. Cecil Everley was tall, willowy, blond, and in his youth, which had passed, must have been good-looking. He and Marie-Laure only shook hands. "But I assumed that it was Cecil Beaton you were with," she said to Roro. "It's too sly of you not to have said."

Roro laughed and exclaimed, "Don't be idiotic!"

Whereupon Marie-Laure slowly drew off her white gloves one by one, dropping them and her pocketbook onto a stool covered in red velvet. "Suddenly I have the most frightful headache," she said. "I couldn't possibly go out to dinner. You will have to excuse me." And withdrawing to a farther corner of the room she added, "And so I will bid you good evening."

There was nothing for us to do but accept her dismissal and depart, so one after another we said goodbye and turned to the door, Roro and Cecil leaving first. But then Marie-Laure called out, "Lucian, you and your friend stay for a moment. I have something to tell you. And do close the door. Roro knows the way." Sitting down in an armchair beside the fireplace, she took up her goblet of champagne and said, "There's nothing like a sip of champagne to cure a headache, is there? It's like magic. I feel better already."

Lucian laughed, poured more wine from the bottle into all of our goblets and said, "Francis says champagne is the elixir of eternal youth."

Marie-Laure also laughed.

I contrived to snicker slightly but more from embarrassment than amusement, startled and shocked at the hostess's overt rudeness, which put me decidedly ill at ease as a guest for the first time in her mansion. Besides, I didn't know who the unwelcome ones were, not to mention Francis, and no effort was made by my companions to explain what had happened. They seemed to take my presence for granted, paying little attention to me, which was what I could most have appreciated under the circumstances, leaving me at ease to be smitten by the beauty of Goya's blond-haired, dark-eyed son, his tight striped trousers and pearl-gray tailcoat, imagining I might never have a chance to return his languorous gaze. How, indeed, could I have known that in time he would become as familiar to me, as responsive, moreover, to my soulful admiration, as half the people I knew?

But before we had time to finish our champagne, Marie-Laure stood up, took her gloves and pocketbook and said, "We'd better be going. I reserved at the Méditerranée for nine-thirty, and Baka is waiting with the car."

But Lucian said, "Let's show James the upstairs first. I'd particularly like him to see the Balthus." So we went back through the gallery and up the marble staircase. At the landing hung a large Picasso figure painting of the Negro period. Probably executed about 1908, I thought, but cautiously refrained from comment. On the upper floor we passed through a pair of tall doors, faced with bronze on the inside, entering a very large salon. The walls were covered with paintings. To the right a huge Rubens. Between the windows a wonderful early Chagall of a green pig. And on the far wall the magnificent portrait of the viscountess by Balthus, her countenance a mask save for the sly, penetrating gaze, a painting that bids fair to be a masterpiece. I exclaimed over it. Then we went back downstairs.

Baka was the chauffeur, the car a large Chrysler. Only fifteen or twenty minutes had passed since Marie-Laure's cavalier pretense that she felt too unwell to dine with Roro and Cecil, and as we came outside to get into the car there they both were, standing at the street corner to our left, not fifty yards away, obviously at a loss for something to do. No situation could have seemed more awkward, for they certainly couldn't help seeing us, but Marie-Laure and Lucian behaved as though the other two were either invisible or, worse, nonexistent, climbing into the back seat of the car, its door held open by the chauffeur —rather sullenly, I thought—and I had no choice but to climb in after them. Still, I couldn't help feeling compassion for the humiliation gratuitously imposed upon two persons presumed to be the viscountess's friends, and I wondered whether such a woman could actually be the lady of rare sensibility and remarkable attainments of whom I had heard so much. There were times when I thought she was, others when I felt certain she wasn't, and I would still like to know.

The Méditerranée was a restaurant, then chic and excellent but since gone downhill, where we had dinner, and in those years in the main dining room hung a large painting by Balthus of a ferocious cat seated by the seaside, knife and fork poised to devour a jet of fish spouting from adjacent waves onto his plate. The place specialized in seafood. During dinner there was no mention of Roro and Cecil. Marie-Laure turned her entire attention upon me, asking all sorts of questions, many of them indiscreet—which was their fun and interest—about my past, my family, my ambitions, my resources, my friends, my intimacies, etc., etc. This was clearly a game, and something of a test, meant to be impertinent and to find out how far it was possible to go without getting one's goat, but at the same time there was no mistaking the warmth of her curiosity. Above all it was clear that one should avoid the slightest appearance of being intimidated. In fact, I felt, a soupçon of insolence might add appreciative savor to the personal repast. So I said, "Of course, when somebody lives with treasures and masterpieces every day the way you do, he becomes blasé. For instance, all those gold boxes in your salon, I don't suppose you even see them anymore."

There was a distinct pause, into which Marie-Laure introduced the hint of a frown overlaid with the suggestion of a smile, and said, "I only look at them to count them, the last thing I do before going to bed."

And yet, when some years later every last one of the gold boxes was stolen, her feelings of bereavement seemed almost as if for an old friend. The theft was never solved. There was no sign of forced entry, and nothing else of value disappeared. Some people said that the burglar had been a boyfriend of Jean Genet. It was too bad; the magnificent room never again had quite the same aura of careless splendor. And then a little later the Goyas were relegated upstairs to a situation almost of insignificance on a side landing of the staircase. But that was for reasons beyond the reach, as it were, of feelings of bereavement and which, indeed, might understandably have seemed to deny the life enhancement of masterpieces.

Marie-Laure paid for the dinner. Her chauffeur was waiting outside and I was dropped off at the inexpensive hotel where I then lived. Soon afterward Lucian returned to London, leaving with me the unfinished and unsigned portrait drawing and an etching inscribed: "To James with love from Lucian."

Robert Veyron-Lacroix was a distinguished harpsichordist who gave concerts all over the world, often with the flutist Jean-Pierre Rampal, and became a respected professor at the Conservatoire. He was a loyal friend to Marie-Laure, and all of us saw him often. Cecil Everley was the boyfriend of an American millionaire who had married the grandniece of Pope Leo XIII, enabling her and their five children to live in great splendor. His wife was often described as the Marie-Laure of Rome. The Francis referred to by Lucian, believer in champagne as the elixir of youth, was Bacon, needless to say, and his belief has been ostentatiously vindicated by his example, as countless bottles of bubbly never diminished his vitality till sudden death at age eighty-two.

Not long after that first meeting with Marie-Laure I left Paris for three months, then in October went to the United States, not returning to France till March 1, 1951. Soon thereafter I ran into the viscountess at a party. She remembered the evening with Lucian and we had a chat. I continued to run into her here and there. She invited me to her house for lunch, after which we sat in the grand salon at the top of the staircase, and I was able again to admire the Rubens, the gorgeous green pig by Chagall and the portrait of Marie-Laure by Balthus. But then I went again to America, traveling all over the country and through parts of Canada, absent from France this time for more than a year. So it was not until the spring of 1953 that I resumed acquaintance with many people I'd met in Paris.

Living there in those years was a young American composer named Ned Rorem. As yet he had achieved no professional distinction; it would come later. For the moment he was famous mainly for his beauty, which was so exceptional that even Ned contemplated it with emotion. To make friends with him was easy, because he interpreted amicable attitudes as tributes to his appearance and felt that they deserved the reward of intimacy. And in fact he longed to be liked or, even better, to be loved, which would prove that nature had rightly selected the recipient of her alluring gift. Companionable but nobody's fool, hardworking and hard-drinking, ambitious and shrewd, Ned quickly made plenty of friends in Paris. If they happened to be famous, rich, useful and awed by his angelic countenance, so much the better. I didn't record the circumstances of our meeting, but I do remember assuming during my first years in Paris that one could make the acquaintance of absolutely anybody if the desire was keen enough, and I think that that was very nearly true. Marie-Laure and Ned inevitably met, since she was supposed to be a patroness of all the arts, and it was said that she succumbed to an instant passion for the beautiful musician, though of course nothing sensual came of it, as Ned sought gratification solely in the longings of his own sex. Between us there was never anything more than good-natured camaraderie, because I didn't see sexuality in his good looks. The three of us went out together occasionally even before I left for America in 1952. When I came back, I found Ned living in Marie-Laure's house, where a comfortable room with a piano had been arranged for him up a flight of back stairs from her own apartments, overlooking the leafy square, and she had given vent to her humorous perspicacity by bestowing upon him the nickname of "Miss Sly." It was Ned who first set ajar for me the portals of the Place des Etats-Unis, for his status in the house was such that he could invite guests on his own initiative. Later, the mere momentum of social and artistic life in Paris in those years carried me along, but most especially was I made welcome by the unpredictable viscountess when my relationship with Dora Maar grew close. This was in the late autumn of 1953.

Marie-Laure and Dora had known one another then for something like twenty years, having first met among the Surrealists. Both of them possessed personalities of exceptional singularity and unconventional self-reliance. I think there was a certain rivalry between them, the competition being principally for prestige conferred by the celebrity of their lovers. When Dora became Picasso's acknowledged mistress, she achieved quasi-royal status in the milieu frequented by both women. Marie-Laure indubitably was envious and liked to relate that she had once suggested to Picasso that they jump into bed together, saying, "You'll be Goya and I'll be the Duchess of Alba," but this historic consummation never took place. I never believed that tale. Marie-Laure was archly prone to prevarication if she imagined it might enhance the stature of her persona. When Picasso brutally broke off relations with Dora in favor of a girl half her age, the viscountess probably felt a certain gratification, but she was too profoundly feminine and sporting to let it show, and the two women doubtless became better friends thereafter. Besides, Marie-Laure continued to have lovers, whereas Dora was alone in the world. Then I came along, and even to Dora, I think, her solitude seemed less. For a time.

The summer of 1954 Dora and I spent together in the Provençal village of Ménerbes, her house there a gift from Picasso in happier days. And during the month of August, Marie-Laure invited me to stay at Hyères, where her vast establishment had been but partially renovated after use as a hospital during the war, only eight or ten bedrooms and three or four salons made habitable, the swimming pool, squash court, gymnasium and all the rest left in semi-ruin. But it was a very agreeable large house within the remains of a huge one; the walls were covered with works by Picasso, Juan Gris, Klee, Miró and Max Ernst, the gardens luxuriant and the food unparalleled. Ménerbes by comparison was monastic, and I was glad of a temporary change, indolent days and the lively company of my hostess, Ned and other guests. So I lingered. And one languorous afternoon while I lay reading on a divan in the large salon Marie-Laure came in and sat down beside me. She wanted to talk to me about Dora, she said. We talked about her at length. It was only little by little that I became aware that Marie-Laure was far more interested in finding out all she could about my relationship with Dora than in discussing the personality or tribulations of her friend, and unfortunately, being impressionable and irresponsible, I told her more than I should have. And without quite saying so I suppose I made it sufficiently clear that we had not been to bed together, a clarification hardly necessary inasmuch as my hostess could not have failed to know that my sexual preference was similar to Ned's. But at the same time I was flattered to feel that she was interested in *me*. That she was too interested for my comfort, however, presently became clear, and there was nothing for it but to risk rudeness by making an abrupt exit. She didn't hold it against me. In fact, as I grew to know her better I realized that she liked and respected her friends somewhat in proportion to their readiness to resist her whims and make light of her displeasure.

"It's hard work," she used to say, "earning one's erotic daily bread." She made hard work of it, to be sure, and worked hard at it. It was the only hard work she ever knew.

My close and affectionate friendship with Marie-Laure began that summer and lasted without interruption or misunderstanding until her death. Just how close and trusting our friendship was may be deduced from the intimate knowledge of her life which she shared with me. I believe she shared it with quite a few others as well, for she was anything but averse to talking about herself, her experiences and feelings, because the more she talked about herself, the more she could assume that she was the authentic protagonist on the stage of her own devising. It was astute of her to realize what could be made of her temperament and personality in terms of a character who defined some social and intellectual aspects of a specific era. One may contend that she contributed to the era nothing more than this definition, in itself an abstraction of no enduring consequence, but she was sufficiently discerning to realize that what is transitory has its value and that to become emblematic of that value might bequeath to her life a subsistence beyond the tomb. She recognized and exploited the fact that she had been born at exactly the right time. Forty years earlier or later there would have been no place for her, nor would a young lady of her milieu have ever envisaged, perhaps, the business of being Marie-Laure de Noailles. After all, she had Picasso, Balthus, Dali, Giacometti, Max Ernst, Miró, Buñuel, Breton, Aragon, René Crevel and all the rest, including the German officer, as members of her supporting cast, and all of them would have been just as out of place in another era as she would.

There has been talk of preparing a full-length biography of Marie-Laure. But I don't believe that her story possesses the wherewithal even for a shortish book or that her life will ultimately be seen to provide sufficient material for one. A biography needs a hero or heroine, an individual whose existence has transformed the world, a Keats or Mozart, Alcibiades, Cleopatra, Emily Brontë, the Bishop of Hippo or countless others whose names fill encyclopedias. Marie-Laure was not of their company but ardently would have liked to be, and the truth is that she very nearly might have been. She possessed the aspiration, the basic talent, the intelligence, the opportunity, the material facilities. What she lacked, and lacked to a decisive degree, was strength of character, without which every other attribute is bound to lead to obscurity and disappointment. Along the way, to be sure, may be enjoyed all manner of brilliant illusions, mundane honors and grand but empty promises, and these may be mistaken by some for ultimate satisfaction of the original aspiration. But never in the long run by a lady so shrewd as Marie-Laure. The idea of her biography would have appealed to her. However, I like to believe that common sense would have led her to object that her life was interesting principally because she interested, amused and entertained men and women of greater interest than herself. To do her justice, I think, the unassuming, critical scrutiny, the anecdotal and candid narrative—not excluding a portion of gossip— will be fairest and most revealing. And if it is circuitous, somewhat lacking in logic and structure, that was the way with Marie-Laure herself, which made it easy for those who liked her to accept her as she was, something, to be sure, that some people found next to impossible.

I liked her. I liked the splendor, the aura of limitless wealth, the

great works of art, the good talk and good food, the easygoing hospitality, the exceptional variety of interesting people, the plain, plentiful
fun and, of course, I very much liked being liked. That she in turn was
fond of me I never for a moment doubted once our friendship became
a fait accompli, though it was possible to wonder whether people
weren't rather interchangeable for her so long as they were congenial,
and if any serious inconvenience arose friendship flew out the window.
In the spring of 1957, for example, I was staying alone with Marie-
Laure at Hyères, and one afternoon in the bathtub began to feel rather
bizarre. A doctor was summoned before dinner. After a brief examination he announced that I had the mumps, a disease usually affecting
only children but which can have a serious effect on adults, and admittedly contagious upon close contact. After this diagnosis I never
caught a glimpse of my hostess. My evening meal was served in my
room, and the very next morning I was bundled off to the municipal
hospital in Hyères, an establishment at that time hardly modernized
since the Second Empire, smelly and none too clean, where I spent
ten very disagreeable days. My suitcases and car were brought down
from St.-Bernard by Marie-Laure's chauffeur. A close friend, unafraid
of contagion, came to meet me in Cannes and we set off for Italy. In
Genoa my testicles swelled to the size of kiwis, causing much pain,
and I spent another ten days in bed, this time, at least, in the luxurious
Hotel Columbia. I didn't see Marie-Laure again for six weeks, and
then she said, "You gave me quite a scare. I was worried for weeks.
Did you know that mumps in an adult can cause deafness?"

"And sterility," I said.

But a certain benefit came from this experience, for as a consequence I learned that Giacometti had also had the mumps after puberty
and did become sterile, a fact essential to his biography which I probably otherwise would never have learned. Fortunately, my hearing is
excellent, and sterility has never troubled me a bit more than it troubled
Alberto, which was not at all.

Marie-Laure's lover when I first knew her was an extravagantly
ugly painter called Oscar Dominguez. A Spaniard from the Canary
Islands, Oscar had come to Paris well before the war to participate in
all the Surrealist shenanigans and had proved his scorn of convention
during a café brawl by blinding in one eye a fellow artist named Victor
Brauner. A giant of a man with a bellowing voice, Oscar had been born

with an abnormally enlarged skull, jawbone slightly askew and thick, rubbery lips. He drank continually to excess, his eyes were always bloodshot, and when he was intoxicated his conduct and conversation were often outrageous. At a soirée given by a prim Parisian interior decorator, he interrupted the performance of a troupe of Balinese dancers by removing his trousers and underdrawers and capering around the dance floor. Some of those present said that it had hardly been worth making such a spectacle to exhibit so little. Marie-Laure made a show of being outraged but was in fact delighted. As a painter Oscar was a mediocrity, but he had a flair for dexterous brushwork and pastiche. His work was irretrievably influenced by Picasso, who obsessed him and with whom as a fellow Spaniard he managed to establish an uneven and uneasy camaraderie. During the war he earned extra cash by painting fake Picassos for sale to the Germans, an expedient which the elder artist seems not to have held against him. But this facility for fakery was to have tragic consequences.

Marie-Laure's liking for lovers who were creative personalities was certainly in part a reflection of her desire to attain recognition for herself in the same capacity. When we became friendly she had given up writing, though she published at about this time a novel written earlier and entitled *The Squirrels' Room*, which is dedicated to "The Memory of the Incomparable Henry James, whose Secrets no one yet Knows." As for secrets, this novel contains an episode which describes a young wife finding her husband in bed with another man, a discovery ultimately leading to suicide. Having set aside literary aspirations, Marie-Laure decided to make a creative mark for herself as a painter, this pursuit perhaps appearing less arduous. She was also no stranger to the quest for immortality that creative friends could promote by making works of art in her likeness. In addition to portraits by Picasso, Balthus and Dali she possessed quite a number by lesser talents like Berman, Bérard, Fernández, Marie Laurencin, Fenosa, etc. Giacometti had drawn, painted and sculpted her in the late forties. Her name, indeed, appears frequently in the notes he wrote to himself at that period. He made a considerable number of drawings of her, two sculptures and one painting. The painting was exhibited in 1950 in Basel, erroneously labeled a portrait of the artist's wife, Annette. Alberto was casual about such errors, but it is strange that he never took the trouble to correct this one, as the unlikeness to Annette is unmistakable, and the painting remained at the Basel Kunsthalle, where it is still labeled incorrectly. Neither of the sculptures of Marie-Laure was ever cast in bronze during the artist's, or model's, lifetime. I once asked Marie-Laure why she didn't urge Alberto to have them cast, a proposal to which I felt confident he would agree, and she said, "Oh, that's ancient history now. I can't be bothered." Something odd had gone wrong between the artist and his model. I suspect it must have been something of a very intimate nature, as Giacometti almost never made portraits of people toward whom he did not have feelings of, at least, affection, and it was very out of character for Marie-Laure to express indifference concerning a portrait of herself. It's too bad that her private collection of likenesses did not include a Giacometti.

Marie-Laure and the viscount were profoundly attached to one another. People who knew them well felt that he found vicarious enjoyment in her scandalous liaisons and unconventional behavior, that perhaps he envied that robust resolve to do as she pleased. Frequently apart, they communicated almost daily by telephone or letter, often both. But the viscount could never escape from the confines of his caste. He had his coat of arms sculpted in high relief on the ceiling of his bedroom, and one wonders with some compassion what gratifications may have been his when he gazed upward from his solitary bed at that heraldic emblem of archaic privilege and power. Behind his back Marie-Laure made great fun of this self-indulgence, but I don't think she would ever have done anything deliberately to wound him. To embarrass him, on the other hand, probably amused her greatly, as she was perverse, more intelligent than he and the more powerful personality. She was a true connoisseur and aesthete, whereas he didn't care deeply about art. What he prized was good taste. His politeness was certainly exquisite, and yet a more concentrated scrutiny seemed to reveal an indifference that was virtually an expression of contempt. I recorded a conversation we had one day in his car after lunch at the Place des Etats-Unis. He explained to me with a certain pathos how it had become next to impossible to give dinner parties due to difficulties in the protocol of seating caused by the prevalence of false titles and illegitimate children pretending to be legitimate. Such problems would not have given an instant's pause to his wife.

The viscount must have been sorry he had no son to inherit the prestigious title, a viscount whose title went back to the Middle Ages

being far more lordly than a mere count. The father, having supervised
the upbringing of the two girls, must have hoped that they would make
brilliant marriages. Given the name and fortune, even royal alliances
were not inconceivable. Laure, the elder daughter, married an obscure
but supremely elegant bourgeois named Bertrand de La Haye Jousselin, with whom she was very happy. They had two sons. She was a
chic, prim, supercilious woman, referred to her mother's artist friends
as "Mama's hoboes" and died of cancer not yet aged sixty. Nathalie,
unlike her sister, cared little for society but was fanatically devoted to
animals, especially horses, and aspired to be a champion equestrienne.
She impulsively married an Italian named Alessandro Perrone, whose
family owned the principal Roman newspaper, *Il Messaggero*, and who
soon proved to be an unfaithful and incompatible husband. They nonetheless also had two sons. Nathalie hated life in Rome, suffered such
serious falls while show jumping that her health was permanently
impaired and eventually returned to France, divorced, old before her
time. One day at lunch Marie-Laure said to her, "It's terrible for a
woman like me to have a daughter like you." What was terrible, of
course, was the cruelty as well as the accuracy of the remark, identical
to one I had heard made by Picasso to his son Paulo. But at least
Nathalie had the spunk to reply, "And don't you think it's terrible to
have a mother like you?" Paulo had been less defiant, remaining silent.
Marie-Laure must have admitted to herself that Nathalie had legitimate cause for grievance, because that evening she said to her, "I've
decided to give you the big Picasso that hangs in the staircase." No
work of art, however, could compensate for the maternal humiliation.
But Marie-Laure believed that art could be life's ultimate justification,
redeeming error from ignominy and righting unintentional wrongs.
The next time I went to the Place des Etats-Unis I noticed that the
Picasso had disappeared, replaced by a fine Klee.

Improbable as it may seem, Marie-Laure sometimes found herself
short of money. Since free access to her capital had been legally withdrawn from her after the ruinous affair with Markevitch, she was
dependent upon her husband for cash, and he was known to be punctil-
iously economical though not quite miserly. Exactly what arrangement
prevailed between them I cannot say, but there were times when Marie-
Laure wanted funds not forthcoming in the usual manner. Her residences, to be sure, were overflowing with possessions that could easily

be converted into ready money. An excess of treasure, in fact, might have been considered to have accumulated, so that a painting or object here or there would hardly be missed. That was Marie-Laure's attitude, blithely disregarding her knowledge that an inventory existed listing every item, no matter how trifling, to be found in all the Noailles residences. Not desirous herself to go about the workaday business of hawking her possessions for sale, she turned to others to do it for her. Knowing that I was well acquainted with Parisian dealers and sometimes bought and sold pictures on my own account, she several times asked me to sell things for her. One of these was a painted stone bas-relief by Henri Laurens, a very beautiful work of about 1920, now in the Museum in Copenhagen. Also a small painting by Mondrian of 1926 or 1928, an austere work, black lines on a white ground with a small rectangle of gray, in pristine condition. I had a terrible time finding a purchaser for it. This was in 1955, and I finally had to let it go for $3,000. There were in addition a number of drawings by Klee, Max Ernst, Dali, etc. So it was no secret among the dealers that the Viscountess de Noailles occasionally made sales via her friends. She never haggled over the price or expressed dissatisfaction if it was low, and she always insisted on my accepting a very generous commission. Her generosity, in fact, was exceptional and an interesting, contradictory aspect of her nature. Though unusually acquisitive and possessive, she was virtually extravagant in the largesse she distributed to those she cared for, especially if they happened to be in straitened circumstances.

Despite her recognition that literary work was more difficult and challenging than her temperament disposed her to undertake, Marie-Laure was phenomenally well read, having, for example, finished all twenty-four volumes of Henry James's New York Edition as well as every French, German or Russian classic, plus plenty of Dickens, George Eliot, Hardy, and she could recite from memory poems by Andrew Marvell, Petrarch, Mallarmé, etc., etc., etc. Painting, after liberation by Picasso and the Surrealists from representational discipline and the constraint of any tradition whatsoever, seemed to offer easy access to the dignity and, if possible, the glory of creative endeavor. So Marie-Laure set out to make herself a painter of repute, devoting to this task the resources of her considerable intelligence as well as her social and financial status. Despite a literary and artistic cultivation unique in her milieu Marie-Laure was no intellectual. The dominion of ideas did not attract her. It might almost be accurate to say that her intelligence was physical rather than mental, instinctive rather than inductive. This singularity of mind endowed her with an exceptional curiosity, allied to which were a perverse impulse to mockery and a determination at the same time to be taken very seriously herself. A fusion of characteristics, one might have thought, not calculated to bring about spiritual fulfillment of the highest order.

Having known the artists as well as the writers of the Surrealist group, and possessing plenty of their works, Marie-Laure, with Dominguez, a practiced *pasticheur*, at her side, was able to put to good use in her own painting a lot of tricks of technique which they had originally perfected. Both in Paris and in Hyères were studios well stocked with all the materials an artist could conceivably need, and they were put to use. The viscountess did not intend for an instant to be regarded as an amateur. Nor did her paintings show her to have been one. She had a talent, a skill, a flair for putting paint on canvas and was able to transform the tricks of her friends into a manner, if not a style, recognizably her own and relatively original. Close scrutiny, however, revealed that a part of Max Ernst, a part of Bérard, parts of Miró, Masson, and even Dominguez had been adroitly blended to produce an effect of independent and fanciful invention. Marie-Laure often asked me to come into her studios and comment on the works in progress or already finished. When criticism is requested by artists, especially by those not of well-established reputation, and sometimes by them, too, what is usually wanted is praise or, at least, encouragement, not candid analysis of weaknesses or failures. And what Marie-Laure expected was praise. She possessed neither the will nor the clairvoyance to stand apart from her creations in order to see them not only as works of art but also as images of her own character. Had she had the courage to do this and the self-discipline to make both her works and her commitment to art the principal raison d'être of her existence, then she might have been able to develop a style entirely her own and become a truly original artist. In every sphere of experience, however, she had grown too accustomed to facility to submit herself to such a stern regimen. This was obvious to me and must have been obvious to everyone who cared very seriously for art. So I told her on the whole what she wanted her to hear while urging that she work harder and more conscientiously in order to eliminate the easy mannerisms and effects too visibly reminiscent of other artists. It was wasted advice. In order to please and encourage her I even bought one of her paintings, because a monetary outlay seemed to her the most authentic affirmation of esteem. As an artist Marie-Laure was never more than a highly talented dilettante, her work a means of making life more entertaining via this semblance of serious dedication.

Whether or not she was herself aware of this superficiality we will never know. She certainly did not allow others to assume any such awareness or to make light of her efforts. Her fortune and social position permitted her to bring to bear sufficient pressure to assure regular showings of her work, not only in private galleries but in the annual Salon de Mai, which was presumably reserved for artists of proven merit, even Picasso willingly exhibiting there. And this added facility doubtless did nothing to strengthen her commitment to an admittedly Sisyphean task. She always signed her pictures, as her writings, with her forename only, not wanting to seem to trade on the prestige of her husband's surname, but of course everyone knew that the Marie-Laure who painted was the Viscountess de Noailles. And that is rather a pity. For her it would have been almost a drama had her resolve been more staunch, because her paintings are not without a pleasant verve and a certain decorative charm, and if her name had been Martin, her fortune modest, she might have made a creditable career for herself. After all, her work is far more honest and accomplished than the slick trash churned out by someone like Leonor Fini, who has contrived to have herself taken semi-seriously and made a fortune. Marie-Laure, alas, wanted to be an artist, an aristocrat and the protagonist of her own theatrical production, all at the same time. Picasso was as protean as that, but he had the advantage, and the affliction, of genius, whereas Marie-Laure had only her longings and her millions. They were not enough.

Marie-Laure knew, and liked, lots of women, but she far preferred the company of men and was much more indulgent with them than with members of her own sex, especially if they were young and beautiful. Once one had become an accepted member of her intimate circle it was possible to take her hospitality virtually for granted. Lunch at the Place des Etats-Unis was served precisely at one-fifteen and I often called at a quarter to one to ask whether I might come. Unless the guests already numbered twelve, the reply was usually yes, and on one

Double portrait of Gertrude Stein and Alice B. Toklas, taken by Cecil Beaton [*Sotheby's, London*]

(above) Portrait of Gertrude Stein, by Pablo Picasso, 1906 [*The Metropolitan Museum of Art, Bequest of Gertrude Stein, 1946. 47.106*]; *(opposite, top)* Gertrude in front of the Picasso portrait [*James Lord*]; *(bottom)* Gertrude, Paris, 1946 [*Horst P. Horst*]

Portrait of Alice B. Toklas, by Dora Maar, Paris, 1952 [*Yale Collection of American Literature, Gertrude Stein Collection*]

Alice and James [*G. Boigontier*]

(above) View of Skyros village from the beach in front of Errieta's house [*James Lord*]; *(opposite, top)* Errieta's house, with mill at rear [*James Lord*]; *(bottom)* Errieta seated under the pergola [*James Lord*]

(top) James, seated on the roof of Errieta's house [*M. Richard*]
(bottom) Larry Hager [*James Lord*]

occasion when there were already twelve a small table for me alone was set beside Marie-Laure's place. Invitations to stay at Hyères were quite as easy to come by. Many of the most amusing, dramatic and/ or farcical of our experiences with Marie-Laure took place at St.-Bernard, because there one was in her company almost all the time. And there she felt more at liberty to behave without constraint according to the mood or whim of the moment. When I first knew her, Marie-Laure was frequently prone to drink more than she should have. We all were, especially Oscar and Ned. And that increased the fun or sometimes heightened the drama.

One August evening in 1957 we were sitting in the library, Marie-Laure, Oscar, Ned, Robert Veyron-Lacroix and I, having what was supposed to be one last drink before going to bed, when suddenly Robert leaned unsteadily toward his hostess and said, "You're fat."

A moment of shocked silence followed this obvious but crude statement of fact, then Marie-Laure, recovering from surprise, replied, "It's true, but I'm rich."

"Rich, yes," cried Robert, "and fat and Jewish. A rich, fat Jewess. A rich, fat, ugly Jewess. You have no idea how ugly you are. Why, you're almost as ugly as Oscar." His voice now had risen in pitch almost to a shriek while Ned and I endeavored unsuccessfully to tame this incomprehensible outburst. But there was no calming him, and he went on: "You could exhibit yourselves in the circus and add to your riches. The richest uglies on earth, and travel from continent to continent, famous at last. Even I would pay to see you. I'd even play some snatches of Rameau for you to dance to."

Marie-Laure never lost her composure but she sighed, passed a hand across her face and said, "Robert, what possesses you?"

"You don't give a fuck," he shouted, suddenly bursting into tears, "none of you give a fuck, and I don't give a fuck either, and I'm going to kill myself." Whereupon, gasping and sobbing, he leapt from his chair, adding hysterically, "I know you all detest me, and I'll be much better off dead." Then he rushed from the room.

"A flimsy little fairy," said Oscar.

"Be quiet, Putchi," said Marie-Laure. "This is grave. You never know. When people talk about suicide, sometimes they do it. We must take precautions and be quick about it."

But we were not quick enough. Robert had gone to his room, and had had plenty of time to take whatever pills may have been at hand. Marie-Laure was distraught. Her love for her friends, though sometimes perverse in expression, was strong and sincere. She said that Robert must immediately be taken to the hospital. No risk was to be run. The household was roused. An ambulance came. Robert was taken away, semiconscious, on a stretcher. When he had gone, Marie-Laure carefully combed his bathroom and bedroom in search of any dangerous medicines, putting all she found, even aspirins, into a metal box.

Oscar in the meantime had taken advantage of the confusion to serve himself several more drinks. I retired with relief to my room as soon as Marie-Laure reappeared, but sleep did not come as promptly as it might have, because the sweet quiet of the hilltop was rent till late by the clamor of an altercation between the viscountess and her bellicose boyfriend.

In the midmorning Robert returned rather sheepishly from the hospital. He had not, apparently, swallowed anything that would harm a housefly and did not, fortunately, remember very clearly what had happened. When he inquired, Marie-Laure said only that he must have had an attack of indigestion and she had feared it might be something more serious. Her nature was, indeed, a strange mixture of malice and self-effacing kindness.

One day in the large salon it seemed to me that there was something amiss. And suddenly to my astonishment I saw what it was. In that room, among many other pictures, hung three drawings by Picasso, one collage of the Cubist period,* one large beach scene with bathers from the twenties,† and a sanguine nude of the Classical period.‡ All three had naturally been framed under glass, and in each case the glass had been shattered, as if by a single blow of some sharp tool. I called Marie-Laure, pointing out the damage. "It's Oscar," she said. "He's obsessed by Picasso. Uncontrollably obsessed. As if by breaking the glass on the drawings he's killing the artist. Madness." We inspected the drawings carefully, and none had been damaged despite shattered glass, save the large beach scene, which was very slightly torn, damage which could easily have been repaired, though it never

* Zervos, Vol. II-A, No. 501.
† Zervos, Vol. IV, No. 170.
‡ Seemingly not in Zervos.

was. Marie-Laure immediately summoned her butler, Henri, instruct-
ing him to have the chauffeur take the three drawings down to a
framing shop in the town, have the broken panes replaced and the
pictures back in place before lunch, by which time it was possible that
Oscar would not have appeared. Within two hours the three drawings
were back in their places and, indeed, there had as yet been no sign
of the certainly impenitent vandal. He slouched into the dining room,
bleary and flatulent, just as we were sitting down at the round table.
Maybe he, too, I thought, had experienced a convenient attack of am-
nesia. The one who had without doubt forgotten nothing was Marie-
Laure, and I couldn't help wondering what thoughts and emotions
must be hers while she pondered, as she had to, the symbolic aggression
with which she had to contend. Her composure was impenetrable. She
chatted and joked and smoked cigarettes. But she must have asked
herself questions to which the answers cannot have been those which
a subtle and creative individual may wish to fathom.

At about seven o'clock the butler came to my room to tell me that
the viscountess wished to see me at once downstairs in her bedroom.
I found her pensive. She was distressed, she said, about Oscar and the
smashed panes of the Picasso drawings. She felt that Picasso must
appear to Oscar as a sort of living symbol of his own failure as an artist.
But she wondered what she herself could do to help, and all in the
world she wanted was to help. She had an idea. As Oscar's paintings
found no buyers, he had very little money. Of course, from time to
time she gave him some, but in her peculiar situation she did not have
large amounts at her disposal, and she felt that perhaps a large lump
sum at this moment might restore his morale, allowing him to feel
that in no sense could he be considered a profiteer or gigolo, since she
was happy to share her wealth as well as her life with him. I thought
this a very bad idea and that Marie-Laure was deluding herself, but
as a friend I did not feel it was my place to try to dissuade or disillusion
her. To me Oscar seemed a hopeless case, though I had no idea then
of how very close to the end of hope he in fact was, or of the responsibility for this fact that might be imputed to the one who believed
herself so sincerely determined to help. As I well knew, when in need
of extra cash, Marie-Laure was always ready to sell a work of art. And
that was her idea now. Moreover, she had already selected the work
she was disposed to sell, and selected it with a view to its symbolic,

almost poetic, relevance to the particular situation, for it was an oil painting by Picasso. It hung in the long, rather dim corridor that led from her bedroom to the entrance hall, where no one could see it very well, was a Cubist picture of moderate size, measuring only about sixteen by twelve inches, not one of the finest productions of that finest era of his creative life, a bit empty in structure and drab in color but a Cubist Picasso nonetheless, which certainly could command a considerable price. Marie-Laure asked whether I would try to negotiate the sale, since she felt that it would in every respect be crude and perhaps unkind to entrust the business to Oscar. I said I would be glad to do all I could, didn't expect the sale to be difficult and wouldn't even need to take the picture away with me immediately, as it was certainly reproduced in the Zervos catalogue raisonné of Picasso's work, which would be quite a sufficient selling point for the time being. Marie-Laure declared herself well pleased and no more was said of the matter during the remainder of my visit.

When I returned to Paris, one of my first errands was to call on Heinz Berggruen at his gallery in the rue de l'Université. Heinz was the obvious purchaser for a Cubist Picasso, sure to be more generous than Picasso's regular dealer, Kahnweiler, who was well known as a skinflint. When I explained that the purpose of my visit was to offer for sale a Cubist painting by Picasso, Heinz immediately said that he was a buyer at any price within reason. From the library adjacent to his office he brought Volume II of the Zervos catalogue and I quickly found a reproduction of the picture, No. 245, described as *Head of a Young Girl*, dated 1911, and listed as being in the collection of the Viscount de Noailles. Heinz looked quizzical.

"And how did you come by this painting?" he asked.

I told him that I didn't have physical possession of it as it still hung in the house of the viscountess at Hyères but that she had authorized me to negotiate its sale.

"There's something wrong," said Heinz.

There couldn't be anything wrong, I protested, because I had had the painting in my hands only recently, and it was the very one reproduced in the volume that lay open on Heinz's desk.

"But it's not," said Heinz, "because I already own that painting and have had it for nearly a year."

"How is that possible?" I exclaimed.

"It was sold by Oscar Dominguez to another dealer, from whom I bought it," Heinz said, "and since everybody knows of Oscar's skill as a forger I took precautions, had tests made, and the one I have is the original. In fact, I took the same precautions with another little Picasso I bought directly from Oscar not long ago, and it was right, too."

"Could I see a photo of it?" I asked.

"Certainly." It was in Volume II-A of the Zervos, No. 501, the small Cubist still life.

"That picture is also still at Hyères," I said.

"Copies," said Heinz. "Think it over. There is Dominguez, a failed painter but an expert forger, living in a house filled with genuine pictures of great value. What in the world could be easier than for him to substitute copies for the originals, which he then sells? And he has no compunction, because he willingly gives receipts stating that the Viscountess de Noailles has authorized the sales."

"But what am I going to tell her?" I said.

"Well," Heinz murmured, "it all depends on the quality of your friendship. Of course, you could find some way to say nothing, because it isn't very agreeable to have to tell a lady that her boyfriend is stealing from her. On the other hand, where art is concerned I always feel that truth is the heart of the matter. So I can't make a decision for you. But let me know what happens."

The dilemma was formidable. A bearer of bad news is often blamed, while the one who conceals falsehood and theft becomes an accomplice. Fond of Marie-Laure, knowing her to be vulnerable beneath the veneer of sophisticated composure, and anxious not to disrupt our friendship, I didn't know what to do. So I turned for advice to Giacometti, with whom by then I had become friendly, because I already felt, and have never ceased to believe, that he could positively distinguish what course of action was right or wrong in any situation.

"I can't tell you what to do," Alberto said. "Marie-Laure can live very comfortably with a lie, and theft is not a serious issue in the logic of ethical priorities. What matters is the human element."

"Which is?"

"Well, it's simply whether you respect her or not."

"I do respect her," I said.

"Then it's simple," said Alberto.

"So I have to tell her?"

Alberto smiled but would not commit himself. I knew him well enough by that time to know that his determination to respect the human element could at times lead him to behave in a way that to some people would have seemed heartless.

So I went to the Place des Etats-Unis, and in front of the fireplace in her bedroom, where two armchairs faced one another and we often sat to talk, I told her everything. I even told her that I'd discussed it all with Alberto. She said that I'd done right, that it would have been a betrayal of our friendship to conceal the truth from her. It was impossible for me to tell how she felt, how this unexpected, unpleasant revelation affected her. Inquisitive, I said, "What will you do?"

"I'll live with it," she replied. "I can live with it. I'm like Alberto in that way, at least. I, too, respect the human element."

"And Oscar?"

"Why, he also will live with it. If I can, he can, and maybe it's for the best, after all, for us both: a sort of exorcism of the Picasso demon."

And that, I assumed, was that. What Marie-Laure said to Oscar I don't know, but she can hardly have failed to say something, since she expected him to live with the knowledge as ably as she did. I saw them together several times after this and discerned no alteration in their manner toward one another. Oscar was preparing for an exhibition at the Rive Gauche Gallery and there was much enthusiastic talk of recognition at last. Then early in November I left Paris for a four-month visit to America. It was there that I heard the pitiful news. On New Year's Eve in his studio on the rue Campagne-Première, Oscar had gotten into a bathtub full of hot water, slashed his wrists and ankles and bled to death, aged fifty-one. His corpse was not found until the following afternoon. What led to this pathetic, desperate act neither I nor anyone else will ever know, as he left behind no explanation or apologia. His exhibition had been a failure, not a word of comment having appeared in the press while he waited every day for some notice to be taken. After his suicide, of course, the papers were full of him, an article on the front page of *France Soir*. I couldn't help wondering whether the Picasso demon might not also have been in some way a causative element. For Marie-Laure to say that she could live with what Oscar had done was one thing. For Oscar unquestionably it can only have been something else. And it is very possible that this tragic event had its determinant effect on Marie-Laure's life thereafter. It was impossible to doubt that she had been deeply devoted to Dominguez. She arranged to have him interred in the Bischoffsheim family mausoleum alongside her father and grandparents. Perhaps this was an act of contrition.

The bereaved viscountess returned as soon as possible to Hyères, and it was there more and more as the years passed that she clearly felt most at ease with herself, with her friends and with the spectacle of her existence. From St.-Bernard on January 20, 1958, she wrote, half in English, half in French, as follows:

> Dearest James,
>
> The drama was too awful to be spoken of before a long time. No commentary is possible.
>
> What is happening to your book? And are you satisfied? I think only of my friends and of the future. I do not have the vocation of unhappiness.
>
> I embrace you.
>
> [Signed with a drawing of a laurel leaf, her heraldic emblem.]
>
> Ned wrote a very good letter.
>
> Dora very religious.

Indeed Marie-Laure had no vocation for unhappiness. Living for the moment, she invited it to do for her anything it could, prepared for her own part to respond with zest both to its gifts and to its demands.

There lived in Nîmes during these years a couple named Jean and Mimi Godebski. He was a nephew of the celebrated Misia Sert, patroness of the arts, intimate of Diaghilev and a prima donna of Parisian society. So naturally Marie-Laure was well acquainted with Jean and Mimi God, as she liked to call them. And one day not very long after Oscar's suicide she invited them to drive over from Nîmes, a rather long drive, for lunch. They asked whether they might bring with them a young friend, a request by definition granted at once. The unknown guest was a young man of about thirty named Jean Lafont, a handsome, well-built fellow with sandy hair, high cheekbones and slightly slanting eyes, a Slavic look inherited from his Russian mother. He was an enthusiast of bullfighting and his ambition was one day to own a ranch where he could raise bulls for the ritual of the arena. Oscar also had been, like his idol Picasso, an ardent aficionado. So Marie-Laure was no stranger to the Iberian passion for "death in the afternoon." The other guests that day were Georges Auric, the composer, and his wife, Nora, also of Russian descent, beautiful, charming and crafty.

Perhaps it was the evocation of bullfighting that led to talk of Oscar. By this time Marie-Laure had evidently become sufficiently inured to his absence to make commentary possible. At all events, during the course of the meal she remarked, "At present it's going to be necessary for me to find a new lover."

Whereupon Jean Godebski said to Jean Lafont, "Why not you?"

"Do you like women?" asked Marie-Laure, having a very sharp eye for handsome men, however virile in appearance, who didn't.

Nora Auric, who knew that Jean Lafont had, at least occasionally, had affairs with women, said, "Yes, he does like women."

Just how much he liked them was always to remain problematical, but he certainly preferred the company of beautiful young boys, and there were many of them in his entourage throughout the decades to come. However, they never interfered with his relationship with Marie-Laure, which had its start on that winter day at St.-Bernard and there-after progressed apace.

The viscount, as ever something of an accomplice in his wife's affairs and scandals, and perhaps himself more interested than by sole concern for her welfare and his reputation, having become aware that Marie-Laure's infatuation with Jean Lafont was not a fancy likely soon to pass, made inquiries, rather as a father might have sought information as to the suitability of a fiancé for his daughter. And his acquaintances in Nîmes told him that Jean was a very decent, dependable man, not likely to be motivated beyond reason by the prospect of material advantage. So it, indeed, turned out. Despite Marie-Laure's eccentricities, her dalliances with other young men as the years wore on and the occasional quarrel over matters of no importance, Jean remained faithfully by her side till the end. The Noailles bought a ranch in the Camargue and Jean became its very efficient manager, but Marie-Laure knew that whenever she wanted or needed his company she could count on it. And in her later years there was probably no other person of whom that could be said.

When I returned to Paris in March of 1958, Marie-Laure had

come back from Hyères and Jean Lafont was already now and then to be seen at the Place des Etats-Unis. Ned had by this time realized that he must make his career at home, giving up Europe and drink simultaneously, decisions which the decades have amply ratified. He has become almost as well known through the publication of his candid diaries as by performances of his music. At Hyères the diary was kept in notebooks which were left open on the desk in the main salon, and everyone was invited to read what had been written. As the entries concerned Ned, his feelings, thoughts and impressions almost exclusively, readers were few, and the author complained. When Ned went back to New York, the room which had been his in the palatial house was soon set aside for the visits of Jean Lafont.

It came out after Oscar's death that the two Picassos were not the only pictures at Hyères of which he had made copies in order to sell the originals. There were works by Klee, Léger, Laurens and perhaps others even now unsuspected. His own paintings, the entire contents of his studio, went up for sale at auction at the Hôtel Drouot. Many of the things were sold in lots, unframed, canvases rolled up and left in heaps, drawings pell-mell pawed over by sensation seekers, and the prices were preposterously low. It would have broken Oscar's heart. But the auction was well attended. Seated near the front of the room, and the most persistent, successful but discreet bidder of all those present, was the Viscount de Noailles, as if to demonstrate by the large quantity of his acquisitions that an aristocratic appreciation of art takes staid precedence over vulgar curiosity. And of course the collection formed that afternoon by the viscount for a song is today worth a fortune, because Oscar's prices have risen steadily as popular taste has accorded classic status even to the semblance of Surrealism.

A certain semblance of Surrealism, however outmoded the actual rites had long since become, sometimes characterized Marie-Laure's behavior as she grew older. She remembered with nostalgia the outrageous shenanigans of the thirties, and Oscar's example remained persuasive. She liked to surprise, to shock, to scandalize, and she knew how.

There was a fourth-rate painter in her entourage called Felix Labisse. Though married to an amiable Belgian heiress named Jony, he was an inveterate womanizer and had had a brief fling with the viscountess herself. One evening after dinner at Hyères we were sitting around in the salon, Felix, myself, our hostess and one or two others, chatting, when Marie-Laure without a word got up and left the room. Felix's mistress of the moment was a very beautiful young mulatto, absent that evening, as was Jony also. After a few moments Marie-Laure returned, now stark naked—by no means a figure of beauty—walked into the room, turned round once or twice, then departed without having uttered a word. We were all so astonished that nobody could find a thing to say before Marie-Laure returned, attired as before, and sat down with a quizzical smile of satisfaction on her face. Then we did make free to ask what in the world was meant by her bizarre exhibitionism. To which she calmly replied, "I just thought it would be good for Felix to see a white woman."

Ingenious practical jokes, especially if spiced with a bit of malice and a bit of justice, amused her greatly. We all had a friend in those days who went by the nom de plume of Henri Hell, a man of surpassing self-satisfaction, neither handsome nor well groomed, who boasted that he had never failed to take to bed sooner or later any man he desired. He was also fond of recounting the details of his relations with the famous persons whom he assiduously cultivated. At the same time, however, he took pains to prevent those who had made no names for themselves, like me, from becoming acquainted with these celebrated personages. Still, there were moments when he made himself as agreeable as the next man and he could talk about Proust, Saint-Simon, Pergolesi, Scarlatti, Pontormo or Chassériau with perfectly fluent familiarity. I had met him through Stephen Spender, a mutual friend; he was kind to me during my first years in Paris and I with some reluctance allowed him to add me to the roster of easy conquests he could boast about. We all called him José, for that was in fact his real forename. Of the famous persons with whom José was friendly, the most famous was Francis Poulenc, and he was consequently the one most jealously kept from contact with those judged unworthy by José. Poulenc, of course, having been a friend of Bérard, Cocteau and all the Parisian beau monde, had known Marie-Laure long before he ever heard of José and was occasionally to be encountered in her house, where his jolly bonhomie and good-natured raillery added much to the fun. His friendship with José, we knew, was based largely upon the determination of the latter, who had a serious knowledge of music, to write a book-length study of the composer.

In the summer of 1956 I and my oldest friend had rented a house near Azay-le-Rideau, spending two and a half months there. We were aware that Poulenc owned an estate reputed to be charming at Noizay, not thirty miles distant, but didn't feel that we knew him quite well enough to telephone. Instead we went to see Max Ernst and his bibulous wife, Dorothea Tanning, at their farmhouse in the tiny village of Huismes. Sometime in August we received a telephone call from José, staying with Poulenc at Noizay, who suggested that he would enjoy coming to spend a night or two with us. As we had plenty of room, we said yes. José had no car and didn't know how to drive, so we proposed that we should come to Noizay and fetch him. That, he replied, was out of the question, because Poulenc detested having strangers visit his house and would be disturbed even by the briefest coming and going. No, José said, he would take a bus from Noizay to Tours, only about ten miles away, where we could meet him. And that is what happened. José's visit was agreeable enough, and he talked at length about the beauty of Poulenc's house, the excellence of the food and wine and the delightful conversation of the host.

Some years previous to this time Poulenc had met and fallen in love with a young soldier. When this fellow's military stint came to an end, he presently felt disposed to marry and set himself up in some sort of business. Poulenc sensibly made no objection to these arrangements but proved his affection for the young man by buying him a house and assisting him to go into business, the nature of which none of us ever knew. As it happened, the young couple resided at no great distance from Hyères and Poulenc came regularly to the South to visit them, staying in a nearby hotel. And while there he sometimes telephoned Marie-Laure and came to call at St.-Bernard. So it was that we found ourselves there together one day during the Easter week of 1958. I had not seen Francis since José's visit to Azay-le-Rideau, and one of my first concerns was to tell him that while I understood his need for complete tranquillity I nonetheless had regretted not having caught so much as a glimpse of him.

"But that's perfectly absurd," Francis protested. "I begged José to have you come to Noizay, and he told me that you led the life of a hermit, hated any sort of sociability, and that he was only accepted as a guest because James had such a passion for him."

"What a lie!" I exclaimed. "Why, I only to went to bed with José once, because he was so insistent that it was easier to do it than to refuse. And I wanted nothing in the world more than to come and see you. Ah, that José is a sneak. Just wait till the next time I see him. I'll give him an earful that he won't forget in a hurry."

"Please don't do that," said Francis. "I don't want to be the cause of bad feeling, and all the same we're rather fond of old José, aren't we?"

"Fond but fault-finding," said Marie-Laure. "Now, let's see what would fit the circumstances. José has been quite naughty, so he must be punished, and the punishment must fit the fault."

"But we don't want to do anything to hurt him," Francis protested.

"Come, come," said Marie-Laure, "is the composer of *Tiresias's Tits* going to prove squeamish? We won't hurt him. We'll just tickle him enough to cause a little well-deserved discomfort. Let's see. Let's see. He claimed that you couldn't see James because he lived like a hermit—a lie—but that he could go because James had such a passion for him. Another lie. Lies of passion. José's exclusive passion for Francis. And how would it be if we simply turned the passion around and let José simmer a bit in the contradiction?"

"But how do we turn it around?" Francis inquired.

"It's as simple as good morning," said the viscountess. "We fabricate a love affair between James and Francis, then let José speculate on the appearances and see what happens. What could be more fitting?"

"I like it," said Francis.

We all liked it.

The first thing to do, said Marie-Laure, was to manufacture an initial scrap of evidence. Nothing better than a picture to do the work of words. Someone must have a camera. I did. The viscountess arranged the mise-en-scène. Francis was to sit in an armchair on the terrace and I on his lap with my arms around him. This pose easily and satisfactorily assumed, Marie-Laure came forward, took Francis's right hand and set it suggestively between my thighs. "Just a nuance of something more than familiarity," she said, and she snapped the shutter several times herself, delighted by her role in this deception. "And when the photo is developed," she said to Francis, "we'll send you a copy, then you can place it somewhere in your apartment in Paris where José is sure to notice it, a rather compromising place, say, in the corner of the mirror of your bedroom. And I'll wager it will gnaw

at his entrails like the Spartan boy's fox, but he won't say a word. And
then later there will be opportunities to manufacture evidence even
more compromising."

"It's very good, very good," said Francis, "assuming, of course,"
he added, turning to me, "that you don't mind being romantically
linked to an old party like myself."

I was very pleased and said so, gratified, too, to prepare a little
well-deserved exasperation and jealousy for José.

I ran into him two or three times that spring. He was cordial as
ever but there was also an intimation of curiosity and intrigue that he
couldn't quite bring himself to articulate. So I assumed that he must
have seen the photograph, which had turned out quite well, but was
either too timid or too vexed to mention it. I, however, had no inhibition
and, though I had not seen Poulenc again, thought to sprinkle a bit
of pepper on the situation by saying, "I'm rather worried about
Francis."

José showed his surprise. "And why, may I inquire, should you
be?"

"He doesn't take proper care of his health. Much too overweight."

"You need not worry," José said. "He's not yet sixty and strong
as a bull."

"Oh, yes, he *is* strong, isn't he?" I said, and that was the end of
our conversation.

I spent that summer in a house on the plateau above Aix-en-
Provence, not far from the Bibémus quarries, where Cézanne painted
many masterpieces. And it was there toward the end of August that I
received the following note from Francis:

> *Noizay, Indre-et-Loire*
>   *For goodness' sake, send me by return mail a compro-*
> *mising note or at least an envelope with your handwriting.*
> *José-Henri gave himself away yesterday. "Did you or didn't*
> *you do it?" I lowered my eyes like someone caught in the*
> *wrong. "This is not like you . . . It depends." He chewed his*
> *fingertips and ripped off three hangnails.*
>   *A thousand affectionate greetings*
>   *Francis*
> *P.S. I gave out that you had come to Avignon to see me.*

So I immediately sat down and wrote the most compromising but vague and ambiguous letter I could devise and sent it off at once. Four days later I received another note from Francis:

26 August

Dear friend,
   Your letter arrived this morning ten minutes before the departure of Henri for Paris. Smelling salts were not wasted when he read your letter. We really ought to tell him the truth! As he is discretion itself he didn't ask me a single question and was satisfied with a simple "Well!"
   He worked marvelously here and his Francis Poulenc *seems to me perfect. A thousand greetings as I await your visit* here.

Francis Poulenc

Whether or not José ever found out the truth about the "romance" that Marie-Laure had invented to punish him for his foolishness I doubt. The last time I saw Francis was at a birthday party given for me by Georges and Nora Auric. Marie-Laure and Jean Lafont were naturally also there. I asked Francis if he had revealed to José the details of the practical joke we'd played on him, and he admitted with some embarrassment that he'd never yet had the courage to. And only two years later he was dead, aged but sixty-four. There had been reason, after all, to be concerned about his health.

If one did not hesitate to telephone in Paris half an hour before lunch to ask to be invited, by the same token Marie-Laure often made free to summon her guests at the last minute. It was almost always for lunch; in the evenings she habitually went out, leaving house and servants free for her husband's and daughters' convenience if they chanced to be in Paris. So I was not surprised when she called late one morning to bid me come to lunch. This happened to be inconvenient for some reason and I resisted. But she was insistent, telling me that one of her guests that day was to be the wife of an American general from St. Louis who had done favors for her husband during the war, a complete stranger, speaking not one word of French, on her first visit to Europe. So it was essential that I should be present, being a countryman to this woman, able to speak to her in her own language. Needless to say, Marie-Laure spoke impeccable English and it was very likely that most of the other guests would be reasonably fluent. My presence was not indispensable, but I suspect that my shrewd hostess foresaw a boring guest and wanted to shift the conversational burden away from herself. I agreed to be at the Place des Etats-Unis in half an hour.

We were ten in all. As I had expected, most of the others spoke quite adequate English. The general's wife arrived shortly after I did. She must have been about sixty, was attired without the slightest concern for creating an attractive, much less a stylish, appearance, wore no makeup, weighed about twenty-five pounds more than was becoming, had on a tweed hat that matched her pocketbook and shoes with thick rubber soles. In a word, she was dowdy, a typical American matron from the Midwest, her origin emphasized by her accent. At the same time it seemed that she was the quintessence of kindness, naïve good nature, eagerness to please and provincial unsophistication. Needless to say, she had never even imagined the splendor and opulence of a house such as Marie-Laure's, which the proprietor herself sometimes referred to as a palace. But so much grandeur definitely did not leave the general's wife at a loss for words. On the contrary, the more she saw to admire, the more she voiced her admiration, but her expression of it, unfortunately, was not in keeping with the aura of supreme refinement which she meant to extol. She gushed. She said, "Oh, it's so beautiful." She sighed and gasped and clapped her hands and said, "I've never seen anything like this. What a dream! What a marvel!"

Now, Marie-Laure liked people to be impressed by the sumptuous setting in which she enacted her various performances and was quick to detect the least pretense of supercilious indifference. But at the same time she expected the admiration of her guests to be expressed by subtle understatement and in terms befitting the exquisite and magnificent things which in dramatic profusion were there to be admired. It thus soon became plain to everyone save the general's wife herself that she was an unwelcome annoyance to our hostess. Marie-Laure barely spoke to her and pointedly paid attention to all the other guests.

But the lady from St. Louis was not to be struck dumb by being ignored. Garrulity is not punctilious about its beneficiary. And there were those who had no choice but to listen. Consequently it was a relief when André, the butler, flung open the salon door and loudly announced, "The luncheon is served."

We trooped across the gallery through the library and into the small dining room with its blue-glazed walls and marble table. Marie-Laure placed the general's wife opposite her, which was correct, and me to the lady's right, presumably as the logical target of her loquacity, which I at once became. The arrival of food and wine, however, placed some restraint on her verbiage, especially welcome as her conversation had become quite personal, leading to the indiscreet questions which are a staple of American small talk. One of the curiosities and the principal treasure of the dining room was an extraordinary eighteenth-century clock that hung directly above the table. It was in the shape of a large, octagonal, gilt bronze and blue enamel birdcage, the dial and hands for telling the time on the bottom of the cage, visible to those seated below, while within the cage itself perched peacock-colored mechanical birds that could be made to warble by pulling a string. It was this remarkable object that brought about the undoing of the general's wife. She had—yet again—never seen anything like it. Being her neighbor and countryman, I received the frontal flood of her vocal wonderment. In an effort to stem it I caused the birds to warble, but this only augmented the inundation. And it carried across the table.

Marie-Laure, having till then nearly ignored her loquacious guest, leaned forward and said, "So this is your first visit to Europe?"

"Yes, my first," replied the unsuspecting lady, "and I don't mind telling you that having lunch in this fabulous house is probably going to be the high point of the whole trip. It's so fantastic I could kill myself for not bringing my camera to take a few snaps to show to the folks back home. Nobody will ever believe that I actually had lunch in a place like this. I don't mind telling you that in St. Louis there's nothing to compare with it."

"And where are your travels to take you?" Marie-Laure inquired.

"Oh, you know, the places everybody goes. I've already done London. The American Express arranged my trip. That makes it all so much easier, because that way you get to see everything and don't miss the high spots. But I don't mind telling you that I never thought I'd see anything like this place."

"And after Paris where do you go?"

The attention of the entire table was now concentrated upon this interrogation, as everyone present save the general's wife assumed that some premeditated mischief was in the making.

"I go to Italy."

"And where in Italy?"

"Only the places that really matter, the high spots, you know, Venice, Florence and Rome, and that's it. Then back to old St. Louie, Louie." She laughed.

"You mean to tell me that you're going to miss Bologna?" Marie-Laure asked severely.

"Is that a must? I've never heard of it."

"Bologna has been one of the greatest centers of learning in Italy since the Middle Ages," said Marie-Laure, "and it is especially important for women. No self-respecting woman who has the opportunity should fail to spend a few days in Bologna because we all could benefit from learning the Bolognese specialty."

"Is that something to eat?" asked the general's wife.

"For women with healthy appetites, yes, definitely," replied the viscountess, snuffling with laughter.

"Pasta?"

"No. Penises."

Even for those accustomed to Marie-Laure's occasional conversational excesses this was rather extreme, bringing talk around the table to an abrupt stop in nervous expectation of what might come next. The general's wife was mute.

"Bologna, you see," continued the imperturbable, implacable viscountess, "in addition to its famous university possesses Europe's best school for prostitutes. After all, those girls have to learn their trade like anyone else, and they come to Bologna to study the local specialty, which is nothing more than fellatio. You may think it's easy to take a cock in your mouth and suck it. Not at all. I'm told this practice is widespread in the United States. So maybe you are already acquainted with the refinements?"

The general's wife with an expression of glum misery shook her head but did not utter a word.

"Well, it's really very simple once you understand the technique. The whole trick, you see, once full stimulation has been achieved, is to get the head of the penis over into your cheek and massage it at the same time with the tip of your tongue. I'll show you how it's done."

Taking a spoon from the table, Marie-Laure inserted it into her mouth and distended her right cheek with the bowl. "It takes a bit of practice to get the thing just right. One must be very careful not to bite. And that's why a few lessons in Bologna can change a woman's life, because there's nothing men like better than a professional blow job. Believe me, my dear, I speak from experience. And the instructors in Bologna are very handsome young men. Now, you wouldn't want to miss that, would you?"

The general's wife kept her eyes fixed upon her plate and did not reply. Moreover, she did not say another word during the remainder of the meal. General conversation, indeed, was slow to resume. And when we all stood to go upstairs to the large salon for coffee, the general's wife passed straight through the hall without a murmur of farewell or thanks and disappeared beneath the porte cochere. The abruptness of her departure left behind no doubt that, provincial and naïve as she may have been, she had very well understood that her hostess had deliberately provoked and ridiculed her.

And Marie-Laure, of course, understood exactly the same thing. Several of us, while we were drinking our coffee, remonstrated with her, reproving her for having been gratuitously unkind, even cruel, to a person who had done nothing to offend. But Marie-Laure had a profound dislike of being criticized or put in the wrong, and possessed a shrewd flair for justifying her misbehavior. She said, "That silly woman has come to Europe to see the sights, the American Express tour. What do you think will make the least impression on her? San Marco? The Palazzo Vecchio? The Sistine Chapel? Not a thing. It would all be spaghetti in her brain. But she'll remember me, because I provided her with the only real shock she'll receive in all of Europe, the only hint that the old continent is still populated by real people, not robots on the American model. And maybe that will make her wonder about her compatriots in St. Louis. And if she wonders hard enough, just possibly she might turn out to be a changed woman. Highly unlikely. But possible. So I've offered her a chance. The chance of a lifetime. How can anyone criticize me for that? I've not been cruel but generous. And anyway, maybe now she'll give the general a good blow job, and it's a well-known fact that men appreciate skill in that department."

We laughed, allowing her to assume that right was on her side. It was specious, of course, but, coming from her in her house, not without sardonic humor. And perhaps, after all, a bare possibility did exist that the shock of brutal vulgarity in such refined surroundings might waken in the matron from St. Louis a livelier appreciation of values to be perceived in incongruity and paradox. Still, the deliberate humiliation of a guest had been painful to witness.

In the first years of our acquaintance Marie-Laure still made efforts to present to the world an elegant and insofar as possible attractive appearance. Mademoiselle Chanel in person supervised the confection of her clothes, her hair was dyed and dressed by Alexandre and she wore a considerable variety of remarkable jewels. Without question she was a striking figure, and the impression she made certainly was enhanced by the knowledge of who she was. But then the ineluctable wastage of the years did its job, with a certain ironic collaboration, it's true, from the lady herself. In short, she let herself go. Though she ceased to drink, she ate more. The food in her houses being superb, she stuffed herself—table manners atrocious, often smoking while she ate—and consequently grew fat. To make things worse she developed a fibroma, a benign tumor of fibrous tissue, protruding from her belly, which made her look almost obese. It would have been perfectly simple to have this fibroma removed, but Marie-Laure had a horror of doctors, illnesses, operations, hospitals, and refused to have anything to do with them, with the result that her good health became a matter of luck. She once remarked that in order to make herself presentable she would have had to undergo seventeen operations, most of them cosmetic. She had trouble with her feet, abnormal growths having developed on both just behind the big toe, making it impossible to use without extreme discomfort ordinary footwear for women. Instead she wore soft, flat-heeled slippers, of which she possessed a large collection, but these had the unfortunate effect of making her gait rather awkward, so that she seemed to plod rather than to walk normally. As she smoked incessantly, her teeth were not always as impeccably white as one might have wished. Finished were the days when she dressed in Chanel suits. Now she wore ample peasant skirts run up by her maid from fabric bought in the marketplace at Hyères, which did nothing to hide the fibroma. Except for one immense diamond ring, worn only on the rare occasion, all the fine jewelry disappeared, replaced by eccentric brooches and a collection of cameo bracelets. Of makeup she wore rather too much, and this was not always applied with the skill that feminine artifice wants. Her hair, ostentatiously auburn, was dressed in spit curls to conceal the excessive height of her forehead. Instead of a crocodile purse from Hermès or Dior she took to carrying her wallet, compact, lipstick, cigarettes and matches in small wicker baskets. When going out, she often wore a scarf over her head, knotted under the chin, and all in all it's no wonder that people frequently remarked that she could well have been mistaken for a gypsy fortune-teller. That, to be sure, would rather have pleased her, because at the same time there was no mistaking that she was indubitably the Viscountess de Noailles, one of the most notable personalities in France. Her photograph appeared often in the newspapers and no matter how little she may have looked like a glamorous movie star she was always pleased, snipped out the photo and pasted it into her scrapbook. Having long been eccentric in her behavior, she had now transformed herself into an accomplished bohemian. If the family regarded her artist friends as hoboes, what can they possibly have thought of her present incarnation? In any case, as there was no telling now what she might say or do, she was rarely invited to the formal functions still observed with decorum in the Faubourg St.-Germain. Not considered exactly an outcast, she was observed from a safe distance as an aberration, and that state of affairs suited her very well. Rather than dine with any exalted personage from the *Almanach de Gotha*, she far preferred the company of Max Ernst, Man Ray, Balthus and the interior decorators, hairdressers and various hustlers who made up her clique and claque, and who never remonstrated when she told, as she was prone to, how she had been obliged to pierce her maidenhead all by herself, provoking a deluge of blood, as the viscount lacked enthusiasm for that ritual.

Jean Lafont had become the viscountess's official *amant en titre* less than six months after the disappearance of Oscar. But this did not prevent him, or her, from enjoying the occasional extracurricular diversion. There was a painter named Piero Graziani who caught her fancy for a time. His canvases depicted clouds, pink, blue, violet, emerald green, variegated clouds, clouds and clouds. Piero was novel among Marie-Laure's lovers by virtue of being heterosexual. Maybe that's why he didn't last very long. He received the gift of a station wagon and presently was seen no more.

Of all Marie-Laure's possessions those that she prized the most, those incontestably the most precious and prestigious, were the two large paintings by Goya, the life-size portraits of his son and daughter-in-law which had always hung in her octagonal salon. Acquired by her grandfather Bischoffsheim in 1880, they had been with her all her life and they unquestionably represented a vital aspect of the mise-en-scène of her personality. To lead one's life against the backdrop, as it were, of two such powerful masterpieces challenges their possessor to create an individual aura of comparable imaginative authority. Marie-Laure was clearly aware of this challenge, and she met it, though in fairness to the paintings one must acknowledge that the aura she created was not always as lovely as they were. It is unlikely that Marie-Laure worried much about what would become of her Goyas when she was no longer present to be mirrored in their glory, because she heartily detested the ultimate reality of death, most particularly her own. To say that she lived for the Goyas would be hyperbole, but she did feel that they brought to her life a dimension not conferred by any of the other works of art in the house.

I was with her one summer afternoon in Hyères when the telephone rang in the library. She answered. It was the viscount calling. I did not leave the room, having already heard one side of countless conversations between the wife and her husband. They chatted casually about trifles for a few minutes, but then suddenly Marie-Laure sat up straight in her armchair, as if stung by a hornet, and cried, "No, no, no!" Then her husband spoke for a minute or two. "Never!" she cried. "Not the Goyas. They're mine and I'll never, never let them go." But she was silent again, listening to her husband for quite a long time, and she sank back into her chair. "You want me to die," she murmured at length. "That's what it means. So it's all been decided behind my back. Is it the price I have to pay?" Her husband then spoke at length, while she listened, nodding now and then, and finally she said, "Very well, Charles. I agree, because I have to, but you must understand that I understand, and that's the price you and Laure will have to pay. I can say no more about it now, or ever, perhaps. So goodbye." And she hung up the telephone.

Since I was present she explained. Her husband and his lawyers had decided that in order to forestall eventual payment of inordinate death duties it was prudent to transfer now to her heirs legal title to some of her most valuable possessions. Thus, the two Goyas were presently to become the property of Laure de La Haye Jousselin, the elder daughter, though they might remain in Marie-Laure's home till her death. "For me," she said, "it will be as if they cease to exist. Such is the cruelty of great wealth. It lives for your death."

The next time I went to the Place des Etats-Unis the two Goyas had been removed from Marie-Laure's salon. For the rest of her life they hung on the narrow upstairs side landing of the grand staircase on either side of a mediocre Van Dyck, difficult to see and easy not to notice, rather woebegone, I felt, in their expedient exile. Where they had been other paintings were placed, one of these a superb Géricault, but the salon, needless to say, was never again the same. After Marie-Laure died, the Goyas were shipped to the country château of the La Haye Jousselins and next to nobody I know has ever seen them since.

It would be tempting, and facile, to tell Marie-Laure's story by stringing anecdote after anecdote, but monotony and distortion would be the outcome. However, there is one anecdote, a lengthy one, that I cannot resist relating not only for its intrinsic absurdity and humor but also because its circumstances and implications suggest so much that was essential to the development and performance of Marie-Laure's persona. She is not at all the principal actress in this anecdote, merely a witness, but without her it would hardly seem to have the same grotesque and pathetic resonance, and indeed her presence had from the first been solicited as the leading link in the chain of incident.

In the month of August 1961, I spent a week or more alone with Marie-Laure at Hyères. One day before lunch the telephone rang in her library. After some conversation she asked her caller to hold the wire and said to me, "It's an American lady named Mrs. Livingston who wants to give a dinner for me in three days' time. I've never met her, but she keeps inviting me. Shall we go?"

I said, "Why not?" Being alone with Marie-Laure was not always sure entertainment, so the prospect of some exotic sociability was alluring.

Having accepted the invitation on condition that one male house-guest be included, Marie-Laure put down the phone and told me all she knew about our hostess-to-be. Mrs. Livingston was—and, for all I know, still is—an American lady of ample means who, being either divorced or widowed, had not long before bought an estate near St.-Tropez and was busy establishing herself as a person of social consequence in that already very overcrowded area. As the Viscountess de Noailles was one of the most notable residents of the Riviera, and since formal introductions had long since ceased to be indispensable to the merriment of society, it was natural that Mrs. Livingston should have labored to add Marie-Laure to her list of honorific acquaintances.

Even for August in that warm part of Europe the day of Mrs. Livingston's dinner party turned out to be fiendishly hot. Toward evening the viscountess and I set out in her automobile for St.-Tropez, a distance of only thirty miles but over poor and twisting roads. Local gossip had meanwhile told us that Mrs. Livingston's estate consisted of a very large farmhouse, with adjoining vineyards, which the American lady had at great expense lately transformed into a luxurious summer residence. Night had come by the time we got there. As we approached the place by a long drive lined on either side by mimosa trees, our headlights showed a large, typical Provençal building. At the front door stood a young man in a white jacket with gold buttons and epaulets, wearing white gloves.

"That's a very bad sign," said Marie-Laure, and it's true that she was in a better position than most people to know that servants in livery, especially on the Riviera, were so much a part of the irretrievable past that even to have called them a thing of it would have seemed a provocation.

We got out of the car and went inside through the door which the white-gloved young man held open for us. And what was our astonishment to find that suddenly we seemed not at all to be in the South of France but in Southampton, Long Island! The interior was entirely done in chintz, draperies, upholstery, table coverings, cushions, while flowered carpets in harmonizing colors lay on the tile floors. In heavy silver frames on round tables were photographs of ladies wearing huge picture hats. Agog to have netted, if not quite landed, a social catch as sizable as the Viscountess de Noailles, Mrs. Livingston was at pains to make us welcome. A tall, slender, blond person of about fifty, she was of an evident American distinction very suitable to Long Island but appearing ever so slightly anemic on the earthiness of Gallic soil.

The diners were ten in all, half of them American. Most eminent of these was Mr. James McCormick, tycoon of the reapers, with his brassy French wife, then a Mr. and Mrs. Charles Spofford, he a New York lawyer and trustee of the Metropolitan Opera, our hostess and myself. There was a German gentleman who had something to do with the opera and claimed close acquaintance with Herbert von Karajan. The French, in addition to Renée McCormick, were Marie-Laure, a colorless baron said to be Mrs. Livingston's beau and the Count and Countess Pierre de Fleurieu. The count had been an authentic hero of World War I, having left on the battlefield one of his arms, and wore the crimson insignia of the Légion d'Honneur.

Drinks, particularly welcome on such a stifling evening, were served on silver salvers in the drawing room by the young man in livery and by another, old enough to be his father, in identical attire. Conversation was no more than it's likely to be in such circumstances: sluggish. Never one to endure boredom with tolerant politesse, Marie-Laure was not trying hard to be sociable, though acquainted with several of the French guests, but she did manage to admire an exquisite Louis XV painted fan displayed on one of the tables. Mrs. Livingston was pleased. "It was a gift to my grandmother from Mr. Morgan," she said complacently.

To hear dinner announced was a great relief, a relief quickly dispelled, however, by the discovery that instead of dining out of doors on a cool terrace we were to eat in a smallish room where all the draperies were drawn, illumination provided solely by candles, of which there must have been several dozen. The heat was, in a word, unbearable. Perhaps somewhat less so for the ladies, as this was the season when lounging pajamas were the rage, and all save Marie-Laure were attired in loose-fitting creations of this sort. For the men, all of whom wore jackets, the situation was otherwise, perspiration profuse. Mrs. Livingston had given Marie-Laure the place of honor directly opposite her at the oval table, but in a signal lapse of savoir faire had placed me to Marie-Laure's left. However, I didn't care what assumptions might be made about my intimacy with my hostess and thought myself lucky to have a dependable conversationalist beside me.

Dinner got under way with welcome platters of lobster salad and excellent white wine, served by the two men in livery. The table was of marble, there was also a marble-topped console, and it did seem as dishes and platters came and went that there was excessive clatter and rattling of silver and china. But the discomfort of one's body took a maximum of attention, little left over for notice of undue noise. Then came the roast, a rack of lamb strongly redolent of garlic and infernally unsuited to that August night. It was served by the older man, and properly he first held the platter for Marie-Laure. As he leaned down to do so, he said in a very loud, though slightly slurred, voice, "It's not me that stinks, it's the meat." An audible intake of breath ensued around the table, then silence, while an expression of ineffable contentment suffused the features of my friend the viscountess, who liked nothing more than grotesque incongruity, for the butler did, in fact, very perceptibly stink. Of liquor. Mrs. Livingston looked aghast and wiggled her hands. Marie-Laure took a thumping portion of roast, whereupon the butler continued to pass his platter and the younger livery came along with some kind of vegetable. When the servants had gone out of the room, their unhappy employer explained that a lot of drinking got done in the kitchen, that she had hoped against hope nothing would go wrong and implored her guests to be understanding. We were. This was made easier by the fact that intoxication in the kitchen presently led to shouting and other kinds of ominous commotion. The hands of our hostess became more and more wiggly, her visage ashen with worry, but the baron told her not to fear, as we would brave it through. Marie-Laure looked at me and I looked at her, our glance meant to signify that bravery, while being the somewhat indigestible portion of good manners, might also satisfy the appetite for a bit of good fun, and we smiled in complicitous anticipation, little guessing what comedy was to come.

Salad materialized without catastrophe, though every plate to reach the table was accompanied by unnerving anticipation of same. Then it was the turn of dessert, a frothing concoction of fruit and cream brought forth by senior livery on a silver platter. By some tipsy miracle of equilibrium this vessel circumnavigated the table about halfway before reaching the Countess de Fleurieu, at whose shoulder a tragic tilt occurred, causing a veritable Niagara of cream to go cascading down the front of that lady's pale blue lounging pajamas. Her shriek rose as if from the pit of Hades. "My pajamas!" she screamed, wildly mopping their irreparable creaminess. "My pajamas! My pajamas!" Her husband, the count, began to berate the bungling butler just as he would have upbraided an incompetent soldier in the field, declaring him a clumsy oaf who had no idea of how to serve. A pertinent observation, perhaps, but liquor, not discipline, prevailed. "Well then," cried the mutinous subaltern, "you can serve yourselves." And he dropped the platter, which came down with a calamitous crash onto the table, sending up a geyser of cream. The butler bolted from the room. Mrs. Livingston's hands were now in a frenzy of wiggles. Marie-Laure chortled out loud. From the kitchen came sounds of drunken pandemonium. Whereupon the Count de Fleurieu raised his single remaining arm in a gesture recalling climactic moments in the trenches and cried, "All the men to the kitchen!" as he leapt to his feet. Decades have done nothing to diminish in memory the unutterable absurdity of that instant when to my astonishment—and shame—I saw that every man, including my own ridiculous self, had risen in obedience to the count's command and prepared to invade the kitchen. Therein, alas, now dwelt authentic enemies.

This is what we saw. On the floor, looking decidedly trampled, lay the white jacket of the older man. The younger stood in a corner, appearing but halfheartedly belligerent and not especially drunk, while beside the refrigerator a middle-aged woman swayed and moaned, murmuring, "We're not animals. You can't treat us like animals." The older man roared obscene insults and swore with a vengeance. Pierre de Fleurieu denounced him with strident disdain. So ensued a shouting match, which seemed unlikely to get anyone anywhere, and most particularly not likely to allow for dignified retreat by Mrs. Livingston's male guests from a terrain where they had no business. Then it was that Mr. McCormick intervened, suavely asserting an authority made dynamic by knowledge of all those reapers in their invincible dominion upon the Great Plains of North America. He pronounced appropriate irrelevancies meant to calm tempers on both sides, an effort entirely lost on the kitchen, but effective as to the ludicrous platoon from the dining room, which was only too anxious to abandon an untenable position. We retreated. The scene of erstwhile strife was deserted, the ladies having retired to the salon. In the stifling dining room the only sign of life was the flicker of those innumerable candles casting their unreal light upon the debris of misbegotten sociability.

To save the soirée now was unthinkable, but a gallant try for redemption came along in the form of a tray of liqueurs passed by

Charlie Spofford. This made, at least, for a delaying action of gentility, during which we were able to learn a bit more about what had brought down her doom upon Mrs. Livingston. Having purchased the farmhouse and adjoining vineyards from an absentee landlord, she had thought in her practical American naïveté that it would be wonderfully convenient to keep on as servants in the refurbished domain the selfsame persons whose business it had previously been to work the land as tenant farmers. The latter, thinking no doubt that a good thing could be made of a proposition so patently prompted by idiocy, had agreed. While the property was being done up to suit a nostalgia for the eastern end of Long Island, its owner went off to Italy in search of suitable livery for her resident servants, because the French had long since given up the manufacture of such unrealistic apparel. And when she had got the former peasants, father and son, all dressed up in their fancy suits, she thought that she had turned a very neat trick of domestic expedience. Now, alas, she would have to reckon with what she had wrought.

Marie-Laure was delighted by the comeuppance of so much witless trifling with social usage, but her pleasure was not of a variety that called for any further savoring at the source. Having learned the particulars, she was anxious to withdraw both her person and her prestige from this compromising locale. With no nod to tact she turned to me and announced, "We're leaving." Mrs. Livingston, who could clearly see in the departure of her most exalted guest the dashing of lofty aspirations, wiggled her hands and hoped for happier opportunities in future to entertain the viscountess. Never one to miss an occasion for making the most of somebody else's embarrassment, Marie-Laure snatched from a side table the Louis XV fan she had admired at the start of the evening and cried, "I love this fan. Do you mind if I take it along as a souvenir of your delightful soirée?"

"Oh, please do, please do," sighed the abject hostess.

Whereupon we summarily said good night all round, went out by the front door, which we had to open for ourselves, and got into our automobile. Driving away in the odorous dark of the Riviera, which all at once felt delightfully refreshing, we talked about what had happened and as we sped along, laughing, found that in spite of herself Mrs. Livingston had given a very good party. In addition to which Marie-Laure had managed to make off with a rare and valuable *objet de vertu.* Perhaps it was the value of the souvenir that caused her presently to grow pensive. She, the mistress of a palatial residence in addition to her concrete castle and a retinue of servants that numbered near twenty, not to mention one of the great fortunes of the world, sighed as she waved J. P. Morgan's fan and then she said, "It's people like that who are responsible for Communism." I recalled that Marie-Laure was a direct descendant of Donatien Alphonse François de Sade, the notorious marquis, and thought with regret that Mrs. Livingston would never realize that this infamous social outcast had symbolically been present at her table on that memorable night in the person of her most eminent guest.

Purloining precious objects from the houses of friends, or of mere acquaintances, by means of extravagant admiration, fawning politesse or brazen cupidity was nothing new to Marie-Laure. Possessions were a projection of herself which had an almost physical capacity for assuring her that she was truly the person she wanted to believe in. If a semblance of shameless rapacity sometimes presided over the acquisition of a gift, the recipient could forgive herself the more easily by considering that her possessive passion was aesthetic rather than material and that her ability to analyze and reflect upon an artistic effect was likely to be more discriminating than that of the donor.

There lived in a large house on the outskirts of Hyères a gentleman well past middle age named Monsieur Eiffren, noted for being president of the Automobile Club of the Var and for having employed a painter to decorate the walls and ceilings of several rooms in his home with copies of the more sensual male nudes from the Sistine Chapel, including, of course, Adam. Monsieur Eiffren was pertinacious in his cultivation of the viscountess, and she occasionally dined at his house, resources of conviviality at Hyères being limited. And by dint of shameless vociferation of her enthusiasm she had once contrived to have her host offer her an exquisite Meissen horse which had decorated his dining-room table and now graced hers. One summer evening, Marie-Laure, another friend and I went to dine *chez* Monsieur Eiffren. On our way through the garden toward his front door the viscountess noticed a nineteenth-century marble statuette of Cupid writing on a tablet, the whole about eighteen inches in height and executed with a certain grace and charm. By an almost incredible and perhaps unhappy coincidence a nearly identical statuette stood on the terrace outside the library at St.-Bernard, the only difference being that the viscount-ess's Cupid was reading a book, not writing. That it would be mirac-ulously logical to unite the writer and reader occurred to Marie-Laure instantly, and before we had reached Monsieur Eiffren's threshold she said, "I must have that Cupid. It belongs with its brother. I must have it. I shall have it."

We were not the only guests that evening. Some of the others were already acquainted with Marie-Laure. She paid them little attention. All her charm, which when conscientiously exerted could be winning indeed, was lavished upon her host, who did not yet suspect any ulterior motive and responded with radiant contentment. We stood about for some time drinking champagne and Marie-Laure pronounced Mon-sieur Eiffren's Michelangelos quite as fine as the Pope's. In her resolve to acquire the Cupid in the garden the viscountess was obviously pre-pared to go the limit. But she held back the onset of her campaign until dinner, knowing that she would be seated to the right of her host and could press him in a situation allowing for no retreat. And we had not gotten very far with our fish before the offensive began: fulsome admiration for the Cupid, which much pleased Monsieur Eiffren, who had very lately acquired it from the famous Lucien Blanc in Aix-en-Provence. But then came the frontal assault, the fantastic coincidence of the Cupid's twin perusing a book on the terrace at St.-Bernard. And what a desperate shame that the brothers should be separated. Surely Monsieur Eiffren could appreciate the lovely justice of their reunion, nor was it necessary to specify on what terrain that happy conjuncture would take place. Monsieur Eiffren, mindful perhaps of his Meissen steed, gave not the slightest hint of any such appreciation or the least desire to effect a reunion. Instead he talked about a rally of automobile elegance that he was organizing. Didn't the Noailles have a Rolls-Royce or Bugatti that could be brought out for the occasion? Marie-Laure allowed a brief automotive truce, but very soon the Cupid campaign resumed. It did not give promise of success, though the viscountess deployed every aristocratic, alluring, snobbish tactic she could devise, and by the end of dinner Monsieur Eiffren had allowed not the slightest intimation that the writer in the garden might ever travel up the hill to be united with his bookish twin. Having made her craving almost humiliatingly plain and been rebuffed, the only tactic remaining was a display of pique. Marie-Laure seated herself in the corner of a sofa and gazed irritably at the ceiling. Someone sat down beside her and endeavored to initiate a conversation, but she did not reply. Coffee and herbal tea were offered by a handsome waiter in a silk sport shirt. She shook her head. And after twenty minutes of sullen mutism she abruptly rose, knowing that her chauffeur would be waiting at the gate, waved her arm imperiously at her friends to follow and headed toward the door, bidding Monsieur Eiffren a brusque good night as she passed beside him. Clearly unsettled by this cavalier and untimely departure, our host followed us outside, murmuring embarrassed respects. So we formed a little procession along the garden path, Marie-Laure in the lead. Inevitably we came upon the lovable *casus belli*. Marie-Laure stopped before it, exclaiming loudly, "I adore this object. It would be ideal on my terrace. I must have it. I'm just going to take it."

Its owner, having naturally heard this outburst, surrendered to force majeure and said, "Oh, my dear, if it could give you pleasure, then it's my pleasure to make you a gift of it."

"You are really too kind," sighed Marie-Laure. "But I must be sure I won't be depriving you of something you specially cherish."

The defeated but gallant man said, "My dear, you know I cherish your friendship and pleasure more than any material object."

The viscountess smiled broadly, almost laughed and shouted, "Clément, Clément!" (the name of her chauffeur). "Come here and put this object in the trunk of the car."

It was quickly done. We said good night to Monsieur Eiffren. Not a hundred yards had been traversed before I set about berating our euphoric hostess for what I judged to have been no better than polite theft. Predictably she disagreed, asserting that anyone who could live with such appalling copies of works of genius was not entitled to the slightest benefit of a doubt when it came to appreciating an object even of relative and decorative quality like the Cupid. That was sophistry, I said. What mattered was Monsieur Eiffren's obvious reluctance to part with his statuette, not his taste, whether good or bad. But Marie-Laure was determined not to be put in the wrong, and our discussion continued even after we had returned to St.-Bernard and Clément had placed the writer beside the reader, a union admittedly most pleasing, each Cupid adding to the somewhat saccharine charm of his twin. I insisted that fairness required that reparation be made to the despoiled party. Marie-Laure was willing and said she had just the thing to please Monsieur Eiffren far more than the studious little Cupid. It was a rare edition of a homosexual story by Jean Cocteau, entitled *The White Book*, published in 1930, illustrated with drawings by the author of libidinous young men with large members and dedicated by Cocteau to Marie-Laure. She would have it delivered by Clément in the morning.

By this time our conversation had taken us from the library through the hall and down the long corridor to Marie-Laure's bedroom. No doubt she was right that Monsieur Eiffren would much rather possess *The White Book* than the purloined statuette, but I nonetheless felt that its acquisition had been outrageously high-handed. So I said, "And how would you respond if someone came to your house and admired a possession of yours with such insistence that his desire to have it for himself became almost a demand?"

"It's simple," said Marie-Laure. "If I believed that his imagination was sincere and of a quality equal to the quality of the object, I'd give it gladly."

"Well," I said, "I've always admired this drawing. There's nothing in the world that would give me greater joy than to have it." And I plucked from the wall beside me a study by Degas after some antique sculpture, no doubt executed during his early years in Italy.

"Then it's yours," said Marie-Laure.

Astonished, delighted, but stunned by wonderment at my good fortune, I held the drawing high in the air and said, "Oh, Marie-Laure, do you really mean it?"

"No," she shrieked. "No, no, no. Put it back on the wall immediately." I did as I was told, slightly disappointed but not very surprised. At all events, Monsieur Eiffren did receive *The White Book* and sent an effusive letter of thanks.

She liked contests of the will, challenges to her power and prestige, and respected those who had the effrontery to defy her—so long as they did so with suitable deference. Her servants on the whole were respectful and obedient. They put up with a good deal of willful capriciousness, but it went without saying on both sides that she was more dependent upon them than they upon her. One autumn day in Paris as we were going toward the dining room she glanced into the garden and noticed that the paths were littered with crisp dead leaves from the chestnut trees. "All those dead leaves," she said to the butler, "are most unattractive. Have them cleared away."

The servants had a manner of addressing Marie-Laure as if the conventional term of address and the title were a single word, so that "Madame la Vicomtesse" became "Mamlavicontez," and André said, "Very well, Mamlavicontez." When we came back from lunch, not a single dead leaf was to be seen in the garden. "But now it looks too barren," Marie-Laure protested. "You should have left just a few dead leaves here and there to create an artistic effect."

"Very well, Mamlavicontez," said André, smirking almost imperceptibly. "I'll send a footman out into the square to collect a few dead leaves and we'll scatter them about."

"Don't be insolent," said Marie-Laure, smirking herself, and we went upstairs for coffee.

In the spring of 1961 I entered upon a serious relationship with an American from Oklahoma named Larry Hager. Marie-Laure did not much like her friends to acquire new lovers or mistresses, as her own successes in this department became more and more problematical, and although she usually agreed to receive them she could be aloof and condescending. And so she was at first with Larry, who reacted to the grandeur of the Place des Etats-Unis with more becoming aplomb than the lady from St. Louis, he an authentic escapee from the Dust Bowl. Consequently I saw the viscountess quite often alone or with other friends. One evening in June the two of us had dinner together in a Left Bank restaurant. I had promised to rejoin Larry well before midnight. But when we had finished dinner and were in my car, it then being close to ten-thirty, Marie-Laure announced that she wanted to go to the movies. Some film was playing on the Champs-Elysées that she longed to see. I told her that I had an after-dinner engagement and couldn't possibly accompany her to the movies.

"But I want to go," she insisted.

"Well, I can drop you at the theater if you like."

"Certainly not. What a rude suggestion. A lady does not attend the theater unaccompanied. I want to go to the movies, and as my escort you are obligated to accompany me."

"That sort of old-fashioned protocol doesn't apply to us. Our engagement was for dinner, not dinner and the movies. I'm going to drive you home, and that's all."

"In that case," said Marie-Laure brusquely, "I can only consider our relationship compromised. Why, it's nothing at all to take me to the movies. There are quantities of people in Paris who would leap at the opportunity."

"I explained to you that I have an engagement."

"Of what sort takes little imagination to guess."

"That's neither here nor there."

"You are compromising our friendship for nothing."

"It's not nothing, and I refuse to be coerced by your whim."

"Too bad for you. Think it over. If our relationship is no longer the same, you have a lot more to lose than I do."

"Not at all," I said. "*You* think it over. If anyone has anything to lose, we both lose the same thing, which is simply a friend who has stood the test of time. And there are never many of that kind around. It would be a pity to lose one simply because of a missed movie."

Marie-Laure was silent for a time, lit a cigarette, puffed at it deeply, then said, "Well, at least you can come into the house and have a brandy with me before you go off."

"I'll be happy to," I said.

So we sat in her bedroom on either side of the fireplace, sipping brandy, and chatted about things of no consequence for thirty or forty minutes. And from that time onward she was much more friendly toward Larry.

By this time Marie-Laure had long since become a celebrity, a status frequently mistaken for authentic fame by persons lacking the wherewithal to attain the grander condition. And it was as a celebrity that Marie-Laure achieved her true fulfillment as a personality and probably her greatest satisfaction—sad to say—as a creative individual, because she was able to project to the public the image of herself that she personally felt to be most provocative and interesting. She was acquainted with the people who wrote gossip columns in the newspapers, and her name appeared in them often, her photograph also, sometimes on the front page. In France there was no royal family to crystallize the dreams and fantasies of the populace. People like Marie-Laure had to do that, and she did it with incomparable verve. None of the others could compete with her in originality or talent. She had something to say about everything, and if, as sometimes happened, it didn't prove entirely intelligible, few people cared, since her role was not to be sensible or cogent but simply to be picturesque. And that led fatefully into the snare of eccentricity. She had repudiated her past, her social status and her familial responsibilities with all the aggressiveness characteristic of great innovators. Now that she was entirely independent to make of her freedom whatever she chose, her innovation was her eccentricity, and by the time she was sixty it had begun to be clear that she didn't very much care what she said, whom she saw or how she behaved. There were moments when her talk went beyond the border of incoherence, but if it was disconcerting, it was often funny and could be attributed to Surrealist nostalgia. That is probably why at about this time we started calling her—behind her back—La Mère Ubu, for she did often recall the grotesque, nonsensical protagonist of Alfred Jarry's play *Le Père Ubu*, a work beloved by Breton and his disciples.

Her companions became a little more difficult to explain away. The mixture had usually been casual and impromptu but almost always included the select few who assured that conversation would be lively and cultivated. That era was now past. True, some of those who had made it liveliest and most cultivated were now gone or had little liking for the newcomers who floated in on the wave of gossip. Some of these were inexplicably crass. They may have been good-looking or glib, but their presence in that house seemed to contradict everything that it had originally been created to exemplify. The viscount must have been appalled. It was a fact that the most fleeting encounter with Marie-Laure at an art gallery or in the bar of the Hôtel Pont-Royal—a chic meeting place in those years—could now be engineered to produce an invitation to the Place des Etats-Unis, where the magic of La Mère Ubu could transform total strangers into lifelong friends within a fortnight. There was a handsome young actor named Pierre Clémenti who for a time was an habitué. His manners were deplorable, but the ruder he was, the more Marie-Laure seemed to enjoy his presence, so there were some who assumed that her hunger for erotic daily bread was not yet quite appeased. And then there was a witty young would-be writer called François-Marie Banier, who had the appearance of a Botticelli angel, the conversation of a juvenile Cocteau and the temperament of a latter-day Rastignac but who could not be considered in the category of daily bread, as he invariably appeared with his friend, a very handsome interior decorator. Also, alas, there were commonplace businessmen and their even more ordinary boyfriends, plus a baroque assortment of arrivistes of all four sexes. And the dullest of the dull old hangers-on still did their ritual dance and laughed when expected to.

An extravagant example of Marie-Laure's determination to get herself talked about and to participate, however frivolously, in events that were being talked about occurred during the student riots which convulsed Paris throughout the month of May 1968. These disturbances, upon occasion of extreme violence, paralyzed the city for several weeks, caused considerable damage and greatly embarrassed the government, which seemed powerless to prevent the duration of what appeared to be a state of anarchy. This appearance was an appearance only, however, for the government's semblance of indecision was motivated by the desire to avoid serious casualties, by an awareness that the student agitation had no popular support or practical purpose and by the time-honored knowledge that all this excitement, this defiance of established rules and regulations, this exhilaration of bluster and audacity would in due time, aided by a few cosmetic concessions, wear itself out. It was entirely a tumult of the young and ingenuous, centered, of course, in the Latin Quarter, especially in the Odéon Theater, which the students had sacked and where interminable jejune harangues were to be heard day and night amid a rather jolly uproar. Indeed, as time went on, the atmosphere of carnival became more and more pronounced. In all of this grown-ups were well advised not to meddle, but many mistakenly fancied that the dawn of a new order needed their counsel, while others foolishly thought that a midnight march, a brush with the police and a display of sympathy for the high jinks of students young enough to be their children not only would be exciting but would restore the ebullience of their own youth. The allure of such fun was irresistible to Marie-Laure, who had herself conveyed to the Odéon by her chauffeur and endeavored to engage the students on hand in some sort of dialogue. They were nonplussed, of course, by the Mère Ubu irrelevance of her observations and their response was a mix of atavistic respect for a person who was obviously a grande dame and of derision for an individual who hadn't the good sense to keep out of a situation in which her pretense of participation was ludicrous. The encounter, in any case a fiasco, was not prolonged and ended in the farcical retreat of Marie-Laure. But what mattered was that it got into the newspapers, the attitudinous viscountess once more appearing to be a figure in the forefront of eventful circumstances. And so things went in the last years of the sixties, all of us feeling with varying degrees of melancholy that our old friend had little by little ceased to be the person so entertaining, cultivated, cunning and self-reliant whose company and hospitality had enlivened our lives.

On January 14, 1970, I had lunch at the Place des Etats-Unis. Jean Lafont was present, also Man Ray, the Surrealist photographer, now become a pompous windbag, and his charming, patient wife, Juliet, together with a lawyer from Chicago intent on getting everything he could from Ray and a young painter nobody seemed to know very well. The conversation was, for once, principally in English, Ray in his native tongue less tiresome than when speaking French. Marie-Laure was in excellent humor but didn't make much sense. After lunch she insisted that Jean and I accompany her to a frame maker's shop, where a great deal of pointless palaver was pursued before I could politely take myself away. Exactly fifteen days later, the 29th, I had arranged to have lunch with Annette Giacometti. We met at her apartment in the rue Mazarine and walked to a brasserie called Balzar in the Latin Quarter. On entering I noticed Jean Lafont seated with two of his friends at a table to the left of the entrance, and as Annette and I had to pass by him to reach our table I said hello. Jean looked up at me without rising but held out his hand, and when I had shaken it, he said, "Marie-Laure died at ten-thirty this morning." The statement was made in a manner altogether matter-of-fact, as if he were announcing some minor political event in a distant land. I was stunned, asked for details. She had had a stroke the previous evening, Jean said, spent a restless night, was attended by two doctors, had another stroke in midmorning and died. That was all. Annette meanwhile had seated herself at our table. The luncheon was not easy to get through.

It is, or was then, in any event, often customary for deceased persons to be prepared by undertakers in their own homes and then visited by those desirous of paying homage and bidding a final farewell to their erstwhile friend. This ritual was respected in the case of Marie-Laure, the visit taking place the very next day after her death. To me it seemed rather morbid. I was reluctant to return to the Place des Etats-Unis under such melancholy circumstances. Others went, however, most of our mutual friends, "Mama's hoboes." But I did not. The next morning, however, I had a change of heart, telephoned the house and was told by André, the butler, that I might still make the visit if I came before noon.

At ten-thirty, the very hour of Marie-Laure's death two days before, I reached the house. Greeted by André in the vestibule, I was asked to sign a book, which already had many pages filled with signatures. The previous day had been busy. But that morning I was alone. In the octagonal salon waited Marie-Laure's eldest grandson, Edmond de La Haye Jousselin, stiff and formal, obviously displeased with his role as usher into the presence of his dead relative. When we had shaken hands, he indicated that I was to go into the bedroom alone.

How often I had sat with her in that room which so strongly bore the impress of her personality, its walls covered with such an eccentric assortment of her possessions: paintings by Cranach and Picasso, drawings by Ingres, Delacroix, Dali, postcards of bullfighters and Madonnas, a collection of miniature tortoiseshell mandolins, ex-votos of noses, ears, fingers, toes, etc., etc., etc. And there in front of the fireplace we had talked and talked. She had told me countless stories about her life, which was now over. She had left that room forever, and yet she was still grimly present, for her corpse lay outstretched upon the bed beneath a stiffly starched white sheet. Her hands, joined upon her breast, were holding a black wooden cross. Only her face was visible beneath a thin white veil. The undertakers had worked well, for her features looked composed, tranquil, serene, the very image of one who has peacefully passed into the hereafter. The room was dim. I sat down in an armchair placed by the bedside, thinking of the past, so many pleasures and incidents and oddities now also consigned to the embalmment of memory. However, the moment was touched neither by sentimentality nor by solemnity. She would not have appreciated either attitude. I remained for about five minutes, then returned to the salon, said goodbye to Edmond and went back through the gallery to the hall.

There I came upon Emma, a tall, thin woman of about fifty who had for many, many years been Marie-Laure's personal maid. She and I had always had cordial relations with each other and, having learned from André that I was in the house, she was waiting for me, as she wanted me to know how Mamlavicontez, in fact, had died. What she most wanted, of course, was to share her grief, and the desolation she felt was unmistakably profound and sincere. Marie-Laure had not always been an easy or considerate employer, but she was well liked, respected, even admired by her servants. André stood by but said nothing. So it was from Emma that I learned of Marie-Laure's screaming, "I don't want to die, I don't want to die." And she had clutched Emma by the arms, as if by holding close a living person she could hold on to life itself. To demonstrate the passion of this desire Emma drew back the long sleeves of her dress, showing on both forearms deep scratches from the frantic fingernails of her mistress, who had also pulled her hair and ripped her dress. But all the screaming, scratching and ripping had only made the fatal end more miserable for everyone. "We have lost a great friend, a great poet, a great artist," Emma said, and it probably helped her to believe that. Very dignified, as always, André said simply, "There is nothing to say." Indeed there was not, and so I left the house.

In addition to respectful and laudatory obituaries a mortuary announcement appeared in the press on behalf of the family in accord with socially accepted practice. It surprised and shocked many of Marie-Laure's friends and read in full as follows:

We are requested to announce the sudden demise of
MARIE-LAURE BISCHOFFSHEIM
Viscountess de NOAILLES
which occurred in Paris on January 29th.
A service will be celebrated on Monday, February 2nd,
at the Church of Saint-Pierre de Chaillot.
Neither flowers nor wreaths.

It was, and is, customary in France for death notices to include the names of all the surviving members of the immediate family, spouse, children and grandchildren. But in this case not a single name appeared. In addition, the prominence given to the maiden name of the deceased, who had legally borne for nearly half a century the title and name of Viscountess de Noailles, which appeared below the name Bischoffsheim, suggested that the family had at last found itself free to repudiate the embarrassing and scandalous Marie-Laure. This was both shameful and foolish, for despite all her shortcomings as a respectable aristocrat, she had been the most colorful, cultivated, creative and—in her own way—distinguished person to have attained prominence in that rather effete clan within living memory. But the prominence attained had everything to do with Marie-Laure Bischoffsheim and nothing to do with the Noailles, for she had succeeded in making herself a character whose existence was her own unique theater.

The funeral took place as announced. Saint-Pierre de Chaillot was the church of Marie-Laure's diocese. It is a large one and seemed at the time perfectly adequate. When the viscount died eleven years later, however, his funeral service took place with pomp at the Madeleine, well outside his diocese, and the grandest religious edifice in Paris after the Cathedral of Notre-Dame. One noticed the difference which in death a semblance of social amenity and aristocratic equivocation could make. Anyway, the church, though crowded, was not quite full. But all those who had been her friends, and many who were the friends or relatives of her husband, were present. The service was not long. The priest spoke of "our sister Marie-Laure" and commended her soul to the mercy of the Almighty. There was some music. Then all present one after another passed by the casket to sprinkle it with holy water from a mortar while making the sign of the cross with the pestle. Every surviving relative stood in line to the right of the altar in order to receive the condolences and shake hands with those come to pay their last respects to the deceased. The last person in this line was Jean Lafont, and we all thought it very seemly and sensitive of the viscount to have included him.

It had been specifically requested that none of those attending the church service should follow the hearse to the cemetery, and everyone accepted this as the simple expression of a desire to avoid prolonging an already distressing occasion. There may have been more to it than that. The morning was cheerless, chilly and gray. Some of us lingered in front of the church until the casket was carried out and loaded into the hearse. It drove away, followed by a number of limousines conveying members of the family. A few of us walked up the Avenue Marceau to the *café-tabac* at the corner of the rue de Chaillot. We ordered coffee and glumly sat there for some time, all mournfully aware that life in Paris without Marie-Laure could never again conceivably be the same for any of us. She had been more than herself. She had been a pivotal figure in the cultural and social life of Paris, and a very great deal of what was vital and innovative in her era had one way or another turned around her. There would be no one to take her place. We realized that at once. And in the more than two decades since her death no one has taken her place or presumed or pretended to. The loss was irreparable.

We found out after a time why, perhaps, we were asked not to come to the cemetery. Because Marie-Laure was interred in the mausoleum of her Bischoffsheim forebears in the section of the Montparnasse Cemetery, the twenty-eighth division, set aside largely for the Jewish dead, surrounded by Blocks, Blums and Lehmanns. Neither her mother nor her husband reposed there with her, only her father, her Paine grandparents and Oscar Dominguez, whom she had thus welcomed into her family when no other means of making amends was possible. The plaque indicating the presence of Marie-Laure's remains is engraved in keeping with the precedent of the newspaper announcement.

MARIE-LAURE HENRIETTE ANNE BISCHOFFSHEIM
VICOMTESSE DE NOAILLES
31 OCTOBRE 1902–29 JANVIER 1970

Perhaps it is customary in France for the dead to be separated from those supposedly nearest and dearest. I don't know. But I was not the only one to be shocked.

On the fifth of June of that same year I went to the Place des Etats-Unis to have lunch with Charles de Noailles in order to talk to him about Giacometti, as I was then just beginning my lengthy researches for the biography published fifteen years later. I found an old man, his head bent forward, fingers deformed, very wrinkled, with thin white hair. But the sense of overpowering distinction and impregnable politeness was as strong as ever. We ate alone in the dining room where I had so often eaten with Marie-Laure and ten or eleven others. It was surpassingly strange to be there without her. The viscount had interesting things to say about Alberto, and to my surprise he also spoke of Marie-Laure with respect and, I thought, some nostalgia. She would never again embarrass him, but maybe to his surprise he found life less lively without her. It was she, he said, who had initially wanted to collect contemporary art and who selected almost all of the paintings, he being from the first more interested in sculpture and objects and in the end caring only for gardens, of which he had created two, one in Fontainebleau, the other at Grasse. After lunch he allowed me to step into Marie-Laure's salon for a moment. It was unchanged but seemed to exist in a vacuum, unsettling and mournful, the stage upon which no performance would ever again take place. The viscount said that it was sad to see the room empty and that something important in Parisian life had come to an end with her death but he added that it had been time for her to go because her health had deteriorated seriously, and he was glad she had died quickly, as she was not a person who could easily have endured being an invalid. I agreed and said goodbye. I never saw the viscount again or ever afterward entered that house.

Ten years later on the twenty-ninth of January, the anniversary of Marie-Laure's death, I had lunch with two friends who had also been close to Marie-Laure. My idea was that we should afterward visit the Montparnasse Cemetery, find the Bischoffsheim mausoleum and leave some flowers there. I had expected that we would not be alone in remembering and commemorating this anniversary. After all, the viscount and both daughters were then still living. The day was bright and windy. To reach the cemetery was not easy, as there was a student demonstration in progress on the Boulevard du Montparnasse, and we had trouble driving through it. Marie-Laure would have liked that. At the flower shop near the cemetery entrance I bought a small white cyclamen. We had difficulty in finding the mausoleum. Above the portal were the names Paine-Bischoffsheim. Not a single floral tribute lay on the steps below. We were surprised, considering the hundreds of people who had enjoyed Marie-Laure's friendship, humor, intelligence and hospitality. Not to mention her family. The small pot of cyclamen blossoms looked pitifully inadequate on the granite step before the double doors. We peered through the glass panes. Inside on the left- and right-hand walls were plaques engraved with the names of those interred there, and between them an altar with a wooden crucifix, beneath it a pot of artificial violet flowers. We remained for a few minutes, then got into my car and drove away.

It seemed so hard to believe that nobody else in Paris should have paid tangible homage to Marie-Laure's memory ten years after her death that I visited the cemetery again two days later. Only my forlorn and solitary cyclamen stood on the step of the mausoleum. Already the blossoms had begun to wither.

La Mère Ubu

Twenty-two years have now gone by since Marie-Laure's death. Those who knew her still speak of her often, lament her loss and agree that nobody has taken her place. We think it sad that she might be forgotten. After all, she was much more interesting than the grandmother immortalized by "that bore Marcel." Alas, Marie-Laure, who so longed for fame, never encountered her Proust.

On June 25, 1992, I again visited the Montparnasse Cemetery. It seemed fitting to do so as I reached the end of this account dedicated to the memory of the friend who lay interred there. The afternoon was radiant, the air in the cemetery sweet and the walkways among the tombs deserted. I found the Paine-Bischoffsheim mausoleum at once. Its portal now stood open. The interior was grimy with dust and detritus. Heaps of brown, withered leaves had collected in corners. I went inside. Everything within bespoke abandon, neglect, indifference, forgetfulness, disrespect for the dignity due even in death to one's forebears.

Marie-Laure's descendants have been categorical in their refusal to make available her papers and journals to those who wish to memorialize her. I have been told—by persons who should know—that there has been some elimination of material deemed too scandalous. Well . . . even Byron's journal was burned. But one can't help reflecting that these selfsame descendants are living among treasures collected by her, are supported in luxury on the wealth bequeathed by her and, whether they like it or not, are regarded with an interest more lively than they would normally excite because of their connection with her.

I left the mausoleum and the cemetery with a weight in my chest but glad that *she* at least could not see what wanton lack of care prevailed in her final resting place. So the scandalous, embarrassing forebear was in perpetuity to suffer symbolic rejection. But then I recollected that the corpse of her famous ancestor, the Marquis de Sade, had been hurried into an unmarked grave, his remains exhumed without ceremony a few years later, whereupon a quack phrenologist made off with his skull, losing forever the receptacle of that extraordinary brain. The marquis had been far more embarrassing and scandalous than she was, his legacy to civilization far greater. But maybe, when all has been sifted and said, it may seem that in keeping with her character as his direct descendant Marie-Laure also merits the tribute of remembrance.

4

Errieta's Risk

[E R R I E T A   P E R D I K I D I]

Having traveled for a fortnight across the South of France and around northern Italy, searching fruitlessly for some peaceful place to spend the summer, Christian and I reached Trieste on June 30, 1959. Our idea then was to put the car aboard a ship and voyage comfortably to Athens, where I had a friend who could suggest some ideal spot in the islands. But the port of Trieste was paralyzed by a shipping strike, so we had to leave the car in the garage of the Grand Hotel and take the train, still then called the Orient Express, a hapless misnomer, as the trip from Trieste to Athens in conditions of tedious discomfort took sixty hours. I had sent a telegram to Aleca, and she was at the station with her ancient Citroën to meet us. The cool, sweet gardens of Ambelokipi, where her villa stood, were then virtually in the suburbs of the city, Athens not yet having become the swollen nightmare of urban ugliness and ruinous pollution it is today. All Greece, in fact, was still for a few more years to dwell in ecstatic tranquillity, unaware of the peril underlying its clean blue sea, golden shores and ancient traditions of hospitality. Then the tourist tidal wave did more damage in a decade than the Romans and Turks had done in two thousand years.

Aleca Diamandopoulos had been a considerable heroine of the resistance against the Nazi occupation and again during the subsequent civil war against fascist subversion, risking her life many times. Now she lived with her aged mother, a lover named Vico and a captious female cousin in the large but rather run-down villa with a fragrant garden. When I fell ill in Athens some years before, my friend John Craxton, the English painter, had asked Aleca to take me in so that I could recuperate in more comfortable and cordial surroundings than provided by my cheap hotel. I was treated as a member of the family. They were eccentric. And that is why I had not hesitated to telegraph Aleca, warning of my arrival with Christian. She insisted we stay at the villa and said at once that she knew of the most peaceful and beautiful spot in all the Grecian isles, of which she had visited the majority. If possible, she insisted, it was there, only there, that we must plan to spend our summer. She would send a telegram at once to learn whether accommodations were available.

Aleca played only a supporting role in the history of Errieta's risk, though characteristically the support was decisive and given during a time of danger. She told me parts of the story that Errieta would probably have been too modest to mention. As for Christian and me, and the friends who later followed us to the island, we played no role at all. We only listened.

Having said a word about Aleca, I might briefly do likewise for Christian Davillerd. We had met at a party in January, found each other attractive and became lovers soon after. He was employed in the fashion industry, was good-looking, well built, a few years younger than I, interested not at all in literature or art but companionable and imperturbably good-natured. Aged then about thirty, he gave no indication whatever that he would later succumb to uncontrollable alcoholism, recover eventually, endeavor without success to become a monk, devote himself for a time to the care of handicapped children, then one night walk into the sea never to return.

Aleca received a telegram telling her that we would be welcome. It came from the island of Skyros and was signed by Errieta Efstathiou. Aleca had become acquainted with her in the context of resistance to fascist elements during the civil war. Afterward she had several times visited Skyros, and Errieta's house there, in which rooms were for rent to the occasional visitor during the summer. This was the ideal spot Aleca had in mind for us. Trusting her advice, I asked her to send a telegram to say that we would arrive on July 11. She added that we would find the lady of the house an exceptionally gracious, friendly and interesting individual. How accurate was this judgment I only began to grasp as time did its work and I learned her story, which I want to try to save from oblivion.

Travel from Athens to Skyros in those days was not easy. The island lies in a group called the Northern Sporades set well out into

the sea beyond the northern coast of Euboea. It was necessary to leave
Athens early in the morning and cross the Attic plain in a slow, ramshackle bus that stopped at every village, no matter how humble, and
sometimes at mere crossroads. After several hours we reached the
narrow strait between the mainland and Euboea, had a most inadequate lunch and crossed to the town of Khalkis on an ancient ferry.
There we took another bus across the mountainous island on very
narrow, curvaceous roads, driven with maniac recklessness by a young
fellow who laughingly scorned the nervous protests of his passengers,
several of whom were sick. At last we reached the little port of Kimi,
where a good-sized ship was waiting to take us over to Skyros, forty
miles away across the choppy sea. Our first glimpse of the island was
not prepossessing, as the ship put in at the small port of Linaria, where
only a few houses, a store and a taverna stood along the rocky hillside.
Yet another bus, even more ramshackle than the first two, waited there
to take us about ten miles across the island to the town of Skyros. En
route we ran over a chicken, providing great merriment to most of the
passengers. The bus left us outside an ugly, brand-new hotel above
the beach. Our trip had lasted twelve hours.

The village of Skyros is built along the steep slope of a high hill,
its houses packed tightly together along narrow alleyways, all cubes in
shape and painted bright white. I always thought that village looked
like a Cubist glacier in permanently arrested motion on its high hillside.
At the summit stood a building that appeared once to have been a
fortress—there was a Lion of San Marco set into the stonework above
the entrance—but later got transformed into a monastery, where in
my time a few antique and disheveled monks still guarded some priceless icons and Byzantine ivories. Inquiry at the hotel told us that Mrs.
Efstathiou did not live in the town but farther along the beach. Her
house would be easy to find, as it stood back on a low bluff above the
beach just beyond the spot where a small stream ran down into the
sea. And the house was easily recognizable because it was built against
a round tower which in other times had been a windmill. It was only
a few hundred yards distant. We found our way down to the beach
and trudged along, lugging our suitcases, the fine white sand seeping
into our shoes. Luckily the stream was narrow enough for us to jump
across. Not far beyond it a rather steep path between oleander bushes
led up the bluff, which at that point must have been about eight or ten

meters above the level of the beach. And there before us stood the house of Mrs. Efstathiou. At first glance it did not appear to be the image of enchantment described by Aleca. L-shaped, with but a single story, a vine-covered pergola in front and the round tower, the former windmill, to the rear, it looked like many a modest house found by the seashore all around the Mediterranean. I felt disappointed. But there we were after a very tiring journey, so we would just have to make the best of it. That initial sense of disappointment, I think, may have been the very best introduction to Errieta and to Skyros, because it made for such a breathtaking contrast to all that followed.

From the house appeared a slender, slight, white-haired woman attired in a simple skirt and white shirt, advancing across the sand, hand outstretched, smiling amicably. This was Mrs. Efstathiou. She greeted us in faultless English, spoken with an accent of impeccable refinement. I was surprised. When I introduced Christian in French, she spoke to him in that language, though with less assurance than in English, which proved, in fact, to be virtually her mother tongue. All others, even Greek, she spoke with a slight English accent. She led us across the terrace beneath the wisteria-laden pergola and into the house. It was plain and unassuming but possessed an air, an atmosphere, a character that asserted deliberation and taste. The principal rooms were but three: a spacious, airy living room, a large bedroom at the front with windows overlooking the sea and a smaller bedroom with one window opening upon the dunes, also a bathroom and kitchen. Then there was the tower, which had been converted into three bedrooms, one on top of the other, with an outside staircase opening upon a wide terrace. The furnishings were of the simplest but, like the house, they had the strong character of their simplicity. It was evident that this was the residence of an individual with a decided view of proportion and harmony. In the living room were many books, a large but modern icon and an extraordinary embroidery of birds and beasts in a multicolored landscape.

Mrs. Efstathiou said that all the rooms were then available, though she expected other visitors later in the summer. We could have our choice. She herself during the summer slept on a couch in the living room, while her husband preferred to sleep outside on a cot beneath a stunted pine tree halfway between the house and the edge of the bluff. I selected for Christian and myself the large room with twin beds at the front of the house and asked also to reserve the smaller bedroom, in which to do my writing. The rental was modest. As for meals, we could have breakfast and lunch at the house but would have to take our dinners at the hotel, which had just opened, or at one of the small tavernas beyond it along the edge of the bluff. No electricity existed in the house, only oil lamps, although, oddly enough, there was electric wiring in all the rooms. Running water, both hot and cold, was plentiful. We went to sleep that night to the chiming of the waves.

Christian liked to spend his days in the sun and the sea, whereas a modicum of swimming was enough for me, and I wanted ample time both morning and afternoon for writing. When the words came with difficulty, which was often, I would sit on the terrace, gazing in a trance of enchantment across the peacock-blue sea toward the hazy fingertip of the island while blossoms from the wisteria vine occasionally fell around me and I very quickly understood why Aleca had described this spot as the most beautiful in all the islands. Our hostess, as we immediately came to consider her, often joined me. It was a pleasure to be able to speak my native language, and I felt that she shared it. We quickly became companionable, or even more than that, and used our first names as naturally as if we had had no other expectation from the beginning. I realized at once that she entirely understood my relation with Christian and saw nothing amiss in it. As for her husband, George Efstathiou, she rarely spoke of him at first. I met him that summer only once. He was very much younger than she, about forty, exceptionally handsome, but very withdrawn, I felt. Sometimes if I got up at daybreak to go to the bathroom I saw him asleep on his cot under the pine tree, his black hair blown backward by the dawn breeze, but he had always disappeared by breakfast time.

We were joined later that summer by two friends from Paris, Michel Richard, a diplomat and expert on French Protestantism, and his friend Jacques Cervione, a doctor and novelist. Lodged in the tower, they responded immediately, as I had, to the enchantment of the house and the island. Jacques had long been a member of the French Communist Party, though by this time had left it, but he remained deeply concerned with political events and was a committed idealist. He and Michel came to Skyros every summer that I did—there were only three—remaining, however, considerably less long, and maybe that is why they never grew to be as intimate with Errieta as I, that and a certain difficulty on her part in speaking fluent French. Still, Jacques in particular became very attached to her, and she to him. They had long conversations together, and it was from Jacques that I learned certain details of her story. I met Zaccharoula, too, of course, though I couldn't converse with her. But she communicated much without words, for she was an artist. Also during that summer a Greek painter named Manolis Calliyannis stayed for some weeks with his wife and two sons in the tower. He was a man of decided leftist political convictions, made acquaintances in the village and heard a lot about Errieta and George. I later saw something of him in Paris, and he contributed telling details to the story. And then during the summer of 1961, the last summer I spent on Skyros, we had the visit of Jenny and Julia Caracolos, cousins of Errieta, and while listening to their family talk I also learned a lot. By that time, to be sure, everything had gone wrong for Errieta and I already knew what was essential. In 1966, nonetheless, I made the acquaintance of a musician and Communist politician named Mikis Theodorakis, who had been very active during the civil war, imprisoned on Makronisos and tortured, and he described that period with understandable passion. My friend Michel Déon, the French novelist, spent four months in Skyros in 1965, living, in fact, in the house which had been Errieta's, and naturally became acquainted with George, learned a lot about him and about Errieta and repeated it to me. In his book *The Rendezvous of Patmos* he describes the stay on Skyros. In 1968 I met Vassilis Vassilikos, the novelist, and Michael Cacoyannis, the film director, both of whom added to my knowledge of the background. Still, it was Errieta herself who little by little told me most of what I want to try to preserve from the graveyard of forgetfulness. I can't say why she told me so much. The majority of it came during that last summer, when she could see that I was unhappy, and maybe that made it easier for her to confide in me. Needless to say, there is much that I would like to know that I don't know. At the time I recorded a great deal in my journal but one can never record everything, and regrettably there will be omissions here and there, missing links and speculative asides. For instance, I know nearly nothing about what happened to George during the battles in Albania and later against the Germans in Epirus, experiences which significantly affected his outlook and temperament. But I myself saw something of warfare in France and Germany. The faces of the dead and of their killers are not very different from one country to the next.

I spent about six months in all on Skyros. What I learned about Errieta did not come consecutively, but I shall try to tell her story chronologically, because in the sequential timing of episodes and experiences resides much of their meaning and emotion.

1

Aristides Perdikidi, Errieta's father, was one of the wealthiest Greeks of Smyrna, owner of the largest tannery in Asia Minor, employing hundreds, a family business dating from the early era of Phanariot influence. Errieta was the elder child, more than ten years older than her sister, Julia, the only other offspring. Her father, having hoped, of course, for a son, treated her somewhat as he would have treated a boy, allowing her, for example, to drive the tilbury and talking to her of affairs his wife said were "men's business." Myrtle Tanser, the English nanny from Cheltenham, said that Errieta would never be a proper young lady, as she was far too headstrong. But the young girl laughed. When the fruit trees were in bloom, they rode out in their landau to Bornova and sang snatches from Gilbert and Sullivan en route. Mrs. Perdikidi wore organdy and played excellent croquet. In the summer they sailed to England, went for picnics in the Lake Country and Errieta recited long passages of Wordsworth.

Then came World War I. Mr. Perdikidi said that the Young Turks were too cocky for their own good, had gone into the war on the wrong side and would pay a terrible price for their railroad. Colonel Lawrence presently came along to help prove him right. He was not worried. Smyrna, Homer's birthplace, had been predominantly Greek for twenty-five hundred years. Persians, Romans, Mongols, Crusaders had all come and gone. The Greeks remained. And after the war a Greek expeditionary force arrived to reclaim from the wreck of the Ottoman Empire the hegemony which had long ago been theirs. The Turks, humiliated and dispossessed, decided to fight back, but such fighting as there was took place far from the Perdikidis' croquet lawn and went well at first for the Greeks. Still, Mrs. Perdikidi worried and thought it might be wise to go for a time to England. Her husband and elder daughter said it would be dishonorable to flee at the slightest hint of trouble. But then Mr. Perdikidi came home one day from the Cercle Européen and said the news was bad. A terrible defeat had been inflicted on the Greeks about three hundred kilometers east of Smyrna, half their army slaughtered or taken prisoner, the rest in undisciplined retreat toward the coast, pillaging, butchering and burning as they fled. Refugees and wounded were already straggling into the city, bringing lurid tales of horror from the interior. Business ceased. Merchant ships in the harbor disappeared overnight, empty. British, French and Italian warships still serenely swung in the roadstead, but a Greek hospital ship had ominously been added to their number.

Mrs. Perdikidi implored her husband to leave. The servants had already disappeared. There was still time. They could find a way, drive south in the Daimler to Ephesus and hire a boat there to ferry them across to Samos. But Mr. Perdikidi could not contemplate the abandonment of everything his forebears had for generations labored to build. After all, Greeks and Turks had for centuries done business together on the Aegean shore. Could all this be undone in that pleasant September of 1922?

It soon became clear that it could. Overnight the straggle of refugees became a frantic horde, camping in the city streets around fires over which they had nothing to cook. Then the remnants of the Greek army arrived in headlong confusion, pouring without pause toward the harbor, where they went on newly arrived troopships, followed in craven haste by all the Greek civil servants and police. The populace was left at the mercy of war's fortunes.

The first Turks arrived on horseback, gaunt and fierce, waving their sabers, followed by lumbering lines of baggage camels. There was no fighting. Kemal entered Smyrna the following day, his car decked with olive branches. That seemed an auspicious sign. He issued a proclamation sentencing to death any Turkish soldier who harmed a noncombatant. Optimists thought that things might turn out safely, after all.

The first screams of "Fire!" came in early morning. A strong wind blew from outlying hillsides a billow of black, oily smoke. Mr. Perdikidi told his wife and two daughters that they had ten minutes to gather what they could carry and not to try to bring the silver. Their mansion stood on the boulevard that ran around the crescent perimeter of the bay. Between it and the water thousands of refugees had already been encamped for days. At the first cry of "Fire!" they began screaming hysterically and gesticulating toward the warships that still stood close at hand but which, flying neutral flags, remained agonizingly uncertain as a last hope. The crowd pressed frantically toward the jetty, hoping that boats would quickly put out to save them. The four Perdikidis, hugging a few satchels, were physically powerless to approach the water's edge. Held fast in the panic-stricken mass of people, they were compelled to halt forty or fifty meters from the jetty. This saved their lives.

By nightfall the entire city was ablaze. Along the waterfront the crowd grew denser and denser, the screams of terror louder, while from the English flagship not far away came as a catastrophic irony the lilting strains of light opera music played by the naval band. Sometime after midnight, when the hunger, the stench, the noise had long since become intolerable, the entire line of buildings along the waterfront erupted into flame with a volcanic boom. The crowd, screaming in terror, recoiled in an irresistible shock wave toward the quayside. Those closest to the edge were either trampled underfoot or driven into the water, where, exhausted, stunned by fear or by others falling on top of them, many drowned. The Perdikidis, clothing torn partly off and possessions wrenched away by the brute violence of the mob, were pressed to the very brink. But there by force of terror they managed to remain. Below them in the water were people screaming, thrashing and dying. The roar of flames was deafening but, above it, more piercing and dreadful, sounded the wailing of the trapped crowd. Now the fire stretched in fifty-meter flames for two kilometers along the waterfront, spreading faster and faster, houses and warehouses burning, shops, cafés, bazaars all burning, the burning rooftops collapsing and crashing inward, flinging aloft fiery whirlwinds of debris that were scattered, burning, along the quay and into the crowd, while the surface of the sea shone like flaming copper and even the impassive warships gleamed luridly in the firelight.

Toward dawn without warning boats suddenly put out from the warships and came to the quayside. Bluejackets leapt out, struggled to enforce order and began helping dazed survivors into their boats. The four Perdikidis, being so dangerously close to the edge of the jetty, were in one of the first. Behind them in the crowd began a wild stampede toward the boats. Men plunged into the water to swim. Women threw their children into already overcrowded boats. The sailors had to fight back the mob. But the Perdikidis' boat had already drawn away. As it moved outward, a young fellow with long mustaches gripped the rail and tried to haul himself aboard, tipping the craft dangerously, and one of the sailors hurried to push him back. Still, he struggled frantically, pleading to be let aboard. Then a white-haired man in a caftan squatting close by brought out a long knife and with a single violent stroke severed the youth's four left-hand fingers, which had been gripping the rail. He fell back, screaming, waving his mutilated hand, which spewed blood. The boat moved imperturbably onward. Mrs. Perdikidi fainted. Julia was sick. The white-haired man wiped his knife on the skirts of his caftan, put it away, then from the bottom of the boat one by one picked up and threw overboard the severed fingers. No one addressed to him a word of reproach.

In the smoke-dark dawn the Perdikidis lay among hundreds of others on the deck of the English flagship, the *Iron Duke*. Errieta never forgot the name. When it weighed anchor and steamed serenely from the magnificent harbor, they looked back at the charred walls, blackened domes and scorched minarets, the still-smoldering ruins of their native city, their home, and they knew that none of them would ever see it again.

Not wishing and not having to be numbered among the million or more refugees who eventually returned to Greece from that catastrophe known ever afterward as The Catastrophe, refugees returning penniless to a homeland where they were blamed for having failed to implement the Grand Idea of Panhellenic Sovereignty, the Perdikidis traveled to France. At Menton they took a small villa and waited for the shock of loss to be dissipated by time. There was enough money, at least, to live on in acceptable comfort, for Mr. Perdikidi had invested abroad. He was no longer himself, however. The doctor said that spring would set him right. It didn't, nor did the summer, and in November he almost imperceptibly ceased to live. The ladies went to England. Mrs. Perdikidi and Julia settled in a small cottage near a town in Kent called Tenterden. Errieta did not wish to resign herself at age twenty-seven to the uneventful tranquillity of life in the country. She took a bed-sitting room in Knightsbridge not far from the Victoria and Albert

Museum. She attended concerts, lectures, made some acquaintances and, being Greek, after all, sometimes wondered why she remained so far from that land, longing often to hear the melody of the Homeric sea. However, she was aware that Greece was troubled by violent political strife, coups d'état and countercoups, a struggle between liberal and reactionary elements. She thought of herself as a liberal, opposed to any kind of oppression or interference in the right of every individual to live as he wished. Among her acquaintances were a young Greek painter and his wife who felt even more strongly than she did about the elemental rights of the individual. They invited her to attend some meetings with them. When she did, she found that they were Communists, and that his father was a professor of political science at London University, a well-known adversary of political corruption in his homeland, from which he was a virtual exile. The painter and his wife were evidently in London to keep him company. In the late twenties it was easy, especially from a considerable distance, still to believe in the Communist ideal of disinterested devotion to the betterment of humankind. Errieta found herself in active sympathy with it, but she declined to join the Party. It was not in her temperament to be a joiner, and even less to accept the discipline of adherence to opinions or convictions dictated from above or from afar for reasons often obscure.

What she found impossible to forget was the sight of those four severed fingers being flung into the water. They seemed to symbolize the cruelty, the bestiality of which men were capable. The fire, the loss of their home, even the death of her father, all this she came to accept as melancholy evidence that her century was unlikely to be a peaceful one. But the severed fingers suggested something more terrible. They appeared in her dreams. Being Greek, perhaps, meant that a belief in omens was true to life. Errieta's hair had been jet black before that night. By dawn it was laced with streaks of gray. At first her mother had thought that these were ashes from the conflagration. But no. The change was permanent. It aged her.

She had never been beautiful. Thin rather than slender, with not much of a figure, a prominent, beaked nose, small mouth, wiry gray hair, she definitely did not embody the Grecian ideal of female allure. But her eyes, though protruding, were wonderfully blue, her smile was exquisite, her laughter, when it came, a perfect trill. What she had in abundance was charm, which outlives beauty, also intelligence and exceptional courage, which when fused with charm in the crucible of experience produces character of unusual strength. So she did not go unnoticed. Whether in those years before she first came to Skyros she had any romantic attachments I do not know. It seems likely, because she was not lacking in initiative when the decisive encounter occurred.

She traveled on the Continent, visiting France, Switzerland, Italy, Spain. She contemplated the masterpieces of art and architecture in those countries, read the great literature, attended concerts and operas and, in short, became a cosmopolitan lady of unusual cultivation. She thought often of visiting Greece but did not do so, as if some premonition told her that the time was not yet right. What premonition could conceivably have told her when the time might be right, in view of what was to come, lay beyond even the most oracular of Grecian prophecies.

But then in the spring of 1936, a period of inauspicious political turmoil not only in Greece but also in Spain and, even more ominously, to the north, Errieta's painter friend and his wife persuaded her to accompany them to Greece for the summer. Why she agreed after having waited for so long she didn't know. It was an impulse. Her mother disapproved, contending that conditions were unstable, worrisome, remarking also, when Errieta refused to be dissuaded, that Miss Tanser had been right: she was too headstrong for her own good. The three friends traveled by ship, a slow voyage in those days. They visited the principal sites of Greece's antique glory, even hiking up the mountainside from Andritsaina to see the lonely temple of Bassai. To spend the major part of the summer on the remote island of Skyros had been the idea of the painter and his wife, whose names were Phaedon and Clio. Someone had told them that the light there was particularly fine. They had to travel all the way from Piraeus by boat, a long, dirty, fatiguing trip. Coming round Cape Sounion, approaching the barren isle of Makronisos, Phaedon pointed to the mainland, and said that over there lay Laurium, where the silver mines which had produced the wealth—and glory—of ancient Athens had been worked under conditions of unspeakable brutality by twenty thousand slaves laboring naked on their bellies in the narrow tunnels. And was so much suffering, he said, redeemed by *The Republic*? Errieta told me that Phaedon had been especially given to asking questions which had no answers.

He had written to the mayor of Skyros of their desire to spend the summer on his island, asking whether a good-sized house near the shore might be available for rent. It was ready when they arrived, standing near the spot where the hotel would be built twenty years later. And there was a young girl from the village to keep house for them. The cost was negligible. They were made welcome by the mayor in person, a man of immense girth by the name of Spiro, who did not impress them as friendly despite protestations of eagerness to be of service. It appeared that there would be nothing to interfere with a summer's sojourn of uninterrupted tranquillity. In these years there were no tourists and very few travelers. Skyros, moreover, had no ruins, no hotels, no modern comforts and next to no history. Errieta and her friends confidently expected to be the only outsiders on the island that summer and were not unhappy at the prospect of being more or less cut off from news of the world beyond. Therefore they were both surprised and displeased to learn from the serving girl soon after their arrival that they were not the only "foreigners" present. A German and his wife had already been on the island for a month, occupying a large house in the center of the village. This unwelcome news aroused a determination to avoid making their acquaintance. But it is nearly impossible on a small island to preserve one's privacy, and the smaller the place, the greater is the curiosity of its inhabitants.

Errieta enjoyed strolling on the beach in the late afternoon. And there, of course, she was easy prey. The German had on a tropical helmet, a wrinkled linen suit, and carried a camera. He seemed to be pacing rather than walking across the sands. Without overt rudeness there was no avoiding him. He held out his hand and she had to shake it. His name: Reichel, and he made a little bow. She told him her name. Speaking excellent English, he made some remarks about the unexpected pleasure of meeting people from the outside world in such a remote spot. Errieta agreed and made as if to turn away. His manner was unattractive, like his appearance: fleshy, red-faced, perspiring. But he was persistent. He would be very pleased, he said, if she and her friends, the young artist and his wife, would come to his house one day for lunch. Decent food was difficult to come by on Skyros, but Frau Reichel did wonders with what was available. Errieta answered that she could not reply for her friends, would have to consult them, and perhaps in the event of some future meeting a time might be set.

She felt that this was short of outright refusal. The German declared that any day in the next month would suit him perfectly, that even if the artist and his wife were otherwise occupied he would be happy to have Mrs. Perdikidi by herself. Miss Perdikidi, said Errieta. Well then, said the German, he would send his servant girl the very next morning to learn what day would be convenient for her and, if they so wished, her friends. Whereupon with another bow he made off across the beach.

Errieta was not only annoyed by the Teutonic lack of tact but also at a loss to understand why the man should be so persistent. It seemed that he must have some ulterior motive, as if he wished to make the acquaintance of herself and her friends for reasons that had nothing to do with sociability. None of them had the least desire to accept his invitation. On the contrary. But Clio and Errieta felt that it might be simpler to accept a single invitation, to be formally polite but not in the least friendly, without the slightest intention of agreeing to a second visit or even repaying the first, and thus have done with the German promptly rather than allowing his overture to loom unpleasantly over the summer. Phaedon said he didn't like it, but he agreed. So when the young girl appeared in the morning to learn their answer, they said they would be pleased to come to lunch the very next day and learned from the messenger the location of their host's residence.

The village of Skyros, when Errieta first went there, was undoubtedly very much as it had been for a century or two, and probably little change had taken place when I arrived some twenty years later. The cobblestoned streets, so narrow in places that it was possible to touch the walls on either side in passing, seemed more like tortuous corridors than streets. The whitewashed houses were immaculately stark and clean, emphasizing the severity, beauty and modesty of the village. Doorways and windows often stood open, allowing one to look in at the small rooms, their elementary furniture and pristine walls decorated with icons and the occasional copper utensil. Women sat on their thresholds spinning coarse yarn on dangling spindles, darning or embroidering, all dressed in black with black shawls covering their heads. Young or old, these women appeared to accept their circumstances with a resourceful stamina which through generation after generation had but reinforced their servitude. Toward the center of the village the street widened. Here were a number of tavernas, stores, a barbershop and a post office, through the open door of which could be seen in

1936 the ubiquitous portrait of King George. Policemen in uniform
and unshaven islanders in their blue pantaloons sat smoking beneath
thatches of interwoven rushes before the tavernas, sipping occasionally
from minuscule cups or glasses. Not a single woman was to be seen
here. When Errieta and her friends passed, uncomplimentary remarks
certainly were made by the hidebound Skyriots.

Finding the German's house proved easy. It was larger than most
of the others. Again speaking English, he greeted his guests in a large
room with windows looking out to the sea far below. The furnishings
were simple: a plank table and benches of rough, unpainted wood and
a few of the low, carved chairs typical of the island. For the sake of
added convenience he was even then having a set of plain shelves
installed. And the carpenter was still at work, taking no notice of the
recent arrivals. Reichel complained about the quality of his work, observing nonetheless that it was cheap because the carpenter was very
young, inexperienced, and had poor tools. They talked about England,
Mrs. Simpson and the king, Reichel remarking that a country in which
such a situation could arise must be in poor political health. Still, he
did concede that it was remarkable for anyone to sacrifice so much for
love, remarkable but senseless. Errieta already regretted having come.
Phaedon said something about anti-Semitism and the remilitarization
of the Rhineland. Frau Reichel came from the kitchen and was introduced, a stocky, stern blond woman who spoke no language but German. The meal was ready. When they took their places at the table,
the carpenter ceased his pounding and sat down on the floor in a far
corner of the room, took out from his toolbox some bread and cheese
and a small flask of wine. The Reichels and their three guests served
themselves from a platter of excellent roast lamb and potatoes.

Errieta protested that it was not only embarrassing but indecent
for them to eat seated at the table and, moreover, to enjoy a fine meal
while the carpenter sat on the floor and had no food but bread and
cheese. Reichel apologized, saying that the awkward situation was
entirely the boy's fault. The carpenter had asked whether he could eat
in the corner and Reichel had agreed, never thinking that the presence
of a workman would prove offensive to his guests. But the awkwardness
could easily be remedied. He would tell the boy to take the rest of his
food out into the street and finish it there.

Errieta exclaimed that that would be intolerable. The carpenter should be asked to join them at the table and share their meal. She looked at him carefully and was surprised to observe that in addition to being very young he was extraordinarily handsome, indeed beautiful, though dirty and dressed in rags. Reichel replied that such a thing was out of the question, as workmen must know their place and it was no kindness to them to pretend that it could be otherwise. Phaedon said that if he were the carpenter he would definitely prefer to eat on the floor, and Errieta reflected that they had been fools to accept the invitation. But the usages of politeness kept them at the table until the meal was over. They stood up to leave quickly enough to suggest that they had not enjoyed themselves. By this time the carpenter had resumed his hammering, surely unaware of having caused discord between the German and his guests. On the threshold Reichel expressed the hope that they might all meet again soon. On such a small island it was likely, Errieta replied.

Phaedon was angry. The man was not only a swine but probably a Nazi, he said, and might turn out to be dangerous. His presence on the island seemed suspect. He had been here more than a month and was obviously planning to stay longer. Why? Errieta did not know and had no desire to find out. But it was she who had the opportunity to do so.

It was less than a week after the unpleasant lunch that she met the German again, once more on the beach, but this time had no chance to avoid him, as he appeared suddenly from behind a clump of bushes at the base of the bluff. She was the victim of her good manners, she thought. Reichel complained of the monotony of life on the island. Then she had the opportunity to ask him why he stayed on. He said that he was composing a thesis on Homeric themes, and that, as she undoubtedly knew, Ulysses had sent from Troy to Skyros for the son of Achilles, Neoptolene. It was a minor detail, but the very monotony of the island was conducive to concentrated literary work. Errieta felt dubious as to the truth of this story, having noticed the absence of any books in Reichel's house. Perhaps that was why he needed shelves. And the Homeric reference was too trifling to be convincing. Not that she cared two straws one way or the other. It was no surprise, however, when he asked whether she and her friends would once more accept an invitation to lunch. On the verge of refusing she had an idea. It was doubtless a foolish idea but the element of poetic justice made it seem irresistible. She asked whether the carpenter was still at work. Yes, said Reichel, because he was very slow, being inexperienced and provided only with the crudest tools. But he had the advantage of being cheap, if she needed any work done. Well, she said, her friends were now too occupied with their daily routine to go out for lunch. She, on the other hand, would be pleased to come. He was delighted. And she was sure, she added, that he would be equally pleased to fall in with a lady's whim. Oh, of course. Then would he be ever so kind as to invite the carpenter to sit at the table with them and share their meal? The German went even redder in the face than usual. What she requested, he said, was contrary not only to custom but also to common sense. Errieta replied that neither common sense nor custom had ever been among her strong points, whereas ordinary human decency was a vital issue for her. If he did not deign to grant her request, then she would be most regretful. The polite implication of duress was plain. Reichel didn't like it. They would have to speak Greek, he said. Good practice for them both. Very well, Reichel reluctantly agreed, the carpenter would have his meal with them, but he saw no good coming of it. Errieta pronounced herself delighted, agreed to appear two days later and felt that she had achieved a little victory for human betterment.

Her friends said that it was absurd, agreeing with the obnoxious German that no good was likely to come of her whim, and predicted that she'd regret it. She laughed and said she'd take the risk. When they insisted on her lack of judgment she tartly replied that she would keep her appointment, and that was that.

The carpenter had obviously been informed of the unprecedented break with custom, because as soon as Errieta was led into the room he put down his tools and turned to face her. There was no knowing what the German had told him. He came forward, tall, his face impassive under the thicket of dirty black hair, eyes lowered, silent. Reichel made the introduction. George Efstathiou, Miss Perdikidi. It was up to her to establish some social ease. Smiling, she held out her hand to him. After a moment's hesitation, he very briefly touched her fingers with his. She saw a livid cut on the back of his hand and mentioned it. He blushed, saying something to the effect that cuts come before skill, and looked away. She responded with some casual banality. He lowered his heavy lashes sullenly and did not reply.

It appeared that the meeting was unlikely to be a success, which must have pleased the host, who talked to Errieta about Europe and topics of which the carpenter could know nothing. She had to answer and felt like a fool, thinking Phaedon had undoubtedly been right and that Reichel must see her discomfort. What made things worse was the probable assumption of the young man that he had been drawn into a situation in which he as a person was irrelevant, thus ridiculous.

The shelves were almost finished. Heavy and rough, yet they suited the austere room. Errieta admired them, passing her fingertips along the planks. The carpenter may have been pleased, for he said that he could have done better but had only the poor tools which had been his father's.

Then it was time for the meal. Once again roast lamb and potatoes. George ate with noisy haste, using knife and fork only incidentally to help his fingers, gulped wine and paid not the least attention to his companions. He was evidently very hungry, and in fact didn't look well fed. But proud. And for the first time Errieta had an opportunity to observe closely his remarkable physical beauty. It was like a gleam that came from him despite the dirt and the wretched clothes. He appeared to be utterly unaware of it. Then to her surprise she found that she was deeply touched by this youthful perfection, which seemed to reach her awareness like music, with a vibrant conviction of some promise that heretofore she had never known. So she felt that there was nothing to regret, after all. She and the carpenter would never share an understanding, but she felt that her principles had been vindicated. When he happened to glance at her, she smiled; then he looked away immediately, scowling. The meal lasted longer than she would have liked, because the boy was so hungry. When it was finished, she hurriedly said goodbye and did not offer to shake hands, trusting thus to make it clear that this visit was her last.

It had been a fiasco, she acknowledged to her friends, and indeed she had ventured along the road paved with good intentions. But no harm would come of it. And they all had a good laugh at her expense.

At some little distance along the beach snaked a small stream which by its apparently perennial irrigation nurtured a sort of oasis on that low-lying, rather barren end of the island. Back from the shore stood a few poplars, fig, mulberry and pine trees, trailing vines and close to the sands a high stand of rushes. This watercourse clearly filled a larger bed in winter and above its high mark a track of beaten earth led down to the beach. Boys leading goats or donkeys sometimes passed along it. This was the way Errieta now took to begin her afternoon stroll, safe there, she thought, from the odious German.

On the far side of the stream up a sandbank stood an abandoned mill, round, white, bereft of arms, with a conical roof. Errieta looked up at it daily. Its abandonment seemed to beckon and offer some intimation of romantic eventuality, but for the time being she felt no desire to approach more closely.

From afternoon to afternoon, she had noticed, the configuration of the water's edge could be strikingly different according to the varied action of the surf, one day flat, the next angularly humped. Banal as she knew it to be, this observation delighted her, for it seemed to draw her closer to the life of the island. At its northeasternmost extremity, the beach turned backward and swept on in another tawny arc for more than a kilometer.

She sat down on the sand. It was near sunset. Over across the bay Mount Dhafni was drawing up purple shadows from the sea. The personal aura of the island had begun to surprise her, for she kept meeting in herself reminders of other places she had loved—Smyrna, Menton, London—and now half forgotten. She lit a cigarette. From a distance she recognized the young man by his defiant, rolling stride across the sand, though she had never seen him before out of doors. As he came closer, his face dark and lowered toward his bare feet, it was obvious he would not speak to her. She was astonished but amused to recognize that she felt a little intimidated, not a familiar feeling, and for that very reason she called out as he passed, "Good evening." He only sullenly nodded. "A very fine evening," she added.

Then he did reply, saying that she had better return home, as the dark came very quickly.

She offered him a cigarette. To accept it he had to come close to her, blushing as he took the cigarette and packet of matches. She was conscious of his resentment, and it touched her. He had some trouble lighting his cigarette in the breeze, so she told him to sit down. He refused. Surprised, she asked why. For her honor, he said. She laughed. If people saw them sitting here alone in the dusk, he said, her honor would be lost and she would never be able to find a husband. But how, she asked, did he know she was not already married? The German

181

had told him, he said. Then had he never found himself alone like this, she inquired, with a woman? Never, he said. In Skyros in those days it was unthinkable for an unmarried man and an unmarried woman to find themselves alone together. The woman would thereafter always be considered dishonored.

So she insisted that he sit beside her, and she lit his cigarette. He was ill at ease. The advantage was hers, but she could not make anything of it, for his physical self and his beauty stood between them. She asked him about his work. She could feel his suspicion but he said that it was difficult, as his father had died before being able to teach him much, leaving only inferior tools. The only other carpenter on the island was an old man, and soon he would be left alone to do more than he was able to. His situation was unjust. He flung away the half-smoked cigarette. But he could not say what he felt. His resentment was too keen.

Errieta was taken aback. She sensed something akin to eloquence in his anger and bitterness. She heard his fingers digging in the sand beside her, and suddenly the boy's physical nearness was like an amazement, a fever of awareness. When she spoke to me of this much later, she did not use those terms, but the meaning was clear. She asked whether he spoke of his feelings with anyone in the village. Never, he said. There had been a schoolteacher named Stelio in whom he was able to confide, whose friendship he could count on, but this man had been transferred two years before to Volos on the mainland. Both his parents were dead, and he had been an only child. Besides, nobody would care what he thought. He was poor.

Poverty need not be decisive, she said. Beliefs, convictions, thoughts were important.

Thoughts would never change old tools into new ones, he exclaimed.

To be sure, she said, thoughts were not material property but they were a commodity for which people would pay. And sometimes the price could be high. What she meant to say, she added, was that she would gladly buy new tools for him.

He angrily flung a handful of sand away from him in the twilight and said that when he had new tools, they would be bought by his work, not come from a foreigner who felt pity because he was poor.

Errieta said, "Neither is poverty a bar, but a man may benefit his country whatever be the obscurity of his condition." She asked whether he had heard that statement before.

He sullenly replied that he had. The schoolteacher had taught him Pericles' Funeral Oration.

So she added, "There is no exclusiveness in our public life, and in our private intercourse we are not suspicious of one another, nor angry with our neighbor if he does what he likes; we do not put on sour looks at him which, though harmless, are not pleasant." Were not those words good guides to conduct even today?

Words! Words! They pay for nothing, he said, adding that he did not need new tools so badly that he must lie down in his poverty like a dog at the feet of a foreign woman.

She told him that he spoke like a silly boy. The pride of poverty was simply ignorance and prejudice. Perhaps she had been a fool, but he was a coward.

He leapt up. He would not listen to her. His answer to her offer was his contempt. Then he ran off across the sand along the edge of the water until his wild figure was lost in the oncoming dusk. Walking back to her house and her friends, Errieta was pensive. In this primitive place here was an exception. How exceptional an exception only experience could tell. But it seemed that his remarkable beauty had made his character remarkable, and she realized not only that she was moved but also that she wished to know more. This was troubling. His youth, his solitude, his suffering were not the only aspects of his being that had impressed her.

The following afternoon when she came to the beach she did not see him. This was no surprise. She accepted her foolishness. Like the aftermath of a childhood prank, awkward as a bruise but endearing. She lit a cigarette and expected nothing, after all. But her expectancy was quick as light when she heard the sigh of footsteps in the sand behind her. She did not turn. He stood beside her. After a moment she asked whether he had changed his mind. He tossed his head, the Greek gesture meaning no. Then why had he come? she inquired.

To tell her he would not tolerate being called a coward.

She imagined he might have changed his mind, she said, about the tools. She touched the sand beside her, but he waited a minute before sitting down, hugging his knees with both arms and frowning. She thought it was absurd, because in truth he was only a boy. Eighteen, perhaps, no more, and she a good twenty years older. She told him that she was not offering him tools but an opportunity, something, she said, that might make a difference to his life. She held up a single grain of sand. Even something as small as that might make all the difference in the world, she said, if placed in precisely the right position. Did he not wish to make something of his life?

Yes, he said. The schoolteacher had often talked of this to him. He wanted his life to have the shape of a handful of fresh earth when pressed so tight that it took the shape of the hand, then you could see the force of your life in the form of the earth, and things might grow from it.

Errieta was startled. So he would accept the new tools, she said.

He bent his head to signify assent, and then looked around at her and smiled and said she must have known that he would agree.

No, she said. She had thought he was too proud. But she was thankful he also possessed common sense. And as if to say something more she placed her hand on his arm. Then before she sensed the mistake he had roughly kissed her.

Whether it was immediately that they became lovers or only in the succeeding afternoons I never learned. Errieta was unusually candid about her life and herself, but there were realms of intimacy naturally skirted. Besides, the time of the start of their intimacy is irrelevant. What was important was that it began. Equally important, no doubt, was their indifference to the opinion of others and to the eventualities of the future. Indeed, probably neither of them paused to ponder the momentum or meaning of what was happening. It would assert itself in its own way and time.

The storekeeper in the village was a man called Nikos. It was from him that the new tools would have to be ordered. He was a brutal, tightfisted man, concerned with profit at any price, who had refused credit to George's parents when they were close to starvation, and he would guess where the money for the tools had come from. The German also would guess. The village would know. It would be deemed dishonorable, be called a scandal. Errieta said that Pericles would never have accepted such a definition of dishonor. There would be a new Greece one day; the old prejudices would die. The schoolteacher, Stelio, also believed this, George said, and he had gathered a small group of men in the village who shared his beliefs, and it was for this reason that the mayor, a treacherous pig, had had Stelio transferred to Volos. Errieta said she would be pleased to make the acquaintance of these men. That would not be easy, as she was a woman, but George promised to see to it.

Beyond the far point, where more distant beaches stretched cleanly onward for kilometers, there were a number of huge, truncated outcroppings of rock which in antiquity, he explained, had been quarried to fortify the Kastro, the buildings at the summit of the village. In the lee of these rocks the water was calm. Errieta proposed that they bathe here. He was reluctant. They had no bathing attire. She made fun of his modesty. So in the late afternoon they confidently bathed naked in that remote spot where no one from the village ever ventured.

Her friends observed the change in her and made tactful inquiry. But she put them off, maintaining that the transformation they observed was due to the peace and beauty of the island. It so delighted her, she said, that she had been thinking of buying something here, perhaps the abandoned mill that stood up on the bluff beyond the stream. Several times recently she had clambered up there to visit it. Inside among the high rafters and Piranesi shadows of tumbledown machinery a few shafts of sunlight fell upon the immense millstones in their sheen of dust. In front of the mill a level sand plot stretched some fifty meters as far as the brink of the bluff. She stood there often, gazing at the outflung end of the island, lying like a giant's arm or the silhouette of some prehistoric monster upon the horizon, while the rippling bay continually changed its hue.

One afternoon while Errieta was absent, the painter and his wife received an unexpected visit. It was the mayor, Spiro, who had ridden down from the village on his donkey. He apologized for having come without an invitation but insisted that his intrusion was motivated by the best of intentions. Phaedon and Clio reluctantly made him welcome, offering a glass of wine. There was some banal preliminary talk about the beauty of the island and the cordial reception accorded by the islanders to outsiders. Well, that brought the mayor to his point. The island was not accustomed to the ways of the outside world, with which it had little contact, being without radio or electricity, receiving only occasional newspapers by the weekly boat. Therefore it might happen that a foreigner could transgress island customs and should take heed not to go too far. The man had obviously come to deliver some kind of admonition. Phaedon asked him to say what it concerned and be done. "Fornication!" exclaimed the corpulent official. What nonsense, said Phaedon, demanding an explanation. Spiro was only too pleased to oblige. He spoke of Miss Perdikidi. Both Phaedon and Clio exclaimed indignantly. Yes, of Miss Perdikidi, seen fornicating on the far beach by Kostandi, the boy who herded his goats. He had been beaten severely to make sure he spoke the truth, then beaten again so he would not tell all the village. But people would find out, and things would go badly, especially as she was a foreigner. Others like her had been content to live in Turkey till the Turks would have no more of them, and then they suddenly remembered they were Greeks, when no true Greek could ever forget what was suffered for centuries from the Turks. Skyros was not a place that tolerated lechery.

Phaedon demanded to know who was the man if this accusation was true.

Efstathiou, the carpenter boy. And what made it worse was that this foreign woman, old enough to be his mother, paid him for his favors. He had only recently ordered from Nikos, the storekeeper, and paid cash money for a complete new set of carpentry tools, the finest tools money could buy and such tools as he might never in his life have been able to afford. Miss Perdikidi paid well, but the boy was very handsome, of course, and very young. He was known to have questionable associations, however. The former schoolteacher and a few others were thought to have dangerous ideas.

Then what, Phaedon inquired, in addition to disclosing indiscreet gossip, would have been the purpose of the mayor's visit?

Friendly advice, he said. It would be in the best interests of the foreign woman and of the island were she to leave Skyros without delay. This was not an official order, he added, but the courteous advice of one who had at heart the best interests of all concerned.

In that event, said Phaedon, nothing remained but to thank the mayor for his consideration.

When he had gone, Errieta's friends didn't know what to say. Their regard for her was such that it can never have occurred to them to question her motives or intentions, and now they understood the change they had observed. What troubled them most was to decide whether or not they should tell her of the mayor's visit and warning. They realized that Skyros was a backward, brutal place and could be dangerous. But they decided all the same to keep silent, feeling that Errieta was principled enough to determine right conduct for herself. So she did not learn of the threat till later. But the knowledge came all too soon, and with it awareness of the danger.

From the first Errieta had taken upon herself the chore of walking up to the village two or three times a week in midmorning to fetch the mail. This would have been a pleasant though sometimes fruitless errand but for the surly discourtesy of the man who presided over the post office. Behind its jerry-built counter he eyed Errieta with insolent sloth at each visit, obliging her to spell out her own name as well as Phaedon's every time, and demanding to see the identity papers of the recipient if there were any letters, which he always tossed rudely onto the counter. She at first attributed this gross behavior to the natural arrogance of petty people in positions of trivial authority, took no notice of it and treated the man with patient courtesy. She smiled, spoke of the weather, asked obvious questions about Skyros, lingered in the post office longer than necessary. To no avail. The sullen, slovenly post-master took stock of her with swarthy disdain and responded, if at all, as rudely as ever.

Then one day she forgot to bring the essential identity papers, and it happened that there were two letters, one for Phaedon, the other for herself. The postmaster curtly refused to hand them over without being shown the usual documents. Those were the regulations. Errieta pro-tested that he had seen the papers a dozen times and knew perfectly well who she and Phaedon were. The postmaster laughed and said that he knew not only who she was but *what* she was. Skyros had seen the likes of her before, he said, foreigners who came to the island to buy pleasure. Just two years before, a yacht had come with two or three Englishmen, and they had had half the young fellows of the island to straddle them for money, then sailed away. Just like her with the carpenter she paid for her pleasure. He laughed again and flung her letters onto the floor.

Aghast with mortification and rage, Errieta stooped to pick up the letters. Not knowing what to say, she said nothing, turned to go and found herself face to face with the very last person on the island she would have liked to see: Herr Reichel. He bowed, murmured a greet-ing, but she strode by him without a word.

The letters had caused her humiliation, but the news they brought was worse. Early in August, with the collusion of the king, an army general called Metaxas had brought off a coup d'état, suspended the constitution, abolished civil rights and assumed dictatorial powers. Phaedon's father warned that the situation could become dangerous for people with political convictions such as theirs. It might be wise for him and his wife to return to England. Errieta said she would miss them. They were surprised. Would she not travel back with them? No. She thought she might stay on here indefinitely. They asked what could induce her to do so, though they knew. She was diffident, but they were her friends, so she told them everything. As yet she had not spoken to George of marriage. The suggestion, she knew, would have to come from her. It would not be easy.

Meanwhile, she had made the acquaintance of three young men who, like George, had been favored students of the schoolteacher Stelio. Their meeting had taken place after dark in a small, poor house on the far side of the hill, and in addition to the clandestine atmosphere there was at first an air of caution, if not of outright mistrust, which Errieta naturally assumed to be due to the fact that she was a woman and in their view a foreigner. George must have stoutly vouched for her. Still, she possessed the convincing authority of her age, her fortune and her experience of the world, while the four young men, hardly more than boys, had never left Skyros. They spoke of conditions on the island, its backwardness, stolid resistance to change, inequality, poverty and ignorance. They aspired to work for a modern, just and prosperous Skyros. Errieta advised them to keep their opinions to themselves and not rashly to expect, or even endeavor to bring about, any improvement in conditions in Skyros till radical change of the political situation in all Greece should one day yield more liberal social legislation. She didn't say so, but she thought that George and his friends were dreamers and might make serious trouble for themselves. She admired their dream, however, and told them that they were men of honor. She had a premonition of danger. Her own convictions were entirely in sympathy with the young men, and yet she felt that they and their island might have been better off without their dream. But she was herself a committed and resourceful idealist. And Skyros had now become the focus of her own dream.

What George's thoughts and feelings must have been during those last weeks of summer can only be guessed at. He could hardly have been expected to ask himself rational questions concerning the future and come up with logical answers. He was young, callow, inexperienced but by nature passionate almost to the point of madness, proud and daring. Nearly destitute, living in one room with one chair, one bed, one oil lamp, he had been among the lowliest of Skyriots, destined by the hierarchy of the island to remain so forever, his beauty worth not a drachma when it came time to acquire a wife. But then Errieta had appeared out of the blue. He knew she was not beautiful, was old, was foreign, and that their relationship would be deemed dishonorable by everyone. But in the context of his feelings none of that can have made an instant's difference. He was certainly happy. Probably he was frightened, too, and ashamed. Errieta seemed to offer him the prospect of a personal fulfillment he never could have anticipated before, because she believed in him. What it was she believed in he didn't know, but her belief became his glory. And then it must have seemed that, after all, he need not be too fearful or humiliated, because Errieta had known the great world and whatever it was that she saw in him was his priceless gift to her. So he could seem to walk on wings like the ancient god, guide of souls.

Errieta's friends wondered how George might adapt himself to life in the world beyond Skyros. For him, she said, there was no such world. His home was here. Here he would have to prove himself and make his life. But this island was not home to her, they said. Here she would never be accepted save by him. She, who had been accustomed to Covent Garden, the National Gallery, the reading room of the British Museum, to the rue de Rivoli and the Spanish Steps, she could not make this obscure, remote, benighted little island her home, could she? Errieta said that they must not forget that she was Greek, that she had been born beside the sea and could make her home wherever it pleased her heart to reside. Besides, having already loved London, Paris and Rome, how could she not love the home beloved by the one who pleased her heart? Phaedon said that she was a dangerous romantic.

The proposal had to come gently from her, allowing him at the same time the indispensable assumption that, because he was a man, he was her superior, possessing the power, acumen and fortitude to determine in all matters what would be best for them both. This cannot have been easy. The measure of Errieta's perspicacity and worldly wisdom was that she succeeded. Words of love certainly must have been exchanged, and little did it matter whether the emotions corresponding to these words were on one side or the other altogether equivalent. In love affairs they rarely are. What mattered was the pledge to the future, a future as indeterminate and unreliable as life itself. And consequently they agreed to be married. It was obvious to everyone that this ceremony and attendant arrangements could not possibly take place in Skyros. If the affair was a scandal, the marriage would constitute an outrage. Already George had been jeered at by youths in the village, while older men disdainfully turned away their faces.

The new tools, however, had in due course arrived from Athens, and now George was without competition as the most skilled carpenter in Skyros. Where good value was concerned considerations of virtue could be set aside. He worked hard, was shrewd enough not yet to ask too much money and cared not two straws for the hypocritical esteem of the mayor, the storekeeper or the postmaster. Knowing that he was young and that a miracle of money and devotion had been lavished upon him, he saw that he could afford to wait with confidence for the fullness of life. And never for an instant did it occur to him that this should be found anywhere but on the island of Skyros.

If the village would neither welcome nor accept Errieta, she had no desire to make herself amiable to the village or impose her presence upon it. She would dwell apart, fearing neither isolation nor solitude. She consulted George, and he, having himself very little for which to thank the village, gladly agreed to have his home at some distance from it. This saved his life, which is to say that Errieta saved it, though they were for the time being blissfully unaware of a risk. It was she who chose the spot which would become their home: the ruined mill beyond the stream and set back from the bluff. She would buy the mill—not in her name, of course, as all property must belong to the husband—and they would build a house around it, a spacious, pleasant dwelling with large rooms and high ceilings and windows facing toward the sea. The mill, as it turned out, belonged to an aged widow in the village, who was only too happy to exchange it for a modest amount of ready money. George, Errieta and her friends made plans and set out stones in neat lines around the mill to mark the locations of the rooms. That the husband-to-be, and owner, was a carpenter would make much simpler the building of his home, and his elation, he being still very boyish, was a joy to Errieta. Much equipment and material would have to be shipped from Athens, of course, for the house was to be provided with modern plumbing, heating, a bathroom, the comforts taken for granted in the outside world. They would even install electrical wiring, sockets and lighting fixtures, though no electricity existed as yet in Skyros. But it would come someday, Errieta said, and they would want to be ready. Skyros could not remain forever mired in the backward and reactionary ways of the past. It all seemed very simple and happy then. George was surprised and pleased by the competent, self-confident and yet modest manner in which his bride-to-be made decisions.

But they were not to be altogether alone in this part of the island. During her rambles Errieta had noticed a small house some distance farther upstream from the beach, hidden among fig trees, vines and an amazing profusion of flowers. This was only the home of old Zaccharoula, George explained, a woman who had had troubles in the past, now lived there alone and was said not to be right in the head. She was seldom seen in the village, avoided contact with others and would be no bother to them. Errieta thought it might be agreeable—and very likely useful—to have at least one neighbor, especially, perhaps, one considered a lunatic by the village, and she was curious about the nature of the past troubles. Without ever having seen her she welcomed Zaccharoula into the prospective company of her friends.

The date of their departure for Athens did not seem to be pressing. The weather was still fine. They went bathing every day and ate lobsters in the little taverna at the foot of the path leading up to the village. But one morning they learned that prudence dictated their leaving the island as promptly as possible. And this advice came from the person whose concern for their well-being they would least have liked to welcome or trust, the one to whom nonetheless they owed incommensurable gratitude, which made the matter but more galling. It was Herr Reichel, the German pacer of the beaches, who came to their rented house and knocked on the open door. Why was he still in Skyros? Errieta wondered. She always suspected him of being a spy, someone sent by the Nazis to scout the place in case of future hostile necessity. But she never knew, and it was true that he did warn them. After a few phrases of conventional politesse he ventured to say that they were probably uninformed of certain political realities which it would be prudent to heed. Phaedon immediately took offense, mentioned Spain and the despicable assistance provided there by Germany and Italy to the fascist forces. Reichel shrugged and observed that he had obviously been correct in assuming that his interlocutor was the son of a well-known exile revolutionary who in London made seditious declarations to the press. To which the young man rashly replied that, indeed, such was his honor. The German answered with excessive courtesy that the fact would have better been kept secret but was known in the village and that, whether they were aware of it or not, men suspected of Communist sympathies were being arrested throughout the country and deported to arid prison islands. It was this information, which as one man of conscience to another, no matter what their political opinions, he had felt bound to convey. Regarding their personal attitudes, these were temporarily irrelevant. Whereupon he performed a stiff bow, did not offer to shake hands, turned with military precision upon his heel and departed. None of them ever saw him again or learned what had become of him.

To leave Skyros in a hurry was not easy. They would have to find donkeys, a boat secure enough to take them to the Piraeus, more than two hundred kilometers distant, a couple of boatmen, sufficient food, water, fuel. George knew the man for the boat. An excess of money took care of the rest. Forty-eight hours after Reichel's visit, George Efstathiou left his home for the first time. Looking back at the island as he had never seen it before, silhouetted against the vibrant horizon, he must have felt an extraordinary exaltation, going as he was to confront the great world, to be wed and then discover himself a man of substance. At the same time, though, he cannot have helped feeling that he was running away, and this would undoubtedly have troubled him. To be considered a coward was what would have seemed most intolerable to a Greek of his background and generation. Phaedon was certainly not so naïve and knew that, depending on tactical conditions, strategic retreat may require as much courage as frontal assault. He was doubtless more worried about Errieta than about himself. He knew of the clandestine meetings with George's young friends, who might be very dangerous because they were surely hotheaded and ignorant.

As for Errieta, she cannot have failed to realize as the boat pitched and splashed toward the open sea that this was the definitive moment toward which all the events, the emotions, the decisions and desires of the past months had ineluctably been leading. Now there could be no turning back, no afterthought, no regret. Not that there was the least likelihood of any reservation. That would have been altogether contrary to her character. She saw things as they were, and perhaps she perceived an element of folly, or madness, in her conduct. But that would not have intimidated or restrained her. Nothing had frightened her since that other boat ride, fleeing from the burning city of her birth, when a man's severed fingers were one by one tossed overboard. No. She saw herself as an ugly woman of middle age in love with a youth of passionate integrity and incomparable beauty. And she surely asked herself elemental questions, though she was too wise to expect conclusive answers. The course upon which she had embarked she would now have to see through to the end, and only a fool could have fancied that this might not entail a serious risk. But she was also wise enough to know that those unprepared to take great risks have very little in life worth risking. Consequently it would have been with a thrilling sense of fitness that she looked forward to the eventualities of the future.

2

Athens was a nervous town in the autumn of 1936. General Metaxas had made it painfully plain that his dictatorship was no laughing matter. Those who opposed him were summarily dealt with, and the opposition was assumed to consist principally of Communists or any with Communist sympathies. Arrests were frequent, indiscriminate and arbitrary, anonymous denunciations abundant, while taverna waiters, street vendors, tramway conductors, even beggars were all presumed to be informers. Maniadakes, the chief of police, was reputed to be a man of infamous brutality, prone to punishment without due process of any kind. Those suspected of Communist connections were required to sign a statement of recantation. Any who refused, and many upon whom suspicion merely appeared to weigh, were deported to prison islands, where their treatment was said to be harsh. And just in case there might be any misunderstanding as to the spirit of the regime there was a restaurant in Patission Street where loud martial music played constantly, swastika banners adorned the walls and opposite the entrance hung a huge photograph of Adolf Hitler.

Phaedon had friends ready to run the risk of hiding him temporarily. They could not know whether the police in Skyros had sent word
of his presence to the authorities in Athens. In any case, he was determined to leave Greece immediately after Errieta's wedding, travel
as rapidly as possible to Spain and join the forces fighting fascism
there. His wife despaired but did not attempt to dissuade him. George
was astonished. It didn't seem natural, or even comprehensible, to him
that a man, and a Greek, moreover, should go so far to fight for a
country not his homeland. Errieta tried to explain the idealistic motive,
but George said that it was contrary to common sense.

The marriage took place at the Church of St. Pantaleimon, an
ugly, huge, obvious place for that ceremony, which Errieta despite the
reverence she felt for its purpose could not help considering a conces-
sion to bourgeois convention. What was sublime in the symbolic union
of two beings, she felt, could not be consecrated by orthodox ritual.
But she realized that it would be capital for George. He wore a black
suit, the first he had ever owned, purchased the day before in Hermes
Street, while she had on a plain white frock. They stood side by side
before the priest, wearing on their heads crowns of jasmine blossoms
attached by a white ribbon. The only guests present were Phaedon,
Clio and a few friends of theirs, not ten in all, one of them an energetic
and good-humored woman named Aleca Diamandopoulos. Afterward
they went to the Hotel Grande Bretagne, had a fine meal and drank
several bottles of champagne. And the next morning they drove in taxis
to the Piraeus to say goodbye to Phaedon and Clio, who got on board
a ship bound for Marseilles, whence Phaedon alone would make his
way to Barcelona. Mrs. Diamandopoulos invited the newlyweds to have
lunch at her villa, where they drank a light white wine from Patras
and endeavored—with some success—to look with optimism toward
the future.

Errieta had been pleased but not surprised by the ease with which
George adapted himself to the new and strange. The modern world
had happened to him all at once, the electricity, automobiles, elevators,
radios, telephones, and he reveled in the discoveries. Also he was awed
by the remaining splendor of his country's glorious past, the Acropolis
and Parthenon, the golden marvels from Mycenae, the marble likenesses of long-dead heroes and triumphant athletes. There came, it
seemed, almost overnight a new and stronger gleam to his youthful

beauty. Errieta was not so foolish as to imagine that this was due entirely to his new status as a married man, but it must have had something to do with it. A few days after the ceremony they sat down together at the table in their hotel bedroom and she explained to him in detail her financial situation, making it clear, as she knew he would expect, that all of her resources were now equally his and that he might make independent decisions as to their expenditure. And a good deal must now be spent to purchase the necessary fittings for their new home.

It had been with some hesitation that Errieta had written to her mother and sister of her marital intentions, a letter posted, in fact, on the eve of the ceremony. Consistent with her character, she had been entirely candid, concealing nothing of George's origins, circumstances and age. The replies, when they came, were just as she had expected. Mrs. Perdikidi regretfully considered her daughter's decision folly, predicted that it would come to a melancholy conclusion but nevertheless hoped against hope that she might find happiness on the unheard-of island where she now elected to live with a man young enough to be her son. However things might turn out, though, she was never to forget that a dependable and loving home would always await her in Kent. Julia, on the other hand, was very happy for her elder sister, foresaw that all would be bliss for bride and groom forever and asked for photographs, which their mother had pointedly omitted to do. It was, of course, out of the question that Mrs. Perdikidi should travel to Greece, or travel anywhere more distant than Brighton, for that matter, and therefore Errieta was urged to come "home" for a visit as soon as convenient. She replied that the business of building her own home would detain her now for a long time in Skyros but that one day she would without fail pay a visit to her mother and sister.

Of the materials necessary to build their house only the most primitive were to be obtained in Skyros. No seasoned lumber, no decent hardware or steel nails and screws, no plumbing fixtures, no copper pipe, boiler, bathtub, no tile, no finished sashes or jambs, no cabinetwork of any kind would be available there. It would take a ship of considerable size to transport everything necessary, and luck was with them, for they were able to find in Athens everything needed. Errieta was indignant that Skyros should be so lacking in elemental building materials. Why should George not supply them, she suggested, as he was a carpenter, after all? It was unrealistic to suppose that conditions on the island would forever remain so primitive. What was needed was a modern carpentry mill, supplied with power lathes, electric saws, all the most modern equipment, imported wood and hardware, so that when electricity finally came to Skyros he would be ready and there would be no competition. George caught the excitement of the possibility. In an instant he imagined himself a prosperous entrepreneur. And might not such a mill also provide facilities for grinding the island's wheat into flour? Together the husband and wife exulted over their prospects.

When the ship bringing them and all their supplies from Athens put in toward the beach below the ruined mill a little crowd assembled to watch the unloading of the cargo. Nothing like it had ever before been seen in Skyros. The stack of hardware, tile, brilliant copper pipe and boiler, basins, tables and chairs, chests of drawers, barrels, boxes, crates and the white enameled bathtub on its shiny claw feet in the sand, all appeared fantastic in the autumnal sunshine. The Skyriots did not like it, for to them this looked like hubris and they grimly anticipated that fate would in time exact the appropriate retribution. One among them, however, and to the surprise of none, had a more workaday view of this household in the making. It was Nikos, the storekeeper. He offered Errieta his hand and promised any assistance that might be needed, to which she politely replied that he should consult her husband. He proffered sugary felicitations and requested to be allowed to send a demijohn of Samos wine, the best. She accepted.

There was no shortage of men to work on the construction of the Efstathious' house. George worked alongside them, not shirking the most arduous tasks, while Errieta came almost every day to watch, bringing cakes and wine, and ask discreet questions. The workmen at first resented her presence as they resented also George's good fortune and the fine house they were building for him. But little by little they were won over by the lady's serene modesty and generosity, by the carefree devotion of the young husband to the older wife and by the humble delight they took in the construction of their home. When the renovation of the ruined mill was begun, Errieta asked that one of the ancient millstones be carried out to the edge of the bluff. It would make a pleasant seat from which to survey the ever-changing views of the sea.

She was amazed by the simplicity with which all her past life had fallen from her in the presence of a daily joy that she had neither expected nor known to exist. She possessed completely all that she could dream of desiring. The strangeness within the strangeness was that she couldn't tell for certain what this was, and she foresaw that she would never know till she had experienced it to its very end.

Children, she thought, would come. At least one. A male child, she was aware, it would have to be. She wasn't growing any younger, but there were plentiful instances of women past forty bearing children. And a child would represent the creation of happiness within their happiness. She had faith, but she and George never spoke of it.

When told that the wiring, the sockets and switches were for electricity, the workmen laughed, knowing that it would never come to Skyros. But the house was built, finished. Errieta and her young servant girl prepared a banquet for the workmen. A few days later George and his wife slept for the first time in his house. It was nearer the sea than the one they had been renting in the meanwhile. Lying in the front room in the dark, in that room where I also slept for nearly two hundred nights, they listened to the flux and reflux of waves on the beach below, wondrously peaceful and lulling. What they had created was a kind of paradise all their own.

During the construction of the house Errieta had several times seen Zaccharoula peering furtively through the bushes above the stream and had tried to approach her. But the other woman had always scurried away with surprising fleetness, and Errieta did not wish to pursue. She remarked on it to George, who reiterated simply that their neighbor was loony. She had had an accident, he said, in her youth that had affected her mind. An accident? What sort of accident? Errieta wanted to know. It had had to do with her family, her brother. George seemed evasive. His wife insisted. It was an unfortunate story. But that was the way of the island. Though hard to imagine now, Zaccharoula as a girl had been very beautiful. So there were numerous young fellows of the island who had had their eyes intent upon her. And one of them, as it happened, had been appealing to the girl, then about sixteen or seventeen. How it came about that he was able to speak to her nobody knew, as young women were strictly watched over by their families and forbidden to have anything whatsoever to do with young men lest their honor be ruined forever and any chance of one day finding a husband utterly forfeit. Yet somehow Zaccharoula communicated with her admirer, and they agreed to meet one afternoon on the beach, where they walked hand in hand for half an hour. That was all. But of course they were seen. They hadn't even attempted to hide their meeting. So naturally the family found out and Zaccharoula's brother, a young man called Demetrios, a few years older than she, determined to punish her for the loss of her honor. He lashed her wrists together at one end of a long rope, fastened the other to the saddle of his horse and galloped off across the open country beyond the village, dragging his sister behind him. Not very far, but it seems that she lost consciousness. There was no serious injury, no broken bones. But when she came to herself, she could not speak. So it went for several months. Then little by little she found her voice again, but it became apparent that she had lost her mind. The family owned the little house by the stream, where no one for years had wanted to live, and Zaccharoula was installed there. All this had been years before. She lived alone, seeing next to nobody, and supported herself by selling an occasional embroidery, for she had always been expert with the needle, and that skill had not been forgotten when she lost her mind. It was a terrible, terrible story, Errieta said. And what, she asked, had been done to the beastly brother? Why, nothing at all, George said, as Demetrios had only been concerned to vindicate the honor of his family. Errieta said that it was an outrage, that the brother should have been sent to prison at hard labor for many years. But he meant no harm, her husband protested. And the young man who had strolled with Zaccharoula on the beach, no retribution had been inflicted upon him, Errieta supposed. No retribution, no, George said. Pitiful Skyros, Errieta exclaimed.

But it would change, she asserted, and George could help it to change. That was what Stelio, the schoolteacher, had said. But how was he to transform the customs and conventions of the centuries? By becoming prosperous and setting an example. He himself had already changed, and the man who can change himself can change nations. Now that their house was finished it was time to think of building the carpentry mill. And if Skyros should not have electricity, then they would buy a generator of their own. George had already selected an advantageous site for the building at the bottom of the path which led uphill to the village, and they bought the land. The building required would have to be a large one. When the probable costs of construction and equipment had been carefully estimated, Errieta explained that this outlay would require at least half of their remaining capital. They agreed that the expenditure was justified. Work on the foundations began, and Skyros may have thought that George Efstathiou was getting above himself. However, he was courteous and kindly. There were none, when the talk of the tavernas was done, to find serious fault with him, no matter that he had been bought and paid for by the foreign woman.

As there was no bank in Skyros, money came to the Efstathious via the post office. It was George who most frequently received it, a relief to Errieta, who had not forgotten the gross rudeness of the postmaster. However, she did go there occasionally, finding the man as offensive as ever, and was surprised to observe that he must have married, for in a rear corner of the room there usually sat a fleshy woman dandling a baby girl on her knee.

News of events from the outside world came to Skyros late, if at all, and seemed almost to concern happenings on another planet. They heard of the annexation of Austria by Hitler, then of Czechoslovakia, and of the revolt against Metaxas in Crete, which was brutally suppressed. But Skyros went about its business as if its isolation would also keep it forever remote from bloodshed and catastrophe. Flocks of storks flew over the island as they always had, springtime came in an instant and the hillsides were awash with short-lived wildflowers. Work on the carpentry mill, being a far more considerable undertaking than the house, progressed slowly.

Having heard Zaccharoula's story, Errieta determined to make friends with her, no matter how difficult and ticklish a business this might turn out to be. So with increasing frequency she made her way past the little house upstream, surrounded with dahlias, cosmos, oleanders. Zaccharoula must have been exceedingly wary of intruders upon her solitude, and it was months before Errieta caught occasional glimpses of her, though sometimes she reached the house just in time to hear the door click shut. And if she lingered to sniff the flowers, she might see a twitching of the fine lace curtains. Among the books which Errieta had had sent from England were a number of volumes of reproductions of works of art. She remembered that Zaccharoula was an expert needlewoman. One of her books by chance was a French study of medieval tapestries, especially those in the Musée de Cluny of the lady with the unicorn, of which there were a number of passable reproductions in color. It was not a rare or precious publication, but Errieta thought that no other even remotely like it had probably ever been seen in Skyros and that it might be just the thing to touch Zaccharoula's wounded heart. And so one day when the twitching curtains told her that Zaccharoula was at home she placed the book on her whitewashed doorstep and hurried away. A week or more passed, during which Errieta was careful never to approach Zaccharoula's home; then one morning when she opened the door leading into the courtyard behind the house, between it and the tower, she found on her threshold, held there by a round stone, an embroidery which she recognized at once, even before she picked it up, as an image of the lady with the unicorn. But it was an image transformed, simpler but more fanciful, with garlands of brilliant flowers entwined round the unicorn, which very much resembled a goat, and round the lady, whom Errieta thought rather resembled herself. It was beautiful, exquisitely worked, at the same time both primitive and sophisticated. Errieta had never seen anything like it. She was delighted, grateful, moved and felt that she held in her hands the work of an artist. How astonishing to come upon a product of authentic inspiration in a place where the very notion of art cannot have had much meaning. She showed the embroidery to George, who only smiled and said that it was funny but would not find a buyer in the village. Errieta remarked that neither would a painting by the Douanier Rousseau.

That day in the late afternoon she went to Zaccharoula's house and knocked on the door. It opened at first just a crack, then very, very slowly wide enough to reveal a short, fat, stooped and squinting woman, attired wholly in black, with a black kerchief binding her gray hair. Errieta smiled and handed her a rose. Zaccharoula bowed, opened wide her door and gestured to Errieta to enter. The interior was amazing, for all the walls and part of the ceiling were covered with embroideries. Not the traditional designs sold in the village but extravagant images of people and animals and flowers, some of them upside down, floating on the sea or flying through the sky, donkeys with wings, flowers with faces, people with four arms and no feet, a world of imagination and fantasy. Errieta was struck speechless with wonder. For some time she went from wall to wall and back again, studying each embroidery, and finally faced Zaccharoula, paused for a moment, then put her arms around her and kissed her on both cheeks. Whereupon tears came into the eyes of the older woman and trickled down her weathered face. Holding one another's hands, they sat down upon a small bench and for some time did not speak. At last Zaccharoula said, "You are a foreigner, myself a madwoman. Is it possible for two such to become friends?" Then they laughed and laughed until they were breathless. Zaccharoula brought tiny glasses of water and pomegranate conserve and that was the beginning of their friendship. They saw each other almost daily, talked with zest of nothing and everything, and they were both astonished at the happiness so simply and unexpectedly found by two women of such different circumstances. Perhaps it was the extremity of the difference that made for the firmness of the bond.

News of disaster travels fast, isolation notwithstanding, and Skyros learned of the war in Europe only forty-eight hours after the Nazis attacked Poland. Since the abortive uprising in Crete, George had occasionally asked his friends from the village who were more free in their thoughts than the others to come to his house for conversation in the evening. Now they were more than three, and they always came singly after dark, because it was acknowledged that their way of thinking could bring them trouble. There were men in Skyros whose opinions were anything but liberal and from whom no compassion could be counted upon toward those with whom they disagreed. Aside from the opportunity to express a passionate longing for change and hatred of the Metaxas dictatorship, the nocturnal meetings at the Efstathious' house accomplished nothing. Errieta was present, but she seldom participated in the conversations. She was aware that they could bring no positive result, because these young men had no political organization, no program and above all no leader. Under these circumstances, she thought, the fewer clandestine meetings that took place, the better. But she refrained from speaking her mind, even to George. What Skyros needed, she felt, was some Communist organization. She had no illusions about Soviet Communism, not after the trials and sinister rumors of mass oppression, but Greece was not Russia. The only effective resistance to the Greek dictatorship was Communist resistance. She had heard from her friend Phaedon, who after the debacle in Spain had returned to Athens, where he was living under a false name and trying to organize opposition groups.

Snow fell in January. The stream became a raging torrent impossible to cross. Nikos sent a boy to toss over loaves of bread and tins of meat for those stranded on the far side. The muddy water bore down uprooted saplings and rose almost to the threshold of Zaccharoula's house. She said, "It is the apocalypse." But it wasn't. The spring flowers bloomed as always, and Skyros remained as ever in its beautiful isolation.

Then one lovely day the security of even so remote a spot no longer could be taken for granted. Italian troops attacked Albania. There were rumors that an attack on Corfu was imminent. The Albanians put up a little resistance at Durazzo but none elsewhere, so the invaders easily reached Tirana and established a government there. Authorities in Athens were alarmed but general mobilization was not yet considered necessary. General Metaxas enjoined the country to remain alert, prepared for any emergency but calm. The Italian minister assured the Greeks that the territorial integrity and political independence of their country would be respected absolutely. Great Britain and France offered unilateral guarantees of support.

Errieta recognized that now it was only a matter of time. What the worst might turn out to be only time could tell, but that, she said, was what they must prepare for. And already then she began to set aside reserve stores of sugar and salt, coffee and tea, flour, oil, rice, tinned meats and fruit. George refused to believe that the situation could grow serious. Why, even in World War I nothing of any moment had happened to Skyros except that some English hero who had died on shipboard was brought ashore and buried somewhere on the other side of the island. Errieta knew that. His name was Rupert Brooke. This time things would be different. Already the Nazis had conquered Holland, Belgium and France in less than two months. They would certainly not stop at that. And the Italians would follow in their footsteps. They would not have forgotten that their ancestors had conquered Greece, for Mussolini openly aped the Caesars.

Mrs. Perdikidi and Julia wrote of the bombing of Britain, though they were safe in their obscure village. They urged Errieta to come to

them. She had retained British nationality despite her marriage to a
Greek, whose nationality she also acquired, and was now the bearer
of two passports. Her mother and sister pleaded with her to come to
England, bringing with her, if she wished, her husband. But Errieta
saw the danger to Greece, in which George would inevitably become
involved, and she would never leave the country so long as he was
there. She wrote reassuring letters to her mother and sister, not be-
lieving what she said.

There were, of course, incidents to begin with. Italian planes
bombed Greek ships. Italian troops were reported massing on the Al-
banian frontier. Greek officers' leaves were canceled, and garrisons in
the north placed on alert. In Epirus and western Macedonia all the
men between twenty and thirty-five were being mobilized. In the tavernas the young men of Skyros talked of nothing but the coming war
and their part in it. George Efstathiou was one of them. No one mocked
him now because he had sold himself to a foreign woman old enough
to be his mother. The carpentry mill, though far from finished, would
obviously become an important business one day. That fact made for
a marked change in George's stature in Skyros's eyes. It was said, to
be sure, that he and a number of others had dangerous opinions. But
no man could question his patriotism.

One sunny Monday morning in October the war came to Greece.
George had sometime before gone to the mill, but Errieta still lay in
bed, listening to the slight clatter from the kitchen, where the servant
girl, Elpinikia, was preparing her breakfast. Suddenly the church bells
of the village all simultaneously started clanging, and she knew immediately what that meant. So when George came racing up from the
beach, she was ready. It was war, he cried. Italian troops had attacked
at dawn in Epirus. The news had come over the new wireless in the
mayor's office. General mobilization. All men of fighting age to report
to the army center in Volos. Boats would be leaving Linaria that very
day. In less than a week they would probably be at the front. Errieta
saw that he was thrilled. She would not argue. But he must be prepared,
assuming preparations for war to be thinkable. She begged him to be
careful. He promised. His heavy overcoat should go with him—it would
be cold in the mountains—a packet of food and a goodly sum of money
in his wallet. It was all done in less than an hour. He kissed her quickly,

then was gone. She went to the edge of the bluff where the millstone had been set down and from there she could see him running along the beach. Then he disappeared.

She did not expect to hear from him. He had been engulfed in the irrational abstraction of combat, and there was nothing to be done but wait it out. The news had no personal meaning. Greek forces did well at first, compelling the Italians to give up what territory they had taken and to retreat into Albania. Fighting was merciless in the icy mountain passes. Five months after their initial attack the Italians' strategic situation began to look critical. Then the Germans had to come to their aid, striking southward through Yugoslavia into Greece. By the end of April all the country was in Nazi hands. Crete fell in May.

During these six or seven months, as she expected, Errieta had heard nothing from her young husband. And even in later years I don't know that he described to her very much about what had happened to him during the war. She told me only that at the end he had been in a place called Votonasi, where the Greek and German generals were settling on terms of surrender, and a Greek lieutenant had told him to get rid of his uniform and keep off the main roads if he hoped to reach home. It was his money, which till then he had had no means of spending, that saved him. He managed to reach Volos, where he found his onetime schoolteacher, Stelio, who hid him for a few days and said that the worst was now to come. There would be resistance to the Nazi occupation, but the resistance would not be united. Communists on one side, royalists on the other. Change and progress versus reaction and oppression. Stelio took for granted which side George, Errieta and their Skyriot comrades would support and befriend.

Zaccharoula had never doubted that George would return home unharmed. She reassured Errieta daily. The two women drank tea together every afternoon, sometimes in one house, sometimes in the other. They talked and talked. Zaccharoula now went often to the village, observing carefully what went on there and overhearing gossip all the more easily since everyone regarded her as simpleminded, a misapprehension she was careful to cultivate, guessing it could be useful someday and, in any case, obdurate in her contempt for the villagers. So she was able to tell Errieta everything that happened in Skyros, who was friendly with whom, who was another's enemy, who lay at death's door and who had given birth to an infant of what sex. It was a never-ending story told with a sense of the picturesque quite in keeping with the eye that invented the extraordinary embroideries. "What would I do with a radio," Errieta once remarked to me, "when I can turn on Zaccharoula?" She did not have the same sorts of stories to tell as her friend, but she had known the outside world and found that descriptions of London, Rome, the Alps, the Eiffel Tower and the canals of Venice, no matter how many times repeated, never failed to delight the imagination of a woman whose own travels had taken her no farther than two or three kilometers from her birthplace. Errieta also observed that in all of Zaccharoula's talk no mention of her family or of what had happened to her long ago ever was made.

The Italians, presumably as their reward for having been so ineffectual, were assigned to occupy the islands. A small troop arrived in Skyros, commandeered several houses, requisitioned some food, though not too much, and sat slouched in the tavernas, drinking white wine. Zaccharoula reported that they would make no trouble because they lacked the mien of conquerors.

It was the two hundred and thirteenth day of his absence, an azure afternoon in May, when George Efstathiou returned home from the war. Thanks to Stelio he had come in a fishing boat from Zagora, embarking after dark, sailing without lights, taking bearings from the stars and passing to the north of Alonissos, where enemy patrols were less likely to spot them than in the channel between Skiathos and Skopelos. Oh, he had been lucky. And wasn't his good luck Errieta's? Yes! She was overjoyed. He was safe. For them the war was over. Now it would be fought by others. Not so, said George. The war would never be over as long as an enemy of Greece remained on Greek soil, and it would have to be fought by every patriot according to his conscience and his capacity. Errieta perceived that her husband was no longer the youth who had left home seven months before. She worried but agreed, because the unimportant island of Skyros, she thought, would never become a battlefield. So she allowed herself simply to be happy because the man she loved had come safely back to her from the bounds of carnage. George, too, was happy. To be reunited with his wife had been the longing of every soldier.

Moreover, there was work to be done. The only other carpenter on the island, old Zanettos, had died during George's absence. Now there was only one carpenter in Skyros, equipped with fine tools, and many demands for his skill. A good thing, too, said Errieta, for no more remittances would be coming from England due to the war and she had spent almost all the ready money for the supplies which filled her cupboards. George promised her that she would never want for anything. Already he had taken on an apprentice, a young fellow called Vyron, who worked hard and learned quickly.

The carpentry mill stood just as George had left it, walls complete and several roof beams in place but open to the sky, the floor unfinished, doors and windows empty holes, a huge husk of a structure.

One autumn night—this must have been late in 1942—George and Errieta were awakened by a tapping on the shutters of their bedroom. He went to the window and asked in a whisper who it was. A messenger from Volos, sent by Stelio Vetsanopoulos, was the answer, and there was some secret password. George put on his trousers in the dark and went round to the front of the house to admit this emissary. Errieta remained where she was, aware that this was men's business, but she felt alarmed. Stelio's messenger did not stay long. When George came back to their bedroom, Errieta asked what the man had wanted. She would see in the morning, George told her, and when she did see, she realized that her sense of alarm had been only too well founded.

On the dining table lay a dozen pistols, a pile of boxes of ammunition and a large bundle of pamphlets. The messenger had been a strong man to carry so much. But the situation henceforth, said George, would call for many strong men. He would distribute pistols to all those who could be trusted. As for the pamphlets, they would find their way through the village, and nobody need know exactly where they came from. They were statements of the Communist position, which called for active resistance against the enemy, *and* against those who sided with the forces of reaction, working for a return of the king and all the old injustices when the war would be over. Already the Nazis' situation had begun to disintegrate. They were on the run in North Africa, Algeria had been invaded and in Russia their position had begun to look perilous. A new spirit was abroad in Greece. In every city, every town, every village, throughout the islands as well as on the mainland, organized administration of Communist resistance groups was being established, its army named ELAS. The reactionary force was called EDES. Already there had been skirmishes between the two. Not all the ELAS men—and women—were Communists. They had half a dozen bishops, a score of regular army generals and many junior officers with them, not Communists but patriots, committed to a transformed nation in the future. There could be no return now to the grievous fatalism of the past.

Errieta understood and sympathized. But she was afraid. She recognized the risk for George. Noble sentiments were one thing, pistols another. Precautions must be taken. That meant a hiding place. For him. But he must not yet know it as such. She searched the house and recognized the place at once. In their bedroom was a closet, narrow but long, its ceiling as high as the ceiling of the bedroom. If a false ceiling were installed in there, a man might easily be hidden above, not to mention firearms and incriminating pamphlets. Errieta was not by nature an alarmist, but she had no intention of allowing her husband to make himself more vulnerable than necessary, and she realized now that peril of Smyrna proportions could come even to remote Skyros. Fortunately George was a carpenter. She would only have to prevail upon him to make the hiding place without understanding that it was for him. She discharged young Elpinikia, the servant girl, on the pretext that even so modest an expense had become extravagant. Then she asked George to bring some lumber to the house, matching planks, but only one at a time. For shelves, she said. When there were enough, she explained what she wanted done. He didn't see the use of it, so she insisted that some safe place for weapons, pamphlets and extra food must be prepared. To set her mind at rest, she said. He complied, priding himself, once the work was begun, on making the false ceiling appear permanent, immovable and inaccessible while at the same time it could be easily opened and closed by pushing upward or downward at precisely the right spot and no other.

An anonymous postcard mailed from the Piraeus had told them soon after George's return from the war that Phaedon and Clio, in hiding in Athens, had had a son, named after the faraway professor. George and Errieta were happy for their friends, but before long the news from Athens became a résumé of horror. The German occupying forces lived off the land, confiscating without compunction whatever they needed or wanted. Less and less remained for the sustenance of the civilian population. In part this was retaliation for acts of terrorism and sabotage carried out by resistance forces in the mountains of Thessaly and Epirus. Hostages were shot, villages burned, Jews deported. In the capital people began to go hungry, then to starve and die. Women clawed through garbage cans and children fought ferociously for apple cores or ends of bread tossed from the armored cars of the Wehrmacht. Emaciated cadavers, sometimes savagely gnawed by starving dogs, lay along the sidewalks. A hundred, two hundred were dying daily. At dawn the handcarts of the charnel house would come jarring along to gather up the corpses. And not more than a year after the arrival of the first anonymous postcard from the Piraeus came another to announce that the writer's son had died of hunger.

Errieta wept. If only she had been able to send some of the food she had so providentially stored away, or some produce from the garden vigilantly tended with Zaccharoula's help, or their goat or a couple of chickens and doves. It was monstrous. She and George were in no danger—as yet—of starving. But this news brought another awareness, more painful still.

No hopeful illusion could now conceal the fact that an Efstathiou son would never be born from the union of George and Errieta. From their life together no other life would take form and meaning. Both of them must have become aware of this at about the same time, and it was a measure of their regret and sorrow that no mention of it ever was made by either of them. But they knew, and it made a difference.

Zaccharoula brought gossip from the village. She had become a sly and resourceful eavesdropper. George was talked about. People said that he was leader of the Communist resistance group in Skyros. But this was simple speculation. Some were for him, others against him. No matter. The war remained distant. The Italian soldiers drank what little wine was left and were no more bellicose than bumblebees. Rumor had it, though, that on the mainland fierce battles were taking place between EDES forces that favored the king and the ELAS army opposed to his return, virtually a civil war, with terrible brutalities on both sides, as cruel as the Germans'. Errieta implored her friend to listen carefully to everything said by the villagers. A chance remark might make all the difference in the world. Oh yes, Zaccharoula would listen, and she laughed, for apparently people were surprised to see the madwoman now so often in their midst.

From one day to the next something went wrong with the Italians. They looked sullen and apprehensive. The explanation came soon enough. Italy had surrendered and its soldiers consequently faced a highly uncertain future. Zaccharoula brought the ensuing bad news very early one morning to Errieta and George. A troop of German soldiers had landed the previous evening at Linaria and were even then marching across the island. The villagers were fearful, knowing that Germans would not be so easygoing as their erstwhile allies. Errieta asked George to remain in the house until they knew more. He was reluctant, eager to go to the village to see what would happen. But she insisted. Zaccharoula said that she would go to the village. She had nothing to fear from anyone, being loony, whereas George was now too well known as one who had something to do with the resistance. So he grudgingly acquiesced.

The Germans wasted no time. A sergeant went round the village, marking with red chalk the doors of houses to be requisitioned, nineteen in all, the occupants being allowed just one hour to vacate their premises. The mayor was ousted from his office, which was taken over by the officer in charge, a captain. They were all very young, their looks angry and hostile. The Italians were arrested and set to building a stockade on the far side of the village where they would be imprisoned. Notices were posted in the center of the village. Any person taken in acts of overt or covert aid to the resistance movements would be executed on the spot. For every act of terrorism ten hostages would be shot. The island fishermen were forbidden to take their boats more than five hundred meters from shore, to embark from any points except two, one at Linaria, the other directly below Skyros village, and they were further forbidden to remain at sea after dark lest torpedo boats fire upon them without warning. The islanders were ordered to keep well clear of the beaches, which would be patrolled by sentinels with dogs day and night. Surveillance would be strict. Firearms of any kind were supposed to have been surrendered to the Italians when they occupied the island, but if any remained in private hands they would be accepted without reprisal if surrendered within forty-eight hours. Thereafter any person found in possession of a rifle or pistol would be executed as a terrorist.

Zaccharoula was frightened. These Germans were evil, she said.

Already they were interrogating men in the village, and the questioning went badly for some, because screams and groans were to be heard through the closed windows of the mayor's office.

Errieta understood the implications instantly, and she, too, was frightened. The danger to George was clear and must be dealt with promptly. He said that he and his friends had long ago agreed that in case of any grave danger they would take their weapons and meet in a cave on the far side of the island, a spot nearly impossible to discover save for those who knew the island intimately. He would go there at once. No, said Errieta. It might already be too late to move freely about the island, and armed, without risking one's life. As the Germans were meticulous and ruthless, it was very possible that they knew the island intimately. Remember Herr Reichel. They had dogs, machine guns. And of what use could George and his few brave friends possibly be in their remote cave, where they would die of hunger if they were not found out? George insisted that he had given his word. And what good would it do, his word, asked Errieta, if he forfeited his life to keep it? His honor would not be forfeited, he said. The dispute was settled by force majeure. Zaccharoula had exceptionally acute hearing. She ran outside, returning immediately to say that a group of Germans were approaching along the beach, had almost reached the stream.

Not an instant was to be lost. The hiding place Errieta had persuaded George to make ready must now be put to use. He did not argue. The clothes were taken out quickly, the false ceiling opened, George stood on a chair and disappeared into the darkness above, closing the aperture after him, and the two women hardly had had time to replace the clothes in the closet before a pounding came on the door opening toward the front of the house. Errieta went to open, while Zaccharoula shut herself in the kitchen.

The German captain stood outside, a young fellow, no more than twenty-five, with a peaked cap and pensive, pale blue eyes. He saluted and said in English that he understood Errieta to be a foreigner. A Greek married to a Greek, she said in Greek. And Mr. Efstathiou was a leading member of the Communist resistance, was he not? If so, without my knowledge, replied Errieta, speaking English with hesitation. As you must be aware, she added, Greek women do not participate in the affairs of their husbands. And where was Mr. Efstathiou at present? demanded the German officer. She said she did not know, as he had departed that morning before she awoke. In any event, the captain politely requested permission to search the house. Certainly, said Errieta. Three soldiers did the job, and they were extremely thorough. In the kitchen they found Zaccharoula seated on the floor, nodding her head and murmuring to herself. Errieta explained that this lady was a neighbor, regarded by the villagers as simpleminded but harmless. The captain said that simple minds might be a blessing in times such as these. Errieta took note but did not respond. In the bedroom the soldiers turned the bed upside down and plunged their trench knives into the mattress. They took all the clothes from the closet, pounded the walls and ceiling with their rifle butts and appeared satisfied nothing was concealed there. George had done his work well. They also searched the tower. When they had finished and found nothing, the captain apologized for the inconvenience caused. The mystery of Mr. Efstathiou's absence remained, however, and would necessitate future searches. His orders were categorical. The resistance had inflicted severe losses of personnel and equipment and could not be tolerated. Even in so small a place as Skyros. Indeed, a man named Argiris Kampas had been found in possession of a pistol, ammunition and Communist literature. He would be executed the following morning. But Kampas was a poor cobbler, father of four children, cried Errieta, and certainly there must be some mistake. He had denied nothing, said the captain. Exceptions could not be made. It was most regrettable. Nobody could say how the war might turn out, but perhaps Mrs. Efstathiou knew of German reverses in North Africa and Russia. What must be must be. Errieta bowed her head, the captain saluted and that was the end of their first meeting.

When the Germans had gone, George came out of his hiding place. He had not heard the mention of Argiris Kampas, so Errieta said nothing. She realized that she must become utterly pitiless and selfish. George would have to remain in hiding so long as the Germans were in Skyros, for it was evident that someone must have denounced him. And he realized, he must realize, what the alternative would be. He railed and swore and stamped and pounded the walls. But he realized. The hiding place must always be ready, especially after dark, in case of sudden incursions. And at all times, both day and night, all the shutters of the house should be kept closed and locked. Zaccharoula came from the kitchen, pleased with herself for the impersonation of a madwoman. Henceforth, she said, Errieta and she would have to keep a sharp lookout in case the enemy soldiers should come back.

George fretted over the fate of his friends who might have gone to the cave, feeling he had betrayed their trust. But now it was too late to help them, insisted Errieta, and no good would be done to anyone if he were taken prisoner. He could hardly deny that. Still, it was demeaning to skulk in safety when others were risking their lives. That, declared his wife, was schoolboy sentimentality, not worthy of a grown man who had already witnessed the disasters of war. George grudgingly assented.

The next visit of the Germans came a week later, at the hour of the midday meal. Cunning, calculated to apprehend the fugitive while eating or to find some culinary proof of his presence. But Errieta had thought of this. She and George ate from the same plate and luckily had almost finished their meal when Zaccharoula came in a flurry to warn of the approaching enemy. This time she slipped away through the bushes. George was safely in the hiding place before the knock on the door. The captain, having saluted, apologized for the intrusion. Oh, Errieta said, she had expected it. The search was somewhat less brutal and thorough than before. And had Mrs. Efstathiou any knowledge of her husband's whereabouts? inquired the officer. None, she said. Perhaps he had gone to the mainland or to Euboea, as he may have learned that he was being pursued. Perhaps. Perhaps. Though the sea was patrolled constantly by torpedo boats ordered to sink any craft encountered beyond the five-hundred-meter limit. Alas, it would be necessary to search again. Military necessity. Mrs. Efstathiou must understand. Oh, she did, she said, she understood, and the captain must feel no scruple about performing his duty. Indeed not, he said, and then to her amazement it seemed that his eyes suddenly became glassy. Was it possible that those were tears? But before she could tell he had saluted and turned away.

It was more than a month before the Germans came again, this time in the late afternoon, and from her hiding place among the oleanders Errieta saw them, only the captain and one soldier, approaching along the beach. Hurrying to the house, she saw George well installed in the hiding place before the knock came at the door. The captain's salute, polite as ever, was the prelude to a surprise, for he asked whether he might come inside. Certainly, she said. The soldier remained in front of the door under the wisteria vine, which had now lost most of its leaves. Closing the door behind him, the officer made a slight bow and removed his cap. His dark hair, she saw to her astonishment, was streaked with gray. Errieta stood facing him. He had not come to search her house, he said. Ah? Then what was the purpose of his visit? It was to tell her that he realized Mr. Efstathiou was in hiding somewhere on the island and that he felt certain she knew where. But how, she inquired, could he have reached this certainty? By observing her. She was nervous but not anxious. A woman who truly feared for the life of her husband could not feign composure such as hers. He knew. Then what, she asked again, was the purpose of his visit? She must be aware, he said, that there existed means, infallible means, of compelling people to impart any information wanted. But he was not disposed to resort to them. The purpose of his visit, in short, was to inform her that henceforth her house would not be subject to search and that consequently Mr. Efstathiou would have nothing to fear if only he kept out of sight. Errieta laughed. The trick, she said, seemed transparent, assuming, of course, that she knew the whereabouts of her husband. The captain replaced his cap and said that he knew better than she how truly he deserved her contempt. Having offered her an assurance, however, which could cost him his life, he felt entitled to make a request of her in turn. Would she be willing to receive him again, alone? And for the sake of her security and repute in Skyros he would come only after dark, when the curfew was in effect. Had she, she asked, any choice? And what would be the purpose of this future visit? He smiled, and Errieta thought she had never seen an expression of such ineffable sadness. The purpose, he said, might be to discover whether or not the world existed. In that case, Errieta replied, a welcome must be taken for granted. Saluting, he told her that she might expect him in two weeks to the day; then he was gone.

George was suspicious. Errieta herself felt misgivings, but at the same time recognized that there was no option. Moreover, if the captain proved as good as his word, they would have no worry till the war was over. There was a risk, to be sure, but it tempted her.

Exactly two weeks later, the evening meal finished, George safely settled in the hiding place, made more comfortable now with cushions and blankets, the expected knock came at the door. Errieta went to open it and stepped back quickly in alarm because for an instant she had not recognized the man who stood outside. It was the German officer, but he was attired now in civilian clothes, a dark brown corduroy suit, and bareheaded. In order to emphasize, he said, the unofficial nature of his visit. He brought with him a bottle of brandy. Errieta invited him to be seated, but he declined. She brought two glasses. They drank, she sparingly, he quickly and repeatedly. For some time he strode back and forth in the spacious room without speaking. At last he said that he could no longer believe in civilization but that in this room in Errieta's company he could entertain the illusion. Why, he asked, was that? She replied that she had no idea, though she had a very good one but suddenly felt such compassion for this distraught young man that she could not bear to express it. After a good deal more striding back and forth in silence and several glasses of brandy, the captain murmured his apology for intruding upon her. He had no right to do so, he said, and would not return. Errieta told him that he would be welcome if he desired to come. He need only tell her when his visit was to be expected. So they agreed that if he intended to come, it would be only after dark on the last day of each month.

George began to find his constant confinement within the house extremely irksome. Sometimes he grew irritable, short-tempered, and reproached Errieta for having compelled him to hide like a coward while she received an enemy officer. But then he would beg her forgiveness, because he knew that she had saved his life.

The German captain did not come on the last day of every month, but he came several times, always in civilian clothes, and was very little more communicative than during the first visit. But at least he did eventually agree to cease his striding and sit down. And Errieta remembered that once he had said that the existence of the world was connected to the relation of good and evil in it. I don't know that she ever learned his name. She refrained from asking questions. He was obviously a man of exceptional intelligence suffering from a terrible mental strain. He always brought brandy and drank a lot of it. Errieta had had shipped from London before the war her ancient phonograph and a small supply of records. One evening she asked whether he would like to listen to a Beethoven quartet. He replied that he would rather kill himself. It was he who told Errieta that the Americans and British had made a successful landing in western France, that the Germans were everywhere in retreat, would before long be leaving Greece, that the war would soon be over. But then, he said, really serious troubles would be in store for Greece. Opposing political factions would never settle their differences peaceably.

On the last day of July—this would have been in 1944, some ten months after the Germans' arrival—he came again. But this time in uniform. To remind them both, he said, of his true identity. And to say goodbye. His troops and their Italian prisoners would be leaving the island within a few days, would be lucky to reach Salonika and get safely through Yugoslavia. Then Greece would be free. The British already had landed men on Samos and Leros. He wished to thank her. For what? she asked. For having almost—almost!—persuaded him, he said, that the world existed. He wished, in addition, to tell her something. Before being wounded he had been on duty in Russia and Poland. Had witnessed things there known to few. After the war she would hear terrible stories of what the Germans had done. He wanted her to know that these stories would all be true but very, very far from the truth, because no truth could ever be equivalent to the terrible things done. And so he would say goodbye. Would she be willing, he asked, to shake his hand? Of course, she said. And while she held his hand in hers she saw—and this time was certain of it—that his eyes were filled with tears. Then he stepped back abruptly. Instead of touching his fingertips to the visor of his cap to salute her, as he had done before, he flung up his right arm and in a hoarse whisper, almost inaudibly, said, "Heil Hitler." Turning away before she could respond, he went out the door and strode into the darkness.

So the war was over for Skyros, having cost the life of but one man executed by the Germans shortly after their arrival. Few other localities had been so fortunate. More than a thousand villages lay in ruins. All large road bridges were destroyed, olive groves, forests, vineyards had been laid waste. At Yefira partisans suspected of setting a charge under the railway culvert had been roped to the tracks and run over by the night train. Eight hundred men and boys had been murdered on one evil December 13 at Kalavryta. Women whipped to death for pilfering rotten potatoes on the dock at Volos. How many thousands dead of hunger in Athens?

Errieta cautioned George against reappearing too quickly in the village. It would not be fitting for people to know that he had been hidden all this time by his wife while his companions, perhaps, had risked their lives or starved in the mountains. Zaccharoula must try to learn what had become of those who had been meant to rendezvous at the cave. By extraordinary good fortune they had survived and came back one by one. They had escaped thanks to the daring of an old fisherman named Stefanos in Linaria, who ran them across to Euboea one stormy night in November. So what was George to say? He rebelled against lying to his comrades. Then he must tell as much of the truth as they would want to learn. He would say he had stayed in hiding in Skyros in order to keep watch on the Germans. His hiding place? Oh, nothing is easier for a man who is not being pursued than to hide. If he had not been afraid of being denounced, he might even have ventured into the village. But in the village were those who would willingly have seen him shot like the unhappy Argiris Kampas. Nikos, the storekeeper, for one. The postmaster, Vergottis. The mayor. To say that much would be enough, Errieta felt, and in fact it was more than enough, for George's comrades were so happy to find him alive that they inquired very little about his adventures, being eager to relate their own.

In October a band of ELAS men landed at Linaria, a captain and some twenty soldiers with bandoliers across their shoulders and grenades at their belts. It was announced that a village meeting would take place the next morning at the school. The ELAS captain read a proclamation stating that it was the primary duty of all citizens to ensure order and a peaceful political life for the country. There would be elections, and when that time came it would be well for everyone to remember that ELAS partisans had done more than any others to free their homeland from its enemies. Let all who would do honor to themselves as loyal Greeks be mindful of this. Errieta said that that sounded ominous.

3

Between two storms in November came a detachment of British troops. Their commanding officer, a lieutenant aged about twenty, called upon Errieta, having heard, he said, that there was an Englishwoman on the island. She explained, invited him into the house and expressed some surprise at his arrival, the Germans having left Skyros three

months before. He replied quite simply that the British liberation of
Greece was in fact a formality, as the enemy was already on the run
by the time they landed. So they were here merely to ensure order,
nothing more, till elections could be held and proper national security
forces were well in control of an integrated situation. Errieta said she
had supposed that the forces which in effect freed the country must be
capable of ensuring order. Well, that was just the rub, observed the
lieutenant, for they were mostly Reds, weren't they, these ELAS chaps?
And they could take over the country in a quarter of an hour if they
wanted to. Which is what you are here to prevent, I presume, said
Errieta. Well, free elections, the uncoerced will of the people, that was
what the war was all about, wasn't it? Indeed! But the British had not
come to prevent or to foster anything. ELAS, after all, had about fifty
thousand men, while the government's loyal Mountain Brigade had
only a few thousand, the British even less. So it would hardly be an
even match. And if ELAS didn't expect to have things their way, they
would take over the country at once, wouldn't they? The plan was to
disband all military forces in Greece and then to organize a new national army. But ELAS seemed a trifle chary about turning in its arms.
What he really wanted to know was whether there had been any active
resistance movement in Skyros. Errieta replied that as a woman, and
a foreigner, she was hardly in a position to know. Probably Skyros was
too small a place to make a difference, the lieutenant speculated. A
few activists in the woodwork, no doubt, but that was standard. Besides,
he had only forty men. Andros would be his next stop. He thanked
her for her cooperation, took up his cap and stick, saluted and departed.

George, with his apprentice, went to work in his unfinished mill
with the frenzy of a young man newly released from confinement.
Nothing else concerned him. He returned home at dusk, departed at
dawn. His friends were disappointed at his lack of interest in the political developments in faraway Athens, which so preoccupied them.
And developments there would soon compel even the unconcerned to
be concerned.

General Scobie, commandant of all British forces in Greece, had
forced the appointment of the rightist General Vendires as chief of
staff of the new Greek army. And many officers of the National Guard
had, as if by chance, been officers of the so-called Security Battalions,
whose men had fought side by side with the Germans against ELAS.

Now they were being armed and trained by the British in case of civil strife. The sole acceptable solution to the problem of military disbandment would be dissolution not only of ELAS forces but also of all royalist army units and armed groups. But the British refused to accept it, and General Scobie issued a decree ordering disbandment of all ELAS forces within ten days.

A mass meeting was organized to protest the order of disbandment. Permission for it had been obtained from the police and the Ministry of the Interior in the afternoon previous to the meeting. But then, at the instigation of the British, the permission was revoked at eleven o'clock that night. Too late to call off the demonstration, and early in the morning, a Sunday, the crowd was already dense in Constitution Square. People bearing placards, flags and olive branches pressed toward the square from the several avenues leading to it. Facing the square were both the Grande Bretagne Hotel, headquarters of the British, and the police headquarters building, its second-floor balcony lined with men in uniform, some holding rifles. There was shouting and shaking of fists at the hotel, while a group of girls began to sing a resistance marching song, but no hint of violence came from the demonstrators. So it was without the least provocation that the police on the balcony began to fire directly into the crowd. Pandemonium ensued, screaming, the crowd stampeding, crazed with fear. But the firing from the police balcony continued unremitting and unopposed for fully half an hour till inert bodies lay scattered all across the square. As soon as the firing ceased, those of the crowd who remained and could move ran toward the police headquarters, roaring and shaking their fists. But then two British tanks came round the corner of the square, moving into position to protect the police building, and the crowd fell back.

More than a hundred lay dead or gravely wounded. Hardly had the priests and orderlies from the hospital arrived when the crackling of rifle fire came on the wind from beyond the Acropolis. That must come from the X-ites, someone said, for they controlled that part of northwestern Athens beyond the ancient Agora. They were members of an ultra-royalist extreme-rightist organization called the X Group and had actively collaborated with the SS during the German occupation. A law unto themselves and unapologetic terrorists, they roamed the country, raping, pillaging and murdering according to their whim.

After the Sunday massacre ELAS was compelled to choose between capitulation and armed resistance. They chose the latter, bringing against them the British and royalist forces. Neither side at first
was prepared to fight. For a week the action was desultory, then ELAS
began to press the British, forcing them to make their stand in an
isolated strip of central Athens some two kilometers long and five or
six blocks wide, including the Grande Bretagne Hotel, the infantry
barracks, the old and new palaces and the two wide avenues from
Constitution Square to Omonia. ELAS controlled the rest of Greece.
Fighting was bitter, bloody, brutal on both sides, and inconclusive.
Meanwhile, two British divisions were flown in. Prime Minister
Churchill visited Athens on Christmas Day and contrived the political
expedient of appointing an archbishop as Regent, which of course was
a commitment to restoration. The reinforced British counterattacked
in strength. ELAS could not hold. After eight days of gruesome street
fighting it was all over. In one night the ELAS men slipped out of the
city, taking with them a large number of civilian hostages. A week
later a meaningless armistice was signed.

George and Errieta experienced none of this. But they heard of it
only too soon and learned the details later.

Mrs. Perdikidi wrote with dismay and alarm from Kent, her letter
taking thirty-three days to reach Skyros. She was appalled by what was
going on in that country which she had never really considered her
homeland. But the English, among whom she lived, were involved.
Could it be true, as Mr. Churchill had said in the House of Commons,
that all ELAS men were "brigands and gangsters," and that he had
instructed General Scobie to treat Athens as a conquered city? What
was one to believe? There were stories of ghastly atrocities. She pleaded
with her daughter to try to keep safe now that the war was nearly over,
then come to England as soon as possible. Errieta replied that Skyros
was the safest place one could reasonably hope to find. Her mistake
became plain only when it was too late to believe that reason might
offer much hope.

The X Group had grown in power and numbers, having seized a
large quantity of arms surrendered after the December fighting, and
they now set about terrorizing the country in expectation of influencing
the elections to come. Former ELAS men were hunted down, beaten,
tried on trumped-up charges and confined to prison islands. Arrests

on hearsay denunciation became common. Men were imprisoned without trial. The so-called forces of order did nothing to interfere. On the
contrary, they often participated. In Larissa, capital of Thessaly, the
Tenth Brigade of the National Guard carried out a two-day reign of
terror, destroyed ELAS offices, burned all the books of the municipal
library and raided the hospital where wounded ELAS men were being
treated, smashing irreplaceable equipment and shouting, "Now you
will die." Many did. Neither the British commandant of the area nor
the local prefect took any action. Having defeated ELAS, the British
and the government they kept in power were hopelessly committed to
the uncontrollable passions which from long before the war had opposed any new order in the country.

One day the war in Europe was over. It was amazing. In Athens
a crowd stood and cheered in the square where a massacre had taken
place five months before. The flags of the Allied nations floated op-
timistically in the blue sky. Throughout Greece church bells rang and
people cheered. But they wondered whether catastrophe could simply
go away like feathery poplar pollen on the golden breeze. In Salonika
some rash ELAS men organized a victory parade with a few British
and American soldiers at its head and crowds singing patriotic songs.
National Guardsmen attacked without provocation, stabbed to death
a young girl and shot several paraders at random. A peaceful future
was not in the making.

If people expected that the end of the war would bring rapidly
improved living conditions, their expectation was vain. Things grew
worse rather than better. The islanders' clothing was mostly reduced
to rags. Shoes, not to mention boots, were worn through. In warm
weather almost everyone went barefoot. Children's feet were bound in
strips of flannel. Boats from Kimi or Volos arrived rarely, if at all.
Supplies came even less often. The shelves of Nikos's store were bare,
and even his back rooms and cellar were emptying fast. Between morning and afternoon, it seemed, the price of one egg or a half *oka* of
lentils could double. The mayor wrote to the Ministry of the Interior
to plead for help. None came. George and Errieta were among the
most fortunate. They had still a little stock of oil and tinned meat, they
had their goat, a few chickens and doves. Fish, to be sure, could be
had from fishermen, now able to go far out in the few boats left in

sufficient repair, and fish saved Skyros from extremities of hunger. But they were costly.

With the end of the war, Errieta's small income, secure from the follies of Greek inflation, once again began to arrive in George's name at the post office. When he went to fetch it, he noted that the portrait of General Metaxas had disappeared, though the king's dour countenance still hung on the wall. The postmaster was as disagreeable as ever, and his fat wife sat in her accustomed corner. But the baby had become an exceptionally beautiful little girl. George asked her name. She had barely time to say that it was Angela before her mother shook her roughly by the arm and told her to be quiet.

George and Vyron continued to work at the mill. It went quickly and well. Before long the building would stand complete. But empty. The machines, not to mention the electricity needed to fulfill their purpose, were still wanting. And heaven only knew when they might materialize. And heaven was too charitable to tell.

The expectation of national elections scheduled to take place at the end of March roused apprehension throughout the country. In the tavernas there were furious altercations. Men who had been lifelong friends began to look on each other with suspicion. Half the walls of Greece were plastered with crowns and accolades to the king accompanied by fierce denunciations of democracy, which was characterized as equivalent to Communism. Moreover, the intimidation of extreme groups like X, supported by the National Guard, the police and the British, promised to falsify election results. The X-ites went from village to village, brutalizing everyone suspected of having had anything to do with ELAS. Men were hung by their thumbs from olive trees or driven naked on hands and feet through the streets. Meanwhile, provoked beyond endurance, guerrilla forces had formed again in the mountains, had already raided towns in western Macedonia and threatened to attack Salonika. British troops and teams of observers went round and round the country, not knowing what to do, as their policy contradicted everything that they had to believe in in order to believe in themselves.

A British cutter put in at Linaria, leaving a company of soldiers commanded by an elderly major. They had come to oversee and ensure the fair and orderly conduct of the elections and pitched their tents at the foot of the hill not far from George's mill. The major called on

Errieta, bringing her a tin of tea, and assured her that there would be no disturbances.

Yet again it was Zaccharoula who came with the warning. She had been taking an altar cloth to the monastery when a band of marauders burst into the village, shouting and brandishing their rifles. Fifty of them, at least. X-ites, someone said they were called; they were searching for ELAS men but didn't appear to care too much who it was they molested, for they had beaten with their rifle butts an old fellow called Nikolaos who had never had anything to do with the resistance and slapped a woman who tried to help him till her face ran with blood. Zaccharoula had fled while they were roping together the feet of a young boy and attaching the other end of the rope to the tail of a donkey. But she had heard them asking where was the house of the man called Efstathiou. George swore. He would take his pistol and go to the village, he said, and have done with some of these outlaws. Oh, dear friend, I implore you, Zaccharoula protested, don't do so, for they are too many. And there are the British troops to keep order, Errieta added, so you must go to the hiding place again, and be quick. Again like a coward, said George. His wife insisted. And when she saw he hesitated, she ordered, which she had never done before. Grumbling sullenly, he did as she demanded. None too soon, Zaccharoula ran out the back door, frightening chickens and doves.

Errieta opened the front door wide and sat down at the dining table. They came almost immediately, four men lunging through the door, pointing their rifles around the room, all of them swarthy, attired in nondescript items of military apparel. The bearded one appeared to be in command. Where was the Communist Efstathiou? he asked. Errieta replied she did not know, had not seen her husband since early morning and it was now late afternoon. He might be anywhere on the island. They could search the house if they wished. They did, smashing crockery and overturning furniture. But what had frustrated the Germans easily foiled these ruffians. The bearded one put the muzzle of his rifle against Errieta's head. You know where your man's hidden, foreigner, he said. Tell me or I'll scatter your brains against the wall. Errieta pushed away the rifle as if it were a gnat and told the man to mind his manners or she would speak to the commander of the British troops. But they are our allies, missis, said the X-ite. What we do is Greek business, keeping order, and the British mind their own affairs,

give Atabrine pills and chocolate. We will find the Communist Efstathiou when he comes creeping out of his hole like a rat. Errieta protested that her husband was no Communist but a loyal Greek citizen.
Then where, demanded the other, was the portrait of the king? The
king, said Errieta, who sat in London drinking tea while Greeks were
starving to death. Well, we shall go but we'll be back, declared the
leader, because we don't intend to leave Skyros Monday morning, and
even when we do go we will come back, while loyal police in the village
will have their eyes open to lay hands on the Communist Efstathiou
when he creeps from his rat hole. Yes, we will cleanse Greece of
resistance rot. And then they were gone.

George came down slowly from the hiding place, sat on the edge
of the bed, his head and arms hanging down. He told Errieta that he
knew what she would want: to hide him again. Yes, of course, she said,
naturally, until the danger had passed. But he was not sure he could
bear it again, living constantly under the threat of discovery, never
leaving the house. It might not be so long this time, his wife protested,
though she thought it would probably be longer. They would find a
dog to keep watch. And as soon as they could manage they would get
away from the island until the situation in the whole of Greece returned
to normal, as it had been before the war. He agreed that they must
go, for the danger to her was nearly as great as to him. He cannot have
failed to realize that all the while she was saving his life she was risking
her own. What he thought or felt about her willingness to do so we
do not know, but he must have understood that the importance to her
of her resolve was in direct proportion to the challenge of the risk.

Errieta was able with half a tin of meat to coax to the house a
wild black dog, and it seemed content to make its home in the rear
courtyard so long as it was fed. It did bark ferociously, snarl and con-
vincingly bare its teeth whenever a stranger appeared. Zaccharoula
was terrified at first. But Errieta suspected that the barking would
probably bring no bite. She went to the village frequently not only to
buy whatever provisions she could but also to put it about that her
husband had left the island.

The X-men departed in January, reminding the villagers that their
votes in the coming elections would tell who deserved to be called
Greeks. Eight days later the British soldiers struck their tents and
prepared to depart. The major called to bid Errieta farewell, somewhat

terrified of the fierce dog, and left with her several tins of bully beef. The village sighed in relief. But too soon. A detachment of the National Guard arrived a fortnight later, requisitioned George's mill—a fact she kept from her husband—and painted crowns on every wall till then overlooked. There had been fighting in the mountains round Lake Vegorritis and in the high Pindus, where the newly formed guerrilla forces were known to have grouped, and the Athens–Salonika railway had several times been dynamited. It was civil war. The elections were to take place on the last day of March. There were speeches at the school, but very few villagers attended, as no one had any doubt concerning the outcome. Five Americans came to the island to make sure there was no intimidation of the electorate. In the tavernas the guardsmen sneered and eyed them with contempt. Not one spoke a word of Greek. To the wonder of none and the consternation of very few the elections gave a large majority to the royalist but so-called Populist Party. There was a celebration in the village, but those elated were mostly the guardsmen, the police and a few who had everything to gain, like Nikos, the storekeeper, Vergottis, the postmaster, and old Spiro, the mayor. They looked forward to the imminent homecoming of the king, which would be decided by a plebiscite of which no one doubted the outcome. The Americans seemed satisfied and went away. Errieta said that it was a spiritual disgrace. George, weary and dispirited from his long confinement, said nothing.

One day the wall of the mayor's office bore a decree headed "Extraordinary Measures for Public Order." The measures included house-to-house searches without warrants and by force, outlawed strikes, empowered the police to impose a curfew at will and introduced the death penalty for any actions considered by the authorities threatening to national security. Even moral instigation of such actions was subject to the death penalty, which could be summarily pronounced at the discretion of special courts-martial.

Errieta returned home and told her husband that now they must leave the island as soon as possible. It was likely the X-ites would come back, and this time there was no telling what they might do. They might even set fire to the house. It was no longer thinkable to run the risk.

But how were they to get away? Errieta remembered the old fisherman in Linaria, Stefanos, who had risked the German torpedo boats to save George's friends. One night she would have to walk across the island to Linaria to find out whether he was willing and, if so, settle on the date. She would go soon. Fortunately there was some money and she had a diamond brooch that had been her mother's. The plebiscite was only weeks away. There was no time to lose. She went to Linaria by the light of a quarter moon and found the fisherman. George's father had once repaired the flooring of his shack and taken only one red snapper in payment. He had not forgotten. He would take them across to Kimi when the moon was down.

The very next night as they were preparing what little they could take with them a ferocious barking came from outside, followed by a volley of rifle fire, yelps, whines, silence. There was barely time for George to get into the hiding place before the front door came down with a crash. Errieta hurried to confront the invaders. There were seven or eight men. She called them brigands and cowards for having shot an innocent dog. They pushed her aside and proceeded to search the house, overturning furniture and smashing crockery. Finding food in the kitchen cupboards, they whooped and seized it all. They also took the blankets from the bed. And where was the traitor Efstathiou? one of them demanded. Errieta called them fools and said her husband had been gone from the island for more than a year. But she must know his whereabouts, the other insisted, and she could be made to talk. She calmly said that she knew nothing. Then another spoke, saying that they could at least force a little pleasure upon her, all Communist women were well known to be whores, and he went toward her, waving his flashlight in her face. The others laughed. Errieta stepped backward, but the would-be attacker followed, stretching out one hand toward her breasts, and she could see the grime between his fingers. Stay back, she cried, you must not come close, because I am sick, sick with tuberculosis. She warned of contagion, but they said all women complained of sickness and it was meaningless. How Errieta knew what to do she never knew. Drawing between her teeth the inner flesh of both cheeks, she bit violently through it, choking even as she did so, and spat a mouthful of blood onto the man who threatened her. He jumped backward. She coughed and spat again. She called them robbers and vandals but said that all the same she didn't wish them a slow and terrible death. They grumbled and muttered and after a minute or two trooped outside into the darkness. The next time, one of them threatened in parting, maybe they would burn that pretty house to the ground.

George was enraged. But there was nothing to be done, Errieta said, and no serious damage had been caused. Her mouth would be sore for a few days, that was all. Now it was clear that their departure could be none too soon.

The front door was repaired, the shutters bolted, the windows nailed shut. The goat, chickens, doves were entrusted to Zaccharoula, who wept. They kissed her and were gone.

The fisherman kept his word. As Skyros fell behind them, both George and Errieta looked back at the black silhouette. It was the second time they were leaving the island as fugitives, and they had lived through years of peril. It must have seemed to them both that only their devotion to each other could have enabled them to survive.

From Kimi they had to cross most of Euboea on foot, going slowly, because George tired fast, having had no proper exercise for so long, and had to rest. But they were lucky. The villagers they encountered were kind. The ancient tradition of hospitality toward strangers was still strong at that time in those remote localities. And they were helped by money. In some places they stayed two or three days while George regained his strength. It took them nearly three weeks to reach Athens. Thus they had plenty of time to consider what they should do when they got there. To go to a hotel seemed out of the question, as there was no knowing whether or not George was officially listed as a man wanted by the authorities, and his arrest, even by regular police rather than X-ites, was a danger they could not afford to run. They would have to find a place where they could reside in security, now both in hiding but far less vulnerable than they had been in Skyros. How to go about this was the question. Somewhere in Athens, living under a false name, was Phaedon, whom they had not seen for a decade and could hardly hope to find. But then Errieta remembered that at her wedding had been a friend of Phaedon's named Aleca Diamando-poulos, who had invited them to her villa in Ambelokipi. Perhaps she was still there and might know where to find Phaedon.

They had some trouble locating the villa. Aleca, of course, was still there, and she remembered very well both Errieta and her young husband, found them drastically changed but did not say so. Yes, she knew where Phaedon lived and how to get in touch with him. But it was dangerous. Though Athens might seem peaceful, danger waited at every street corner for anyone who disagreed with the government. For the time being, Errieta and George could stay in Ambelokipi. Oh, they had so much to tell of the war, the civil war, all the terrible and grotesque events of the ten years since they had seen one another.

Two days later Phaedon came to the villa after dark. Errieta recognized him only because she had known that he alone was coming. They kissed and she said that he hadn't changed a bit. He said the same. Then they laughed. It was not easy to talk. Too much had happened to them both that defied the extremes of communication. So they talked about old times in London, the people they had known, concerts at Wigmore Hall, exhibitions at the Zwemmer Gallery. Another life. And the professor? He had been killed by a bomb in 1942, so had not known the worst of what was to happen in his homeland. The worst? It was still to come, Phaedon said. But what could conceivably be worse, Errieta wondered, than all they had already lived through? Aleca and Phaedon shrugged. After a few months on Makronisos, said Phaedon, one of his closest friends had become a police informer and promised to denounce him if they chanced to meet again. Makronisos? Yes, that was the island concentration camp just off Cape Sounion where suspects were sent, and ugly reports of tortures came back to the mainland. They had passed that island en route to Skyros that first summer long ago. Now it was a name that terrified the populace. Then maybe, said Errieta, it would be best to leave the country until conditions became more normal. But both Aleca and Phaedon said for God's sake not to try that, nothing being more dangerous. And even this villa was not entirely safe. They suspected that the police kept an occasional eye on it, as Aleca's active role in the resistance to the German occupation was known. Some secure hideaway would have to be found for Errieta and George. The sooner, the better. Aleca, ever resourceful, thought she knew of a place.

It was in Chalandri, a residential suburb only about eight kilometers away. There Aleca found through a trustworthy friend a small and uncomfortable house set well back from the street in an overgrown garden. Moreover, this friend had three large dogs, fierce barkers all three, and would be happy to loan one of them to her tenants, whom she never met. The rent was nominal and payment could be indefinitely deferred. Errieta and George settled gladly into this refuge, soon making it more comfortable and convenient. Still, they felt homesick for Skyros, missed the sea and worried about the house and mill they had had to leave behind. But they did not expect that their exile would be prolonged. Surely the situation must become stabilized soon, the normal regime of law and order restored. In their new surroundings, where no one knew them, they dared to venture out now and then, and went often to Ambelokipi. Aleca was of inestimable help, providing food, good cheer and occasionally an evening party of sympathetic friends, a luxury almost forgotten by George and Errieta. Remittances from Errieta's bank in London would temporarily be made to Aleca. Phaedon, embittered and pessimistic, they saw seldom, Clio never, for she refused to leave the room in which her son had died of hunger.

The plebiscite took place on a sparkling day of September. British troops, National Guardsmen and police patrolled the polling places. But in the mountains of Thrace and Macedonia armed bands of guerrillas, led by Communist cadres as they had been during the Nazi occupation, waited. And everyone knew that the ELAS army had not disbanded. So the polling was peaceful in an aura of fatalism and fear. Five days later it was announced that seventy percent of the populace had voted for restoration of the monarchy.

So the king returned to his capital, his palace, his people. There were celebrations. The monarch made a proclamation stating that the rules of a democratic regime must be applied equally and without favor. Phaedon laughed, observing that he had said the same thing ten years before and six months afterward instituted the Metaxas dictatorship.

By the end of that year there were ten thousand guerrillas in the mountains. From one side of the country to the other fighting became general. In Macedonia and Thrace, the Peloponnese, even some of the islands. Raiders came down repeatedly to dynamite the Athens–Salonika railway. Government troops were ineffective, for the guerrillas used the same tactics that had been effective against the Germans, and morale was low. There were frequent desertions, mass courts-martial of soldiers refusing to fight and repeated purges of the officer corps.

The elections, the plebiscite, the king's return had changed nothing, achieved nothing. Corruption grew like gangrene. Abuses by reactionary groups like the X-ites went unchecked, while no program for reform or reconstruction of the ravaged country had been proposed. Personal security became a joke. Even the British, having created this situation, acknowledged the grave inadequacy of their handiwork and declared that drastic reforms were imperative: amnesty for political prisoners, restoration of constitutional liberties and a guarantee of new elections. This said, they blandly announced that before spring all their troops would be withdrawn from the country. But if British battalions and pounds sterling were withdrawn, the regime could not survive. Alarm ran riot in the lounge of the Grande Bretagne Hotel.

It was short-lived. Hardly had the first contingent of departing Tommies taken ship than the United States promised to supply what forces might be necessary, plus three hundred million dollars in aid to sustain the British policy.

In Athens no outright fighting took place, but unrest grew daily more and more open. People in the street eyed each other with mistrust. Duplicity and betrayal were the staples of each morning. Arrests were arbitrarily made in hotels, tavernas, shops, streetcars, cinemas and public toilets. The general rumor told increasingly lurid stories of what happened to those who were detained.

One evening in the kitchen Errieta turned away from the stove, stepped on a spoon that lay underfoot and fell backward against the burning stove, where for an instant of excruciating pain she awkwardly flailed her arms before falling to the floor. George hurried to help her to her feet. She groaned but at the same time insisted that it was nothing, a misstep, no cause for concern. Still, it was only with difficulty that she was able to undress and get into bed. In the morning her back was mottled black and purple, livid, and she could barely raise herself above the mattress. George declared that a doctor must be sent for. She would not have it. Her refusal was categorical. No doctor, she said, no stranger, no untoward incident in the anonymous rhythm of their days, no asking of unanswerable questions. For the sake of a clumsy misstep she absolutely refused to take a risk. Perhaps Aleca could get some aspirin. She would mend very nicely in time. Both Phaedon and Aleca, who did indeed bring aspirin, tried to persuade her to have a doctor. They knew one who was trustworthy. But Errieta would not be persuaded. "After all the dangers we'd been through," she told me, "I refused to run a single unnecessary risk." Lying in bed, she read Homer aloud. It was weeks before she was able to sit out in the sun.

Meanwhile, the old king died, replaced by his brother Paul and

Queen Frederika, sometime member of the Hitler Youth. And nothing changed, Athens more and more a capital still at war. Every day American personnel and equipment appeared in the streets in greater numbers. It was no secret that the guerrillas kidnapped hundreds of children and herded them to the mountains, even, some said, as far as Yugoslavia or Bulgaria. They burned towns, hanged mayors, abducted doctors and plundered farmland. Government troops crucified guerrilla prisoners on the mulberry trees at Kanalia. Others they bound hand and foot and threw into Lake Kastoria, and yet others they drenched in gasoline and burned alive. But seemingly no horror could stem the conflict or calm divisive passions. Queen Frederika presented a number of peacocks to the public gardens, and the Sophoulis government talked about amnesty for guerrillas who surrendered their arms. The population talked about the prison island of Makronisos, where it was said that hands and feet were amputated at random without anesthetic.

Mrs. Perdikidi wrote in care of Aleca, communicating parental criticism in terms which added acrimony to octogenarian outrage. It was preposterous, she said, for Errieta to remain in Greece when law and order in that naturally lawless and disorderly country were at the lowest ebb in civilized memory. Moreover, filial concern might legitimately have been expected, after ten years and more, to bring her daughter home for a visit, especially in view of her advanced age, albeit she was in tolerable health. The British press contained appalling accounts of Communist atrocities, and Mrs. Perdikidi hoped that American force of arms would promptly set things right. Mr. Churchill shared her hope. A fond paragraph was appended by Julia, who hoped the same things as their mother and Mr. Churchill but most especially to see Errieta soon. It was an easy letter to answer.

The civil war went on and on. Governments rose and fell, altered not a bit in policy for a new name or progressive statement from one day to the next. In a year the cost of living doubled. A third of the population was virtually destitute. Athens speculators cornered the market in olive oil and tripled the price. Army commanders in the field acted on their own initiative and declined to render reports to Athens. X-ites and other royalist bands still terrorized the provinces and islands, supplied, directly or indirectly, by the regular army, which in turn was supplied by the United States. But the guerrillas could not be defeated militarily. Politically the years were against them. The population had

had enough. Then the Yugoslav frontier was closed to them, Marshal Tito having been repudiated by the Cominform, whereas the guerrillas supported it. And rumor had it that Stalin had promised to leave Greece in the Western sphere of influence. The long-awaited offensive against the guerrillas' Grammos redoubt began in August, when the terrible drought of 1949 had lasted already since spring. In the field were 197,000 troops, supported by planes armed with rockets and napalm, against 17,000 guerrillas. But the fighting was ferocious and bloody, lasting seven weeks. At the end of September the guerrilla headquarters capitulated. The abject survivors were herded into imprisonment. In Athens there was jubilation. The king and queen congratulated their subjects, and the Americans were satisfied that the eastern Mediterranean had been secured.

Aleca, Errieta and George had known that it would eventually come to this. If they were not precisely relieved, they were tired of the danger, the bloodshed and the hunger. It seemed incredible, but they had been in the little house in Chalandri for four years. Now, perhaps, they could set about contemplating the prospect of reinventing their lives. It would take daring and imagination. The civil war was over, yes, but acts of violence, though sporadic, were still widespread. From Macedonia to the Peloponnese, National Guardsmen and X-ites administered arbitrary beatings in the name of the king. Any man who had ever had ELAS sympathies or associations did well to keep them to himself and wait for them to be forgotten or, if one believed in miracles, forgiven.

4

It was obvious that one or the other must soon return to Skyros to find out what had become of their property. It was also obvious that the person to go would have to be Errieta. For who could tell how George might be greeted after so long? He had not been seen in the village for something like seven years, and it was impossible to predict what assumptions the villagers would make to explain such a prolonged absence. Or how they would react to the fugitive's reappearance. Errieta had not completely regained her strength since the accident. She never did. Yet nothing would have been less like her than to mention it. Aleca made the arrangements for her journey. It was far less arduous than before.

When her boat put in at Linaria she felt an emotion that astonished her: the joy of homecoming, and it was as if all the years since The Catastrophe had held in store their provision of feeling just for this moment. Adding to her astonishment was the presence by the jetty of an ancient automobile with the word TAXI painted on its front doors. She took it. The driver was a young fellow she thought she had glimpsed as a child in the village but who did not appear to recognize her. And the donkey track across the island was now a rough but passable road. When they came round the last headland below the village it was dusk, and as she looked up she was yet again astonished, for electric lights twinkled up and down as high as the Kastro. She exclaimed at them. The driver said they had had electricity for a long time already. Errieta immediately thought of George's mill and all the fine electric tools he would now be able to install.

The road ended just above the beach. It was almost dark, but she had thought to bring a flashlight. Everything looked the same: beach, stream, bluff. She lugged her satchel up the path. And there was the house. Wisteria covered the front of it completely. Trees and plants were all larger than in memory. The shutters, windows and doors had been smashed. The interior lay full of broken glass and splintered wood, overturned furniture, scattered books, ripped fabric. But the house itself was intact. Intact. She had anticipated such damage. Or worse. But here was the dwelling place of her life intact. Amid the bedroom debris she dragged the remnants of their mattress onto the bed and lay there fully clothed, listening to the gentle melody of the sea, the house safe around her.

In the morning she went upstream to the little house hidden among flowers and oleanders. The door opened and Zaccharoula stood there, shrieking. The two women embraced and wept. For a long time they wept before being able to speak. Then they told each other their stories. Errieta's house had been vandalized several times, but the last time was now long past. After the first devastation Zaccharoula had been able to save a few items she thought of value. A few lamps, kitchen utensils, some books, linen, one chair and the ancient phonograph with its albums of records. The goat had survived, also a few chickens and a dove or two. Damage to the house didn't appear very serious.

Young Vyron, George's apprentice, now a carpenter of proven skill, would probably be able to make the necessary repairs without much delay. Meanwhile, Errieta could stay in Zaccharoula's house, where she might not be so comfortable but at least warm and dry. As for George's carpentry mill, it was used by every man and his brother as a shelter for goats, but it, too, stood intact. And in the village, Errieta asked, in the village, did people still speak of her with animosity? Would there be danger? Zaccharoula had not heard the name of George Efstathiou pronounced in the village for years. As for danger, it would always be the brother of one's days, would it not? That was the only mention Errieta ever heard from Zaccharoula concerning her own tragedy. Errieta knew that she would have to show herself in the village and see what reaction her reappearance caused.

In the morning she walked up the steep path, and she noticed the steepness. It had not affected her before. Halfway to the village she sat down on a low wall to rest, annoyed and resentful. Her fiftieth birthday had passed, to be sure, during the fugitive years at Chalandri. But was age anything? She went on. To find the village changeless was as natural as the sunshine. In the doorways the women in black courteously responded to her greetings, but that was tradition. The men seated outside the tavernas observed her with indifference. She went into the store. Nikos had grown older and fatter. He was amiable, if not friendly. Skyros had wondered, he said, whether they would one day return. And why in the world not? Errieta inquired. Oh, events, events, troubles. Who could say what unforeseeable consequences might ensue? And her husband? Had he returned home? Not yet, as he had business in Athens. Well, Nikos allowed, it would not be a bad thing for George Efstathiou to come back to Skyros. His carpentry mill, plus the possibility of milling flour, would be a very beneficial thing for the island. Then there would be no danger to him now? asked Errieta. Only envy, said Nikos. She went also to the post office, dusty and flyblown as ever, the slovenly postmaster behind his counter, his slatternly wife in her corner and the extraordinarily beautiful daughter —a caprice of nature, springing from such graceless parents—gazing wistfully out the window. There was no mail for her, of course, but she wanted it known that she would soon be expecting some and that it should not be returned to the sender. And Mr. Efstathiou? He was not with her, Errieta replied. So, sneered the postmaster, he has left you then, and good sense I'd call it. Not at all, she calmly rejoined, not at all. He will be returning soon to his home and his work. Then let him keep the peace, warned the postmaster, as Skyros needs no more trouble. Oh, indeed, indeed, said Errieta, hating the man but knowing the power of politeness. As she turned to leave she noticed with surprise a telephone at the far end of the counter, a black, hump-backed apparatus, and realized that little by little the world of today was forcing its way into Skyros. She was not sure that she liked this sign that there would also be a tomorrow.

Vyron brought a team of boys to clean the house. The wisteria about the terrace was cut back. Replacing smashed doors and windows would take a little longer. Gradually the place began to look as it had always looked. Fortunately the plumbing had not been damaged. Things would have to be ordered from the mainland, but that was easier than before the war. Errieta sat on the millstone at the edge of the bluff, gazing across the bay at the outstretched arm of the island, and she knew why she had so often longed for this place during the years of exile in Athens. It told her the truth. She knew why she had seemingly sacrificed so much in order to make Skyros her home. George's youth and devotion, his need had from the first given her back the other Errieta, the youthful being of variety and promise by whose girlish yearnings she would always measure the fulfillment of time. Neither burning Smyrna nor sheltering London mattered here. It had been a birth, certainly, the only one she would ever know.

Meanwhile George had not been wasting his time in Athens. He visited the woodworking and carpentry mills, took temporary work in several, used the newest tools and studied what techniques might be turned to advantage in Skyros. When Errieta returned, he listened to all the news of the island, asked many questions and pondered the best time to return. A few months would be needed to obtain the machinery he meant to order for the mill. To pay for it would take not half but almost all of Errieta's remaining capital. No matter, said George. Once the mill was working, there would be money and to spare. Errieta surprised herself by feeling some reluctance to convert summarily into lathes and band saws so much of the modest remainder of her inheritance. This, of course, was exactly what she herself had urged and wanted. Still, a peculiar sense of melancholy persisted.

Mrs. Perdikidi was not diminished in assertiveness by the years.

She wrote to inquire and to pronounce, having long since assumed that her daughter's absence, now prolonged beyond a decade and a half, was evidence of wrongheaded eccentricity or derangement or both. Julia added that their mother, while forceful in her opinions, did in her eighty-eighth year grow weak and would be sustained by a visit from her firstborn. Errieta replied with genuine regret that she could not absent herself for the time being.

Phaedon went to England with his wife, whose mind seemed permanently unhinged. He said they would come back, back to Skyros, when Clio was better. But they all knew it was not to be.

At last the machinery George had ordered was all assembled, together with furniture and household effects Errieta had had to buy in order to replace those broken or stolen. All this would voyage by ship to Linaria, while they went by the faster, easier route overland to Kimi. How long before had it been when they had made the selfsame journey on foot?

The goats were evicted from George's mill, the machinery installed, electric cables brought down from the village. George worked hard, as there was at once much demand for the finely smoothed planks, lathed wood and finished building components that his machines could turn out quickly and cheaply. He made agreements to mill all of the grain from the western wheat fields, receiving in payment a percentage of the flour. From the pine woods in the center of the island he bought trees, hauled to the mill by donkey. Very soon he had to employ two assistants. The people in the village had greeted his return at first with reserve, if not outright suspicion, but as they soon recognized that he was on his way to considerable prosperity they became more cordial. He was invited to drink coffee and ouzo in the tavernas, the men made jokes and no one asked where he had been during the years of danger.

Errieta realized that George no longer told her everything, consulted her, asked for her opinions and judgments. This was natural, she told herself, after fifteen years of marriage, and she must accept the change. It was in her as well. Her hair had turned completely white after the accident, and her flesh hung loosely on her bones. One might have thought her ten years older than she was. The pain in her back came and went. She mentioned it to no one, but Zaccharoula, who was too observant to miss much, guessed. George noticed nothing.

Errieta had engaged a strong and conscientious serving girl called Annoula, who did most of the hard household work. Thus the life that they had known in Skyros before the war resumed as it had been except that it was not at all as it had been. Errieta never spoke to me of the intimate aspects of her life with George, though she spoke of almost everything else, nor did any other person ever refer to it. But a decisive transition must have taken place. The husband was a powerful young man, while the wife seemed almost to be approaching old age. She was lively, talkative, serious, intelligent, amusing, but she was not young.

George observed that their house was now one of the few on the island without electricity. It was unreasonable, he said, since the wiring had been installed when the house was built, and the municipality would pay for the cables if he paid for the poles. It wouldn't require more than a dozen, fifteen at most. Errieta said no. She didn't want electricity now, or need it. Lamps had been enough for so long. They would be enough still. Annoula filled them, trimmed the wicks and washed the chimneys. George pointed to the wiring, the switches, the empty sockets that hung from the ceiling, but Errieta said that it was too late. He did not insist, for now he came home only to eat and sleep. There was talk in the village, he said, of building a tourist hotel. It would mean much work for him, added prosperity for the island. Tourists in Skyros, Errieta remarked, would surely signal the end of an era. It had already ended, of course. The occasional traveler had always turned up. Like herself, Phaedon and Clio long ago. And Herr Reichel. George remembered. Perhaps Errieta might rent rooms to the tourists. That would bring in a bit of money and provide an entertaining diversity to the routine of her existence. He was aware that it must be dull for her being alone all day. It was not dull, she said. There was Zaccharoula. And she had taken in a stray cat.

Mrs. Perdikidi continued to write. With the asperity of old age she ventured to wonder whether she would ever see her elder daughter again. Errieta replied with picturesque news of the island and accounts of the time-consuming activities that occupied her and her husband, much of which she invented for the sake of her mother's peace of mind, and her own.

Having observed that the taxi did a tolerable business, the storekeeper went to Volos, bought a used Opel bus, brought it back to Skyros and put it in service running back and forth between Linaria and the village. Construction of the tourist hotel began, and it did in fact keep George very busy, so that often he did not return home for the evening meal, sending a boy to advise Mrs. Efstathiou, and sometimes even slept at the mill in a small back room where he had set up a cot. It was in the spring of 1957 that George learned at last, while in Volos to order fittings for the hotel, what had become of his old friend Stelio Vetsanopoulos, the only person before Errieta who had treated him with human decency. Stelio had been arrested in 1947, deported to one of the prison islands, Makronisos or some other, nobody seemed to be sure, and had died there. Of pneumonia, stated the report sent to his family. George mourned for him. Errieta was surprised by the intensity of his emotion.

Large white ships now dropped anchor twice weekly in the bay at Linaria. Tourists were ferried ashore in small boats and transported across the island by bus to the now at last completed hotel. There were not very many at first but the Greek tourist agency advertised. Of the rooms available few stood empty for long. Errieta let it be known that she would be willing to take in visitors unable to find lodgings else-where. Before long she had as many as she could comfortably cope with, sometimes more. Her hospitality being exceptional, people like Aleca told their friends, who told still others. And that is how Christian and I came to her house in Skyros in the month of July 1959. We stayed until mid-September.

As the summer progressed it seemed to me that our hostess under-went some change. It was difficult to define. I still didn't know her very well. I had then learned only the outlines of the story of which I have now related everything I know except the conclusion. The details, nu-ances, suppositions and assumptions were still to come. It was in early August, I think, that the change became noticeable. Errieta grew less forthcoming. Our conversations were no longer so spontaneous, in-teresting and jolly. She spent hours seated on the millstone at the edge of the bluff, gazing fixedly across the bay, as if awaiting some sign or harkening to some signal. I remembered she had told me that severe winter storms sometimes washed away great chunks of the bluff and that during her first years on the island an old, old man had told her that a chapel had once stood nearby but had been engulfed in one night by a terrible storm. And sometimes, she said, she imagined she could hear its sunken bell tolling, as in the piano piece by Debussy. Maybe, I thought, that was what she was listening to, that tolling beneath the waves. I was thirty-six that summer. Still, I had to get up almost every night to go to the bathroom, a little young for that nuisance. One night I stepped on a dead rat that Errieta's cat had deposited as a token of prowess on the threshold of the room that was usually her mistress's. And so I noticed that George Efstathiou no longer came to sleep under the pine tree.

As Christian and I did not take our evening meals with Errieta, we usually ate in the hotel dining room, where the food was monotonous but digestible, or in one of the small tavernas set along the brink of the bluff beyond the hotel, especially one belonging to a raffish old fellow called Kokalenia, whose fare was less monotonous but also less digestible, and the wine terrible. This Kokalenia, like so many of his countrymen, had gone to America to make his fortune, then returned in the maturity of his years to his birthplace to enjoy it. He had spent more than twenty years in Chicago, and consequently spoke passable English. It was perfectly delightful to sit on Kokalenia's terrace at the end of the day and watch the sun go down while sipping little glasses of ouzo, eating the black olives of the island and spitting the pits over the edge of the bluff. Christian had never in his life enjoyed such a carefree and happy time, having from the age of fourteen always had to work hard and gotten little thanks either for his work or the sexual favors he often had to grant in order to keep it. I think those two months may have been the most enjoyable of his life. It didn't seem to me then that he drank to excess. His greatest pleasure was to walk through the vineyards to the far end of the island, swim naked in the glistening water and lie afterward for hours on the sand.

Kokalenia was proud of his ability to speak English and liked to show it off by plying me with inconsequential chatter, an inclination which I tried to prevent from becoming a habit. But it was from Kokalenia that I learned what had caused the change in Errieta. He knew, of course, that we were staying with her. Jacques Cervione and Michel Richard had joined us by this time and were installed in the tower. One evening when we were happily settled on his terrace Kokalenia said that he supposed we knew that Mrs. Efstathiou was no longer Mrs. Efstathiou. No, we didn't know it. Oh yes, the taverna keeper rather gleefully asserted, for George Efstathiou had obtained a divorce in order to marry the most desirable girl in the village, the daughter of the postmaster, a nubile beauty who would bear many children. The old foreign woman would never be able to give him children, and a normal man wanted offspring, especially if he was prosperous and could provide handsomely for his family. And after all, the old foreign woman had bought the boy as a husband and held him for twenty years, so she'd gotten sufficient value for her investment. That was what was said in the village.

The vulgarity of the taverna keeper's version of the situation only made it more lamentable. Errieta's devotion to her husband, her sacrifice of a totally different previous existence, her decisive role in saving his life and making his fortune: all this I already knew. That he could reject and humiliate her after everything they had lived through together seemed to me inexpressibly callous and hurtful. I did not let her know that I had discovered the reason for the change in her manner. It was not until the following summer that I learned how it came about.

A further cause for melancholy materialized toward the end of August. A telegram from Athens told us that Aleca had suddenly died of a stroke. She couldn't have been more than sixty. But she had never spared herself, had braved great dangers and at least once had been severely interrogated by the National Guard. A valiant, sensitive, idealistic individual was gone, one whose like it would not be easy to encounter again. We mourned her. I think this grief may have distracted Errieta temporarily from her own sorrow.

The walk up to the village was steep and fatiguing, especially under the midday sun, and I went there seldom that first summer. But I did go occasionally, and especially to the post office, hoping for mail, where I found the postmaster quite as surly and uncouth as I'd been told. And after learning of George Efstathiou's intentions I took care to scrutinize the daughter. She had a pretty face, to be sure, and lustrous hair, but her expression was petulant and her figure, though ample and full-breasted, promised to run to excess flesh. Still, she looked as though she could produce plenty of children.

By the end of August, Jacques and Michel had returned to Paris. There were one or two days of rain. The wisteria blossoms had almost all fallen from the vine above the terrace. There was the savor of autumn in the wind and Errieta's sadness was more apparent than ever. It was time for us to think of leaving. Christian had been able to take so long a vacation only because the manufacturer of knitwear for whom he worked was reorganizing his business. As it turned out, this reorganization cost Christian his job, but there was no threat of that as yet. The leave-taking from Errieta and from Skyros was emotional and regretful. We promised to return the following summer. It was not before the last week of September that we reached Paris, having been away for three and a half months.

I wrote to her in October, my letter mainly concerned with plans for the following summer. She replied on the first of November, agreeing to my requests for reserved rooms in July and August of 1960, and mentioning that she was planning to go to England. Her letter was signed "Harrie Perdikidi." I knew, of course, that Perdikidi was her maiden name, but did not find out till later that she had been called Harrie as a girl. It was the only letter she ever signed with that name. A postscript followed:

> *P.S. The change of name is because I have now got a divorce*
> *from my husband. It was in process while you were here as*
> *you no doubt learned from the village gossip. It's sad to end*
> *up so after one has lived many years happily together but*
> *there's too big a difference in our ages and that doesn't work*
> *with a person of my husband's temperament.*

What I replied I don't know. It was difficult, if not impossible, to say anything pertinent, so I wrote banalities. I heard from her again just before Christmas. She had not yet departed, as there was trouble in processing her passport, and then she had had influenza, which weakened her, so had put off her voyage until after the new year.

Early in March I had a letter from England. It said in part:

> *I found my mother and sister very well here—my mother*
> *looking and acting very much younger than she was last time*
> *I saw her but, except for the pleasure of seeing them, I have*
> *had a wretched time here—have been ill the whole time, not*
> *able to go out or do anything. I've only now recovered and*
> *this is the time I should be thinking of returning to Skyros*
> *but I shall put it off till about the eighteenth. I shall be sorry*

to leave my family but very glad to be back in Skyros again.
I get quite homesick for it. And I wonder how my little cat is
getting on without me.

In fact, it was not until April 23 that Errieta reached Skyros. As I
later learned little by little, while in England she had suffered a nervous
collapse caused both by her despair over the divorce and by the necessity of having to accept her mother's judgment—even if it was left
unsaid—that the marriage had been folly in the first place and could
not have turned out otherwise. The benevolent affection of her younger
sister was her consolation and her balm. But it is certain that she was
never again the same Errieta I had known during those first few weeks
in Skyros.

In mid-November I went to America for five months. When I came
back, I found that Christian had lost his job and taken to hard, continuous drinking. There was no question of his returning to Skyros the
following summer. Jacques and Michel, however, intended to come
in August, and several other friends also planned to spend some
weeks.

I arrived in Skyros on the fifth of July, found Errieta changed but
on the surface cheerful. My rooms were just as I had left them, and I
was able to set about writing at once.

That the change in Errieta was profound and permanent became
apparent little by little. She chatted and laughed and managed her
household very much as before, but there was always a somber un-
dertone, as of a distant rumble in the earth signifying the eventuality
of a cataclysm. Not a danger for today or tomorrow but for sometime
in the future, devastating and final. Gradually, through a word here,
a word there, quiet confidences in the late afternoon, implications and
inferences, the circumstances of the divorce became more or less intelligible.

There had been no way of broaching the matter subtly. George
had said one day that he did not wish his sons and daughters to be
the children of an old man. She had understood at once. Remarriage
was the only path to paternity. Yes. Which would require divorce?
Inevitably. After so long and so much? There was no other way. And
when George had told her the name of his bride-to-be, Errieta gasped
with the pang of indignation and grief. And George had hung his head.

But if she hadn't given him so much, he couldn't possibly have asked this of her. If she had ever been selfish, how could he have made this ultimate demand upon her generosity? She must grant it. To have been found wanting then would have been to betray not only that day and all those to come but every day of the entire twenty years past. Had she not from the first accepted and acknowledged that her risk might come to this? Only by letting him go with simplicity and goodwill could she hope to do for him at the last what she had always hoped, and only longed, to do for him. So she had simply agreed to his request. He kissed her and went away. A few days later Vyron came to collect his clothes and personal effects, including his unused pistol and the boxes of ammunition, the pamphlets having long since been burned. Nothing material remained to remind her of him save the house itself and the significance of every part of it, no matter how minute, for his hands had touched each one.

Zaccharoula sobbed and said that it could not be true. Errieta had to console her by explaining that what had come to pass had had to happen in order to fulfill the promise of human nature. As an artist, she said, Zaccharoula must understand that the imperative of creativity could not be set aside simply to accommodate personal feelings. Well, well, that was possible, Zaccharoula said, but she felt like burning every last one of her embroideries to show that personal feelings did not necessarily deserve accommodation. Errieta scolded her for such foolishness. Then they drank herbal tea together and sat a long time in silence, listening to the gurgle of the stream.

It was that summer that Errieta took me to see Zaccharoula's embroideries. They had a unique, magical beauty, somewhat like a blend of the Douanier Rousseau and the early Chagall at their whimsical, colorful best. I longed to have one but did not dare violate their secret beauty by crude inquiries or offers.

Jacques and Michel arrived, and the others. We had a good time together, and Errieta clearly enjoyed having us in her house. She prepared delicious lunches for us, lobsters, rack of lamb, pigeons and all sorts of fish. In the late afternoon we would sit under the wisteria drinking tea and talking of the world. A very great deal of what I have already related I learned during those two enchanting months. Not once did any of us catch a glimpse of George Efstathiou but we heard from Kokalenia that he had married the postmaster's daughter, who was already with child.

Errieta had never completely recovered from the accident to her back. It gave her pain more or less constantly, but she maintained that this was only rheumatism. In Skyros the standard treatment for rheumatism, as well as for many other ills, was to lie on the beach and heap burning-hot sand over one's body, remaining thus, as in an oven, for half an hour or more. It was a common sight to see people lying beneath mounds of sand, only their heads visible, along the stretch of beach between the hotel and the stream. As Jacques was a doctor, Errieta consulted him, but it was difficult without the equipment of a clinic or laboratory for him to arrive at any responsible diagnosis. He told us, however, that he felt Errieta's ills to be more serious than rheumatism.

The others left before I did, but even I departed on the third of September. The leave-taking from Errieta was emotional and sorrowful, for the two summers spent in the same house and my growing familiarity with her story, of which I now felt almost to have become a part, had made for a strong attachment between us. Promising to return the following summer, I kissed her on the cheek. She wept. My own eyes were not dry, and I turned away quickly to follow the boy who was carrying my bags down to the beach. But I looked back from the far side of the stream and, as I had expected, Errieta stood at the edge of the bluff, waving, her white hair blown round her head like a halo by the breeze.

From Athens I went to Hyères in the South of France to stay with my friend Marie-Laure de Noailles. And from there I wrote to Errieta to congratulate her on her birthday, which I knew to be September 15, telling her where she would find the birthday present I had hidden in the house before leaving. This was an anthology of contemporary English and American poetry which I usually carried about with me and which I had myself received as a birthday gift ten or twelve years before. I had inscribed it to Errieta "with all my affection" and placed it in a box on the top shelf of one of her cupboards. Having heard nothing from her by the end of the month, however, I wrote again, once more wishing her a happy birthday and telling her where the book was hidden. Toward mid-October I received the following letter:

Errieta's Risk

Skyros
9.10.60

Dearest James,

I was so happy to get your letter, but it was the first I have had since you left. I never received the birthday letter from Hyères that you speak about. What could have happened to it? I have lost no other letters. I can't understand why this one should have gone astray. And it would have given me so much pleasure because I never thought you would remember my birthday. And of course I had not found the book of poems hidden away in the top of the cupboard. I was delighted with that bit because it was like a child and I love to find grown-ups with a bit of the child in them still. As for the present in the box I was really moved to tears when I saw what book it was, for I'm sure you treasure that book and keep it generally by you and, as I see, it was given to you for your birthday and that you should give it to me! Dear James, I am so deeply grateful for all those affectionate thoughts. I am indeed very happy today.

Don't worry about my staying here alone. I'll be all right. I was only sad because of the parting and because there were things I should have liked to have done and didn't do and because I had that strange feeling of an end. And I'm afraid I overflowed a bit which I shouldn't have done.

But all in all I think I'm better here. It has become almost as much a part of me as the shell of a snail. And maybe a friend will come and stay with me for the winter. She wrote asking if I would have her and I wrote and told her what she must expect in the winter. I have not heard yet if that has frightened her off.

It's blowing a terrific gale today. I'm afraid there will be no mail for a day or two.

I suppose you are busy now typing your manuscript. Will you wait till you get to New York to send it to a publisher? And then how long before it is in print? You need to have patience to be a writer—everything takes such a long time. Will you thank Jacques and Michel for their letters—all so appreciative of their stay here. But I appreciated equally

*much having them here, so charming and friendly. Will you
please give them my affectionate greetings? And to you, dear
James, much love and my most affectionate thoughts.*

Errieta

Early in November I received another letter from Skyros, of which
I record here only the first paragraph, as the remainder is not so revealing and pertinent.

*Skyros
26.10.60*

Dear James,

*It was so nice to get your letter and I so much like to
think of you looking upon this place as a haven—a quiet res-
pite before you sail off again into your bigger, fuller life. May
you come this way again soon! And I shall be looking out for
the light of your ship from afar when it turns in here bringing happy days and harmony and sweet love and pleasant
memories for winter days. And, dear Captain, unload here as
much as you can of such cargo and don't be afraid of being
too forward when you are dealing in such precious stuff. Certainly for the old harbor-master who is sad and half-starved
it is very precious.*

I don't suppose that Errieta meant to be ironic when she suggested
that my life was bigger, fuller than her own. I'm sure she didn't. But
of course the largeness, the fullness of a life is not measured or determined by its events, its voyages, its variety but rather by the dimension of its spiritual components and the structure of its personal and
social commitments. Viewed from the perspective of such primary criteria it seemed to me that Errieta had had a life more full and large
than my own. I still believe that or I wouldn't be trying to preserve the
memory of it. In the same letter I was struck by her suggestion that I
need not "be afraid of being too forward," because in the course of
our long conversations I sometimes thought that perhaps I was, in fact,
being too forward, asking questions or broaching topics that were too
personal and that might trouble or offend. It's true that sometimes she
responded with hesitation or hinted rather than replied, but she never

made me feel that I had trespassed beyond the limit allowed by friendship. And I went far, as is evident from my account. But she must have known that my curiosity was the evidence of my esteem and my affection.

In December I went for a visit to America, and while there my grandmother, aged ninety-seven, died. And a peculiar piece of news came to me from Paris. Christian Davillerd had entered a monastery somewhere in Normandy, intending to take vows and devote the rest of his life to purely spiritual pursuits. I was saddened and shocked to hear this, and the next time I wrote to Errieta I told her of it. She sent back the following letter:

Skyros
11.2.61

Dear James,

Many thanks for your letter. I'm sorry to hear that you lost your Granny. If she lived with you always you will miss her but we can't expect to have Grannies always with us and if she died without suffering and with the affection of those she loved around her that is an enviable end.

I have been so much upset lately. James, what is this news about Christian? He has gone into a monastery and become a monk! I am so sad—so terribly sad about it. Did you know he was thinking of doing this? Why didn't you tell me about him? We could have put our heads together and thought of something for him—some way out of his difficulties. For, of course, he must have had difficulties and must have been very unhappy, poor boy. How dull of spirit I am! I never realized anything was wrong. What was the trouble? Was his work uncongenial? Superficial surroundings can become unbearable if you have a deep and serious nature or if you have a deep sorrow and when one is young it is so difficult to bear things.

Had he been thinking of taking this step for a long time? And is that why he didn't come to Skyros last summer or was it that he couldn't afford the trip? I hate to think that it might have been the latter case and I was so dull that I never thought of such a circumstance so as to tell him that he

Arlette as Garance in *Les Enfants du Paradis* [*Roger Forster, Paris*]

(above) Arlette's house on Belle-Ile; (opposite, top left) Arlette seated
on bench in front of her tower at La Houssaye [James Lord]; (top right)
Picnic at La Houssaye: Arlette seated in the center, James at extreme
left, Lel Bellanger center, and German officer at extreme right; (bottom)
Château de La Houssaye, with Arlette's tower at lower right [James
Lord]

(top) Portrait of Marie-Laure de Noailles by Pablo Picasso, ca. 1923 [collection of Nathalie Perrone]; (bottom) Portrait of Marie-Laure by Balthus, 1936 [collection of Nathalie Perrone]; (opposite) Second-floor landing of Marie-Laure's Paris mansion, with one of the "exiled" Goyas and a slice of Van Dyck

(opposite, top left) Marie-Laure and Oscar Dominguez at Saint-Bernard in front of a wrought-iron cat designed by Oscar [*James Lord*]; *(top right)* Marie-Laure at Saint-Bernard, 1960 [*James Lord*]; *(bottom)* Château Saint-Bernard, central pavilion [*James Lord*]; *(above left)* James and Claus von Bulow on the lawn at Saint-Bernard, 1954 [*Ned Rorem*]; *(above right)* James seated on Francis Poulenc's knees, 1961 [*Marie-Laure de Noailles*]; *(right)* Marie-Laure's tomb, 1992 [*James Lord*]

(above) The author's mother and father about the time of James's birth; *(below, left)* James, rebellious and moody, at age eighteen; *(right)* Mother in old age

didn't need money here. You must always remember that,
James—for anyone—that I can always take one person with-
out pay—and gladly too. But now he has gone beyond our
reach and we can do nothing more for him. I can only give
him the tenderest place in my heart and pray he may find
comfort and happiness and all he is longing for. And though
I can't approve of institutions that take away your freedom
and make you live an unnatural life yet I think the act of
giving up everything is in itself beautiful and strikes favor-
ably in a world where everyone is grabbing to get as much as
he can. But I hate to think of him shut up in a monastery.
He is so young! Has he taken the final vow or is there a term
of probation first? And how much freedom are they allowed?
Can he come and see you or go away for a time? Do write
and tell me everything and when you will be returning to
Paris.

> *With much love, Errieta*

It is a happy thing that she never knew what finally became of
Christian.

Not all of Errieta's letters were expressions of sadness, regret or
sympathy. She had a talent for writing about nothing in particular with
vivacity and warmheartedness, because she spontaneously put herself
into her words. As she herself said, "I always prefer a talking letter to
a newsy one." And toward the end of March, after my return to Paris,
I received a letter from which I quote one paragraph:

I'm very glad to see spring coming and the buds getting
fat and ready to burst. The winter, though so short, was more
than enough for me. We even had snow lying for a day and
such terrible storms and endless rain. The stream was a rag-
ing torrent that uprooted trees and carried them down to the
sea and did much other damage. It was impossible for any-
one to cross it for several days. A loaf of bread was flung
across to me at the narrowest part. For the rest I had to do
with what was in the house. Now that it has subsided some
stepping stones have been placed at the shallowest part but
they are far apart and not flat. You need to be very nimble to

*get across without falling in. I'm expecting the German am-
bassador and family for Easter and am hoping he'll be nimble. There's the further problem of how to get them up here.
The high seas and torrent together have washed away the
lower half of the path leading down to the sea so that there
is now a sudden drop of about two meters. I think a basket
and pulley are indicated. Or can you suggest something better? Your Western mind will probably run to moving stair-
cases and electric elevators! But I like to think of the
ambassador coming up in a basket. It would be such a nice
change for him.*

I encountered an American aged twenty-six and named Larry
Hager for whom I felt an immediate attraction, my only experience of
love at first sight. Two weeks after our meeting he came to live with
me in my small apartment. I had long before arranged with Errieta to
spend the summer in Skyros. Jacques and Michel were to come, as
usual, for a few weeks in August. So I invited Larry to join us and we
flew to Greece late in June. Never having set foot in that country, he
was excited to visit the sites of its antique glory, though I was to learn
the secret of his excitement only later. We toured the mainland for a
week and went to Skyros on the first of July, taking along for Errieta
a Limoges tea service that I bought in a shop next door to the Athénée
Palace Hotel.

Errieta seemed to me more downcast and in less good health than
the year before, but as usual she put upon her condition the very best
face she could manage, and for anyone who did not know her well
this was very good indeed. Larry and Errieta took to each other at
once. I was happy to see two people of whom I was exceptionally fond
become so congenial.

Two or three times a week I walked up to the village to inquire
of the obnoxious postmaster whether I had received any mail. A fortnight or so after our arrival I was surprised to find that there was a
letter for Larry. It bore the postmark of San Diego, California. When
I handed it to him, he read it, made no comment, and I resisted the
longing to ask what it said. I had to wait only until the next morning
to find out. As we lay on the beach together Larry explained to me
that before coming to Paris he had lived for several years with another

man in San Diego in a house which they owned jointly. And by an exquisite irony it happened that this man was Greek, had been born in Athens and taken to America at the outbreak of the war. He had written to say that he was still in love with Larry and was imploring him to return to their home. Having communed with his feelings most of the night, Larry said, he had decided that he must return to California to determine whether or not he desired to resume life with his former lover, and the sooner he set out the better. I was devastated by this revelation, of which I had never been given the slightest hint. When I asked Larry where he felt all this left me, he said he didn't know. He was sorry if the situation caused me distress, but he owed it, he believed, both to himself and to his friend to put their future to the test. And if the test should prove negative, I asked, what then? Well, said Larry, if I was willing to wait to see how things turned out in California, and if they did not turn out happily, and if I still cared for him enough to want him back, then he would return to Paris to live with me. I told him I would wait.

A couple of days later he departed. I stood at the edge of the bluff, watching him as he strode away along the water's edge. He had arranged to take the taxi to Linaria. I watched it climbing like a monstrous beetle to turn around the headland below the village and disappear. And I could not believe that what had happened had actually happened. That is, I couldn't accept it. Neither mentally nor physically could I accept it. I wrote about it endlessly in my journal, repeating and repeating the same phrases, the same inability to accept Larry's departure, the same longing that he should return. But he was gone, and I remained alone with my suffering like a victim and a fool. I was not alone, however.

At the end of the day, as Errieta and I sat beneath the wisteria, sipping tea, after long silence she said, "I understand." Choking, I turned my face away, unable to answer. She never again referred to what she must have observed day after day, but I was deeply comforted though not at all relieved by the certainty of her understanding. In all my life I have never known such distress. It was during this time that Errieta told me the most private and personal things about herself and her life. I think she must have guessed that the story of her own hardships and woes would distract me from my own.

Except for recording what Errieta told me and the tormenting repetition of the same phrases about Larry in my journal I found it impossible to do any writing. So I painted. I had the habit in those years of taking everywhere with me a box of watercolors, brushes and a sketchbook. I discovered that it dulled the pain to concentrate on the shapes and colors of any motif that I selected, and I forced myself to make at least one painting every day.

It was soon after Larry's departure that George Efstathiou came up the path from the beach one evening just as I was setting out to have dinner at the hotel. If I was startled to see him, Errieta must have been even more so. Her composure was impenetrable as she greeted him. When he asked whether he might sit down, she gestured to a chair. I left them together in the twilight.

The next day she told me why he had come. His marriage to the postmaster's daughter had already produced a child, a son. He wanted to bring this baby to Errieta, to show her his offspring, to have her hold him in her arms. She had asked him why he desired this. He replied that he hoped she would be happy to hold in her arms the living personification of his own happiness and that he wanted this happiness to be confirmed in the only home he had ever known or would ever know. To such an appeal Errieta, of course, could only assent. But his wife, he was quick to affirm, would not come near the house, would wait below on the beach while he and his son were with Errieta.

He came late the next afternoon with the child, an infant of eight or nine months, chubby and red-cheeked with a shock of hair as jet black as his father's. I saw them from the window of my bedroom. The wife, as George had promised, remained below on the beach, crouched beside the stream, and in her awkward posture, I thought, expressed hostility and resentment. This was evidently not of the slightest moment to George. Errieta held the child in her arms and murmured to it. To tell whether or not she found pleasure or satisfaction in the physical contact with her former husband's son was impossible, as her expression remained perfectly impassive. And I never would have asked her. Perhaps for her it was a sort of consummation and reconciliation. I wonder. I wonder, too, what may have been George's true motives, conscious or unconscious, for bringing his child to be held in the arms of the woman he had abandoned. Did he mean to be kind to Errieta, to offer her the sentiment of embodying still the beating heart of his life? Or was he unknowingly cruel in compelling her to clasp, to consecrate, to embrace an infant who symbolized the paternal pride and happiness which she had been unable to give him, she who had given everything she had? For the rest of the time I was in Skyros that summer he came often with the child.

A Marxist philosopher named Kostas Axelos, expert exegete of the works of Heidegger, came with his wife to stay in the tower for ten days toward the end of July. One evening when I came back from my solitary dinner at the hotel I found the two of them chatting with Errieta in her living room. She asked whether we would enjoy listening to some music. All said yes. I had often seen the ancient phonograph on its shelf in the storeroom but had never heard it play or asked to, being accustomed to the greater fidelity and convenience of electric systems and long-playing records. Errieta brought in the wooden machine with its large horn, placed it on a low table in the center of the room, then went back for an album of records. It would be Beethoven, she said, one of the last quartets, Number 13 in B-flat major, recorded by Adolf Busch with his brother Hermann and two others more than a quarter of a century before. She wound up the machine by its mahogany-knobbed crank, inserted a steel needle into the head of the playing arm, placed a record on the turntable, pushed forward the rotational lever and very gently lowered the needle onto the edge of the record. The music rose metallically from the horn, uneven and rasping. The record was worn, the machine in poor repair. Yet it was Beethoven, magisterial, sublime. We all sat silent, listening, in the cone of light from the lamp on the nearby bookcase. And in such melody freedom and necessity were reconciled, suffering existed apart from pain. By virtue of awareness, perhaps, all disappointment, all despair could be redeemed from deceit and squalor. And such awareness might even bring the hint of a solution to the problem of evil, a hint only, one which, fortunately, few people need ever contemplate. I remembered the incident of the German officer, his assertion that he would rather kill himself than listen to this music, and I thought that a man who would choose death over consolation must certainly have lived through the absolute negation of life. To sit listening to Beethoven in this lonely house at the far tip of Europe seemed to imply that civilization, even when it came to an end, when the sun was a cinder, would not have been for nothing, and that Errieta was a precious representative of it.

She turned and changed the records carefully, inserting a new needle for each side played. The B-flat major, one of Beethoven's last creations, is a long work. When it came to an end, none of us had anything to say. We thanked our hostess and went to our separate rooms.

Jacques and Michel arrived in August. It was some relief to me to be able to talk to them about Larry. Jacques was concerned about Errieta's health, which appeared to him poor, close to alarming, but she insisted that this was only rheumatism and that she would soon be fit once more. After three weeks my friends decided to leave Skyros and tour the Cyclades. I went with them.

Saying goodbye to Errieta was, as always, difficult and sad but more so that year than ever before. Neither she nor I said anything specific. We understood each other. I left with her my box of watercolors and brushes, thinking it might distract her, as it had distracted me, to do a little painting. She stood at the edge of the bluff, waving, as we walked up the beach toward the waiting taxi, and as we turned round the headland I could still see her, a tiny figure with her bright white hair in the blue distance.

We traveled round the Cyclades. Then I went to stay with my faithful and understanding friend Marie-Laure de Noailles in Hyères. At last I heard from Larry, who told me that he had decided, after all, to return to Paris. In December we went to Switzerland, Germany and Austria, visiting museums, monasteries, palaces, going to the opera and concerts. In January we went to London. During all this time I was remiss about writing to Errieta, or, for that matter, to anyone except my mother. But after the return from London I finally sent off to Skyros a letter describing our travels. In mid-February I received the following reply.

Skyros
11.2.62

Dear James,

It was nice to get your letter and hear all about your trip at Christmas. It must have been very enjoyable, especially with such a nice companion as Larry. And what a pleasant way to study art: to see it instead of only reading about it. (For that, I believe, is what Larry is studying.)

I'm glad to hear that you are writing again. What have you *started on now? And what of all this terrible state of affairs in France?* From the Greek papers that I read it sounds terribly grave and they seem to think that there is hardly any possibility of averting a civil war. The thought of such a thing makes me shudder. I felt very anxious about you all and was very relieved to read yesterday that it was a bit better. I also read that they had made an attempt on the life of the Minister for Cultural Relations who I believe is Michel's chief.*

The advertisement of Greece from Time *magazine was very depressing. I was feeling very blue after the grippe and that turned me a shade bluer. Imagine the beaches plowed up by the footprints of ten thousand tourists each carrying a portable radio and seeking vainly for that lonely spot!! Our age is full of perils: the dictator peril, the bomb peril, the noise peril and now—the tourist peril.*

We have had a rather dull autumn and winter this year. None of those lovely autumn tints. Perhaps because the end of the year was so dry. And none of those beautiful skies with the great rolling clouds gathered over the mountain and rays of light breaking through. Then with the beginning of the year it started to rain and it has been raining and blowing ever since.

Our only other news is that the surly old postman has retired and has been replaced by a young man more surly, more stupid and more incapable. No doubt you think that is impossible. But just come and see . . .

I do hope things will improve in France. Say hello to Larry from me.

And much love to you both.

Errieta

The following summer, instead of going to Skyros, Larry and I went to San Diego, California, where he now owned the small house previously held jointly with the Greek lover. Needless to say, the ethereal loveliness and enchantment of Skyros seemed in San Diego so remote as to be nearly unbelievable. I wrote to Errieta and in mid-

---

* The Algerian war and insurrection.

summer received from her a small parcel containing several watercolor sketches, a still life of fruit, a marine view and a portrait of the serving girl, Annoula. They were quite accomplished. There was also a letter:

> *Skyros*
> *[undated]*
>
> *Dearest James,*
>   *Here are the first sketches I've done. I couldn't decide which one to send so I'm sending them all. Don't be too scathing, dear critic—I haven't touched a brush since I was twenty and I'm only sending them to show you how much entertainment I'm getting from your paints. While I'm at it I'm so absorbed that I forget the time. I even forget that I'm sad! I've also enjoyed the book you left me,* A Death in the Family. *It's a beautiful book, so full of tenderness and the childish outlook is so sweet. What nice things you thought of to give me pleasure! James, you are such a dear. I love you so much. And your friends also but less. I wonder if you can feel how much I thank you for everything and especially for your affection. I think you can—you are so sensitive. It was lovely having you here but now I'm terribly, terribly sad—much more so than last year. As if I had said goodbye forever.*
>   *[unsigned]*

This was the last letter I received from Errieta. I wrote to thank her for the watercolors but had no reply.

In late September, when Larry and I had returned from San Diego to New York, I had a letter from Jacques, enclosing a scrawled note in pencil from Errieta, her handwriting deformed, the handwriting of one who has barely the strength to hold the pencil, who is, in short, dying. Jacques had had a previous letter in which she had sent him the results of some rather vague examinations she had undergone, and he had inferred that she was suffering from leukemia. Was this the result of that long-ago accident in Chalandri while she and George were in hiding? Impossible to say.

That very same day I wrote her a long letter. A couple of weeks later it came back to me with the word DECEASED stamped in black on the envelope.

A Maternal Ordeal

[L O U I S E   B E N N E T T   L O R D]

1

That Gertrude Stein and Alice B. Toklas, Arletty, Marie-Laure de
Noailles and Errieta Perdikidi were all exceptional women cannot, I
believe, be open to question. My mother, Louise Bennett Lord, would
have vigorously denied that she was of their company, for she sincerely
said of herself, "I am a rather humdrum and prosaic person." I, however, her favorite son—pace Ben—am decidedly not of that opinion.
It is a labored bromide that favorite sons, especially homosexual favorites, are prone to consider their mothers exceptional. My purpose
in setting out to write about mine is not only to justify my opinion but
also to suggest that if I succeed in doing so it will be very largely because
the success may be attributed to her. And if my success is, indeed,
hers, then it unfortunately follows that an account of it will have to
take more stock of my life and my doings than would otherwise have
been appropriate, because it is from my experience that my conviction
stems.

Louise Bennett was lucky in her parents. They were prosperous,
good-natured people, devoid of personal distinction but descended
from families well established in the British colonies before 1700. They
lived in Indianapolis, Indiana, were married there in 1890, and my
mother was born five years later on January 3. My grandfather was
the proprietor of a large and profitable company that manufactured
stoves both for cooking and for heating. As children, my mother and
later I were fascinated to visit the foundry and peer into the seething
molten depths of the furnaces. My maternal grandparents had two
children, the other one a son, Edward, two years older than my mother.
She had an unusually happy childhood. There were plenty of docile

servants, fun-loving relatives and friends, parties, picnics, charades, excursions into the surrounding countryside and in the summer all went north to Harbor Point on the upper reaches of Lake Michigan. When she was fourteen, Mother was sent to a boarding school in Greenwich, Connecticut, Rosemary Hall, where she was unhappy. Her adolescence was difficult, traumatic. She became shy, unsure of herself, withdrawing into the secure and consoling company of books. All her life she was an indefatigable reader, in youth especially of poetry and history. The great novels of world literature came later. For Mother's higher education, which she wished to further, a pursuit that neither of her parents had undertaken, Sweet Briar College in Virginia, a relatively new institution, was chosen rather than Radcliffe or Vassar, because my grandmother deemed a mild climate desirable and cared nothing for intellectual endeavor. Mother graduated in 1916, returned to Indianapolis and underwent the trial of a coming-out party, though she was an exceptionally graceful and accomplished dancer. Two years later she met an officer named Albert Lord, originally from Connecticut, twelve years older than she, who promptly fell in love with her. They were married in Indianapolis on May 2, 1920, and went to live in New Jersey, as my father worked in Wall Street, whither he traveled by train and ferry. Their marriage was remarkably felicitous and serene, though not spared from worry, grief and bereavement. My father was a practical man, had received a Puritanical upbringing, had little interest in the arts, at least during his younger years, enjoyed tennis and golf, playing bridge and chess, going to parties and having a good drink. I can remember the furtive deliveries of bootleggers during Prohibition. He had a beneficent influence on my mother, curing her of timidity and cultivating the sociable charm of her nature. They had four children, all boys, Bennett, born in April 1921, myself, born in November 1922, Edward, born in December 1925, and Peter, also born in April but in 1929.

My early childhood was carefree and contented. I was an obedient, lively, amusing child, got along well with my two brothers and there seems to have been nothing about me that could give cause for concern. But when I was about six an abrupt transformation occurred. I became fractious and moody, disobedient, devious and aloof. My mother always wondered what could have brought about this unforeseeable change. It coincided more or less with the birth of my youngest brother, Peter, and I have long wondered whether I may not have felt that his arrival deprived me of an undue share of the love and attention which I was accustomed to receive from our mother. She never seemed to have thought of such an explanation. Considering Peter's tragic fate, however, I don't believe that I ever behaved with hostility toward him or that he received from either parent less attentive care and devotion than the three others.

Then came the time of schooling. A malingerer, cheater and instigator of disorderly pranks, I was a poor student even in the subjects such as English, history and French which most appealed to me. Being unruly and quarrelsome at home, I was sent at the age of nine to a boarding school where military discipline was the rule. I hated it and after two years was expelled. There followed three difficult years at a country day school within walking distance of my parents' house. From this vapid factory for the manufacture of stockbrokers, ministers, rich good-for-nothings and mercantile mediocrities I was also expelled. At age thirteen, after diligent searching by my anxious parents among third-rate boarding schools needful of students during the Depression, I was admitted to Williston Academy in eastern Massachusetts, from which I miraculously managed to graduate after intensive extra tutoring and an additional year of sullen drudgery. All of this, needless to say, caused concern at home. It did not contribute to happiness for me either. Dismay and torment, in fact, became my daily companions when I realized during my second year at Williston that what I felt for the handsomest of my schoolmates was not hero worship but carnal desire. The diaries of those years were filled with the lachrymose effusions of frustration and woe. In 1938 the mere idea of "gay liberation" would have been an odious vagary. It's not surprising that academic application suffered. The one consolation was writing. If I could write, become a writer, an artist in the medium of language, then it seemed to the boy of fifteen that his guilt and shame might ultimately be redeemed. I wrote mostly poetry at first, because when one knows nothing of what is most difficult it seems a logical goal for fatuous aspirants. I dabbled at painting as well. And of course I fooled myself with daydreams of Rimbaud. My schoolmates mocked me.

In 1936 my maternal grandfather, the wealthy manufacturer of stoves, died. His fortune was divided between his wife and two children. As my father had lost both his position and his savings at the onset of the Depression and found only sporadic employment thereafter, his wife's inheritance represented something of a windfall but also a mortifying vicissitude for a husband and father over fifty who had been sternly conditioned to believe that all men should be independent and able to satisfy the needs of their families. His principal occupation thereafter was to manage his wife's investments, and it must be said, I am happy to add, that he did so extremely well, increasing many times over the value of the original inheritance. My grandmother, left alone in a large house in Indianapolis, grew lonely, and since it was unthinkable that she might dwell under the same roof as the shrewish wife of her son she came East in 1939 to live with us, bringing with her a welcome increment of luxury and remaining an integral part of our family until her death twenty-two years later, aged ninety-seven. I grew fond of her, and she of me, for she found me entertaining, but she never approved of me or my doings. While I was at school we occasionally corresponded, and sometime in 1940, having received a letter from her, I impulsively wrote a morbid and self-pitying reply, in which I said that all my energy was being expended on the effort of remaining alive, etc., etc. She returned my letter and wrote as follows:

Dear Jimmy,

 I want you to re-read this letter and see if you are not rather ashamed of having written it or rather being in the mood to do so.

 Of all the boys in the family more is done for you than for any of the others and we get less in return, or rather you yourself are not receiving what we are trying to give you.

 Your studies are important, of course, but working over something you do not like and doing it successfully is of greater value. I am afraid you enjoy giving way to moods—and dramatizing yourself—not a wise or manly thing to do—and a terrible habit to form.

 This is not intended for a scolding letter, but I want you to know how your attitude impressed me.

 Brace up, and take what comes like a man, and not like a weakling . . .

 Do write me a nice cheerful letter, and tell me what got into you to send this doleful one.

Of the numerous letters from which I intend to quote excerpts I have selected first this one from my grandmother, with whom I shall not be greatly concerned, because it most bluntly suggests the quandary with which my family was unhappily confronted. From my mother and father came many admonitions more or less similar. From my mother, for example, approximately of the same period:

Dear Jim,

Dad, Grandmother and I have discussed the question of your tutoring in geometry and have decided that there is very little use in our pouring more money into the seemingly bottomless pit which your disinclination to take an education creates. It just doesn't seem worthwhile for your teacher to spend his time and us to spend our money on such a profitless undertaking as trying to make you learn something which you have evidently made up your mind not to learn. It seems too bad, and it is a great disappointment to all of us that you are not willing to make the effort to do a disagreeable task which you know you ought to do.

However, she was seldom so severe and often compassionate.

Dearest Jim,

I certainly did not intend to plunge you into such depths of gloom with my last letter. I had hoped that it would buck you up to a little better effort. I do wish I had better insight and more intelligence to help me help you. I have prayed for it often, but perhaps I haven't sufficient faith. But I am certainly not giving up hope. I know that you have many fine qualities, and all that you need is the spark of interest and enthusiasm which makes the dull, uninteresting work bearable for the sake of attaining a goal for which you really care. For some reason—I don't know why—that spark seems to be lacking in you, but it may come to you sometime just suddenly. My knowledge of psychology is very limited, but as I understand it people have to have an emotional urge—a drive—before they can accomplish anything. We are like machines, with all our physical and mental powers ready to be

*put into action, but it takes fire, electricity or some form of
energy to set us off. And for some reason which I cannot
fathom that energy in you seems to be blocked.*

*It might help you to go to a psychologist and talk it over
and see whether you can find out why you haven't more energy and ambition. What do you think? Generally speaking,
I don't think it is a good idea for young people to get too
introspective and think an awful lot about themselves, but in
your case it might help. And meanwhile don't feel so discouraged. You know that Dad's and my one thought is to help
you to grow into as fine and good a man as you have it in
your power to be.*

With much love, Mother

But it seems that this period provided a never-ending succession
of parental worries.

*I do hope that you will someday learn (1) not to get into
trouble with the authorities; (2) not to have fights with other
boys. I can think of a number of other admonitions I could
give you, but a lot of moral precepts would not make my letter very welcome, I fear—nor do much good. I hope too that
you will someday shake off your inertia and go at things—
anything—with real determination and ambition.*

The thing at which I wanted to go with real determination and
ambition had by this time grown increasingly clear to me. I didn't feel
that I lacked the activating spark, the fire and the energy needed to
set me off. I intended to become a writer. I wanted it with all the
passion and ignorance of my age, dreaming only of praise and fame,
utterly unaware that a writer's life is lonely and selfish, its rewards, if
any, transitory and shallow. How, to be sure, could I have known? And
naturally I did not know enough to keep my aspirations to myself. My
mother responded:

*About your life work—I am not taking it lightly, but I
do realize that the best laid schemes of mice and men gang
aft agley—and what you plan and hope to do may not be*

*feasible. But if you are unalterably opposed to going into
business and sitting behind a desk, the thing to do is put lots
of effort into fitting yourself for whatever you do want to do.
Because, unfortunately, there are more openings for people in
the uninteresting occupations than in the more exciting and
stimulating ones. So you have to be extra good to get anywhere in them. However, even a dull job can be inspiring if
you put imagination and spirit into it. But those are bridges
which don't have to be crossed yet, and you undoubtedly
know what your job now is.*

Yes, I knew what it was, but I had no taste for it, or for much of
anything else. I read Poe and thought surcease of sorrow sounded
inviting, wrote imaginary suicide notes and brooded over the bravery
of Van Gogh. One year I went the whole winter without an overcoat
and sometimes lay down in puddles of icy slush, thinking as I spent
hours in cold, wet clothes that I would catch pneumonia and die, but
that was the one and only winter when I never had a single cold. My
mother must have surmised.

*I hope that things are going better with you now, and
that you are no longer in the slough of despond into which
you seemed to be plunged for a time. Don't worry too much.
Other people have failed to comprehend mathematics and yet
have grown up to be useful and happy people . . .*

And again:

*How are your studies coming—geometry in particular? I
have been looking over a diary which I kept when I was in
college, and I gather that even at the advanced age of twenty
I was not the serious student I remember myself as being. So,
while I certainly don't want you to follow in my footsteps—
when those steps went astray—nevertheless I did finally develop a real interest in my work and got through college
more or less creditably. So perhaps you will do likewise.*

Along with these letters checks were frequently enclosed, unexpected but very welcome additions to my regular allowance and cheering evidence that maternal care went beyond the sensible advice I continued to receive.

> *About your life work: circumstances will certainly have a very great influence on that, but any effort which you may exert in learning to express yourself clearly in the English language will be time well spent. So it will not be amiss if you state that you want to make your "life work" writing or journalism or something of that sort.*

In addition I got good advice.

> *I cannot help wondering why you are given so few of the older novels to read—Dickens, Scott, Thackeray, etc. If you don't read them now, you probably never will. And I do not see how you can have any foundation for the study of English literature without some knowledge of the standard classics. The newer books are many of them interesting and should not be totally disregarded (as contemporary books were when I went to school) but certainly it is just as one-sided to read only modern books. But perhaps I do you wrong, and you have read a lot of standard works which you have not mentioned.*

I hadn't, and her prediction concerning Dickens, Scott and Thackeray was all too accurate. Still, I kept on writing poems and even had the temerity to submit one of them to some small magazine. The inevitable rejection slip came back promptly and was inadvertently opened by my mother.

> *I am afraid that you are going to be very much annoyed at me for the inadvertent opening of the enclosed letter. I supposed that it was an advertisement which it was unnecessary to forward. I was, however, much interested and pleased with your bit of verse. Although I am a rather humdrum and prosaic person I have always loved poetry, and would like noth-*

*ing better than to be able to write it myself, but needless to
say I have no talent for it. I am very glad that you are trying
your hand at it, and hope that you will not be discouraged
by a rejection—which is not surprising for a first (or is it a
second or third?) effort.*

She may have had no talent for writing poetry, but she felt true
respect for achievements of the intellect, and in fact had determined
to further the cultivation of her own now that parental tasks had become
less pressing, all four sons away at boarding school.

*I have decided to take some kind of a course at Colum-
bia just to keep my rusty mental equipment from total disintegration, and am now in class waiting for the teacher. I
haven't decided yet exactly what to take, so am visiting
around before making up my mind. This class is called "European Political Institutions." Last week I went to one on
"Modern European Drama."*

As the time for my graduation unbelievably approached there was
not only surprise but satisfaction at home.

*You certainly have improved wonderfully—in studies
and in many other ways—in the last two years. As Grandmother was saying the other day, you may be the pride of the
family yet.*

I never provided an instant's pride to my grandmother. My few
publications before her death were more embarrassing to her than
gratifying, I think. No matter. She possessed not the least respect for
artistic endeavor, esteemed her friend and neighbor Booth Tarkington
only because his books made money and the sole intellectual achievement of her lifetime was to shake the hand of Henry James at a reception after his lecture in Indianapolis in 1905. She certainly never
read one of his books. Her husband read O. Henry and *The Saturday
Evening Post.*

By this time, of course, the catastrophic war in Europe had begun,

Poland, Denmark, Norway, Holland, Belgium, France, Yugoslavia and Greece all having been overrun by the seemingly invincible Nazis.

Of my three brothers the only one with whom I was close while young was Peter. "He seems to have developed a great admiration for you," my mother wrote. He was the sole member of the family who shared my passion for classical music, though my parents in later years became devotees of the opera, and I persuaded him to take piano lessons, as I did. Peter and I went for long hikes together in the summer, sat on mountaintops and shared dreams of doings that would amaze the world. Though at different schools, we corresponded, and Peter sent long lists of the symphonies, concertos and sonatas he preferred. He learned to play an accurate though unfeeling version of Beethoven's *Appassionata*, not the easiest of sonatas. In retrospect our closeness seems peculiar, as Peter's true passion was mathematics, mine literature. At all events, after two or three years I became aware of an aloofness on his part, and unable to account for it, I asked him for an explanation. Apparently while in the miserable throes of unrequited adoration for one of my good-looking schoolmates I had said, "You must never become too attached to anyone, because if you do you're sure to be hurt." And Peter had taken this to heart. He must have been ten or eleven at the time. Thinking back now, more than half a century later, on that relatively brief but happy era of our fraternal camaraderie and its abrupt end, I can't help wondering whether that may not have been more important than I know, or want to know, even today. Of course, I never discussed this with our mother although only too often we spoke of Peter.

It was customary in those years, as also in these, I presume, for young men of college age to take jobs during their summer vacations with the idea that the experience of employment would help to prepare them for a lifetime of the same when the college prelude was finished. Such a prospect appealed to me not in the least. I wanted to spend my summer in the lovely town of Paris, Maine, writing poetry and painting an occasional picture. My parents were not of one mind regarding this desire. Mother wrote as follows:

> *I favor your pursuing some of your artistic efforts this summer, while Dad thinks that you should have some work which would prepare you to a certain extent for the kind of*

*regimentation which will be inevitable if you go either into
the army or into a job. The ideal thing, we decided, would
be for you to have really strenuous work along the line of
your interests. If we were sure that you would really work
hard at any one of your avocations I believe Dad would feel
differently—but the idea of your fooling along, putting in
maybe one or two hours a day at writing or painting, is certainly not a prospect which offers much chance of self-
improvement for you—and after all if you don't develop your
character and will power sufficiently to force yourself to take
the drudgery necessary to prepare yourself to do the things
you like, how are you going to have anything about you
worth expressing? That is an involved sentence, but what I
mean is that a vague, immature love of beauty isn't enough
for an artist or writer. He should have reserves of strength
and endurance and fortitude in his character or his self-
expression will be only a superficial sentimentality.*

Gertrude Stein, who knew what she was talking about when it
came to the literary life, once remarked that it was important for a
writer to spend an appreciable amount of time doing nothing. Especially in the formative years, I think, that is so, but my parents, of
course, didn't see things as Gertrude did. About necessary drudgery,
reserves of strength and endurance and fortitude, however, all capable
writers—and many incapable ones, alas—discover soon enough that
a lifetime of servitude is to be their lot. Anyway, I got what I wanted
that summer. It was the last I spent in the beloved Paris of my boyhood
before becoming acquainted with the beloved Paris of my manhood.
In the fall of 1941 I entered Wesleyan University, and as with all
institutions of education I hated it, drew undesirable attention to myself
and was miserable. I didn't expend on my studies at Wesleyan one bit
more effort than I had at Williston, but I received excellent grades,
and this unpredictable result came about because I was little by little
learning to write. Compelled to take at least one course in science, I
had chosen geology, and even in this tedious subject I did well, writing
long essays about the beauty of stratification, the mysterious migrations
of sand and the superhuman drama of earthquakes and volcanoes, all
of which had very little to do with the material of study, but the kind-

hearted professor was bemused and gave me a high mark. The same technique proved even more effective in other fields. My parents were doubtless surprised, certainly relieved and even more gratified.

> *Dad and I were more pleased than I can say with your report. It is wonderful that you are doing such good work, and even though you said in your last letter that you "just sit around and don't do much" I can't believe that you aren't getting a lot more satisfaction out of life than you did when you were doing so poorly in school. You* must *be doing more than sitting around or you couldn't get such a good report . . .*
>
> *I was very pleased at what you said about a letter from me making you feel better. My letters are usually so dull— there is so little which goes on here to interest you—that I often wonder whether you boys care anything about my letters. So it makes me very happy to think that you do like to receive them. Don't feel too downhearted, Jim. Dad and I are not at all discouraged about you. In fact, when I think of your making honor grades in college and doing distinction work in English I feel proud as Punch.*

By this time Pearl Harbor had been bombed, the United States had declared war on Japan, Germany and Italy and the eventuality of military service had become an immediate concern for every young man in America. But those attending college were not among the first to be called.

My dear mother would not have been pleased, and emphatically not proud as Punch, had she known that the description of my academic efforts as sitting around and not doing much was as truthful as I cared, or dared, to be. I spent time writing, of course, and in addition to poems had begun to compose short stories. What also occupied me while sitting around and listening to the *Eroica* symphony on my record player was getting drunk. Lonely, friendless and hopelessly in love with an older boy to whom I never dared speak more than half a dozen times, I was deplorably despondent. With the help of alcohol, I found, I could imagine myself the master of my fate, captain of my soul. I favored Four Roses, and sometimes in case of urgent want I carried around the campus with me a pint bottle in a paper bag. Luckily for me the youth of that era had never heard of heroin or cocaine. My mother must have had some intimation of my state.

> *I hope that you will try to make a few friends among the boys. It is good to steer a middle course between rushing headlong into friendship and being so stand-offish that you never know anyone. You know you are very good company when you let people find it out, and you will enjoy the companionship of a few kindred spirits if you will only take the trouble to ferret them out and cultivate their acquaintance.*
>
> *Thank you for having your hair cut. Do keep it combed down flat—like a gigolo, as you say.*

Rushing headlong into friendship was all that I yearned to do, but the friend toward whom I longed to rush barely recognized my existence, and friends of the variety I really desired were definitely not of the kind my mother had in mind. Of kindred spirits in a student body of seven hundred boys aged between seventeen and twenty there were undoubtedly a number, but I was unhappily unable to put my finger, so to speak, upon a single one, for all of them were no doubt just as fearful as I of making themselves known. I could cut my hair and look like a gigolo, but to my sorrow nobody proposed to keep me. Of all this my parents as yet knew nothing, and I told them nothing. My letters gave only vague hints of what was happening to me. Mother wondered.

> *I hope that you will find time to write a really detailed account of your activities and your experiences up there. You know we are interested, but we can't get much idea of what you are doing from a letter saying merely, "Everything is horrible here."*

Parental curiosity would have been very miserably repaid by a detailed account of my activities and experiences. Everything *was* horrible, and eventually they were bound to learn why. It took a little courage to tell them, but I had no choice and did have some help. Even in a crowd of seven hundred a loner gets noticed, and I made no effort to be inconspicuous. So it was that I found myself summoned by the

Dean toward the end of the summer semester which had been added
to the regular curriculum because of the war. He was a kindly, sensitive,
shrewd man named Victor Butterfield. He had heard of my drinking,
guessed the reason for it but led me to tell him myself what it was. He
recommended that I be treated by a psychiatrist, and when I explained
that I could not contemplate telling my parents of such a necessity he
volunteered to call my father himself and advise him that psychiatric
care would be beneficial. But he added that I must myself assume the
responsibility of explaining to my father what it was that made such
treatment necessary.

Thus my father and I sat down together in the living room of our
house in the midsummer of 1942. It was boiling hot. We were alone
in the house, as all the rest of the family had gone to Maine. The
shades were drawn and most of the furniture was covered with dust
sheets. My father asked what was troubling me. I replied that my
problem was more or less of the sort commonplace among boys of my
age. So it must have to do with girls, said my father. Well, no, it didn't,
I told him with great difficulty, my trouble was that what most boys
felt toward girls I felt toward other boys. My father made no more
comment than to say, "I see." After a pause he added that he felt sure
this was only a passing phase, that of course I should consult a
psychiatrist—he would make the necessary arrangements—and he felt
sure that in the end everything would turn out to be all right. That was
the conclusion of our conversation, and never once in the ensuing
thirty-one years was the subject again broached between us.

How my father came to select the psychiatrist to whom my treatment was entrusted I do not know but suspect that he must have
inquired among his friends in Wall Street. The man's name was Irving
H. Pardee. He was of middle age, hearty in manner, exuding an aura
of suave self-assurance, well dressed and good-looking, with a luxurious office on Park Avenue. It may seem irrelevant—but is not—to
say that in those years I was accustomed to use an odorous aftershave
lotion called Old Spice and had applied some of it the morning before
I went for my first afternoon meeting with Dr. Pardee. When I entered
his office and after a formal greeting had taken my seat facing him
across a large mahogany desk, he leaned forward and said, "You know,
real men don't wear perfume." From that instant, needless to say, I
detested him. We met three times a week thereafter for most of the

remainder of the summer, and I was careful to use no Old Spice before
going to his office. The therapy he evidently deemed fitting for my case
consisted largely of lengthy descriptions of the desirability of women,
the voluptuous delights they could provide and the pleasures to be
found in the depths of the vagina. There were moments, indeed, when
he sounded very much like a procurer, and I wondered whether he
might not be on the verge of providing me with a prostitute. At the
same time he dwelt with marked repugnance on the nastiness, im-
morality and illegality of fellatio, sodomy and any sort of sexual fond-
lings between males. In short, Dr. Pardee was a fool, a fraud and a
contemptible trifler with the psyche and I am almost prepared to believe
in hell for the pure pleasure of hoping that he will roast there forever.
When I felt that a sufficient number of sessions had been spent in his
noxious company to practice a deceit, I told him that I felt much better
and that, after all, my homosexual fantasies had been but a final man-
ifestation of adolescent ambivalence. He agreed, seemed very well
satisfied with his treatment but recommended that after my forthcoming return to college I visit a psychiatrist in Hartford called Dr. Gosselin,
to whom he would write.

My parents must have been informed of all this, for they saw
Pardee, paid his bills, which were certainly outrageous, and even went
to see Gosselin in Hartford. This man was by no means so crass as the
Park Avenue dunce, but his competence didn't go much beyond kindliness and good intentions. He also felt that my case could be corrected
by conversational appeals to common sense. When I assured him that
this would do no good, he said that at our next meeting he would begin
a series of hormonal injections which would stimulate my masculinity.
I never saw Dr. Gosselin again. My parents were disappointed, but
they specifically avoided ever referring to the reason which made psychiatric care desirable.

> *Dad and I were disappointed to hear that you did not
> care for Dr. Gosselin. We liked him very much. Dad is call-
> ing Dr. Pardee today to ask for his advice and we shall let
> you know right away what he says.*

Advice from that mountebank was the very last thing in the world
I wanted, and I was fearful that if it was given I might have to follow

it. I continued to hate college and, of course, myself, and mournfully wondered how I could ever hope to have a bearable existence. Even Four Roses had ceased to provide effective solace, so I gave up drinking and tried to think of some radical way out of my self-made predicament. My mother sent letters of tender sympathy.

> *Too bad that you were feeling so low-spirited. You are right that boys of your temperament often go through periods of great depression at your age. However, if they can get hold of themselves and have enough character, will power or whatever it takes to rise above their personal feelings and learn to sublimate (that's the psychological word, I think) their causes for melancholy, they are often much more sympathetic, outgoing individuals than those who have slid along on the surface of life. The danger is, of course, in getting bogged down in your own emotions and becoming a self-centered, introspective person, thinking and caring about no one else. That is why it worries me that you do not make an effort to have friends. However trivial and shallow you may consider the other boys, I feel sure that an effort to get on a friendly footing with some of them will amply repay whatever difficulty you may have at first. Won't you make a trial at making a few friends before Christmas?*

The war was much on everyone's mind. After three years of Axis victories it suddenly appeared in the fall of 1942 that a turning point might have come when Rommel was routed by Montgomery at El Alamein and the Americans successfully invaded Algeria. Able-bodied young Americans were being drafted into the army, air force and navy by the millions, and it was evident that my turn would come, though I could have obtained considerable deferment still on the basis of being a college student in good standing. I knew, moreover, that I could avoid military service altogether, as homosexuals were not accepted into the armed forces. Dr. Pardee had explained that that crucial test of my masculinity would confront me. But it never occurred to me to multiply my shame and guilt by advertising my abnormality and incurring the reputation of a shirker. Feeling certain that the army could not possibly be more hateful than college, I decided to escape from Wesleyan by enlisting. Parental response to this decision was predictably varied. My mother wrote:

> *My feelings about the situation are very mixed. I am pleased and proud, and at the same time can't help being disturbed at the prospect of your enlisting. However, I know that it is the right and manly decision which you have made, and I am very, very proud of the spirit you are showing, especially when I know that it isn't easy for you. I only hope that the whole wretched war will be over soon and that you will be able to go back to college and finish.*

My father wrote:

> *My "reaction" to this decision is (1) that you are doing yourself great credit in thus manfully facing up to the situation; (2) regret that such a hard choice is forced on you before you have finished your education; and (3) a conviction that you are making the right decision in what may well be one of the critical periods of your life, a decision which I am confident will be a source of satisfaction to you in later years.*

Both of them, dear people that they were, obviously had no inkling of my true motive. My father's last sentence, however, was uncannily prescient. This was definitely one of the critical periods of my life, and my decision brought me in later years, and brings me still today, all the satisfaction I could conceivably have hoped for. If I had waited to be drafted, it is virtually certain that I would never have had the military career, if it can be called that, which by the quirky chances of army snafu allowed me to live in France for six months or more virtually as a civilian, find friends here and ultimately come to make this country my home. When I appeared at the enlistment center in New York on November 5, 1942, I was naturally subject to a physical examination, which included an interview by an army psychiatrist. This consisted of a single question: "Do you like girls?" I said, "Yes," which was not a lie.

A Maternal Ordeal

In December of 1944, having become a member of the Military Intelligence Service, I was sent to the picturesque, uninteresting town of Quimper at the far end of the Breton peninsula, and while there I became acquainted with the chief doctor of the local insane asylum for men, a good-natured and hospitable man of about forty named Paul Mondain but known to all his friends by the nickname of Pluto, which he had chosen for himself because he felt that he somewhat resembled the dog of that name in the animated movie cartoons of Walt Disney. I quickly grew friendly with Pluto and his family and he later came to my aid when once again I wanted to escape from college. My parents by this time had three sons in the armed forces. My older brother Ben was in the navy, my younger brother Teddy was a paratrooper. Concerning him, I received a letter sent from Paris, Maine, by my mother and which I received in Germany early in June 1945, almost a month after the war in Europe had ended.

I am sorry, Jim dear, to have very bad news to write you. Teddy has been killed. It is so hard for me to believe it. I feel as though he might walk in the door any minute. This is the hardest thing which Dad and I have ever had to bear. Our lives have been so happy. Sorrow seems always to have passed us by. I suppose it should make it easier to think of all the blessings we still have—each other and three fine sons— but that does not make the one who has gone any less dear nor the loss easier to bear.

We received the telegram while we were stopping at an inn in Massachusetts on our way up here day before yesterday. It said only "Killed in action in Luzon" and the date given was May third. I had received a cable for Mother's Day from him on May seventh, but it may have been sent some time before that. He was in a hospital all through April and a letter about the first of May said that when he went back to his division they were in rest camp. He must have been killed very soon after they returned to action. The telegram said that a letter would follow, which will probably give us some details, not that it matters much, except that I hope it was quick and painless.

*We plan to leave here next Tuesday on the night train. I
don't know just when we will come back again.*
With best love, Mother

Teddy was without question the most attractive and promising of
the four sons, just as I was the least promising and most unaccom-
modating. He was handsome, pleasing to girls and very pleased by
them, excelled equally in studies and sports and possessed a sense of
civic responsibility rare in one so young. He was only nineteen when
killed. While at Princeton, the college attended by all three of my
brothers, he had on his own initiative, and despite a crowded schedule
of other work, volunteered to assist in a program for the education and
entertainment of Negro children in the slums of the nearby city of
Trenton, an activity highly unconventional in those days. Very clearly
he was my father's favorite. When I returned home six months later,
I found him a changed man. Though only sixty-two, he seemed to
have grown old. Teddy's photograph in uniform always stood on the
table beside the chair where he habitually sat, and my mother kept it
by her till she died. But I did not sense a comparable change in her.
She had a more optimistic and cheerful disposition than her husband.
Still, she agreed with me that Teddy had been the most promising and
attractive of her children and we often wondered together what he
would have made of himself had the war ended two months sooner.

I returned to college, where I now made a few friends, continued
to surprise myself and my parents by doing well in my studies, was
elected to the Honors College and allowed to do approximately as I
pleased. However, Middletown, Connecticut, seemed very dull after
Paris, France, and there was no one at Wesleyan to compare in personal
excitement with Picasso, Gertrude Stein or even Pluto. During the
summer vacation of 1946 I secreted myself on Cape Cod and wrote
the first of my many unpublishable novels, working ten or twelve hours
a day for seven weeks. I wasn't afraid of drudgery, though some might
have called it self-indulgence. But every creative individual is compelled to indulge the self that dictates his endeavor.

Returning to Wesleyan in the autumn, I began to think how delightful it would be to go back to France, where I could apply myself
entirely to writing, an occupation esteemed over there as honorable
whether productive of wealth and fame or not. To do this would mean

forgoing my degree, because at the end of the autumn semester I would have completed only three years of college. But I didn't care two straws about becoming a Bachelor of Arts—I knew myself destined to be a bachelor anyway, and of arts to boot!—and thought a degree would never be of the slightest value to me. Nor would it have been. My parents saw things differently, my father in particular, who had been deprived of a college education by the necessity of having to support his widowed mother and unmarried sister, and my mother also, who respected academic achievement per se and was even then continuing her studies at Columbia under such eminent professors as Jacques Barzun and Lionel Trilling. But I was stubborn. There were long conversations—it would be unfair to call them arguments—about my material status, my artistic aspirations and my resolve to see them fulfilled. Oddly enough, my professors at Wesleyan, including the ever-helpful Victor Butterfield, agreed that I would probably have more to gain intellectually by devoting myself entirely to writing while living in France than by sticking it out in Middletown. I was twenty-four years old, and little as they may have liked it, my parents acknowledged that decisions concerning my future were my own to make. However, they both emphasized that I should be under no illusions about their preparedness to pay for a venture of which they disapproved. That didn't give me much pause, because in the first place I didn't entirely believe it and in the second I was able to get together a reasonable wherewithal of my own by selling a batch of etchings and drawings acquired while in Paris. Moreover, my lodging and nourishment would cost me nothing, for I had maintained with Pluto over the fourteen or fifteen months since our last meeting in Paris a continuous correspondence, and he had repeatedly told me that I would be welcome to live and work for as long as I liked in his large apartment within the asylum walls at Quimper. So it was with a rather complacent sense of satisfaction that I set sail aboard the *Queen Elizabeth* on March 22, 1947.

Soon after arriving in Quimper I received a letter from my mother, concluding as follows:

> *Tuesday will be Peter's eighteenth birthday, which is
> hard to believe, and on next Sunday Ben will be twenty-six.
> It is hard for me to realize that you are all grown up. And*

nice as you are I should like occasionally (not all the time) to
have a gang of dirty, noisy, quarrelsome small boys about.
Such is human nature: nostalgia for the good old days!
     We miss you very much.

                                        Lovingly, Mother

My letters to my mother invariably included lengthy passages pro-
claiming over and over again my creative convictions and aspirations.
She must have grown wearily accustomed to them, as she had grown
accustomed to similar conversations, for such missives had been coming her way by that time for quite a few years. It seems only honest to
say that, whether consciously or unconsciously, I must have felt that
this cumulative humus might eventually bring forth a fruitful harvest
of understanding and support. In fairness to myself, however, I would
deny that such a prospect had anything to do with my determination
to spend time in France. At all events, I had been in Quimper hardly
a month when I received from my mother a letter of which I quote the
largest part.

Dearest Jim,
     I have been thinking a good deal about you and your
work recently. It seems rather strange (providential some
might call it) that I should be taking this particular course in
European culture just at the time when I have the problem of
you and your future support, etc., to solve. A great deal has
been said and I have read more about the subject of how the
body and the soul of the artist can be kept together and func-
tioning while he pursues his art. I have come to several con-
clusions, in which, I am sorry to say, Dad does not entirely
concur. Namely, a. that Art is important, b. that you may or
may not be an artist with something important to say, c. that
no one, least of all an untrained and culturally not very sen-
sitive person such as I, can tell whether a young aspirant has
the spark or not but d. in every cultural period there are doz-
ens of mediocre talents for every first-class one, nevertheless
e. those mediocrities have to develop their talents to the best
of their abilities in order to create the interest, the back-
ground and the cultural climate in which the best talents can

*grow, therefore f. whether you are, as you say, a neo-
Shakespeare or a minor Elizabethan dramatist, so to speak,
it is desirable that you make the effort to say what you have
to say whether it is remembered a hundred years hence or
not, and g. this development has to be financed, and if I can
help finance it my money will be as well invested as in, say,
Atkomatic Valves.* I am willing to finance this artistic enter-
prise within reason, but I fear that I shall have to be the
judge as to what reason is.*

My answer:

Dearest Mother,

 *To begin, I will say that it is not easy for me to reply to
your letter of May fourth, which I received this morning, the
one in which you discuss at length my present and future as
an artist. It is always difficult to respond well to an event
which is profoundly moving, yet I would not be at ease with
myself if I didn't reply immediately. To say that I am grateful
or appreciative or indebted to you seems rather paltry, but
what I feel certainly begins with gratitude. I don't believe you
can imagine what a sense of peace it gave me to read and re-
read your letter, to realize that you have faith enough in me
to say all you said. And it is not only that you will provide
me with the security to work. It is the awareness that you* understand *what I say when I tell you, as I so often have, that
for better or worse writing is my life. Even had there been no
suggestion of financial support your letter would have made
me very happy, as your confidence naturally means more to
me than any other. The confidence of Pluto and my few
other friends is valuable, of course, but it is inevitably different. There is no other person in the world to whom I feel
closer than to you, just as there is nothing that means so
much to me as my work, and it is an incomparable joy when
the two come so happily together. I am only sorry that Dad*

---

* My mother and uncle owned jointly a factory manufacturing such valves.

cannot understand something which to me seems so natural,
but I can't help thinking that eventually he will.

As to the actual content of your letter, everything said is
so well and conclusively said that no specific answer seems
necessary. There is one point, though, to which I object and
that is your contention that you are "culturally not very sen-
sitive." On the contrary, I should say that you are exceedingly
sensitive culturally. The proof of it is in the letter I have here
before me, also in the studies which at the age of fifty-two
you have so imaginatively undertaken, when all your friends
ever think about is playing bridge (I know that you like that
game too—and always win!).

I read your letter to Pluto, and when I had finished he
said, "A letter like that lights up the whole room." It does.
And not only is the room lighted but the entire prospect of my
future. Our future, I should say, because we are partners, are
we not, in my endeavor? If you wanted to give me a sense of
peace, hope and faith as well as of increased responsibility,
you have succeeded wonderfully well.

I'm afraid that all this is a rather unsatisfactory substi-
tute for what I might have expressed in person if I were there
instead of here, but I send it in lieu of anything better, and it
goes not only with my best love but also with my admiration,
respect and humility.

Your devoted son, Jim

It was more than a month before I had any response to this letter,
but I did not fancy that it had been unappreciated. I knew that Mother
was busy with her examinations at Columbia and that she had gone
to Maine in the meantime with my father. She was also busy sending
packages of food, coffee, soap and cigarettes to Quimper, all of which,
especially the cigarettes, were much appreciated by the Mondain family. I had not yet acquired the noxious habit of smoking, to which later
I sporadically became addicted. Life at the asylum was pleasant and
peaceful all during this sojourn. In a letter mailed in mid-June there
came from my mother the following paragraph:

A Maternal Ordeal

Did I ever tell you how much I appreciated the letter you wrote me in reply to one of mine, the one in which you spoke of your sense of peace and security at my understanding of what you are trying to accomplish? Your letter came just before we were going off to Maine, so I may have failed to tell you that it meant a lot to me. I have it here at my desk now, and have just re-read it, and it has made me feel very happy and satisfied.

Inevitably there arose the matter of money. My mother decided to grant me an allowance of fifty dollars a month, which in 1947 was quite enough to cover my expenses so long as I remained a guest at the *"asile."* But it would barely have sufficed were I to have made my residence elsewhere. The location, indeed, of my eventual residence became a more and more frequent issue in letters going back and forth between Quimper and America. Mother wrote:

It is fine that you are so happy and contented, but I hope you won't become so fond of France that you'll never want to come home.

She assumed, of course, that I would sooner or later return and asked whether I would be satisfied to live at home when I did. I wrote that it was not a matter of being "satisfied," that naturally I would be glad to live in Englewood with my family but felt that this would not be to the advantage of my work. There comes a time in everyone's life, I said, when it is desirable to "leave home" symbolically and psychologically, and I felt that that time had come for me. How I was to provide the wherewithal for any such leave-taking was an issue left unresolved. But it seems clear that I did not expect to earn the necessary money myself. Letters went back and forth debating the issue and advancing various points of view. Mine were often pretentious and self-satisfied, but there were some in which I expressed opinions new to me, influenced by my reading and by changes of attitude developed after lengthy ruminations in my journal. One of these brought a happy response from my mother.

Dearest Jim,

*Your latest letter has pleased me more than any I have
ever had from you. You have come around to a point of view
which I have for years been trying to convert you to with no
success. I mean that "success" is a matter of character. It used
to appall me when you maintained that an artist's character
and personality didn't matter. If he could paint or write or
compose skillfully that was all that mattered, his character
was irrelevant. So it makes me very happy to have you appreciate that the very opposite is true. The greater the gifts
the greater the responsibility. Not that I expect you to become
a conventional conformist. That really isn't my idea of the
highest morality, but I think you will agree that altruism and
self-discipline are necessary, and I used to think that you held
them in contempt.*

*I have been pondering on the letter you wrote about
your "future." I thoroughly agree that you should be independent, which does not necessarily rule out the receiving of
financial assistance. After all, no one is completely independent. It seems to me that independence is a state of mind
rather than a state of the exchequer. What I want to do for
you financially is what will be the best for you and your development, and at the same time be fair to Ben and Peter.
The great question in my mind is, "Would it be good or bad
for you to give you a yearly allowance as you want us to,
and if good, then how much?" There are two ways to look at
it, it seems to me (1) this is a period of development, of trying
out to see what you can do, which will be followed by a time
when you can be self-supporting, or (2) if you don't learn to
support yourself now you may never be able to, and, the
world situation being what it is, there is certainly no assurance that one can rely on living on inherited wealth. The
tendency is certainly toward increasing inheritance taxes and
increasing cost of living, and it doesn't seem likely that one
third of what is left after Dad and I die and taxes are de-
ducted will be adequate for you to live on. All this may seem
very low and mercenary to you, but it is the crux of what
worries us. It isn't at all that either Dad or I are unwilling to*

share with you now, or that we don't want to help you and give you an opportunity to develop as you want to. But the thought of you at fifty or sixty getting old and poor and disillusioned does haunt me. This isn't lack of faith in you. It is lack of faith in the world perhaps. Appreciation so often doesn't come. Probably there is nothing I can do about it. But the letters you have written recently about the importance of character development and your appreciation that you are working toward a goal are very reassuring. So I am going to try to forget the foreboding outlined above and take view number 1 of your case. It won't be easy, because I feel sure that Dad and Grandmother will disapprove, and you must be fair and admit that they have your welfare just as much at heart as I. It is only a matter of difference of judgment, and I may be all wrong. But I am willing to take the gamble on giving you an allowance, specifically how much I can't say. We shall have to iron out those details when you get back . . .

Never for a moment was I afraid that my mother's "gamble" would turn out to be a losing one. Despite rejections and disappointments in my professional career, if it can claim in fact to have been one, I remained optimistic, like my mother herself in this, nor did I worry for fear that when old I might be poor and disillusioned. To be so confident was foolish, but it made for an agreeable day-to-day existence. Meanwhile, my mother had other things to think about. She had to decide on the topic of her thesis for the degree of Master of Arts which she had decided to take at Columbia, and she chose to write about life and conditions in Virginia in the seventeenth century. My father thought it eccentric of his wife to spend so much time studying and gave her no encouragement, the only instance I know of when he failed to provide her with his support. Except when the issue concerned me, of course. I was not the only son to cause concern, however. Peter, the youngest, had begun to show signs of neurotic instability. Mother wrote:

You asked about Peter. I do worry a good deal about him. He is still so rude and disagreeable a great deal of the

time, especially to Dad and often to Grandmother. I suppose
the fault was in his early training somewhere. Why he should
feel so out of sorts with his family I don't know.

What decided my departure from Quimper and return home was
my appendix. I had suffered from chronic appendicitis since the age
of thirteen, and it seemed prudent to have the useless scrap of tissue
removed lest it someday burst and cause peritonitis. My parents were
very anxious that this operation should be performed at home. A close
friend, one of America's most eminent physicians, Dana Atchley, told
them that surgery had hardly progressed in France since the invention
of the guillotine, and that I must come home to receive proper care.
The necessary funds for return by air were promptly forthcoming. My
mother wrote, "I hope that you will not be too disappointed in your
home and family." I landed at La Guardia Field on November 14,
1947.

My mother might with reason have formulated her hope the other
way around. What was to be determined, after all, was whether or not
my family would be disappointed in me. The appendix operation took
place without incident, and I settled down at home without protest.
Although I had by letter made an issue of "leaving home," I didn't
insist upon it, and indeed would have been silly to do so. My room
occupied the larger part of the third floor of my family's house, contained in addition to an enormous four-poster bed a grand piano, two
large chests of drawers, a comfortable sofa, several chairs, bookshelves
and a desk. I had an automobile at my disposal, could go to New York
whenever I pleased and heard little criticism when I returned very late
at night and rose in midmorning. I began work on a long novel based
on notes I had made while in Quimper and had a protracted affair
with the wife of the son of some close friends of my parents. This gave
rise to "talk" in Englewood. But no one said anything to me. I spent
the summer in Maine, working at the novel, and that was the last
summer that any of us spent there. My parents, now that their children
were grown, felt that the place was both too large and too far. My
father, having been brought up at the seashore, wanted a summer
home by the water, where he could enjoy sailing, so they bought a
house on Mason's Island near Mystic, Connecticut. Leaving Maine

was an emotional wrench for my mother and me, but the move was a wise one and prepared the way for a later move even wiser.

In the autumn I resumed the heterosexual affair. The woman was named Gina, was in revolt against her bourgeois milieu, intelligent but perverse and, like so many women motivated by carnal vanity, fancied her charms sufficient to make a misguided man forget homosexuality. Her excitable harangues on this topic merely left me irritable and depressed. My mood was not made merrier when the novel on which I had labored for more than a year was rejected by the one publisher I had hoped would accept it. And the atmosphere at home after a prolonged stay did little to improve my humor. When, for example, my grandmother sometimes asked how I intended to spend my day and I replied, "At work," she more than once rejoined, "You'll allow me to laugh." My father was friendly, but it seemed clear to me that he was patiently keeping his disapproval to himself.

I grew morose, confided of course in my mother and suggested that it might be good for me to consult a psychiatrist. She agreed but sensibly decided that it would be preferable to keep this from my father. She asked Dr. Atchley to recommend a competent man. So I did not have to contend this time with a charlatan like Pardee. The psychiatrist I saw was an urbane and charming person called Dr. Z. A. Piotrowski, who put me immediately at ease. I told him my story at length, explaining my troubles, my ambitions, my interests, my hopes. But we didn't talk only about me. Dr. Piotrowski was a highly cultivated man, so we spent a lot of time talking about literature, music, painting, and he was particularly curious to know whether there was any evidence to prove the rumor that Delacroix had been the illegitimate son of Talleyrand. I did some research. There isn't.

After a couple of pleasant months of these pleasant conversations my mother asked whether I would object to her having a meeting with the doctor in order to discuss my case. I didn't, and after all she was paying for the treatment, such as it was. So she went off one afternoon to New York, and I awaited her return with some impatience, for I surmised that much might hinge on what thoughts my mother would have after talking to Dr. Piotrowski. I was right. When she returned, she went to her room and I followed. It was there that all our personal conversations took place, almost never elsewhere in the house, as other people might have overheard us. I asked her what the doctor had said.

It was very simple, she replied. He had told her that I was homosexual, that I had made a reasonably well-balanced adjustment to this anomaly, that the affair with Gina was disturbing and had better be broken off and that in his judgment, if circumstances permitted, the best thing that my mother could do for me would be to raise my allowance, permit me to return to Europe to live and write there in conditions of reasonable comfort but by no means in luxury. And so, said Mother, having thought it over on her way home, that was what she would do. It was the one and only time in our lives that the word "homosexual" ever passed between us. I sometimes wondered in later years whether she had forgotten about it, but I suppose that that is a fact difficult for a mother to forget. Unfortunately, she added, her decision was likely to rouse opposition from my father and grandmother, but she was prepared to face it.

Sad to say, her expectation proved accurate. There was a discussion in my presence between my mother and my father. He saw no reason why I should not continue to work at home and felt that travel to Europe was an unwarranted extravagance. To which my mother replied, "What are we going to spend our money on if we don't spend it on our children?"

"Well, it's your money," said my father stiffly, "and so you can spend it as you please," whereupon he left the room. The moment was a tense, unpleasant one. My mother did not appear as distressed as I felt she might have been, and I must add that in all the years of their long marriage that was absolutely the only time I ever heard any words pass between them which could have been considered unpleasant. That seemed so singular to me that long, long afterward, when my father had already been dead for some years, I once asked whether she and he had ever had a real quarrel. She pondered the question for a minute, then said, "Yes. Just once. We were going to a ball. It was snowing outside. I had on dancing slippers and your father wanted me to put on boots over them. I refused and he insisted. We actually did quarrel. But that was the only time I can remember. And I didn't wear the boots." Of course, she added, they had often disagreed about the children and about politics. But they always resolved their disagreements amicably.

I sailed for France aboard the *Queen Mary* on March 17, 1949. Both my mother and my father came to see me off. Ten days later I was happily installed in my room behind the asylum walls in Quimper. I was away for close to a year and a half this time.

Letters from my mother arrived promptly. She was very good about sending them, and by no means all were concerned with my problems, my work, my future. Many, many of her letters contained only news about doings at home, parties with her friends, golf, her garden, her political activities and inevitably the weather. These do not make for very absorbing reading today, even for me, and would be of no interest to anyone else. Still, they show that she was a very sociable individual, much enjoying the company of people she saw frequently for bridge games or lunches at the country club. As a golfer she was never outstanding, but enjoyed the game. "So much more entertaining than just going for a walk," she said. The gardens, both in New Jersey and on Mason's Island, were among her keenest pleasures, and often in her letters are passages such as this one:

> *The lilacs are in full bloom,* and *the tulips. This is the most beautiful time of the year. Soon the rhododendrons will be out, and then the roses. My garden is doing very well this year. The bleeding hearts are* gorgeous.

My mother strongly believed in civic responsibility. She was for many years a member of the League of Women Voters, an organization to which she gave much time and money. She attended the League conventions conscientiously and was for a time president of the organization in New Jersey. Senators and congressmen received many letters from her on issues which she considered important. And in addition to all this she industriously pursued her studies at Columbia. In July I received a letter that contained the following passage:

> *I am childishly pleased and excited over having received a letter from Professor Krout, my history teacher. He apologized for having been so long in reading my essay (since March) but said, "I congratulate you on the thoroughness of your research and the clarity of your presentation." Isn't that nice? So now I am all set to get my degree next December. I am all steamed up to take another course or two next fall. I may try to get a doctorate some day.*

I was, perhaps, as pleased as she was by the commendation for her talent in writing, wrote to congratulate her and said, "So you see, my passion to be a writer didn't come out of the blue but out of *you!*" She never did try for the doctorate, however, partly, I think, because she received so little encouragement from my father, who felt, perhaps rightly, that in consideration of her numerous activities she was over-working herself. But she continued for several years to attend lectures on history and literature by the professors she found most interesting and provocative. Her letters frequently contained comments on what she had been reading. In early September of 1949, for example:

> *I have just finished the second volume of Parrington's* Main Currents in American Thought. *Very interesting in-deed. He didn't think much of Hawthorne. He bases his judg-ments much more on ethical than on aesthetic considerations. No art for art's sake.*

She still found occasion to criticize and scold me when that seemed necessary, however, writing after my journey to Italy and Paris in May and June:

> *I was disappointed that you consider one hundred dol-lars a month inadequate. I cannot but think that if you found at Quimper that that was not going to be enough you should have given up the Italian trip and saved the money which that cost. It looks very much as though you will spend every cent you can get, and no matter how much is given you you will want more. I thought when we doubled your allow-ance that you would certainly be satisfied, and when one considers that many families live on less than you get just for yourself, I should think that you would make more of an ef-fort to make it do. You don't have to go to hear Marian An-derson twice, nor Heifetz, nor Kirsten Flagstad.*

She was right. I should be ashamed to acknowledge it, but I'm not. I was prepared, and anxious, to spend every cent I could get, and for many years, it's true, no matter how much was given me I did always want more. And more was always forthcoming. Yet I didn't feel that I was being extravagant, and I never was until many years later when it was made possible—by both my father and my mother—for me timidly to begin to be. And how astonished, but perhaps not altogether approving, they would be to know that now, aged seventy, I am able to be considerably generous to my friends, buy expensive works of art when I feel like it and live in a manner very close to luxurious but still well within my means. At last I don't want more than I have.

The time came when I felt that I should no longer accept the hospitality of Pluto and his family, so I packed up my possessions, said goodbye to them and took the train to Paris. Life in the capital, of course, was more costly than in Quimper. My mother worried:

> *I have been thinking about your financial situation and have talked with Dad about it. I don't want you to get down to your last penny. You should have something for emergencies. I am putting two hundred dollars in the bank to your account. That will take care of any doctors, dentists or other emergencies which may arise.*
>
> *I am enjoying my courses a lot. I have just been reading Whitman's* Democratic Vistas. *Have you read it? If you haven't, you have at any rate been influenced by the thought: that a great literature is the crowning glory of any civilization. But I don't know whether you agree that there should be a distinctly* democratic *literature as distinguished from the European, aristocratic tradition.*

In October I went to London for a fortnight, and it was then that a story I had written the previous summer, "The Boy Who Wrote NO," was accepted for publication by *Horizon*, the prestigious monthly review edited by Cyril Connolly. I was lucky, as the story appeared in the very last issue, but Connolly must have felt that it had merit, for he republished it several years later in an anthology of the best material that had appeared during the review's ten-year existence. My mother had not cared for the story when I first sent it to her, finding it "too negative and hopeless." With her positive and optimistic temperament, it was not surprising she had disliked that effort, but it is nonetheless the only tolerably good piece of fiction I have ever produced. And whether my mother liked it or not she was delighted to receive word that it was to be published.

> *Dearest Jim,*
>
> *Congratulations! It really is wonderful that you are going to have a story published, and in such a top-grade magazine, too! I am wondering where I can get a copy when it comes out. Maybe I'll ask Professor Trilling. He should know. I told you that I am not at all qualified to judge about literature in general and your work in particular. But anyway I am awfully pleased and proud. I won't go down Palisade Avenue* shouting, "Attention, all you stupid, bourgeois Americans! My son is going to have a story published in an ultra ultra literary publication in London!" But maybe I shall do a teeny-weeny little bit of boasting in a subtle way when opportunities present themselves. It is nice of you to give me leave, but I shall really be most discreet. I know that it is very bourgeois and American of me to be so pleased by this sign of the great god Success, and it isn't that I value you any more for achieving it. It is really a very selfish satisfaction in having been "right" about you—as nearly as anyone can be "right"—and in feeling that in giving you the opportunity to go ahead and write I was not spoiling and pampering you and ruining all your chances of ever becoming independent, as Dad thought. Grandmother is very pleased too, and sends congratulations. Dad is in Detroit, but I am sure that he will be glad.*

I don't know whether much boasting was done, but there was understandably, and honorably, a little. When *Horizon* was at last available in New York bookstores, my mother wrote:

> *I purchased four copies, not resisting the temptation to remark when the salesman acted surprised at my taking so many, "My son has a story in this issue." And it was a thrill actually to see your name on the cover as big as could be!*

* The principal thoroughfare of Englewood.

A Maternal Ordeal

Though in Europe I was safely removed from the recriminations and diatribes of my sometime mistress Gina, I was not without news of her. It came from a very unexpected source: my mother. She had certainly not approved of our affair, gladly following Dr. Piotrowski's advice by helping me to terminate it. But once I was gone she and Gina saw each other occasionally, discussed the qualities or faults of the stories I sent home, and both women probably enjoyed talking about the faraway, headstrong would-be writer of whom both were fond. Mother even gave Gina occasional help by employing her to type essays written for her courses at Columbia. I thought it an example not only of her broad-minded kindliness but also of her humane interest in people very unlike herself. Gina eventually divorced the son of my parents' friends, leaving their child with him. She achieved very brief notoriety through an affair with Dylan Thomas, then took up with a good-looking homosexual vagrant whom she met in the Sixth Avenue Automat in Greenwich Village and finally she became a Seventh-Day Adventist, going about the Lower East Side asking people whether they were saved.

The first faint flush of literary success represented by the publication in *Horizon* was not followed by great excitement in editorial offices. Still, there were a few stirrings of interest, which I gladly passed along, knowing that they would generate appreciation.

> *That is very good news that you have had some inquiries from editors. You are coming along. It has been—still is, of course—a long, hard pull, and I for one admire your determination and courage in going ahead in spite of all the obstacles. And I recognize, to my regret, that I have been among the obstacles.*

To which I replied:

> *I consider myself phenomenally fortunate in that I've had almost no obstacles to overcome except interior ones. It makes me feel guilty to have you say you think me courageous or determined. It doesn't seem to me that I've had to be. As for your having been an obstacle, I protest violently against such thoughts and would be furious if anyone else*

suggested such a thing. When you suggest it, I'm only sorry. If
at the beginning you had misgivings, what could have been
more natural? I have them still!

Occasionally my mother, despite her misgivings about willful extravagance, sent extra money:

I hope you have received the letter with the bank deposit
slip. In case you didn't I deposited one hundred dollars as a
Christmas present, the twenty-five dollars which Grand-
mother gave you and approximately (I can't remember the
exact sum) two hundred and seventy dollars which was a
balance I had left in the bank in Maine and which I just
made over to you. I must confess that I didn't tell Dad about
that transfer. So you need not mention it in your letters. Just
thank us for the Christmas gift. I don't like being deceitful,
but maybe it is better than stirring up arguments.

I replied with appropriate gratitude and assured my mother that
the best way I could demonstrate my appreciation would be by working
as hard as I could to vindicate her faith in me. She was working hard
herself:

This is a rainy morning, a very good day for studying for
my mid-year exam, which comes on Thursday. I don't quite
know why I am taking it. I just have the feeling that I
should do it, so long as I am taking the course, and a little
curiosity about what it will be and whether I can pass it. I
certainly should, as I haven't missed a lecture, and I am sure
I have done more reading than the average student in the
class, but my poor old brain isn't as agile as those of the
young, and whether I can get down what I know on paper in
some orderly form is a question.
    Next term I think I shall concentrate on Trilling's course
rather than Commager's, though I plan to take both again. I
really think, for general purposes, a knowledge of American
literature is more interesting and (to use a trite word which I
hate) "rewarding" than Constitutional history.

A Maternal Ordeal

I had by this time been in Europe for more than a year, and should have known that sooner or later the issue of my continuing residence here, and my mother's financial support of it, would again cause controversy. It came very gradually. In April she wrote:

> *It would be very nice to have Harper's publish your novel, but I won't feel too disappointed or upset if they don't take it, or even if it doesn't get published immediately. I feel sure that you will get going eventually, and a year or two of delay won't matter too much. Having been reading about F. Scott Fitzgerald, I am not so sure that quick success is a good thing, though of course you are older, and far more stable, than he was. But I can imagine that real success is dangerous at any time of life.*

And again:

> *I have just been reading a great lot of early criticisms of Balzac. One, written by Henry James, struck me. He commented that Balzac, in his youth especially, wrote too rapidly, without reflection, because he had no leisure. Maybe it did Balzac no harm, but I believe that really good work cannot be done under too adverse circumstances. (Maybe that isn't true, but at any rate I don't want you to be worried about money. I think I shall deposit a bit extra for you from time to time. Not much, so don't get your hopes up, but enough so that you won't feel too pressed. I'm not going to deny myself in order to provide you with luxuries, so don't let that worry you. Whatever extra money I may send you will only be that much less for you to inherit later—and it won't be so much less, especially when inheritance taxes are paid.) Don't feel that you've got to be "grateful" for the money we send you. That is such a horrid feeling, and makes one resentful toward the giver, so I understand the best psychologists aver.*

By autumn, however, a very decided atmospheric change had developed, brought on, I suspect, by the combined pressure of opinions held and advanced by my father and grandmother.

> *Dad has gone to Detroit and Indianapolis, so I have not been able to discuss with him your decision to stay in France. But I am sure that he would agree with me that it is time for you to return. I have been giving a great deal of thought to the matter. You did not mention anything about your novel, whether you had heard from the publishers or not. If you have heard, and if your book is accepted, I shall of course be delighted, and in that case you could afford to stay in France if you want. But if it has been rejected, I really think that you should make up your mind to acquire some means of self-support. It isn't, as you well know, that I begrudge you your allowance, or that I don't want to do what I can for you. But I don't think it would be fair to you to let you go on in this way. You have had four years in which to try it out, and I am convinced that the best thing for you would be the experience of being self-supporting. I think probably teaching —French and/or English—would be the best thing for you to do, and that would give you considerable time for writing. Perhaps you would have to go back and finish college. I know that you are going to react violently against this whole program, but I feel that I have taken the responsibility of letting you do as you wanted this long, and I am not willing to go drifting along any longer.*
>
> *I am very sorry, Jim, if this letter upsets you. You know that I love you very much and hate to disappoint you. But I am convinced that this is the right decision.*

The letter did, indeed, upset me, and I made no secret of it. The prospect of becoming a teacher seemed unthinkable, especially as my contempt was still fresh for almost all the practitioners of that profession to whose mediocrity I had unhappily been obliged to submit—no Barzuns or Trillings at Wesleyan, and only a single teacher at Williston for whom I had had any liking or esteem. I was not downhearted, however, because I didn't for an instant believe that my resolve to spend my life writing was seriously jeopardized. Nonetheless my mother's mind seemed made up, for two weeks later she wrote even more emphatically.

> *It is hard to express exactly my attitude about you and your work. I do not at all feel that I have undergone any change in my point of view. I still want and expect you to continue your writing and I still have confidence that you will gain recognition, probably not outstanding popularity, because you obviously neither want nor have the knack for writing "best sellers." All of that doesn't bother me at all. The things which disturb me are these.*
>
> *1. You are nearly thirty years old. You have no means of self-support. If you continue as you are going now, by the time you are forty you probably never will be able to earn an adequate living—unless you can support yourself by writing, which we all hope you will be able to do. It does not seem to me either mercenary or materialistic to want one's son to be able to take care of himself if and when it should be necessary for him to do so. Dad and Grandmother and I live on invested capital. Hers will eventually be divided two ways and ours three ways. Taxes, both income and inheritance, are getting higher and higher. How much you will have I don't know. As things are now it would be enough to support you fairly comfortably. But ten years from now the situation may be* very *different. Dad manages our affairs very well, but of course you don't know and don't want to know anything about business or investments. Therefore the only safe thing for you would be to have safe, low-interest-paying securities. All this leads to the point that you cannot rely on your inheritances for a livelihood. Even if we were much wealthier than we are it just isn't sensible in the present condition of the world to count on always having enough money to live on. Therefore both Dad and I do worry about your future. All of this does not imply a lack of faith in you, nor an insistence on outstanding success. As people get older they probably become more timid, less willing to take a chance, especially for their children whose welfare means so much to them.*

*2. I don't think that it is a good idea for you to expect to
make your home permanently in Paris. I can't help thinking
that it is best for an American writer to live in America. I
have talked with Gina since I got back and she said that she
thought you should come home. Naturally we all want to see
you, but it isn't merely a selfish desire on my part to have
you come home.*

*I hope that you will not misunderstand this letter, nor
feel that my concern about you and your future is in any
sense due to lack of affection for you and willingness to do
all I can to help you. Quite the contrary.*

It seemed evident to me that the views of both my father and my
grandmother had dictated much of what my mother wrote. That she
had discussed the matter with Gina, not yet divorced, displeased me,
because I certainly did not want her in any way involved in decisions
concerning my future, for I knew only too well—and I thought my
mother should have remembered—what considerations would determine her judgment.

Only a few days after that last letter I received another, with the
following paragraph:

*I have been thinking a lot about you, wondering how
you are going to "take" my last letter and what you are
going to do. It worries and distresses me, as you know, to op-
pose you and to have you think that I am unsympathetic or
that I don't care about your work. I can understand that my
letter came as a shock to you. I still feel hopeful that you will
eventually get into a position where you will be able to have
what you write published. But I would feel ever so much easier and happier about you if I knew you were able to support
yourself if the necessity arose. I hope, now that you have had
time to think it over, that you will at least give me credit for
wanting you to do the best thing for yourself, your own future and development. Naturally we would like to have you
back home, but it certainly isn't entirely from a selfish standpoint that we are urging you to return.*

A Maternal Ordeal

My poor mother! The maternal ordeal was, indeed, genuine, and cruel. She was caught in a vise between irreconcilably conflicting ideas and ideals. She twisted first one way, then another, seeking release or, at least, relief from her painful predicament. But there was none. I answered her as best I could:

> *I received your last letter this morning and hasten to an-*
> *swer it. I have not given up my reservation on the* Ile de
> France *for October 23, though I don't really want to come*
> *back that soon. I may be able to arrange to fly. I'll see. In*
> *any case you can expect me by the second week of November,*
> *perhaps sooner. But I must stress that I consider this a visit. I*
> *want to come home to see all of you. But I don't want to*
> *come back to tensions and disagreements.*
>
> *Of course, dear Mother, I understand your point of view,*
> *appreciate your feelings and know that my welfare is your*
> *sole concern. I realize that I am taking a chance. But the*
> *chance has already been taken. It's too late now to turn*
> *back, around or aside. Don't you see? I couldn't. Do you*
> *imagine that I could accept myself as a failure now? Some-*
> *day I may have to. Can you believe that anything else will*
> *matter if that day should come? Anything else, that is, except*
> *my deep remorse at having compelled you to take the chance*
> *with me and at the last let you down. It isn't even a question*
> *of believing in myself. My conviction, my determination are*
> *like the very air I breathe, and there's nothing I can do to*
> *change it. But I'm not going to go on at length about all this.*
> *We will discuss it when I get home, and be assured that I*
> *look forward with the liveliest pleasure to being reunited with*
> *my family. Dearest Mother, please don't worry. It makes me*
> *so sad when I think that I'm such a trial to you. As soon as*
> *my plans are definite I'll let you know. Meanwhile may*
> *everything seem bright—and right!—to you.*

It didn't, alas. I sailed for home on the *Ile de France*, arriving in New York on October 30. During my stay there were numerous conversations with both my mother and my father about what I, and they, should do about my future. None of these made a difference. My father was opposed to what I was determined to do, my unhappy mother wavered. No unpleasantness, however, attended any of those conversations. I was lucky. Both my parents were dignified, generous and kindly people. There was no question of cutting off my allowance. Only my grandmother contributed a note of old-fashioned severity, scolding me harshly for causing by my frivolity and irresponsibility so much distress to my mother. Granny had recently redrawn her will, bequeathing to her six grandsons all the capital remaining to her after considerable gifts to her son and daughter, and she had accorded me just the same treatment as my brothers and cousins, so I kept my peace and let her scold. Besides, I was quite fond of her, relished her stories of nineteenth-century life and often read aloud to her articles from *The Reader's Digest*, for her hearing deteriorated seriously as she neared ninety.

Having stated that my visit was to be considered no more than a visit, I made plans to return to Europe. My parents went to California in February, leaving me alone with my grandmother and the servants. I decided to sail on the *Queen Mary* on February 23, exactly four months after my departure from Le Havre. My mother wrote from Santa Barbara:

> *In case you are still expecting to sail on Friday this is my last letter to you in the U.S.—to wish you a pleasant voyage. Of course I am not angry with you for going but disappointed that you have not been able to adjust yourself to life at home. I can understand that it is not all that you might desire. But whose life is?*

After just two weeks in Paris I traveled south with a friend. In Capri we rented a splendid villa with a large garden and fine views of the blue bay and a smokeless Vesuvius. There I settled down in a vast *salone* to write another novel, this one entitled—prophetically?—*No Traveler Returns*. Not long afterward I had a letter from my mother.

> *I am glad that you are settled at last and hope that you will find life in the Isle of Capri conducive to good work rather than the romantic exploits for which it is famous.*
> *I hardly know how to reply to what you said in your let-*

*ter from Paris about your attachment to me and your feeling
that you must succeed in order to justify my confidence. I, of
course, would like very much to see you succeed, but that is
not by any means the most important thing in my eyes. What
I would like to see most would be a stiffening of the moral
fiber. The qualities in you which disturb me are restlessness,
self-indulgence and egocentricity. But I have said all this before to no avail. So what is the use of repeating it? How
much I am at fault has always worried me. I am sure that
many people think that I should long ago have told you that
you must take responsibility for yourself. But I haven't,
whether from lack of courage, confidence in you or plain
wishful thinking I don't know. I am still willing to support
you, but it does distress me and put me in a very uncomfortable position to have you do the things you do—go off on
this trip, pile up a lot of bills before you leave for clothes
which I cannot believe you needed. It is all certainly very
much in the pattern of the prodigal son, and it is a very distressing and worrying thing for both Dad and me. Of course,
as you very well know we do not work twelve hours a day to
earn the money you spend, but instead of feeling guilty,
which goodness knows I don't want you to feel, you should
do something about leading a more stable and purposeful
life. I know that you think, and I am sure honestly believe,
that writing is your raison d'être, but certainly in order to
write it is not necessary for you to travel wherever you please,
nor, as a matter of fact, to have the kind of company and
surroundings which are the most pleasant and congenial.*

*You will probably consider this a very unkind and un-
sympathetic letter, which I don't mean it to be. But I do
worry so much about you, and wonder whatever is going to
become of you when Dad and I are no longer around to look
after you.*

There was a check included. I replied at once:

*Your good Easter letter came today. Thank you for the
check. Though naturally dismayed by what you say, I do not*

feel that the letter was unkind or unsympathetic. Quite the contrary. It was proof of great sympathy, renewed evidence of your desire to see me live the sort of life that is best for me. I myself would like to see "a stiffening of the moral fiber," and agree that my self-indulgence is harmful. I am not unaware of my faults and weaknesses, and I do strive to overcome them. It will be a lifelong task, and I am grateful for your advice as well as your concern. I can't promise that you will live to see that I am not "the prodigal son," but I believe it.

You will be glad to know that I am working very steadily here and have written more than sixty pages of manuscript in two weeks. I feel this novel to be much more possible than the others and hope to have it finished by the time I come home in the fall.

After leaving Capri I went to Rome and Florence, thence to Vienna and Salzburg, where I stayed with my friend for a month, continuing work on the novel and living in two rented rooms adjacent to a beauty parlor. At the hotel where we had lunch every day the waiter, a handsome blond fellow, was an ardent Nazi, had volunteered for the army when only sixteen, seen service in France, Italy and Russia and been wounded five times. The military life had been hard, he said, but there were good comrades, which was a compensation. "The Americans only have dollars for comrades," he added. From Salzburg we went to Paris, where I bought a car, then drove to the South of France, spending August in a rented apartment at Villefranche-sur-Mer. From there in early September we drove across France to Biarritz, where we stayed with a friend; he accompanied us for a week's tour of northern Spain, including Madrid and Toledo. Autumn was in the air before we returned to Paris, pausing en route to view the magnificent cave paintings at Lascaux.

All of this traveling, unnecessary, to be sure, but enjoyable and cultivating, cost money, more than my allowance permitted me to spend, but I did not heed the maternal injunction not to travel wherever I pleased, with the inevitable consequence that appeals for further funds from home were forthcoming and had the impudence of being sent by cable, which angered my father, not without reason, a cable representing the assumption of a fait accompli. My mother was indignant, reminded me that I had gone abroad without parental consent and again argued that I could certainly live within my allowance if only I made an effort to. "I know *I* could," she added. My mother continued to insist that I need not live abroad. Presumptuously referring to the judgment and example of Henry James, I invoked yet again the European admiration for intellectual endeavor and respect for cultural tradition, both so lacking, I felt, in America, asked for more money and expressed my sense of guilt about accepting it. During this time, and for some years thereafter, I managed to supplement my allowance by doing a bit of dealing in works of art. It was easy then to buy, or find, a Delacroix, Courbet or Monet at a moderate price and negotiate its sale in New York for considerably more. But even these occasional increments of income did not suffice to eliminate the continued deficits.

Both my mother and my father had written letters urging me to come home and "settle down," and I had implied that my reappearance in Englewood could be expected in the autumn. But I put it off, wanting to finish my novel before returning. In expectation of finding a quiet, pleasant place to work I went off to Heidelberg, a town I'd known well while in the army, found an agreeable pension and did, in fact, in a month write several chapters of the book begun seven months before in Capri. By midwinter parental patience was worn out. My mother wrote:

> *Some decisions will have to be arrived at, so please be giving thought to these propositions: 1. We are finally going to insist that you get some kind of job. I am not willing any longer to take full responsibility for insisting that you be allowed to devote all your time to writing and/or such other occupations as interest you while we provide support. Dad feels that that is a very bad thing for you, and I've had the burden of making the decision contrary to his judgment. I am not willing to shoulder that any longer. 2. We will deposit your allowance on March first, but you will have to get yourself home on that. So make plans accordingly. 3. Be thinking about what you will do when you get back.*
>
> *I hope this letter will not seem too unfeeling to you. Believe me, it isn't.*

I never felt that my mother was unfeeling. It was obvious, indeed, that the strength of her feelings was a source of anxiety and conflict for her, and that she contended courageously on my behalf with her inner self. Only five days after having written the ultimatum above she concluded another letter by saying, "Don't be upset by my last two letters. We can work out something when you get home."

If it was, as it was, willful self-indulgence and a disinclination to face unpleasant eventualities at home that prompted me to linger on in Paris, my presence there in mid-February led to a chance encounter which ultimately brought about the fulfillment most ardently desired both by my mother and by myself, for it was then that I happened to make the acquaintance of Alberto Giacometti, a meeting which in time transformed my life.

As for the immediate future, an omnipotent deus ex machina conveniently appeared in the form of the Rockefeller Foundation. One of my pals in Paris, a man whose goodwill and generosity toward me have been unfailing to this day, was well acquainted with the directors of the Foundation and had already received from them considerable encouragement and cash. It was he who thought up a scheme whereby another pal of ours, a writer named André Fraigneau, would be sent on a tour across the United States for a couple of months ostensibly to observe the workings of American cultural institutions—universities, libraries, museums—in order to determine what benefits might accrue on both sides of the Atlantic through closer ties with similar institutions in France. I was to accompany him as a sort of cicerone-cum-interpreter, since he spoke not a word of English. The qualifications of Fraigneau to undertake such a study being flagrantly nil, I suspected from the first that the tour would prove to be a recreational jaunt financed by Rockefeller largesse. That, of course, is not how I presented the matter to my parents, who were duly impressed by the notion that their son was considered sufficiently cultivated and percipient to deserve the magical prestige of Rockefeller patronage. There was no mention of my getting a job when I arrived with Fraigneau aboard the *Queen Mary* on April 14.

My expectation as to the serious cultural purpose of the Rockefeller-sponsored tour was confirmed from the beginning, for Fraigneau's first priority after visiting the Foundation offices to receive a lavish remittance for expenses and indulge in some sociability with the directors was to acquire an expensive suitcase and fill it with a luxurious outfit of clothes purchased from Brooks Brothers. Our journey across the United States and parts of Canada lasted two months, was a lark but did nonetheless include visits to museums and universities. What the directors of the Rockefeller Foundation thought of our peregrinations I had no idea and never learned. The trip is worth mentioning here not only because it relieved some of the paternal pressure on my mother but also because it led to casual encounters with three exceptional women. Fraigneau knew that I was acquainted with an American lady painter named Eleanora Kissell, who had lived for twenty-five years in Taos, New Mexico, and was familiar there with all three of the women who had been rivals for the attentions of D. H. Lawrence in his final years. They were, of course, Frieda, his widow, Mabel Dodge Luhan, indefatigable lionizer of creative celebrities, and the Honorable Dorothy Brett, whose passion for Lawrence had led her to pursue him to that then-very-out-of-the-way spot in the southwestern wilderness. For reasons I never well understood, Fraigneau was more interested in seeing these ladies than anything else in America and urged me to get in touch with my acquaintance in an attempt to arrange it. I did, and Miss Kissell graciously promised to do what was necessary. So we went to Taos, where, indeed, we were introduced one after another to the three ladies.

Mabel Dodge, and her Indian husband, Tony Luhan, were the least interesting. Their house, made of adobe like all the others, was rather elaborate, but the interior was modern and as un-Mexican as a zipper, though an accent of the occult was provided by a commonplace household broom suspended by a string from the center of the living-room ceiling, its significance unexplained. As our visit took place in the late afternoon, large amounts of bourbon whiskey were provided, our hostess and her husband, I noted, serving themselves more liberally than their guests. Mabel's conversation was disjointed and somewhat childlike, as if she had difficulty maintaining for very long any train of thought. Miss Kissell later told us that "serious people" in Taos didn't pay her much heed. Tony spoke almost not at all but fixed everyone in turn with a stare that appeared either disdainful or stoical. There was inevitably talk of Europe. Mabel said she would never cross the ocean again, since passports and visas were too much bother, and, moreover, as a last straw Leo Stein had written her from Florence saying that spaghetti was now made by machines.

Brett was a rather plump little lady attired in blue jeans and wearing a hearing aid, delighted to show us her very messy house and quantities of her paintings, some of them impressive, including fourteen portraits of the flamboyant symphony orchestra conductor Leopold Stokowski. She seemed rather lonely, anxious to talk, especially about her family. A sister, she said, was married to Sir Charles Brooke, the "white rajah" of Sarawak, while her great-grandmother had been born on the battlefield of Waterloo during the battle. This detail, with its Stendhalian resonance, delighted Fraigneau. Though Brett was then a naturalized U.S. citizen, she insisted as we were departing on showing us the enormous rendition of her coat of arms which she had painted on her garage door facing the wilderness.

The last of the three ladies we saw was by far the most impressive, and entirely on her own account, not because she was the widow of the world-famous novelist. A splendid creature, old but robust, she looked rather like a peasant but was unmistakably a noblewoman. She was immediately sympathetic because of her warmth and willingness to talk quite openly and very sensibly about herself, her life with her husband or, indeed, about anything whatever. Her accent was heavy but rich and warm, not at all harsh. She took us round her house, large and tastefully appointed, pointing out a dozen very ugly, somewhat erotic paintings by Lawrence. She said that he had only started to paint seriously when he was about forty, while working in Florence on *Lady Chatterley's Lover*, his favorite among his works because it had caused him the most trouble. She spoke of Lawrence without the slightest hesitation or self-consciousness, remarking that to her he was like someone still living, because her feelings for him had never ceased to evolve. He had wanted to see all the world, she said, travel everywhere, write about Africa and Asia, but died too soon. I was especially interested in her saying that he had not felt that it harmed him creatively to leave his homeland. "His expatriation," she remarked, "was in fact a liberation." As we were leaving she gave me a snapshot of the chapel high in the mountains where his ashes were interred. It had been built by her present husband, an Italian named Angelino, on the San Cristobal Ranch, which Mabel had given the Lawrences in exchange for the manuscript of *Sons and Lovers*. I would have liked to see more of Frieda.

From Taos we went to Cleveland, thence to Niagara Falls, Montreal and Quebec. I was relieved when Fraigneau returned to France early in June, spurning an opportunity—then very difficult to come by—for a visit to the Barnes Foundation.

My parents by that time were installed in their seaside summer home in Connecticut. I remained alone in Englewood, working on my novel, engaged at the same time in a love affair with an out-of-work actor, and visited occasionally by my brother Peter, whom I considered to have become quite eccentric. He was still at Princeton but did not appreciate the social life there, which his two older brothers had so enjoyed. Uncommunicative and brusque, he kept stubbornly to himself and had become obsessively close with his money. Clearly there was something amiss, but I didn't know what I could do about it, and, besides, had preoccupations of my own.

Well before the end of the summer the issue of my future had again become pressing. From Connecticut my mother wrote:

> *It is hard for a parent to know whether a child has suffi-*
> *cient ability to make it seem right to continue to support him*
> *in what to some might seem useless idleness. In our society*
> *there isn't any "leisure class," except for a few wealthy play-*
> *boys who certainly command no respect. I must say, however,*
> *that it seems ironic that no one criticizes athletes for devoting*
> *their lives to sports, which certainly could—or should—never*
> *be regarded as a serious life work . . .*
>
> *You are not proposing to lead a criminal life nor to*
> *break any moral codes—unless one considers that the dictum*
> *"All men should earn their own livings" can be considered a*
> *moral code—and I suppose it is so considered by some. But*
> *not by me.*
>
> *This is the problem as I see it. Is it the best thing for you*
> *that you should continue on this course? I know that Dad*
> *thinks that it is very bad for you, and that he is convinced*
> *that it is wrong to let you go on. I am sure you know that*
> *both Dad and I want most of all to do what is best for you.*
> *The difference is that he thinks some miraculous change in*

your character will be produced by the mere fact of earning
your own living. I am sure that it will not. And, on the
whole, I don't want any change. You are a very sweet, lov-
able person and I am deeply devoted to you. And you are
what you are, for better or for worse. If we made some dread-
ful mistakes in your upbringing, and I am sure we did, they
are past, and the best we can do is accept you and ourselves
as we are—not waste time vainly wishing we were all
different.

I hope you are right about your writing. I want you,
above everything, to realize your highest potentialities. The
paramount question is: will continuing the kind of life you
have been leading achieve that end? I am sure I don't know.

But I did know. My certainty was not a consequence of any rational
decision or determination on my part. It was simply the outcome of
that manic obsession which determines the life endeavor of every creative individual. Whether his creativity turns out to be of enduring
value or even of transient interest is, alas, quite beside the point. I
didn't understand this then. Youth must have generated confidence. I
felt certain that time would eventually vindicate my obdurate resolve
to pursue my vocation despite whatever distress or conflict this might
occasion my mother. But at the same time it saddened me to do so,
and I tried to make that plain.

I am really very sorry that I put you in the position of
having to make a decision, in itself difficult, I know, but
which moreover causes dissension in your personal life. I real-
ize how unpleasant it must be for you to have to contend
with the disapproval of those around you. Believe me, I am
very pained by this. But would you be pleased, after all, after
the years of effort, the thousands of seemingly wasted pages
and fruitless years, would you be pleased if I were to say,
"Well, it was all a mistake, and I'll give up any thought of
ever having a career as a writer"? You would not. Then, then
you'd think of me as spineless, self-indulgent and irresponsi-
ble as do those I need not name. We are what we are, as you
say, you and I, and nothing can change us. To alter a vital

part of one's self is really to repudiate the whole. I have lived
according to my nature as best I could and have struggled to
be, to become, what that nature suited me for. I don't believe
that the struggle has harmed me—on the contrary, I think it
has been all to the good—and I only hope that it has not
harmed you, that it will someday bring you pleasure and—
who knows?—even pride. And should that day ever come, no
matter how far in the future, it will make all the waiting
seem to have been only the more worthwhile, dearest Mother.

The waiting, indeed, did give every sign of being indefinitely protracted. I had returned to Englewood from the Rockefeller jaunt in
June of 1952 and spent the better part of the next year under my
parents' roof and at their expense, working still on the novel I had
begun in Capri. There were occasional discussions about my situation,
my prospects, my requirements, but I must stress that not one of them
ever degenerated into downright argument. Overt reproaches or threats
never were pressed upon me. My father's disapproval was explicit and
I knew that he emphasized it in private to my mother. However, despite
her misgivings she must have continued to shoulder the responsibility
for allowing me to go on as I pleased, because that is what happened.
While working on my novel I congratulated myself for avoiding autobiography, yet that is very much what it turned out to be, the story
of a young American, uncertain either of his purpose or of his destiny,
wandering around Europe, a rather insipid blend, I realized later, of
Tender Is the Night and *The Beast in the Jungle*. Though very certain
of my purpose and optimistic as to my destiny, I also longed to resume
my wandering around Europe. My parents were certainly not prepared
to underwrite once more the expatriation from which they had had
such difficulty in fetching me home.

Another deus ex machina was required. And who could have foreseen that this would materialize via the commemoration of that dour
and irascible genius Paul Cézanne? Of all the artists of modern times
Cézanne alone possessed for me the spiritual grandeur, dogged integrity and breathtaking beauty of pictorial representation that placed him
forever in the company of Rembrandt, Titian and Michelangelo. Having learned that his studio was for sale and in danger of being destroyed, I had determined to do what I could to save it for posterity.

With the approval of the French Cultural Attaché in New York I was able to form an imposing committee of sponsors and appeal to collectors and dealers for funds. The money poured in. It didn't take very much, only about $25,000, though in 1953 that was a substantial sum. Though this sounds, and was, relatively simple, yet it took up a good deal of time, for it was I alone who managed all the practical details of the fund-raising campaign. My father disapproved of this endeavor, feeling that if my profession was to be literary I should devote myself to it exclusively, not waste energy and time on a philanthropic enterprise, for the benefit, moreover, of a country not my own. I persisted all the same, and my parents, being committed to the principle of philanthropy, made a generous contribution. They even attended the reception given in honor of the successful culmination of the campaign. I was summoned to Washington to receive the thanks of the French Ambassador, Henri Bonnet, and informed that the French government would be pleased to invite me to travel to France, paying my round-trip passage first class, so that I might attend the inauguration of a Cézanne exhibition in Aix-en-Provence, the artist's birthplace, the first ever shown there, nearly half a century after his death. I was delighted. My parents could hardly demur. I sailed aboard the *Ile de France* on June 11, 1953, leaving behind the assumption that I would be home again come autumn. This time it would be eighteen months before I once more embarked on the *Queen Elizabeth*.

Already in early September I wrote:

> *Now, I fear, the time has come yet again for a discussion of the "future." How these moments crop up and crop up! And the introductory phrase, I fear, must always make you wince. I'm sorry. Yet I am convinced that my work will proceed most satisfactorily—both for the present and, I must add, for the future—if for the time being I stay on in Europe through this winter, and by "this winter" I mean to suggest a more or less indefinite period which would carry me through at least to the conclusion of my present novel. As you know, I found it more and more trying to go on living in Englewood. (You understand that this had nothing to do with our per-sonal relationship.) Indeed, I don't even know whether I could accept coming back to the U.S. at all just now. Being*

*in American terms and eyes a failure, I find the compulsion
toward demonstrable success, the obsession with material
achievements and the obligation to prove one's worth in some
public way profoundly depressing and demoralizing. Moreover, the cultural life here is of a richness and fertility not to
be found at home, and it is my great good fortune to be more
or less in the midst of it. I do not want to give that up. Not,
at least, for the time being. So, dearest Mother, please allow
your wonderful patience and rare devotion to accept this extended status quo with the firm belief that it will one day
keep its promise to us both.*

And of course she did. What that cost her in terms of stress and
regret I could sometimes guess, when, for example, she sent funds in
addition to my allowance, saying, "This is a sum saved out of housekeeping money and is not to be mentioned in your letters. It is deceitful,
I know, but makes for less tension in the family." I gladly accepted
the extra money, but it added also an extra portion of guilt. I was amply
provided with that anyway, having lived through a prolonged adolescence with the conviction that homosexuality was shameful and vile.
Now I wonder whether it wasn't precisely my homosexuality that
"saved" me. Had I been heterosexual, naturally desirous of wife and
family, the life I have lived would obviously have been inconceivable.

In February, Mother wrote:

*I hope that you are right in your decision to persevere in
your writing. As a matter of fact, I really believe that you are
right, but of course the rightness depends entirely on the seriousness and determination with which you work.*

*As for the drifting, certainly most of us do more or less
drift along on the paths which circumstances and our various
natures lead us to think will be the most pleasant, interesting
and (certainly in many cases) where we think we can be useful. There is nothing wrong in that, and I am not so Puritanical as to think that one should do unpleasant tasks solely for
the sake of self-discipline.*

*I was reminded of our situation today when I read an
account of Whistler's mother, who was not, it seems, the*

*sweet, charming character depicted in his painting. She was
a very determined, self-righteous and Puritanical old soul but
devoted to her son, "Jemmie." I could not but think that perhaps I am a bit like her, but wonder whether my "Jemmie,"
if he ever does a portrait of me, will want, as Whistler said,
"to make Mummie as nice as possible."*

Now that I am endeavoring to create a portrait of my "Mummie"
I have found—somewhat to my surprise—that it is in fact very much
a self-portrait, relying as it does so largely, and effectively, I trust, on
her words rather than mine. And as for making her "as nice as possible," I naturally hope that she will seem to a reader to have been
almost nicer than *is* possible. She certainly seemed so to me. I can
remember only one incident in her long lifetime when she lost her
temper. My younger brother Teddy had had as a small child of three
or four to undergo an operation for hernia, and the very day that he
was brought home from the hospital our nurse, impelled by heaven
knows what provocation, gave him a spanking, which brought shrieks
from the invalid infant, whereupon my mother rushed into the room,
snatched her son from the nurse's grasp and fiercely exclaimed, "Pack
your things and get out. You're fired!" I believe she had just cause.

To me her "niceness" seemed manifest not only in her patient
tolerance of my wayward life—despite occasional misgivings and in-
consistent ultimatums—but also in her discreet acceptance of my personal, private propensities and associations. Never once was a leading
question asked. While living at home, when I often came back from
New York at three o'clock in the morning, the lights in the front hall
were always left burning to greet me, and the next day no inquisitive
remarks were made. My mother cannot have forgotten what Dr. Piotrowski had told her, and she met three of my lovers with imperturbable
aplomb, but she never voiced the slightest comment. In later years,
especially after my father's death, she did occasionally remark that it
might contribute to my happiness if I were to marry, but I realized that
this was only an expression of her fear that I might have to face, as
she did, a lonely and infirm old age. What made her exceptional, all
in all, was precisely that she was so extraordinarily nice, so warm,
generous, thinking and thoughtful, good-humored and humorous, un-
prejudiced, intellectual, modest and incomparably polite a woman.

A radical and permanent change came about in my relation to my parents, and to myself, when the novel so long in progress but at last completed in the early winter of 1954 was accepted for publication simultaneously in England and France, later also in the United States. This sign that I could, after all, legitimately expect to have some future as a writer was profoundly reassuring to all concerned, especially to my father. My mother wrote:

> *Wonderful! I am particularly pleased on Dad's account, as I know he has worried so much about you for fear he has not done the right thing in letting you go on confining your work exclusively to writing. I think one of the chief reasons for the misunderstanding (or lack of understanding) between you two has been that he is very much more sensitive than you have ever realized, and his feelings have often been hurt by your seeming indifference to his opinion. It means a lot to me to keep him cheered up.*

That my father was, indeed, very much more sensitive than I had ever realized was true. But we were entangled in the classic, banal but unhappy Oedipal imbroglio. Later, much later but still not too late, I was able to pay my respects to his sensitivity, a difficult and liberating occasion for us both.

It was during the spring and summer of 1954 that my friendship with Dora Maar—*another* exceptional woman—was most intense. I never thought for an instant about returning to America, although I had been gone for more than a year. Throughout this period, however, there were a number of minor happenings that distracted and pleased my parents, suggesting that I was not a complete wastrel. The Cézanne studio was inaugurated on July 8, and an article by Douglas Cooper appeared in *The New York Times* the following Sunday, relating the event and mentioning my crucial role. So it may have seemed that I had accomplished something, nonliterary though it was, worth doing. Then a review of Cyril Connolly's anthology of the best work from *Horizon* appeared in *The Saturday Review of Literature*, singling out "The Boy Who Wrote NO" and a story by Antonia White called "A

Moment of Truth" for particular praise: "They belong to the currently fashionable category of tales of neurosis, but there's nothing hackneyed about them and they illuminate 'normal' behavior as inferior examples of this genre do not." I had long since decided that it would be proper and natural to dedicate my first novel to my parents. They were pleased.

It is very good of you to offer to dedicate it to Dad and me and I am pleased and touched and would like it. Even though the subject matter may be unpleasant* I nevertheless am sufficiently sentimental to like the idea that you want to dedicate your first novel to us. Dad says that if you are going to dedicate to anyone it should be to me, but I prefer that it should be to us both.

I agree with you a hundred percent that a life devoted to artistic endeavor is worthwhile. And I realize that being a "success" is not a worthy objective in itself. My great worry has been that you might devote the best years of your life to a pursuit which would prove a bitter disappointment, and that then it would be too late to start on a different career. I am more relieved than I can tell you that my fears were evidently groundless. I feel confident that the acceptance of your book is a real turning point, if only from the standpoint of Dad's attitude.

My father's attitude was helped, but not fundamentally altered, by the little signs of success. He was despondent and unhappy about my situation. However, I can't help feeling that there was something inherently pessimistic and despondent in the depths of his nature. He should have known perfectly well that in the long run I would never have to worry about supporting myself, because a dozen years later he made careful arrangements to assure that that would always be the case. Yet he fretted, and this distressed my mother.

I see both your point of view and his. I wish I could help you to understand each other better. You are both fundamentally fine people, but so different.

* Adultery, promiscuity, homosexuality, irresponsibility.

A Maternal Ordeal

The autumn had come, and with it came urgent suggestions that I return home. As it happened, I was ready, for once, to do so, having decided that as an American, no matter how agreeable it was to live in Europe, I must give my homeland a serious trial. In order to do that, it was of course clear to me that I could not go on living at home. I was now thirty-two years old, and I put it to my parents that I must have an apartment, however modest, in New York. This would mean, of course, added expenditure, which further irritated my father. But my mother simply wrote, "Have you any idea where in New York you want to live? I suppose we can scrape up enough furniture. So you won't have to buy any." I arranged to sail for home—aboard the *Liberté* this time—on November 12. On the tenth I fell on the stairway of the Café de Flore and broke my left ankle, a compound fracture requiring surgery. My departure was to be delayed by two months. I went with a friend to Aix-en-Provence to recuperate. My mother was distressed, sent heartfelt wishes for rapid recovery and added, "I don't think I could bear it if anything should happen to delay you again." Nothing did. I arrived in New York on January 12, 1955. To find the suitable apartment in New York took some time, but before the end of March I was comfortably set up at 60 East Eighty-third Street, between Madison and Park avenues, a tranquil residential neighborhood close by the Metropolitan Museum.

Getting promptly to work on another novel, one this time set in America and with a particularly American theme, I awaited the publication in the United States of the first. It had already appeared in England, receiving reasonably favorable reviews, but if I was going to live in America and be an American writer, the response that mattered to me was the American one. Meanwhile, I wrote diligently every day and regularly saw my parents, with whom there was no contention. Oddly enough, they went abroad while I was at home, traveling for two months by car through France and Italy. I met a lot of people, among whom were quite a few well-known figures, whose names I enumerate not out of vainglory but to suggest that in New York, no less than in Paris, it was possible to encounter men and women of cultural eminence. Listed at random in my journal I find Samuel Barber and Gian-Carlo Menotti, Glenway Wescott, Marianne Moore, Stephen Spender, Gore Vidal, Tennessee Williams, Judith Anderson, Suzanne Langer, Thornton Wilder, Aaron Copland, William Faulkner, Virgil Thomson, Dr. Alfred Kinsey, Marlon Brando and William Carlos Williams. There were a host of others, too, very agreeable, whom I saw certainly more frequently than the famous. I was also invited regularly to the Fifth Avenue apartment of Mrs. Murray Crane, who maintained even in her old age the last salon, strictly speaking, to exist in America, and where one could chat with the likes of Robert Graves, W. H. Auden, Padraic Colum and all three Sitwells. So New York was from a cultural standpoint not quite the wasteland I had for so long considered it. Still, I was not content. The unrelieved ugliness of the city oppressed me. And I was still a nonentity so far as any memorable accomplishment was concerned. In America that mattered. In Paris it seemed not to. And from that magic city, the enchantment of which has never to this day ceased to thrill me, I continually received siren messages urging me to return. So I decided to go back. My parents accepted the decision with composure, sorrowful on my mother's part, glumly resigned on my father's, and I sailed aboard the *Queen Elizabeth* on March 3, 1956.

In Paris I easily renewed acquaintance with all of my old friends, saw the Giacometti family, Cocteau, Marie-Laure de Noailles and the rest, including even Rebecca West—one more exceptional woman—with whom I had a long talk about writing and who cheered me by saying that she didn't feel that young writers were nearly pretentious enough, in the best sense of the word, and that no first-rate work could be produced by an author who didn't bear constantly in mind the greatest examples of the past.

My novel had appeared in America before my departure, but there had not yet been any reviews. These were sent to me by my mother and on the whole were laudatory. Needless to say, both my parents were happy and cheered by this—belated—suggestion that their son's headstrong resolve might not, after all, have come to nothing. My mother wrote:

> *It is certainly very encouraging and gratifying, and I am immensely pleased. This is what I have been hoping for years would happen, mostly for your sake, of course, but partly quite selfishly for my own in order to feel some self-justification for having insisted (insofar as I did "insist")*

on letting you go your own way. I feel very grateful to the reviewers.

From my father:

> *All these flattering reviews make me feel that it must be that I don't know a good book when I read one. (Could it be that the faint whisper I just heard is a hearty "Aye, aye!" echoing across the Atlantic?) However that may be, I do send my hearty congratulations.*

Creative individuals are perverse and quixotic creatures. I would have been crushed by negative reviews, as I was to learn in time, but enthusiastic ones did not delight me as I had expected. To my mother I wrote:

> *Thank you for sending the reviews. Such favorable notices, for some strange reason, rather upset me. I have the feeling that I may never again do anything that will seem so good. It may be a silly reaction, but it is how I feel. To a considerable extent I had hoped for some degree of "success" in order to convince Dad and Grandmother that I am not, after all, merely an idler and waster. And, of course, it has been very much for your sake above all in order that you might feel that so much confidence and encouragement over the years—how* long *they have been!—were not abused and misplaced.*

She replied:

> *It* is *very exciting that you are getting such good reviews, and it is of course absurd for you to think that you won't do anything good again. I am expecting the book you are working on to be much better.*

During the period of these exchanges I was settled with a friend in Florence in a very comfortable apartment in a vast *palazzo* on the Pitti side of the Arno, rented from an aged countess—still another exceptional woman—who had danced with Czar Nicholas II at St. Petersburg and had fascinating stories to tell of a vanished world. But by June I was back in Paris. From there I wrote a long letter to my mother, in which I went on at some length, as I was too often wont to do, about my literary ideas and plans. However, I added:

> *I imagine you must become rather weary of my repetitious protestations of artistic resolve, etc., etc. However, I like to tell you these things, as I feel that they do interest you. And if I were not to talk about them to you, then to whom might I? For I'm reluctant to discuss such personal matters with anyone else. With you I can risk seeming pretentious. I may as well add, as I've said more than once, and as I hope you never forget, that I am constantly mindful of, and grateful for, your sympathy and understanding. Grandmother is fond of saying that you are a remarkable person. I agree with her, and think it a tribute to her perspicacity that she is aware of it. I don't want to embarrass you, but if, as you've said, you were pleased by good reviews of my book because you felt "justified," I was pleased for the same reason, as I feel that my work has been made possible not only by your material collaboration but also from the beginning by a collaboration far more intimate. Perhaps I have rendered in tangible form, as I hope to continue to do, some part of your own sensitivity, some part of what it is that makes you remarkable. That, to my mind, would be an accomplishment worthy of honor. Inheritance is not a one-way street!*

Mother may have been pleased by such declarations of filial sympathy and admiration, but she was not immune, alas, to occasional feelings of maternal failure and parental irresponsibility. On December 19, 1956, she wrote:

> *Dad and I saw O'Neill's* Long Day's Journey into Night *night before last, and I haven't quite recovered. Aside from the fact (important, no doubt) that Dad doesn't drink and I don't take dope, the play hits home, not in details but in the fact that we—like all parents, I suppose—haven't really*

*known what the important things were, for us and for you
boys. We console ourselves with the thought that "We have
done our best," but our best isn't good enough. Well, I am
sure it does no good to become morbid and remorseful at this
late date, so I won't bore you further.*

This passage roused my indignation, and I replied:

*I was distressed by your reaction to the O'Neill play. I
certainly don't think you have anything to feel remorseful
about. There are all kinds of parents, certainly, and all of
them make mistakes. Perfection is inhuman. But there are
also all kinds of children, and they too make mistakes. Misunderstanding is never a one-sided affair. I think that parents
must often err in feeling a greater responsibility for their children than circumstances warrant. And children definitely err
—I should know!—in feeling that the responsibility of their
parents is almost limitless. I have often said how truly I appreciate the sincere and selfless efforts that you and Dad have
made, and make still, to do what is best for your children.
Quite honestly I can say that I know of no other parents who
have done as much or as well. So please do not be unduly
stirred by any who, like O'Neill, seek to represent a personal
sense of doom and fatality as a faithful image of the human
condition in general.*

By this time I had finished another novel and sent it off to the
publisher of the first one, who accepted it after some revision. Mother
again felt vindicated, though I observed that she did not seem as pleased
as I thought she should be.

*I am sorry that you thought I was not pleased with the
favorable reaction to your book. Of course I was delighted. I
am afraid that I do not always express my feelings ade-
quately in my letters. When I think of the years during which
I agonized over what I ought to do about you, whether it
was right to let you do as you wanted, or whether Dad was
right in thinking that we should insist on your getting a job*

and doing what writing you could on the side, I believe it is
a greater satisfaction to me than it is to you that you are fi-
nally justifying me in my decision. So any success which you
have is a salve to my conscience as well as a natural booster
of my maternal pride.

Sad to say, the full measure of satisfaction and conclusive boost to maternal pride were still far in the future, but neither of us seems to have doubted that they would eventually come. They came, perhaps, by chance, but I don't believe that chance determines very much, if anything, about the dynamics of creative work. Meanwhile, there was no more discussion as to my future. That die was cast once and for all. My allowance, plus frequent extras, came regularly without remonstrance, and I had come to mention the necessity of acquiring an apartment in Paris.

My brother Peter had recently astonished the family by announcing that he intended to marry. He was then almost thirty and had rarely evinced much interest in girls, or in boys, so far as we knew. But nobody ever knew very much about Peter, as he was so extremely reticent about himself and his doings. He had by this time left Princeton without obtaining his doctorate in electrical engineering, no doubt a bitter frustration. However, he had obtained an excellent position as an experimental researcher with an aircraft corporation in Baltimore, where he had settled, ever more miserly, in the slums. His fiancée was a woman of his age named Peggy, who was teaching young children at a school in Princeton, and he had met her while still at the university. She proved to be an extraordinarily tolerant and sensible wife to an exceedingly difficult, ultimately impossible husband. Just before their wedding my mother wrote:

Peggy is not a silly, love-sick girl, blind to Peter's faults.
She seems to understand him very well, which augurs favor-
ably for future happiness. Whether Peter understands her (or
anyone else) is more doubtful.
*   We have decided to give them (or rather Peggy) a Volks-*
wagen as a wedding present. She expects to continue teach-
ing and will need transportation. Peter talked about buying a
truck and letting Peggy use his old car, so this will forestall

*that piece of idiocy. It seemed foolish to give them furniture
or silver. Nothing can be done with Horner's Lane anyway,
and finally when they get a decent abode we can assist with
the furnishings.*

They were married in Princeton on the tenth of July 1957. I spent
that summer in Aix-en-Provence, working on a new novel, and had
promised that I would return home for a visit in the autumn.

This time I traveled by plane, arriving in New York on November
3. So I was present for the publication of my second novel, entitled
The Joys of Success, a title foolishly insisted upon by the publisher. It
enjoyed no success whatever. The reviews were severely critical, as they
had every good reason to be, for I had attempted a clever, derisive
satire and failed to bring it off. If my mother was as disappointed as I
was, she kindly kept it to herself and assured me that I had only to go
on working in order finally to produce a book of recognized merit.
Rebecca West had said that young writers should be pretentious, and
I certainly followed her dictum on that score. During the next dozen
years I wrote several more novels, long and very pretentious, none of
which—fortunately!—found publishers. I also wrote a play, not an
original work but a dramatic adaptation of Henry James's *The Beast
in the Jungle*, which had never ceased to haunt me—for reasons only
too obvious. It has enjoyed the success that James deserves, having
been produced twice to acclaim in Paris and elsewhere on the Continent but never, oddly enough, in English.

Meanwhile, I returned to Europe—sailing on the *Queen Elizabeth*
on March 1, 1958—and in Paris I presently found a small apartment
for sale in the rue de Lille that seemed suitable. Without much
protest—"your father is resigned," Mother wrote—my parents advanced the money for its purchase. I was asked to sign a note acknowledging the advance as a loan, but Mother wrote, "You know
perfectly well that we aren't going to press you for the money." They
never did, and the day after my father's death, when Mother and I
were going through the papers in their safety-deposit box at the bank,
that note was one of the first things we destroyed, along with a far
larger note, I was sad to see, acknowledging a debt to my mother by
my father.

When I bought the apartment, where I sit writing these words today, thirty-five years later, Mother wrote:

> *Like you I am very glad that the question of your habi-*
> *tation is at last settled, for better or worse, and I hope it is for*
> *better. Naturally I regret that you have elected to live so far*
> *away, but with jet planes whizzing across the ocean at super-*
> *sonic speed the time required for a trip is not as great as it*
> *would have been from here to Philadelphia a hundred years*
> *ago, or maybe a hundred and fifty.*

In November of 1959, having been away for nineteen months this time, I flew home for a four-month visit. It was harmonious and pleasant, no discussions or recriminations, though I could sense that my father still considered my existence capricious and worried about my "fiscal irresponsibility." I still had a good number of friends in New York, whom I saw regularly, and even as far afield as Philadelphia and Washington, where I went for weekends. The visit, indeed, was so agreeable that I returned that same year in time once more for Christmas. To my surprise I found my grandmother walking for the first time with a cane, at age ninety-seven, complaining of a persistent ache in her left thigh. It got gradually worse, so that by Christmas Day she was hobbling about on crutches, and only then did it occur to anyone that X rays were called for. They revealed what every aged person dreads: a fracture of the hip. And then she remembered that she had fallen one night when getting down from the high old bed of her childhood to make herself a cup of cocoa. For nearly a month she had been suffering from her fracture without ever complaining of pain. Hers was the stamina of the nineteenth century. Dr. Atchley was called in. He decreed that surgery, though a grave risk, was imperative, for if confined to bed a person of her age would inevitably die of lung congestion. The operation took place on January 2. It seemed successful at first. Though groggy, the old lady was quite herself. But three days later she suffered a stroke. The doctors said there was no hope. However, she rallied. When I went to see her, she chatted about one thing and another quite normally and spoke of soon returning home. Then she had a second stroke, and this time did not rally. Dr. Atchley said it would now be only a matter of hours. And yet she lived on for four long days while we awaited the end. My mother and I were together at the hospital when it came. The nurse asked us to wait at the end of the corridor until the final moment had passed. After half an hour she called us. My grandmother was a tiny, lifeless, gray figure curled beneath the bedclothes. My mother kissed her on the cheek; then we left the room. It was a gray, chilly afternoon. As we walked back toward our parked car my mother wept. I put my arm around her and we wept together. The funeral took place in Indianapolis, Grandmother's birthplace, where she was buried in the plot of her Holliday forebears close by the grave of one of the slaves her father had brought on from Virginia more than a century before and who had always "belonged" to the family. Two months later I returned to Paris, aware that when my grandmother's estate was settled, always a protracted affair, I would at last have a bit of capital of my own.

One day in April 1961, I chanced to meet an old friend in the street and he invited me to a cocktail party. His apartment overlooked the Seine and had a small terrace. When I strolled out onto that terrace, there were still traces of a Tiepolo sunset along the river. It was an enchanting moment, and I fell in love. The man's name was Larry Hager, American, originally from Oklahoma, aged twenty-six, working in Paris as a ticket salesman for Trans World Airlines. His real ambition was to do something, acting if possible, in the theater, and he ultimately achieved this goal. We lived together off and on for nine years, some of them difficult, but none of that has much to do with the story of my mother, save that all my family at length became acquainted with Larry and rather liked him, for he had a powerful need to make himself likable.

Both of my novels and some stories, translated into French, had been more successful, widely read and popular in France than at home, another reason, perhaps, for my enjoyment of life in Paris. One day I was introduced to someone who asked whether I was James Lord the writer. Pleased by this infinitesimal suggestion of celebrity, I wrote about it to my mother, who replied:

I understand your childish delight on being asked
whether you are "the writer." It would certainly please me to
have someone say, "Oh, Mrs. Lord, are you by any chance

related to James Lord the author?" But whether that ever
happens or not, I am glad to be your mother anyway.

I don't think it ever did happen, but eventually there were compensations that turned out to be adequate, especially in view of the very long time they were in coming.

In the early spring of 1962 my parents decided to take another trip through Europe, this time concentrating on southern Italy and Sicily, then the South of France and the Dordogne. Having seen the sights of Naples, Pompeii, Paestum, too much of Calabria and quite enough of Sicily, they flew to Paris. My father had always dreamed of seeing, not scaling, the Matterhorn, and had brought along his skates in hopes of finding a pleasant pond or rink in Zermatt, for he had enjoyed skating since boyhood—i.e., for more than seventy years—so he went off to Switzerland by himself, leaving my mother and me in Paris. She had written, "My chief object in going to Europe is to see you," and we had delightful days in Paris together, the first we had spent entirely alone with each other for a very long time. Having arranged to rejoin my father in the South of France, we set out in my new car on March 11. The weather was springlike and as we drove along together we laughed and talked and recalled old times, particularly the happy summers in the "other" Paris. I knew that Marie-Laure de Noailles was then staying in her château at Hyères and thought it might amuse Mother to meet this eccentric character of whom she had heard so much and with whom I had grown so friendly. I called Marie-Laure and asked whether we might spend the night of the twelfth. She was delighted, especially as she had no other guests just then and we would enliven her solitude. I, however, once the arrangement was made, began to worry. Enlivening Marie-Laure's solitude could entail highly awkward eventualities. There was no telling what she might say, and she much enjoyed embarrassing newcomers to her milieu. But I counted, with some trepidation, on her fondness for me to avoid any too-outrageous behavior. My mother had long ago written me, "It always seems strange to me to think of your knowing so many famous people and getting along so well and comfortably with them. I am sure I should be very ill at ease in such company." And so I hoped—foolishly—that the formidable viscountess would for my sake be on her best behavior.

A Maternal Ordeal

We arrived at the Château St.-Bernard just in time for tea, a welcome interlude, as Mother was weary after a long day's drive. She suffered from poor circulation and if she was compelled to remain seated for long periods her ankles would become swollen, which though in itself painless made close-fitting shoes uncomfortable. We found the viscountess in the library, her favorite room in the house. Speaking perfect English, of course, she greeted us very cordially, a kiss on either cheek for me, suggested that we have tea and rang for the butler. Before he had had time to arrive, however, she remarked to my mother, "Oh, Mrs. Lord, I notice that your ankles are extremely swollen."

"It's nothing," my mother explained. "I have poor circulation. After a long drive my ankles are always swollen. Fortunately it's neither dangerous nor painful, only unsightly."

"Oh, but it's not at all unsightly," Marie-Laure insisted, "not at all unsightly. But wouldn't you be more at ease with your feet on a stool?"

"Oh, no, please don't bother," my mother protested, though I was aware that at home she often rested her feet on a stool.

The butler having then arrived, Marie-Laure said, "Henri, bring a stool for Madame Lord's feet. Her ankles are terribly swollen and she will be much more at ease with a footstool." So the butler brought a stool and my mother obediently put her feet on it, her swollen ankles thus far more conspicuous than before. "Now," said the viscountess, "I'm sure you're more at ease. And your swollen ankles aren't in the least unsightly. One would never notice them."

"Well, *I* notice them, of course," said my mother.

To my relief that was the end of that exchange. Henri brought tea and exquisite cakes. We made chitchat about one thing and another until after a time Marie-Laure casually remarked, "I must tell you, madame, that I am very devoted to your son."

"I, too," said my mother.

"But I should add," continued the viscountess, "that we have never been to bed together."

"I'm very glad to hear it," said my mother without an instant's hesitation.

Nothing more, fortunately, was said on that score and presently we went to our respective rooms to bathe and dress for dinner. When we came downstairs for a drink in the library, Marie-Laure was all smiles, evidently in an excellent humor. I thought that our hostess was unlikely to test any further the frontiers of embarrassment. When we were seated at the round dining table, however, my mother facing Marie-Laure and I in between, the viscountess abruptly said, "I've often heard that in America there are private clubs reserved exclusively for women, something unheard of in Europe. Is that so?"

"Oh, yes," Mother replied. "It's not at all uncommon."

"And tell me, madame," Marie-Laure pursued, "do you belong to any of these clubs?"

"As a matter of fact, I do," said Mother, "to several."

"Well, I've always wondered," said Marie-Laure, "and you can certainly enlighten me: do these women have Sapphic relations?"

"Not to my knowledge," Mother imperturbably replied.

Marie-Laure laughed and said, "You know, in the short time we've been acquainted I've become quite fond of you. If you permit, I think I'll call you Louise, and you must call me Marie-Laure."

"Why, I'd be delighted to," said Mother.

The rest of the evening was highly entertaining for all three of us, with jokes and stories and amusing anecdotes that kept us up late in the large salon with the Cubist ceiling. In the morning, as we were departing, Marie-Laure kissed my mother as well as me on both cheeks and said, "Now, Louise, when you get back to Paris, James must bring you to lunch, and bring the skater, too."

As we drove across the hills toward Nice to meet my father at the airport I asked my mother what she had thought of our famous and formidable hostess. "I liked her," Mother said. "She's like a little girl, trying to see how much she can get away with and to keep all attention concentrated on herself." When we had picked up my father, very pleased by his contemplation of the Matterhorn and skating on a rink as smooth as plate glass, we went to stay at the Colombe d'Or in St.-Paul.

The next day I telephoned Vava Chagall, eager to show off to my mother as many of my celebrated acquaintances as possible, and we were invited to tea at Les Collines. Vava, having lived in London, spoke good English, and Marc had kept a passable competence from the war years in New York and his American mistress. Our visit was perfectly pleasant, but Mother didn't take to the painter. She thought him far less innocent and straightforward than Marie-Laure despite her perversity and selfishness. His mannerisms were affected, she felt, his air of childlike simplicity insincere and his attitude toward his wife overbearing. We didn't stay very long, and afterward Mother remarked that she would have liked Chagall's pictures far more if she had never met him. I sometimes reminded her of this in later years when we went together to the opera in New York and had to look at his two hideous murals.

Motoring back to Paris via Avignon, Carcassonne and Albi, I managed to have us admitted to the caves at Lascaux, no longer an easy matter then. We went twice to lunch at Marie-Laure's. She called my father "Boy!" and though neither of my parents had ever set foot in a residence so palatial they did not for a moment appear overawed, only rather bemused at the extraordinary contrast between the magnificent house and the bohemian demeanor of its occupant.

By the end of March my parents had returned home. I set out on a tour of Western Europe with Larry that took us through Spain, Portugal, France, Belgium and Holland. It was mid-May when we returned to Paris, and by that time I had some astonishing news to send home. After all the tension and dissension attendant upon my determination to live in Paris I had decided to return to the United States and take an apartment in New York. It would be easy to rent the rue de Lille apartment on an easygoing basis to someone I knew, I could sell my car, pack up most of my belongings and be in America early in June. Parental astonishment was predictable. My mother wrote:

> *Dad can't understand* why *you are coming back and as a matter of fact I don't either, but I shall be very glad to have you nearby, understood or not.*

Understanding must have come eventually, quite soon, in fact, but they never alluded to the reason, or even implied they were aware of it. It was simple. My friend Larry had decided that he wanted to go to New York and study to become an interior decorator. I was loath to be separated from him, therefore decided to go along. We sailed aboard the *France* on June 1, 1962, the last time I traversed the ocean by ship. Larry owned a small house in San Diego, California, where he wanted to spend the summer, and assured me that I would have a quiet room in which to write. My parents loaned us a station wagon and we set out on June 11, stopping en route in Oklahoma to visit Larry's widowed mother, who lived in a small ranch house several miles away from a small town. On the fifth of July I received a distressing letter from my mother:

> *We have had very disturbing news from Peter and Peggy. On Saturday we received a letter from him telling us that he is in a hospital being treated for a nervous condition. He said he had had a shock, which he didn't want to talk about. We finally got his doctor on the telephone yesterday. He said that Peter is making progress but that he definitely needs to be there, that he has "tendencies toward self-destruction." We couldn't reach Peggy on the phone, which worried us, as we feared that there might be trouble between them. But we finally found that she and Carol* are staying with friends, and we had a long talk with her this morning and a letter from her today. Our suspicions were entirely un-founded. She is taking it all wonderfully well, and her only concern is to get Peter well again. The shock, she said, was the stock market collapse, but the real trouble is that he has been working too hard. Probably this has been coming on for a long time. As for the stock market, he only lost paper prof-its, and a good deal of his money is in savings banks. Peggy said that the doctor is encouraging and she is sure he will make a complete recovery. He will have to be in the hospital for two or three months.*

I replied at once:

> *I was very distressed to receive the news contained in your letter of this morning. However, I cannot say I'm sur-prised. Peter has always been excessively tense, incapable of letting go of himself and entering into any experience without restraint. This "breakdown" would seem to demonstrate that he finally found it impossible to continue suppressing some*

* Their first child.

vital aspect of his nature. I am extremely sad to think of all this. For Peter above all, of course, but also for you and Dad. I fear you may be asking yourselves what errors you may have made with Peter, and what part of the responsibility may be yours for this unhappy turn of events. I hope, however, that you are not having such thoughts. As you and I have often said to each other, parents can do no more, and cannot be expected to do more, than what seems to them best according to the ideas and ideals determined by their own development. You and Dad have certainly done that. I only wish there were something I could do to help Peter. I can't but feel that in some obscure way I may have failed or wronged him when we were children together. As you remember we were very close at one time, then we drifted apart. I never understood quite why. Well, we were at different schools and saw each other seldom. But he never seemed quite the same afterward. I don't feel at all guilty about this, yet it does haunt me. Certainly I will write to him, though I wonder how much good letters of sympathy can do.

I wrote a long letter in which I hinted that, perhaps, of all the members of the family, I might best be able to understand and feel compassion for his anguish. I reminded him of our onetime closeness, twenty-five years in the past, and asked him to think of me as a friend eager, if possible, to help, adding that my own experience had made me aware that the security and composure of one's life can disintegrate in a minute and that that awareness might allow me to offer more than mere sympathy.

He answered:

Many thanks for your thoughtful letter. My letter will be brief since my hand will become nervous and start shaking because of nervous tension I have been in.

This hospital is one of the best for treatment and I hope that I will not have any more severe deep moods of thinking, although certain less severe moods may (or may not) work against improving my mental condition.

I certainly appreciate your offer to help me out of this,

but I don't think that this will be necessary with all the doctors and attendants. Many thanks again and I hope that you have an enjoyable time in California.

Love, Peter

Early in August I received the following letter from my mother:

Thank you for your recent letter, enclosing the copy of the one which you wrote to Peter. Letters seem to mean a lot to him, and yours have been very sympathetic and understanding. We went down to Baltimore to see him last Thursday, flying there and back in one day. We had a nice visit with him. At first he seemed quite tense and nervous, possibly because he did not know we were coming. Peggy had telephoned the hospital to ask them to tell him, but the message was not delivered. But later he became calmer and talked quite rationally. The eye which he injured is closed most of the time, though he can open it partway occasionally.* They will probably have to operate on it if it does not improve without an operation.

We had a talk with his psychiatrist, who continues to think that Peter will make a complete recovery. He explained his condition by saying that he is suffering from a "flight from reality," and is substituting fancied worries, the stock market, the Kennedy administration and the Cold War, for the things which really worry him but he cannot face. He thinks but is not sure that the real worry is about his work, especially his fellowship and the research he is expected to do for his doctorate. Having failed to get it once, he may be very apprehensive that he won't succeed this time. But his "obsession," as he calls it, seems to be about schemes for ending the Cold War. Peggy said that he wrote a long paper, about fifteen pages, which he was going to have printed as a paid advertisement in a Baltimore paper. He got terribly worked up

---

* I later learned that he had stabbed himself in the eye with a steak knife, a self-inflicted injury with mythic implications I considered highly significant. But I don't know whether these implications were ever considered so by Peter himself, his doctors or anyone else.

*about it, and got into such a state that he voluntarily went to
a psychiatrist, who later advised that he enter the hospital.
Peggy told us all this when we were in Baltimore. She has a
copy of the paper, but we have not read it.*

I, of course, believed that I knew what reality it was from which
Peter so desperately desired to flee, and felt certain that the war ob-
sessing him was not the so-called cold one, but the scalding conflict
within himself. But I thought that it was not my place to intrude my
suppositions into a situation already fraught with unknown, unknow-
able and unpredictable risk.

At all events, Peter did make a recovery which seemed complete,
even, perhaps, an improvement on his former state. It took time. He
was in the hospital for many, many months. But a year later my mother
was able to write:

*Peter, Peggy and Carol departed on Sunday. As far as
we could tell Peter is back to normal—for Peter. In fact, I
thought he was more considerate of Peggy than formerly. She
is concerned because he is not enthusiastic about his job. We
had a little talk with him, urging him to get into something
else—possibly teaching—if that would interest him more. But
I don't think he will make a change. He is apprehensive
about doing anything new and different. Did I write you that
they have bought a house? Peggy seems very pleased with it,
and I am delighted they are getting out of the neighborhood
they are in.*

Meanwhile, Larry and I had settled in an apartment on the top
floor of a small house on East Eighty-third Street. But I went back to
Europe almost every year, usually in the summer, and the letter from
which the foregoing passage is quoted was sent to me at Marie-Laure's
Riviera château. I kept on writing, while publishers kept on rejecting,
which for some peculiar reason did not hinder either my compulsion
or my conviction and, even more peculiar, seemed not to trouble my
parents in the least.

In September of 1964, as I was en route back to New York after a long stay with Marie-Laure, Alberto Giacometti, with whom over the years I had become friendly, proposed to paint my portrait. Naturally, I accepted, having always longed to possess portraits of myself—I have at least twenty—as if the survival of my likeness might ultimately compensate for the demise of the model. Giacometti did paint my portrait, devoting to it eighteen long afternoon sessions between the twelfth of September and the first of October. Aware from the first day that this experience would be a memorable one, I made in my journal far more detailed notes than usual, having trained myself from an early age to retain long passages of conversation verbatim. When I got back to America, leaving the very next day after the last sitting, I immediately wrote up my journal notes, thinking that some magazine might be interested in the finished text. But it was too long for a magazine, and too short, I thought, for book publication. It happened that the Museum of Modern Art was just then preparing a large Giacometti retrospective exhibition, so I showed my text to a friend who then worked there. He liked it, passed it along to the director of publications and the Museum decided to publish it, entitled *A Giacometti Portrait*, as an adjunct to the Museum catalogue. Of all the things I have written this little book has proved the most popular and highly esteemed. Published nearly thirty years ago, it has been translated into several foreign languages, is still in print both in France and in America and continues to have a steady though modest sale. Having become acquainted with the most eminent art historian of our time, E. H. Gombrich, I offered him a copy, and three days later received a letter of commendation, in which he said, "A thrilling book . . . I couldn't put it down . . . a unique document and intensely moving." No other praise has ever meant so much to me, so I passed it along to my mother, who had never heard of Professor Gombrich, of course, and whose acquaintance with Giacometti was as yet superficial. Still, she was pleased by any approval of my professional labors, no matter how esoteric or useless for burnishing her son in the eyes of her friends.

Peter and Peggy had a second daughter in the summer of 1966, and all seemed well with them. My older brother, Bennett, married soon after the end of the war, had by this time four children, one son and three daughters, and this family also seemed a happy one. I saw all of them fairly regularly during those years spent for the most part in America. They were all, like my parents, friendly to Larry, accepting his presence in my life without comment, though they must have made the obvious assumptions.

On November 27, 1967, I wrote the following letter to my parents:

Forty-five is an age halfway between the beginning of manhood and the end of what used to be deemed reasonable life expectancy. Though one so introspective as I certainly has not waited till now to take stock of his progress along life's thoroughfare, it seems apt to do it again now. And since my very ability to think, not to mention my life itself, begins with both of you, it seems even more apt to share with you a few of the thoughts that occur to me on this occasion.

In the haste and urgency of their need to be themselves and to lead their own lives I don't know whether it often occurs to children that they might do well to thank their parents for having made them what they are, and, in fact, for having made them at all. Of course, it may be that blame seems often more in order than thanks, but it is easier to assign responsibility than to accept it. In any event, I feel altogether on the thankful side, and I hope that to have me tell you so will provide both of you with a satisfaction somehow in keeping with all the care and patience and thought and money you have throughout the past forty-five years selflessly devoted to my well-being. I do mean to emphasize my appreciation of the well-being and my gratitude for the selflessness.

Whatever the difficulties, disappointments and traumas of the past may have been, they are now past. None of us can redeem or change them and their importance is merely historical, if that. But I do want you both to know that, however untoward and willful my behavior at times has been, I now vividly see and greatly appreciate that you always acted in keeping with your disinterested view of my best good. It means much for a child to be able to tell himself this, and it has, I realize, given me with time a continuous sense of emotional and material security which is in considerable measure the source of my relative serenity at present and my resolve to

devote myself ever more conscientiously to the work in which
I have for so long endeavored to find fulfillment.

It gives me an especially profound and lively satisfaction
to feel in the middle of my life that you are both still crea-
tively a part of it, and I am happy to be able to thank you
for having been so always. I hope you will continue to be so
for a long time to come, and that I may eventually give you
cause to be as pleased to have me for a son as I am to have
you for parents.

Six weeks later my mother wrote:

I have just re-read the letter which you wrote to Dad
and me on your forty-fifth birthday. As I told you at the time
I was deeply touched, and so very thankful that you are
aware that, whatever errors we have made (and I'm sure
there were many), we nevertheless tried to do the best we
knew how for you. And though there were worries at the
time, the satisfactions were far greater, because of course we
both love you very dearly. So let's be thankful that all has
come out so happily, as I feel it surely has.

After five years or so of off-and-on life in New York I had had
enough of that city, and my relationship with Larry was no longer as
satisfying as it had been. I decided to go and live in the country, where
I could write in perfect, though solitary, peace. I was able to rent from
a distant cousin in Old Lyme, Connecticut, a fine house built in 1746
not far from Lord Hill. It was entire coincidence that I came to that
part of the country so closely connected with my forebears. The first
Lord ancestor who emigrated to America was Thomas, a smith, aged
fifty, who sailed for Massachusetts from the port of London on April
27, 1635, accompanied by his wife, Dorothy, aged forty-six, and seven
children from four to sixteen years old. The following year he went
through the wilderness with the Reverend Thomas Hooker to found
Hartford, Connecticut. It was one of his sons, William, who settled in
Lyme. Perhaps in part, then, for atavistic reasons I was singularly
content in that large house for several years, worked hard at unpublishable novels during the week and entertained guests from New York

almost every weekend. During the summers I saw a good deal of my parents, as their summer house was less than an hour's drive from Lyme. They came to see me, too, and we played croquet on the lawn under the two-hundred-year-old sycamore trees.

My father was now eighty-five, and one day on the spur of the moment when we were alone together I took the opportunity to tell him that I appreciated how sincerely despite our differences of outlook he had always endeavored to do what he believed best for me. He was so moved that he found it difficult to respond, but his appreciation was evident, and my mother told me later that he had been deeply touched. It was a fortunate thing for us both that he lived to be so old.

Not long after this, though by no means as an outcome of our conversation, my father and mother decided jointly to establish trust funds for their children, which, in my case at least, since I was without dependents, would assure that I need never again be subject to material worry. This was exceedingly generous of them, as it reduced their capital by a great deal, though they kept enough for themselves to live on without the least change of their circumstances. Grateful though I was, and always will be, I couldn't help thinking that all the fuss about money in my earlier years had been based on principle alone, and that the principle had turned out, however understandable, to be unwarranted.

Alberto Giacometti had died of congestive heart failure, aged sixty-four, on January 11, 1966. I was in New York at the time, uninvited to the funeral, and felt that no good could be accomplished by traveling to a remote Swiss village in the dead of winter. But I was overwhelmed with sadness at the loss of the one person encountered in my entire lifetime for whom I could feel unequivocal admiration. Of his greatness as an artist I never felt the slightest uncertainty, but, coming to know him little by little, I reached the conviction that it was as a human being that he achieved his highest and most praiseworthy distinction. Without him the world became for me an inexpressibly poorer place. I was asked to write a memorial article about him for the French review *L'Oeil* and did so. But it never occurred to me that I might undertake to write anything of greater length about this artist and man who had already contributed so richly to my life.

Three and a half years after his death, however, at a time when I had just completed yet another long novel and felt somewhat at loose ends, weary of Connecticut solitude and aware that because of it I was drinking too much, I was approached by an editor in New York who asked whether I would consider writing a biography of Giacometti. He knew nothing whatever about the artist but had seen his photograph and felt that a man with such a face must have had an extraordinary life. Never having written a biography, I had no idea what degree of commitment such an undertaking might entail. Therefore I impulsively said I'd do it. An added inducement was the knowledge that the work would take me back to Paris, for I had had enough of the United States, the turbulent sixties and our demented involvement in Vietnam. Had I had any inkling of the dimensions of the task before me, however, I might have abandoned it before beginning, as I was entirely unprepared for the challenge. But the writing of all those long novels had taught me, at least, to persevere. So I flew to Paris on January 6, 1970, and began the work that was to occupy me exclusively for the next fifteen years.

Research required me to travel around Europe to places where Alberto had lived and where I could meet people still living then who had known him and/or played important parts in his life and career. I even traveled as far afield as Los Angeles, California, and a voluminous journal of interviews accumulated.

In early January 1972, I was in Paris, living in the same apartment my parents had bought for me fifteen years before. The morning of January 5 brought the following letter from my father.

> *31 December 1971*
> *Ben just called with some very bad news. Peter is dead. A close friend of theirs, a Mrs. Flink, called Ben late last night and he is on his way down to be with Peggy as fast as he can get there. It was a suicide. What I have been afraid of for years. We will be calling Peggy as soon as we can pull ourselves together.*
> *We'll write again as we get more information. Maybe we will go down.*
> *Don't think of coming back.*

So my unhappy younger brother had made the flight from reality final. I was horrified and shocked. At the same time I appreciated the deep kindness and thoughtful consideration of my father in having written rather than telephoned to give me the terrible news, for he knew that by the time his letter reached me all the formalities of burial would be finished and that my presence would be of no help to anyone and cause me even greater distress. As soon as the time difference allowed, I telephoned home, spoke to both my mother and my father and, to my great relief, felt that they sounded relatively composed. I also called my brother Ben. He told me what had happened. In the early evening of December 30, while Peter and Peggy were having dinner with their two young daughters, Peter excused himself from the table, saying that he had something to do upstairs. He went to the attic, where he kept the pistols and rifle of which he had always been fond since his days in the National Guard, and there he shot himself in the head. He left no note. I immediately wrote a long letter to my parents, which I quote in part:

> *It was very good to talk to you a few hours ago, and to hear from your voices that you are, after all, more or less all right. As well as can possibly be expected, anyway. I was glad to talk to Ben also. This has been a very deep and terrible shock to us all. But to the two of you, of course, more than to Ben or to me. To Peggy, perhaps, even more than to you. And the two little girls! Alas, there is little one can say. Nothing can alter the stark and awful fact.*
>
> *I am especially consoled at this moment to realize how intelligent and reasonable you both are, how stable and secure in your view of life and grasp of reality. Still, I can't help fearing that you may feel that long ago you might have done something that would have averted this tragic outcome. When a person resorts to an act so desperate and final, then those who are left behind sometimes imagine that if only they had done this thing, or not done that one, if only they had behaved in any of a thousand different ways rather than as they did, then everything might have turned out differently. It is not so. I'm sure you are both too sensible to have such thoughts. But even I have had them, and that is why I men-*

tion it. None of us can be more than we fallibly strive to be at our best, or what we fallibly conceive to be our best.

It is a sad, sad, sad, sad thing that Peter was so unhappy that he could find no other means of coming to terms with experience and with himself. We will never know why, and it doesn't matter now. What does matter—and matters very much—is for the people who loved him to know that they did for him all they could. I believe that they did. Peggy I never knew well, but it was evident that she cared sincerely and deeply for Peter, which must not always have been easy, for he was a strange, difficult being. As for the two of you, I have tried upon occasion to let you know how strongly I feel that you have both in your separate ways been admirable, remarkable parents. I hope that in this very difficult time you will both be mindful of the fact that your children realized and appreciated how truly and deeply you always had their well-being at heart. Ben feels as I do, I know, because within the past year we have spoken of it. As for Peter, I cannot believe that he failed to feel so, for his behavior when with you seemed to me to say so. I noticed this when we were together only last November. But he could not say so explicitly, alas, since it had become impossible for him to come out of himself sufficiently to express his feelings.

So what I want to say to you above all is that as far as your lives are concerned this event must be looked upon as a terrible accident. The psychic determinism which governs all our lives is inextricably complex, and in most instances even foreknowledge would rarely be able to alter circumstances which in times of stress and bereavement one may tend to feel might have been otherwise if only one had had some inkling of what was to come.

My first impulse was to come straight home to be with you. But I realize that in your wisdom you have known what was best for us all. My presence would be only a reminder of what had gone so dreadfully amiss. However, I will be happy to come at any time if you wish it. And in any case I plan to come in April. I shall be thinking of you constantly during

*the coming days. Inadequate as it sadly is, this letter brings
you all my love.*

My father replied:

> *I wish I could write as good a letter in acknowledging
> receipt of yours as you did in sending it. You were so under-
> standing that it was very comforting to have it. I had a rou-
> tine visit with Dr. Atchley on Thursday and he expressed the
> same thought you did, that one is foolish to think that one
> might have taken some action which might have prevented
> this dreadful disaster.*
>
> *I have feared some such thing as this as long ago as ten
> years when Peter had that breakdown and was in the hospi-
> tal so long. At that time I suggested to the psychiatrist who
> was treating Peter that I might take away the pistols and ri-
> fle that he kept at home. But he said it would not do any
> good, because if a person has that urge he will accomplish
> the act somehow.*

My mother wrote a fortnight after the event:

> *Please don't think because I have not written that you
> have not been in my thoughts. It has been so helpful to have
> your understanding letters, your telephone calls and just to
> know that you are thinking of us. Of course you were right in
> surmising that we wondered whether we could have done
> anything, in the distant past or more recently, to help Peter.
> It does no good to agonize over mistakes but hard not to.
> There was our great failure in lack of understanding. But,
> alas, nothing can be done about that now, and morbid
> brooding over it does not help.*

When I went home in April, I was surprised to find both my mother
and my father quite composed. I had no sense that they had suffered
a traumatic bereavement, though we naturally spoke of Peter with
sadness and they told me all the details of his funeral. My father was
then close to ninety, my mother to eighty, and I thought that perhaps

for people of their advanced age death, however tragic, may be easier to accept than when one is young. It was very different, I know, when Teddy was killed. I noticed that my father tired more easily than had formerly been the case. Sometimes after lunch he would drop off to sleep while reading *The Wall Street Journal*. But I also noticed that between them now existed a serenity, a sense of completion and fulfillment, peace, trust and devotion that I found deeply moving. In the room where they sat, each to one side of the fireplace, usually reading, there seemed to emanate from them a sort of ineffable radiance. I have never known anything to compare with it. It was, I suppose, what love brings out at its best in the human condition after fifty years of marriage, and seeing them together as they were then, I thought, was like witnessing a miracle.

I returned to Paris and to my researches for the Giacometti biography. I had been at it now for more than two years and had as yet written not a word of text. My mother and I continued to correspond regularly, her letters for the most part bringing news of family doings, her gardens, parties with friends, my father's health and her political views. Of Nixon she wrote, "We haven't had a president in my memory whom I've disliked and distrusted so much." This before Watergate showed him for what he was and precipitated his downfall. I wrote about my doings and my work. Concerning the latter she commented, "I have re-read your letter but shall not presume to comment on your explanation of your effort 'to explore aspects of the creative personality,' because obviously there is nothing I have to say. You are a creative personality (and one of whom I am inordinately fond) but how or why you got that way I have no idea."

During the late winter of 1973 my mother wrote more and more often that my father grew tired very quickly and had become depressed about his condition. On March 13 she wrote:

> *Dad just doesn't seem to improve. His back is bothering*
> *him again. It was very painful over the weekend. Today it is*
> *a little better but not right by any means. And he has no*
> *strength. This morning he had his breakfast in bed, then got*
> *up and read the paper. But even that tired him so that he is*
> *now (at twelve) resting on the chaise in his office. It is evident*
> *that he is discouraged and doesn't think that he is going to*

get well. He said, "You know old people die." It is sad and disheartening for me. I remember a talk we had last fall when you said that Dad would feel badly, more than most people, if he were sick and unable to keep going, and that is what is happening.

We are going to the bank in a few minutes to put the safe-deposit box, which is now held jointly, in my name. He wants to get everything in order.

Sorry if this letter distresses you, but maybe it is best for you to know the situation.

Hardly had I received this letter than I had a telephone call from my brother, telling me that our father had suffered a stroke on March 18, was in the hospital and not expected to recover. His desire to "get everything in order" had been uncannily and sadly prescient. I flew home the next day, the twentieth. Ben met me at the airport and we drove straight to the hospital. My father was conscious but delirious and did not recognize us. The doctors said that his condition was "stable" but that recovery was out of the question. It was only a matter of time, how long unpredictable. My brother and I asked that "the minimum" be done to prolong things, to which the doctors did not reply in words but signified that this wish would be respected. My mother was obviously and deeply distressed. It would have been very unlike her, however, to add to the distress of her two sons by openly displaying her own feelings.

It was necessary that there should be someone in the hospital room with my father at all times, and it proved that there were simply not enough nurses available to entirely fulfill this requirement, so it was up to the patient's family to keep watch by the dying man's bedside when necessary. As Ben was obliged to return to his responsibilities in Connecticut, this occasional vigil was kept by my mother and me. It was often at night, and the hours were long. Light in the room was kept low, so we could not read, and in any case I don't think it would have been possible to detach one's attention from the wasted figure outstretched in the hospital bed. Much of the time my father was delirious, and in this state often spoke aloud in a rambling discourse, of which a recurrent theme was for some inexplicable reason fishing. "Oh, that great fish," he would murmur. "What a beautiful fish! Oh, the fish, the fish." My mother and I were surprised, because my father had never had the slightest interest in fishing. Even the nurses were surprised. They said that often delirious patients in my father's condition uttered gross obscenities, but he never did, and thus he impressed them as a true gentleman. Now and then there were brief, unexpected moments of lucidity. His eyes would focus and he would say, "Oh, Jim, it's you. What are you doing here?" And I would say, "I've just come for a little visit." At one such moment, however, he stretched out his hand toward me. I took it, and felt his warm feeble grip. "Oh, Jim," he murmured, "I always tried to do my best for you." I said, with difficulty, "Yes, Dad, I know you did." What may have been said between my dying father and my mother, when they were alone together, I do not know.

On Monday, March 26, my father was to be moved from the room where he had been since entering the hospital to a larger, more spacious one. My mother and I were both present. The bed on rubber wheels and accompanying paraphernalia were moved along the hospital corridor by orderlies and placed in the new room beside a window. The orderlies withdrew. My father seemed to be resting calmly, his eyes closed and his breathing regular. But suddenly he gasped, thrust his head up abruptly to the left, his mouth agape, and emitted three or four hoarse gasps, then was silent. I understood immediately that this was the end. My mother cried out, "He's stopped breathing." With my left hand I drew up the sheet to cover his face, while with my right I clasped my mother close to me. Neither of us spoke. A nurse came into the room but I waved her away. Both my mother and I were weeping. Very soon a doctor appeared and led us to his office, where we managed to compose ourselves. It was five-fifteen in the afternoon. After a few formalities we left the hospital. The day was damp and gray. When we reached home, we sat in the library by the telephone, my mother asking me to make the few necessary calls, as she felt unable to. Nor was it easy for me to call my brother, my uncle and one or two of my parents' closest friends. But by dinnertime my mother had regained complete control of herself. I never again saw her weep.

My father had specified that he wished to be cremated and wanted no religious service. He had already several years before, in keeping with his desire to "get everything in order," bought a plot in the cemetery at Saybrook, Connecticut, where he had grown up, and had had a granite headstone installed with his own and my mother's names engraved on it, with the dates of birth, only the dates of death left uninscribed. And there his ashes in a bronze urn were interred in the morning of the Friday following his death. Mother and I returned to Englewood that same afternoon and the next day, ironically, we went to the opera to see *Romeo and Juliet* by Gounod, not by any means a masterpiece.

I stayed on in Englewood to keep my mother company and help her in any way I could for four weeks after my father's death. There were many details to be attended to, not the least of which was the removal of his clothes and many personal effects from his closets and bureau drawers, a task I managed to perform while my mother was out of the house and which I felt sure would be extremely painful for her to have undertaken alone. She thanked me but did not dwell on it. After four weeks it seemed to me that she would be able to manage by herself, a necessity which we both recognized as inevitable. The day before I left we again went to the opera, this time to see *Lucia di Lammermoor.* My parents as they grew older had become very keen on going to the opera, had for many years a subscription, excellent seats, and seldom missed a performance. The next morning the car to take me to the airport was in the drive at the appointed time; I stowed my luggage inside and returned to the house to say goodbye. We were calm, embraced and hugged each other tenderly; then I returned to the car. As it drove away I looked in the rearview mirror and saw my mother rush outside into the forecourt of the house, waving her arms, as if to bid us to stop or to signal some frantic last-minute admonition. But I said nothing, and the driver drove on. I have never been able to forget that brief vision of my distraught mother. When I reached the airport I called her to say yet again goodbye, and she seemed then quite calm. So I returned to Europe to my work and our correspondence resumed.

A week after my departure she wrote:

> *In reply to your question, yes, I am all right. Of course*
> *there are times when I am lonely and depressed, but every-*
> *thing considered I am making out fairly well. It was so won-*
> *derful to have you with me during all that hard time. I*

wouldn't have thought that I could love you more than I already did, but now I do.

And a few days later:

> *You asked me how I am getting on. Pretty well, I think. Of course I miss Dad very, very much, and you too, but I keep fairly busy, and I have never had a morbid dread of being alone, as some people seem to have. I think it has been good for me to have all this Watergate scandal to follow, one very slight benefit in a disastrous affair.*

That summer I went to Greece to the island of Lesbos, where I spent many summers in an idyllic house set among olive groves and towering pines. It was a place of almost primitive simplicity, provided with neither electricity nor, at first, running water, but I have loved very few spots as much as that one and found its total tranquillity very conducive to hard work. My mother never saw it, alas, never even saw Greece. In mid-July, to my surprise, she inquired in a roundabout way whether I did not regret remaining unmarried. She was thinking of my old age, hoping I would not have to spend it in melancholy solitude. I answered, and she responded:

> *Two good long letters have come from you since I last wrote. You are very thoughtful about writing and I am always happy when I see a blue envelope with your familiar handwriting in my mailbox.*
>
> *The first one was written late at night in your little study "in the valley of Eftalou." How poetic that sounds! Wasn't there a Vale of Avalon in Tennyson's King Arthur poems? That was the letter in which you sought to answer my question about marriage, and whether you regret not having a wife and children, and you said that you do not. I am happy to think that you find your life satisfying. Both you and Ben, in very different ways, have developed human relationships which give happiness to your lives—he in his family and you with friends, and with me, I think. No, I don't just think. I am sure.*

A Maternal Ordeal

Before my father's death my visits home had been irregular, due principally to the varying dictates of my work. When my mother found herself alone, however, I decided to return to Englewood twice a year, spending three to four weeks at each visit. I still had friends in New York, to be sure, and enjoyed seeing them, and also saw something of the few friends of my mother then still living, particularly Dana and Mary Atchley. Mother and I also spent much time together, in the evenings watching the television news reports and chatting about world events. We went to the opera and an occasional movie, enjoyed the simple pleasure of each other's company and took strolls around the streets, which had—miraculously—not changed at all since my childhood. At the end of my first visit home after Dad's death, en route by air back to Paris, I wrote the following letter to my mother:

> As you are fully aware by now, I am always glad to be
> able to write letters between departure and arrival, taking
> advantage of the temporary void, with its singular invitation
> to detachment, in order to see and say things more clearly,
> however illusory such a sense of clarity may be. And I hope
> that you are also fully aware—after some forty years of
> initiation!—that there is no one to whom I would rather
> write than to you. That preference has certainly become
> clearer in the last half year, not merely for the obvious reason
> but also because I have myself found a deeper satisfaction in
> my sense of being able to do something that has a more sig-
> nificant raison d'être than before. And so, you see, you are
> always able to offer me more and more in life, to nourish
> and enrich it as you have so beautifully done from the very
> beginning.
>
> I was very happy that you enjoyed our day together yes-
> terday, all of it: from the drive to town, the Matisse exhibi-
> tion, lunch at the Stanhope, the Akhenaten exhibition, tea
> with David Morton and all the rest. For I felt that you en-
> joyed enjoying what I so very much enjoy, and that seems
> wonderfully promising as to happiness for both of us in the
> future. I know that my happiness has always been most im-
> portant to you, but now I want you to learn how important
> is yours to me. I want to show you in my own way (which, of

*course, is the only way I can show it) how glad I am that
you feel at ease with my friends and like them, and I assure
you that you will feel so more and more as you come to
know more of them more and more. And let me add that if,
as you so gently say, you feel that I am "good" to you, I am
in fact only being good to myself.*

*I was happy at my stay with you, and all the more so in
that I am aware of your understanding that I cannot stay indefinitely but that whenever you need me I will be, as it
were, immediately forthcoming. So . . . thanks for everything,
and most especially for being so beautifully and simply
yourself!*

My small apartment in the rue de Lille had begun to seem smaller
and smaller as books and papers concerning Giacometti accumulated.
Consequently I made up my mind to find larger quarters but was
determined to remain in the same neighborhood where I had spent
almost all of my Parisian life. Luck was, and still is, the determinant
factor in finding a desirable Paris apartment, and luck came my way
after considerable searching when I found a spacious, semi-abandoned
top floor in the rue des Beaux-Arts, with a separate but almost adjacent,
smaller apartment on the floor below. I realized immediately that the
top floor could be transformed, with a great deal of work, into a delightful living space, and that the apartment below would be ideally
suited to lodge my mother when, as she promised to, she came to visit
me in Paris. And I also thought that if I should ever find a companion
with whom I wished to share the rest of my life, the smaller apartment
could also house him. Only a small landing separated the two. And
that, indeed, for my happiness is how things have worked out. Still, I
have retained the rue de Lille as a place where I can work undisturbed
and store my large accumulation of papers.

My mother arrived for her visit on the sixteenth of September
1975. It was just two days later that Henry Moore came to lunch and,
not at all to my surprise, but contrary to her onetime protestations,
Mother and the world-famous sculptor got along beautifully. They were
of almost the same age and took particular pleasure in talking about
their early years, so very different, and yet it seemed that they had a
great deal in common. What this was, of course, was the exceptional

sweetness and gentle sensitivity of their natures. I introduced my mother to a quantity of my other friends, and she was invited to tea and dinner parties, some of which she would once have considered a bit rowdy, but she had a good time nonetheless and everyone liked her. She stayed exactly one month.

Our correspondence resumed. Mother was self-conscious about her letters, fearful that they were dull. I replied:

> *You must not be self-conscious about the quality of your letters. To me they would be interesting by definition, because you are in them. But they are also interesting because so vivid in detail about what you are doing, thinking, reading, the people you see and the events that concern you.*

Her reading included such diversities as Proust, of whom as a person she disapproved, Saint-Simon, Disraeli and Gladstone. She also read Nigel Nicolson's *Portrait of a Marriage*, the story of Harold Nicolson's marriage to Vita Sackville-West, though both of them were homosexual. She commented:

> *The book was interesting and he wrote well, but I wonder about his writing such intimate details about his parents. Maybe that is my Victorianism. Would you do the same under similar circumstances? Of course the circumstances are not similar, so maybe you cannot judge what you might do. Too bad that you didn't have such interesting and talented parents. But, as you once said, if we had not been ourselves you would not be you, and I wouldn't want to change that.*

One night I dreamt of my father, and wrote to my mother to describe it:

> *I had such a strange dream the other night. It was about Dad. He had just published a book entitled* A Sea Boy, and Other Stories of the Sea. *There was a long and very enthusiastic review of it in* The New Yorker, *which I read with great satisfaction, especially pleased because in passing I was mentioned as Albert Lord's son and also a writer. I woke up*

*at that point and lay there in the darkness, feeling very
pleased, content and reassured. Do you have nice dreams
about Dad sometimes? I feel a stab of melancholy as I write
that, because I hate the idea of your being sad.*

She replied:

*I was touched by your dream of Dad and his writing of
the book of sea stories. Of course sea stories are exactly what
he would have liked to write. I wonder whether it ever occurred to him to try. He certainly never spoke of it. You asked
whether I ever dream of him. Of course I do, and sometimes
wake up remembering them, but usually my dreams evapo-
rate before I am fully awake and I cannot bring them back.
But you do not need to worry about my being sad. I have
had, on the whole, a very happy life, with so many pleasant
things to remember, that I rarely feel despondent, and certainly never sorry for myself.*

In September of 1976 Mother again came to Paris for a visit. It
was a pleasant one in every respect. Again she met a lot of my friends,
including a young man named Gilles Roy, then aged only twenty-
eight, with whom I had established an intimate relationship almost a
year before, a relationship which has lasted with deep satisfaction on
both sides to this day. Mother occasionally inquired about him in her
letters, anxious that I should not ultimately find myself disappointed.
I never have been, and after her death I adopted Gilles. I also introduced
her to Diego Giacometti, a man whose sweetness of nature was quite
equal to her own, and they spent a convivial hour together, Diego
happy to show his studio and its populace of bronze birds, frogs, ele-
phants, horses and owls. And I took her to lunch with Henri Cartier-
Bresson, the world-famous photographer, by whom, of course, she was
not at all intimidated, and who afterward often remarked on the sweetness of her expression. One evening we went to the Opéra Comique
to attend a performance of Offenbach's *La Vie Parisienne*. It was mediocre but made memorable for me by an incident which occurred
during the intermission. As we were strolling in the foyer suddenly my
mother gasped and rushed from my side a few paces through the crowd.

Then she returned and I asked what had come over her. She replied, "I thought I saw Dad."

She surely missed him more than it was possible—or desirable, perhaps—to say. In one of her letters she had spoken of talking with a childhood friend about the "good old days," then added, "As a matter of fact, they weren't all that good for me." I asked her to explain.

> *In reply to your letter asking me why the "good old days" weren't so very good for me: Of course my childhood was a very happy one, but like yours my adolescence was somewhat difficult, entirely due to my own foolishness. No one could have had more considerate parents, but I went through a period thinking that no one liked me, that I was a complete failure socially, and my mother did care about such things, which made me feel worse. But after Dad appeared on the scene things brightened up, and when I married and moved away from Indianapolis I suddenly found to my surprise [aged twenty-five] that I wasn't really a "sad bird," as my cousin Lucy Holliday once said I was. So out of a long life of almost eighty years there were very few periods of gloom.*

That visit in 1976 was my mother's last to Paris. At eighty-one she found it too tiring and preferred to have me come to her, which I was perfectly happy to do.

In May of 1977 there was a large Henry Moore retrospective exhibition at the Orangerie. I attended the opening, which was crowded with ministers of state, ambassadors, members of the beau monde and intelligentsia. The artist and his wife were besieged by well-wishers. Not liking to intrude and yet anxious to say a complimentary word about the exhibition, which was more beautiful than I had expected, especially the very large pieces on the terrace overlooking the Seine, I edged into the crowd and when Moore glanced in my direction, I said simply, "Splendid, Henry, really splendid." He responded with natural but modest pleasure and then, as I turned away in the midst of the crowd, he took my arm and said, "James, how is your mother?" I replied that she was fine, and Henry said, "Oh, that's good, that's good. Such a lovely lady." When I told her about his query under such pressing circumstances, she replied, "How very nice of Henry Moore to inquire about me! If you ever see him again please tell him that I remember with great pleasure meeting him at your little party." I did see him again, and for the last time, in December of that same year, and one of the first things he said to me was "How's your mother? She's such a sweet person."

By this time my mother had been living in Englewood for some fifty-six years. The town, if not her neighborhood, had changed greatly, she had changed and what had changed most of all was that the majority of her friends were either dead, dying or wished they were dead. Even Dr. Dana Atchley, who, along with his quarrelsome wife, Mary, was her closest remaining friend, had fallen ill with Parkinson's disease. He had been one of the most eminent physicians of his era, whose patients had included the famous and powerful—Greta Garbo, Elizabeth Taylor, Katharine Hepburn, the Aga Khan, Dean Acheson, Charles Lindbergh, et al.—and it was truly pitiful to see him reduced to feeble inactivity. Mother often spent long afternoons reading to him, and one winter gave up her annual trip to Florida to remain and keep him company. But the time came when it was, alas, obvious that she would have no friends left in Englewood. Her summer house at Mason's Island, however, was perfectly habitable in winter, and she was acquainted there with a considerable number of congenial people younger than herself. And my brother, though he would later spend five years on business in Europe, was nearby. So she decided to leave Englewood. "I want to make the move while I still can," she said, aged eighty-three. A year or two later would have been too late.

Meanwhile, as the years struggled along, my work on Giacometti's biography continued very, very, very slowly. My ideals of biographical excellence had been formed by Leon Edel's superb five-volume biography of Henry James and Richard Ellmann's masterful *James Joyce*. Study of these works had led me to realize that I must undertake a taxing and abstruse course of study in aesthetics and theoretical psychology in order to try to understand both the art and the life of my hero. This took much time, and I have always, in any case, written with difficulty. The publishers with whom I had initially made contracts grew impatient and, in fact, wondered whether I was actually doing anything at all. I told them that I sympathized with their impatience, that they were not obliged to wait, that I was the only one whose patience was at stake and that the contracts might be terminated at their convenience. They jumped at the offer, and consequently for several years I had no publisher whatever for the manuscript which so gradually grew longer and longer. Even my mother sometimes allowed herself to wonder whether a finished work would ever result from my seemingly interminable labors. I assured her that it would, adding, "I can say this, really, *only* to you: the book will be finished eventually, and it will turn out to have been worth waiting for, because Alberto will make it so infinitely more than I can. However long the wait, *he* will convince the world that it was not a minute too long. He was a great man and is entitled to a great effort." My mother said that she only hoped she would live long enough to hold the finished volume in her hands, and remarked that it was annoying, when her friends asked what I was writing about, to find that almost none of them had ever heard of Giacometti. I replied that my earnest hope was that my work might help to remedy such cultural privation.

Having moved from Englewood to Mason's Island in the spring of 1977, my mother enjoyed settling into her new "home," having rooms repainted, new curtains made, and installing the furniture sent on from New Jersey, much of which she had known since her childhood. The garden was larger and more attractive and the view out across Long Island Sound, with a lighthouse blinking at night, splendid. And here there were plenty of friends with whom to play bridge, have occasional cocktail parties and enjoy sociable, if not intellectual, relations. She went down to New York for the opera, traveled South in the winter, invited old friends to visit her and made a pleasant, if sometimes lonely, life for herself. Her mother had suffered no ill health until the very end, and the daughter obviously hoped that it would be likewise for her.

Sometime early in 1978 she was stricken with a malady called polymyalgia rheumatica. I never quite understood what caused it, nor, I think, did the doctors, but the symptoms were similar to rheumatism and arthritis, and very painful. There was no known cure, but as a rule remission came of itself after approximately a year. Meanwhile, in order to relieve the pain, a strong drug called prednisone was prescribed. On July 6, my mother wrote:

My polymyalgia rheumatica is fairly stationary. I get
along very comfortably when I take one pill a day, but with
less than that I am creaky. Dr. Boas says that it usually takes
about a year to recover. So I look forward to next April when
I shall feel like dancing a jig.

Alas, she never did dance a jig, she who had been such a graceful and light-footed dancer in her youth. She never danced again at all. From this time onward most of her letters, though they continued to send the usual news of family, gardening, some social activity and, of course, the weather, also brought brief reports of her health, which gradually deteriorated. Before going to Florida in January of 1979 she somehow hurt her back but thought time would bring improvement. When it didn't, she consulted a doctor in Sarasota, who determined that she was suffering from osteoporosis, which meant that her vertebrae had become porous due to lack of calcium and also as a side effect of the powerful painkilling drugs she was taking. She was compelled to wear an uncomfortable brace to support her spine and take less of the drug, but the polymyalgia rheumatica had, as predicted, improved. The back, however, continued to be painful, and arthritis set in across her shoulders. One consequence of these troubles was that she had shrunk four inches in height, measuring only four feet ten inches. "Quite a midget!" she remarked. I went home for the month of March and found that, although her brace considerably restricted what Mother could do—no gardening, for instance—she was nevertheless able to get around tolerably well, lead in appearance a relatively normal existence, drive her car, visit friends and even invite them for the occasional drink or round of bridge. She was constantly in discomfort, however, but that was mentioned, if at all, as a fact of no more moment than a passing cloud. Above all, she remained indomitably cheerful. I returned in August, again in December, and it seemed to me that Mother was unchanged. I was present for her eighty-fifth birthday, a happy event celebrated at my brother's house with many family members present. She was jolly, drank champagne, blew out the candles on the cake and there seemed no reason not to assume that she might continue, as her mother had, to live on as she was for another good decade, at least. It was not to be.

On the second of May, alone in her house, Mother slipped and fell to the floor in her kitchen. To her surprise and distress she found that she was unable to stand up again, however she struggled with the aid of chairs and the pulling out of drawers. Dragging herself into the nearby library, she managed to telephone to a neighbor, who came at once and helped her to her feet. Luckily the fall had not injured her. But it destroyed her sense of self-reliance and convinced her that she could no longer continue to live in her house alone. My brother and I had already endeavored to persuade her to engage someone to come and live with her, a servant or servant-companion. There was plenty of room, and in Englewood she had never been without a servant living in the house. Now, however, she stubbornly refused to consider such an arrangement. When asked why, she said, "I'd have to *talk* to the person."

In the town of Mystic, not two miles from her house, there was a nursing home called the Mary Elizabeth. A number of her friends had had to go there. Having often visited them, she knew the place well and sometimes, driving by it, she had remarked, "I hope I don't end up in there." But now she decided that was what she would do. Unfortunately this nursing home was provided with only a limited number of single rooms, the rest being occupied by two patients, and the only bed available at the time when my mother went to live there was in a double room. In order to have a room by herself she would have to wait until one became available, meaning that someone would have to die. As soon as I learned that Mother had gone to the nursing home I telephoned her. She sounded perfectly calm, but every few minutes I could hear in the background a commotion that sounded like a woman's moaning or screaming. Mother explained that the woman in the other bed, separated from her own only by a curtain, was demented and regularly emitted these groans or screams, sometimes piercing. But there was nothing to be done about it, and she would simply have to be patient until a single room was allotted to her. I asked why she didn't go back to her house until such a room could be had, but she told me that she would lose her priority if she left the nursing home. She was determined to wait it out, and meanwhile was able to leave the room and walk about, even return to her house if someone was kind enough to take her there. She no longer trusted herself to drive a car. The same day she wrote to me:

*I just talked to you, so there is nothing much to say. But
lest you think that all is bad here because my roommate
started screaming at six a.m., I should tell you that I had a
good day yesterday. I walked to the office and back and sat
out in the sun. It was a beautiful day. Bill Crow* came to see
me. He is so kind. He offered to be of any help he could. Ade-
laide† has been here and will come back this afternoon to
take me to my house to pick up some things I didn't think of
when we came here. It was all in a great hurry.*

    That's all for now. So good of you to call so often.

    LOVE *and more* LOVE.

When I went home in June, I found Mother still in the room with
the screaming lady. I had never before been inside a nursing home.
My first visits brought an exceedingly unpleasant shock, and for quite
a long time thereafter, whenever I went home for a visit, the shock
remained intense and troubling, because in such places one sees sights,
hears sounds, smells odors and is altogether subjected to an aura of
suffering, degradation and imminent demise which is profoundly demoralizing. But I came to feel at last that familiarity with such drastic
human situations was, if not uplifting, certainly an illuminating education, providing vivid knowledge of what ultimately awaits us all.
Mother, however, was for some time still able to go to her house or to
a restaurant for meals if someone went with her. She was even able
to have friends come to her house for games of bridge now and then,
and I feel sure she could have gone back to live there if only she had
been willing to accept the presence of a servant or companion. But no.
She was adamant. She would endure the screams of her roommate
until a single room became available, because there was no knowing
what the future would bring and she didn't want to run the risk of
becoming a burden to herself or to anyone else. In the nursing home
it went without saying that being a burden was virtually one's raison
d'être, accepted by everyone, including the inmates, as Mother called
them. Finally, on the tenth of July, a single room was allotted to her.

---

* A friend and neighbor from Mason's Island.
† Another friend and neighbor from Mason's Island.

She spent the remaining eight years of her life in it. Sometimes she entertained fantasies of going back to her house to live when Ben returned from his work in Europe, for it was understood that the house would then be signed over to him. But I feel quite sure that in her heart she knew that she would never leave the place in which she had hoped that she would not "end up."

From this time onward Mother and I "corresponded" principally by telephone. There were some letters, but not many. We spoke together almost every week at least once, and our conversations, like so many of our letters, were very rarely of much moment or interest. We talked about what we were doing or reading, people we saw, world events, the weather, etc., etc. Every now and then, my mother would say, "Do you want to hear something beautiful?" I'd say yes, then she would quote a long passage from Shakespeare or Milton, poetry she had memorized seventy years before at Sweet Briar or lines she had learned lately, especially the Shakespeare, whose complete works she kept in her room, because she wanted, as she said, "to prevent complete disintegration of the memory machine." There was no danger of that. We often spoke of the past, especially of the summers in Maine, all the things a child and his parents invent and share: the magic rock, the castle rock, the cave, the brook with its big pool and little pool, the blueberries on Ryerson Hill, the rolls at the hotel at Poland Spring, climbing Streaked Mountain and the house on wheels. Ben and I loved to clamber into my mother's big bed before she arose in the morning, when my father was absent, and make up stories of the adventures we might have if we lived in a house on wheels that could travel anywhere around the world. Mother always said that I came up with the most imaginative and fantastic stories. We owned an ancient Nash touring car and went for long, adventurous drives along overgrown roads to visit old ladies who made hooked rugs or grew the most extraordinary dahlias. To be sure, we often talked of the same things when I went back to America to see her.

The condition of her vertebrae had deteriorated now to such an extent that she was obliged to sit in a wheelchair when not reclining, as she could hardly stand on her feet unassisted. And it was only when reclining that she felt approximately comfortable, even then *only* approximately. But there was never a murmur of complaint. There never had been a murmur of complaint, and even later, when she broke first her hip, then her elbow as a result of falls in the night, even then never, never was there a murmur of complaint. I once asked her how she could have endured, and continued to endure, her pains and handicaps and confinement without ever complaining or showing any sign of impatience or vexation. She said, "It would do me no good, would it? And it would only make the situation more trying for others."

To transport her from the nursing home to her house or anywhere else after she was confined to the wheelchair became something of a task, for she had to be lifted into the car, her wheelchair folded up and stowed in the trunk, then the operation reversed upon arrival. But both Ben and I happily trundled her about whenever she wished, as her pleasure in getting out of the M.E., as we came to call it, and going to her house or to a restaurant was more than enough reward for so comparatively slight an effort. On one occasion, at least, the effort was somewhat greater, but so was the reward of pleasure. Mother wanted to go to the opera one last time and had tickets for *La Traviata*, one of her favorites, on March 28, 1981, during my biannual visit. We drove to New York, where we were able to stay in the apartment of some friends who were away. Getting Mother into the opera house and settled in her seat, then depositing the wheelchair in the cloak-room, was not simple. The opera, of course, was superb, both Mother and I particularly enjoying the elder Germont's great aria in the second act. The next day we went to Englewood and paid a visit to the Atchleys, both of them in desperate condition but pitifully delighted to see their old friend, perhaps the only one still remaining alive. When we left, Mother said, "I'll never see them again and all three of us know it." She would never see Englewood again either, and she probably knew that, too.

Time passed, and Mother was nearing ninety. Now and then she would say, "Sometimes I wish that I'd go to sleep at night and never wake up." At others she would say, "It would rather amuse me to live to be a hundred." Her body was decrepit, but her mind was acute and clear, more so, perhaps, than ever. She had no fear of dying save that she hoped the process would be rapid and not too uncomfortable. As to the hereafter, she had no belief in it whatever and, like my father, wished to be cremated and have her ashes interred without any religious observance. But she didn't want to die quite yet, because, as she repeatedly told me, she wanted to see my book finished. I assured her that it was beginning to approach its end. She wouldn't have to wait much longer. Meanwhile, I had had the great good fortune to find a publisher who contracted to bring out the biography without having read one word of it, a gentleman of rare good faith and—need I add?—good taste named Roger Straus, who became a close friend, and whose own mother and mine had known each other long, long before at Rosemary Hall. A Dickensian coincidence.

And as Mother grew older it seems that we grew closer. In the summer of 1983, when I could foresee that publication of The Book must be no more than a couple of years away, I wrote to her as follows:

It makes me very happy to know that you know how much I care for you. Often when I'm alone I talk to you— aloud. I say, "Hello, Mama," and then go on to relate— though no longer aloud, perhaps—some incident or thought, because I derive so much greater satisfaction from anything that concerns me when I feel that you are associated with it. Maybe this comes in part from our long habit of talking on the telephone. Needless to say, however, you have always been associated with everything that matters to me, and this from the very beginning, and I have always known in my heart that I could count absolutely on your loving and un- derstanding response to that sense of association. This, to be sure, is vital to any son's belief in himself, his identity and security, thus one of the greatest gifts a mother can bestow. There are others, and it seems to me that you have given me all of them, which provides me with still further cause to dwell gratefully on my good fortune. I do that, you know. And one of the peculiar aspects of it is my strong feeling that the great adventure of life still lies entirely before me. But not at all Beast in the Jungle–*like. I am sixty years old, and yet I feel that my grand fulfillment is still to come. Nor do I doubt that it* will *come. That kind of certainty is rare and precious, another maternal gift: the son's confidence in eventual achievement stemming from his absolute faith in his mother's devotion.*

Then my mother was ninety years old, and her birthday was celebrated by my brother and his family with champagne, orchids and
balloons. Three weeks later I was able to send her a mock-up of the
Giacometti book jacket, the title page and a descriptive text from the
Farrar, Straus & Giroux catalogue announcing publication. That was
my gift, and a significant slip caused me to address the envelope to
Mrs. Alberto C. Lord. I wrote:

> *I know that you have never doubted that The Book was
> being done and would finally get done. Maybe you and I
> were at times the only people who believed that, I because I
> had to, and you because you have from the beginning, from,
> indeed, the very beginning, always shown me that you be-
> lieved in me and were prepared to demonstrate the strength
> of your belief by moral and material support. No thanks, of
> course, no appreciative gesture can ever adequately honor
> such support. But I do want you to know that the prospect of
> your pleasure in the final fruition of this extremely protracted
> endeavor has helped greatly to keep me going when occa-
> sionally the going got hard. And so I thought it might please
> you to see a few tidbits of tangible evidence that publication
> day really is going to come. In the autumn. Early September.
> But if you want to read it before, you can, as there will be
> finished copies in July. So, dearest Mama, after fifteen (count
> them!) years of waiting what you and I have been waiting
> for is at last about to transpire.*

She waited until September. I went to Mystic on Friday the twentieth, and put the book in her hands. I had dedicated it to the memory
of Alberto and Diego, but in the acknowledgments, immediately following my thanks to members of the Giacometti family, I wrote:

> *Through the years, I have been sustained by the confidence and
> encouragement of my mother, Louise B. Lord, and happily take this
> opportunity to acknowledge a lifelong debt which no gratitude can ever
> adequately repay.*

The following Sunday on the front page of *The New York Times Book Review* appeared a very favorable review. One no less favorable had already appeared on the front page of *The Washington Post Book World* the previous Sunday. Mother was delighted. After all, as I had promised, she had not waited in vain. She was ninety, I sixty-three, and the wait had indeed been very, very long, but the vindication was perhaps the more profoundly heartening for having been deferred, all in all, for forty years. Because it did seem now that my life in Paris, my obdurate determination to write and my resolve to live up to the challenge of my subject matter had produced a work of distinction and value. My mother said, "I'm only sorry that your father and grandmother aren't here to see this." I was sorry, too, but the satisfaction that mattered most—to both of us—was my mother's.

The reviews continued to be almost all favorable. One critic said that the book "evokes Vasari's sixteenth-century *Lives*," another that it was "easily on a par with Richard Ellmann's superb biography of James Joyce," yet another that "Lord has written the most moving biography of a modern artist I've read." Inevitably there were a few attacks, one by a fanatical feminist who felt I'd been unkind to the artist's wife and called the book "dangerous." Publication in England, Germany and Italy followed, but not in France, where Madame Giacometti succeeded in intimidating all prospective publishers by threats of legal action. No matter. I had done my work, received much praise and in this sense, at least, my mother's almost lifelong ordeal had had a happy ending.

I believe my mother read *Giacometti* three times. She must have come to a feeling of identity with him almost as great as my own. She read and read in those last years—a great deal of Trollope, and talked about Lady Glencora, Phineas, Madame Max, the old Duke and all the rest as if she'd known them. Much history as well, particularly of England. And at night, when she couldn't sleep, there were mysteries by Agatha Christie.

Upon returning to Paris after the publication of *Giacometti*, I expected to resume writing as if nothing had happened. I found that I couldn't. Something *had* happened, and I didn't know what it was. A well-known fact about writers is that they sometimes suffer from what might be called a postnatal crisis. That such a thing could happen to me had seemed unthinkable. I had always been such a steady worker, whether the works were worth working on or not. But now, after the fifteen years of labor on a single book, I found myself baffled. Week after week I sat at my desk. Nothing happened. I wrote a little of this, a little of that, and threw everything away, tried composing formal letters and tired of it. I tired of everything. I spent much time in bed, listening to music and reading trash. My friend Gilles worried, tried to help, but there was nothing he could do. I consulted a doctor, who advised rest and some kind of medicine to fortify my nerves. It seemed grotesque to think that I might have suffered some sort of minor nervous breakdown, but that appeared to be the case. And when the time approached for my biannual visit to my mother, I felt that I couldn't undertake it. I spoke of this on the telephone but in October of 1986 also wrote to her:

> It is with regret that I sit down to write to you, dearest Mama, about my "condition." In the course of our lengthy telephone talks I have had a sense that perhaps—and I weigh the perhaps—you regard this condition, and most especially the accompanying factor of failure to make my usual visit to see you, as some kind of caprice or whim on my part. That would be very distressing to me, quite as distressing, indeed, as must be for you the disappointment that goes along with my absence at your bedside—because it would only add to the distress I feel already. It goes without saying that you are wise enough and experienced enough to know that psychic troubles can be quite as troubling, and difficult to cope with, as physical ones. I am having a difficult time. It is not serious but might become so. That is why the doctor feels that it is important for me to continue a tranquil routine, keep at work writing insofar as possible and avoid anything that might be either physically or psychically unsettling.

She answered:

> I know that I do not have your gift of expressing adequately my thoughts and especially feelings about you and your condition. I wish that I could do so. In spite of our having spent so much of your adult life separated by the vast

ocean deep I nevertheless have always known that we are deeply devoted to each other.

I think I do understand the psychic difficulties you are experiencing. But I know that you have the strength of char-acter to overcome them. As you say, it may take time. But please do not feel that I in any way blame you. I wish from the bottom of my heart that I could do something to help. Maybe just knowing that my love and thoughts are with you may be of some assistance.

I am sorry if I gave you the impression that I thought your difficulties were only a whim. Perhaps I did think so at first before you wrote me. It seems so hard for me to believe that after the great success of your book (of which I am very proud) you should have a hard time adjusting. But now I do understand. After Teddy's death, which was perhaps the greatest sorrow of my life, I found that working was the one thing that helped. Peter's suicide was dreadful too, but in a way I was prepared for it. But I have always had a sense of guilt that I didn't understand him.

I hope you can decipher this scrawl. Writing is not easy for me.

Your ever loving Mother

Her letter brought tears to my eyes, tears of devotion and gratitude for the spiritual support I had for so long received from her. I wrote to tell her so, repeating once more that I had always felt a very special closeness of heart and mind uniting us. And she did help, I said, and help essentially just by being there, by being interested and kind and thoughtful. Yet again I insisted that she must not feel guilt over what had happened to Peter, for if anyone had failed him, it was Peter himself, though of course I did not mean that in any way as an as-signment of blame. Our frequent telephone talks, I said, were my delight, but added that letters possessed a potential for communication not to be gotten from conversation. So I promised to write more often. I did. But she was unable to answer most of those letters.

By April I felt much improved, though still stymied by the blank page. The trip to America no longer intimidated me and I was anxious

to see Mother. Whenever I went to Mason's Island I spent with her all
the time that she was awake. She took a nap in the afternoon, retired
early. Usually she was seated in her wheelchair and sometimes, if the
weather was agreeable, I would wheel her outside and down a back
street as far as the Mystic River. She made a concerted effort to be
groomed and attired as attractively as possible, never wearing the same
dress more than once in a week or ten days and keeping her hair neatly
washed and waved. She kept flowering plants along the window ledge
of her room, and the proper watering of them became one of the ritual
routines that usually occupy persons whose lives become confined to
very limited spaces. I always sat in the selfsame chair, facing her, while
we talked, and outside I could see through the window a gray granite
Union soldier holding his stone musket atop the monument inscribed
with the names of the men from Mystic who had given the last full
measure of devotion.

During that visit we naturally talked about my spell of nervous
malaise, and Mother told me something that astonished me. She said
that toward the end of his life my father had begun to fear that he was
going insane. He had bought several books on schizophrenia and studied them to see whether he had any symptoms of that malady. He did
not, of course. What had worried my mother was not that he—or I,
for that matter—might go insane but, rather, the fear of it as a dis-
ablement. I remember that during my last visit in Englewood before
my father's death he was reading a volume of speeches by Macaulay
and every now and then would read aloud a passage he found particularly effective. That he might have felt himself mentally troubled
seemed to me absolutely unbelievable. I asked Mother whether she
had ever feared for her sanity, and she said, "What I feared was having
so little mind that the loss of it would make no difference." And we
had a good laugh. We laughed a lot together. Like so many people of
great age Mother remembered her childhood with exceptional vivid-
ness. She could quote numerous silly rhymes she had learned as a
child, and entire scenes from *Alice in Wonderland*. We had good times.
At the end of each visit we congratulated each other for our good luck
in enjoying so greatly the days we spent together.

I returned in August, enjoying that visit particularly for the air-
conditioned comfort of my mother's room while the granite soldier
outside seemed to shudder in the heat.

A Maternal Ordeal

On the first of January 1988, more than thirty years after the inauguration of Cézanne's studio in Aix, remembering nonetheless that long-ago occasion, the French government awarded me the Legion of Honor. My mother was delighted by this official distinction, so I sent her a photocopy of the honorary scroll that I received, bearing the facsimile signature of the President of the Republic. When I went home in April I found that she had attached this copy of the scroll to the wall of her room with thumbtacks. I protested that it was embarrassing to see one's self advertised to all who came and went. Moreover, I said, a mother should be more discreet than to boast about the accomplishments of her children, so I would take down the scroll from the wall. Not a bit of it, said Mother. The scroll was to stay right where it was, and a mother had every right to advertise her pride in her children, having been at some pains to bring them into the world and care for them until they grew able to care for themselves, a business, she added with humorous asperity, in some cases nearly lifelong. The scroll remained on the wall. Again she said she was sorry that my father, who had not approved of my spending time on the Cézanne project, could not be present to see that it had brought me honor. I was described on the scroll as a writer and philanthropist.

I returned again in August. Again we had good times chatting about everything and nothing. I was still experiencing great difficulty in resuming my writing, but I didn't tell her that, and the truth is that despite my difficulties I still felt that the great adventure lay in the future.

Shortly before my birthday in November I received a card from Mother, enclosing, of course, a check, and bearing the message: "I shall think of you on November 27 (as I do every day). With all my love, Mother." That was the last written message I received from her.

Among my various friends to whom I had introduced her were Hilton Kramer, the eminent critic of art and literature, and his kindly, gentle wife, Esta. They found Mother likable, as most people did, and visited her several times when they happened to be near Mystic. Esta, a remarkable cook, was especially kind, sending Mother boxes of exquisite cookies which she relished eating as part of her ritual midnight snack, which also included five—not six!—seedless grapes. And it was to Esta that Mother sent what I believe to have been her last letter.

January 1, 1989

Dear Esta,

*I was glad to receive your letter but sorry for the misera-
ble time you had in Spain. I hope they have called off the
strike, because my son Bennett (Jim's older brother) and his
wife are planning to spend the month of March in Spain. Of
course they will inquire about conditions there before they
leave.*

*Next Tuesday, January third, will be my ninety-fourth
birthday. I never expected to live to be so ancient. But despite
my extreme old age I still find my life interesting. My hearing
isn't good, but with a hearing aid I can hear very well. And
fortunately my eyesight is very good. So I am able to read,
and the library here is very kind about sending me books. I
am now reading* The Spoils of Poynton *by Henry James.*

*You said you might be coming here in the not too distant
future. How happy I shall be to see you! I am somewhat intimidated by Hilton who is such a Brain.*

But I am sure he will be patient with your old friend,

Louise

On Wednesday, February 8, I had the usual weekly telephone talk
with Mother. She was cheerful and we chatted about one thing and
another for some time, but she sounded a little weary and complained
of having caught cold. Two days later, in the evening, my brother
telephoned to tell me that he had been called by Mother's doctor, who
said that her condition seemed to have taken an abrupt turn for the
worse. I said that I could be on the Concorde the next morning and
arrive in Mystic by noon, but he advised me to wait, as the doctor had
diagnosed no particular ailment and felt that Mother's condition might
very well improve. The following day, however, she seemed no better,
but still the doctor said that there need not be any immediate danger.
I decided to fly home, in any case, the following day, Sunday, February
12. Saturday evening, however, Ben called and told me that Mother
had died that afternoon at two o'clock. During the morning he had
said to her, "Jim will be here tomorrow." She replied, "I wish he'd
come today." The end was peaceful. Apparently all of her normal
physical functions had simply ceased. She died of old age.

A Maternal Ordeal

For a long time I had had in mind that ultimately I would want to write a collection of memoirs. Not an outright autobiography, as I don't consider my life to have been very interesting, but accounts of my relations with the very interesting people it has been my good luck to encounter. I started to do this not long after my Mother's death and found that the work went relatively quickly, because, as is obvious, I had for decades saved the journals, letters and notes that would be my raw material. And from the beginning, knowing that I wanted to write about my mother, I felt determined to demonstrate that she was entitled to a place in the cast of exceptional individuals I have known. If I have succeeded, then I will have shown that her ordeal in having had me for a son reached—for us both—the happy ending in which she so courageously believed.

Index